# Spain, 1469–1714

# Spain, 1469–1714

## A Society of Conflict

THIRD EDITION

Henry Kamen

PEARSON
Longman

Harlow, England • London • New York • Boston • San Francisco • Toronto
Sydney • Tokyo • Singapore • Hong Kong • Seoul • Taipei • New Delhi
Cape Town • Madrid • Mexico City • Amsterdam • Munich • Paris • Milan

PEARSON EDUCATION LIMITED

Edinburgh Gate
Harlow CM20 2JE
United Kingdom
Tel: +44 (0)1279 623623
Fax: +44 (0)1279 431059
Website: www.pearsoned.co.uk

First edition published 1983
Second edition published 1991
**Third edition published in Great Britain in 2005**

© Henry Kamen 1983, 2005

The right of Henry Kamen to be identified as author of this work has been
asserted by him in accordance with the Copyright, Designs and Patents Act 1988.

ISBN 978-0-582-78464-2

*British Library Cataloguing in Publication Data*
A CIP catalogue record for this book can be obtained from the British Library

*Library of Congress Cataloging in Publication Data*
Kamen, Henry.
  Spain, 1469–1714 : a society of conflict / Henry Kamen.—3rd ed.
    p. cm.
  Includes bibliographical references and index.
  ISBN 0–582–78464–6 (pbk.)
    1. Spain—History—Ferdinand and Isabella, 1479–1516.  2. Spain—History—House of
Austria, 1516–1700.  3. Spain—History—Philip V, 1700–1746.  I. Title.
DP161.K35 2005
946—dc22
                                                                    2005045833

10  9  8  7  6  5  4  3
09  08  07

Set in 10/13.5pt Sabon by 35
Printed and bound in Malaysia, KHL

*The Publisher's policy is to use paper manufactured from sustainable forests.*

# Contents

# List of maps and figures

## Maps

## Figures

# Preface to the First Edition

I have written this book for students of Spain who may need a survey that takes account of the scholarship of the past twenty years. Constraints of space have created some omissions, and foreign affairs are discussed only briefly; the tired old image of a nation in perpetual decline has also been discarded. If my presentation helps to make readers think in a new way about the past, it will have served its purpose.

Individual chapters were very kindly read and criticised, but not necessarily agreed with, by Roger Highfield, Tony Thompson, Jim Casey and Nigel Glendinning. My particular thanks go to my friends and colleagues in the international Hispanist community whose researches have made possible the revaluation of Spain's history offered here.

For simplicity all terms and place-names are normally given in Castilian (e.g. Cortes of Catalonia, not Corts; Lérida not Lleida), with occasional exceptions where English usage (e.g. Saragossa) and familiarity (Roussillon, or some personal names like Pau Claris) dictated otherwise. Spanish terms used with frequency (e.g. juros, alcabala) are italicised when they first appear but not thereafter. Money in the fifteenth century is reckoned in maravedís; in the sixteenth and seventeenth centuries it is reckoned for convenience in ducats (375 maravedís = 1 ducat), and in the eighteenth in escudos (roughly the same as a ducat). *See* the note on coinage on p. xiv.

H. K.

# Preface to the Second Edition

To bring this new edition fully up to date entire sections have been re-written and expanded, errors corrected, and new research incorporated; but the approach and presentation of the successful earlier version of 1983 have been preserved.

H. K.

# Preface to the Third Edition

In the twenty years since this book was first published, new research has radically changed our perspectives in two important respects. We have become more aware of the political and cultural variety that went to make up the Spanish realms, and now recognise that Spain had a smaller role than was once believed in the rise to imperial power. These aspects are taken into account in the present edition, which has been extensively re-written but without departing from the broad lines of the original presentation.

H. K.

# Glossary

**Alcabala**  Castilian sales tax, levied at about 10 per cent for most of this period.

**Alcalde**  Elected or nominated local magistrates.

**Aljama**  A word of Arabic origin, the ghetto in which Moors or Jews lived apart from their Christian neighbours.

**Almojarifazgo**  Word of Arabic origin applied to the customs duties in the south of Spain, particularly those of Seville.

**Alumbrados**  Illuminists, groups of mystics who minimised the role of the Church and of ceremonies.

**Arbitristas**  Writers who drew up *arbitrios* or proposals for economic and political reform.

**Asiento**  A contract; in particular, contracts by financiers (*asentistas*) to supply money to the crown.

**Audiencia**  See under *Chancillería*.

**Auto de fe**  'Act of faith', the ceremony at which accused were sentenced by the Inquisition, either in public or in private. The burning of heretics was never technically part of an *auto*, but took place afterwards.

**Baldío**  Uncultivated common land which was technically owned by the crown.

**Beata**  Term applied to women who dedicated themselves to a solitary religious life, within or without a religious order.

**Caballero**  Knight or gentleman, member of the lower nobility, usually propertied.

**Capa y espada**  Literally 'cloak and sword', a description referring to the military background of certain public officials.

**Censo**  Used here to refer to the annuities drawn (by *censalistas*) from loans made to individuals or to public bodies; the word also has other meanings.

**Chancillería** Term applied to the Castilian high courts in Valladolid and Granada; other high courts were called *Audiencias*.

**Ciutadà Honrat** A 'distinguished citizen', the highest civic rank, equal to nobility, granted by major towns in the crown of Aragon, especially Barcelona, Saragossa (where called 'ciudadano honrado') and Valencia.

**Consulta** A report summarising the deliberations of each meeting of the governing councils, and sent to the king for information or action.

**Converso** Term applied particularly to Christianised Jews but also to converted Moors.

**Convivencia** 'Living together', a term applied to the coexistence within mediaeval Spain of the three faiths – Christianity, Islam and Judaism.

**Corregidor** Crown-appointed civil governor in main Castilian towns.

**Cortes** The parliament of each realm, normally consisting of three Estates, except for Aragon which had four. By the late sixteenth century the Cortes in Castile consisted of only one Estate, representing eighteen towns.

**Despoblados** Depopulated villages.

**Diputación** In the crown of Aragon, standing committee of the Cortes, with members appointed from each Estate. In Barcelona the committee (*Diputació*, in Catalan) was also known as the *Generalitat*. In this book the word *Diputados* refers to members of the Diputación.

**Ducat (ducado)** *See* the note on coinage at the end of the Glossary.

**Encabezamiento** System of tax-collection by which a region would agree on the total of taxes to be paid (the main constituent tax would be the *alcabala*, q.v.), but exercise full local control over assessment and collection.

**Encomienda** In mediaeval Spain, a grant of land by the king, usually on condition that the holder (*encomendero*) assist in defence. The Military Orders held several such encomiendas. In America the encomienda was a grant not of land but of the labour service of Indians.

**Fueros** The laws and privileges of the non-Castilian provinces of Spain.

**Generalitat** *See under Diputación.*

**Germanía** The union or 'brotherhood' of the rebels in Valencia under Charles V.

**Hábito** Insignia of knighthood, a member of one of the Military Orders.

**Hermandades** System of 'brotherhoods' practised by some Castilian towns as a form of police force.

**Hidalgo** One who has the status of nobility (*hidalguía*), but without denoting rank. In practice, hidalgos were the lowest level of the ladder of noble ranks.

**Jornada** Royal outing.

**Juro** Annuity paid out of state income for loans to the crown. Holders of juros were *juristas*.

**Letrado** University graduate in law, the backbone of the upper levels of Church and state bureaucracy.

**Limpieza de sangre** 'Purity of blood', freedom from any taint of Jewish blood.

**Maestrazgos** 'Masterships' of the Military Orders.

**Maravedí** *See* the note on coinage below.

**Mayorazgo** Entail, settlement restricting the alienation of or succession to a noble estate.

**Medio general** Under Philip II, financial arrangement whereby debts to financiers were converted into long-term juro payments.

**Meseta** Plateau.

**Millones** A tax on basic consumer items, principally meat, wine, oil and vinegar, and voted regularly by the Cortes of Castile as a *servicio* (q.v.) from 1590 onwards.

**Montañeses** From the highland areas.

**Morisco** A christianised Moor – term used from the sixteenth century.

**Mudéjar** A Muslim living under Christian rule.

**Procurador** Representative of the towns in the Castilian Cortes.

**Pronunciamiento** Nineteenth-century term for a military coup.

**Pueblo** Village or town.

**Regidor** Town councillor.

**Remensa** In Catalonia, the money payment (*remença* in Catalan) by which a serf purchased his liberty. *Remensa* peasants were those who up to the fifteenth century were subject to personal redemption.

**Señorío** 'Lordship', applied particularly to jurisdiction over an area.

**Servicio**  A 'service' or grant of taxes made by the Cortes, and renewable only by them.

**Tercio**  Elite regiment in the Spanish army.

**Título**  Member of the titled aristocracy of Castile.

**Valido**  Chief minister or 'favourite', sometimes referred to as a *privado*.

**Vellón**  *See* the note on coinage below.

# A note on coinage

In their decree of 1497 the Catholic Monarchs decreed equality between the three large-denomination gold coins of Spain: the *excelente* or ducat of Castile, the *excelente* of Valencia and the *principat* of Catalonia. Each realm continued, however, to have its separate coinage and currency. In the realms of the crown of Aragon the units were pounds, shillings and pence (*libras*, *sueldos* and *dineros*). In Castile from 1497 the main gold coin was the ducat, the main silver coin the *real*, the main *vellón* (a mixture of copper and silver) coin the *blanca*. Accounting in Castile was, however, done not in these coins but in *maravedís* (coins normally issued in units of two). A blanca, for example, was equivalent to half a maravedí, a real to 34 maravedís, a ducat to 375 maravedís. By the sixteenth century the government moved to keeping accounts in ducats. From 1537 a new gold coin, the *escudo*, was minted and gradually replaced the ducat, which however continued to be used as a unit of account. Where the ducat had been worth 11 reales or 375 maravedís, the escudo was worth 10 reales or 340 maravedís, though its value continued to change in subsequent coinages. After the coinage debasements of Philip III, so-called vellón coins gradually ceased to contain any silver and ended up as copper coins. Treasury accounts normally reckoned vellón and copper currency in ducats, and silver (for payments outside Castile) in escudos, but since the eventual difference in value between the two was fractional, accounts came to be kept indifferently both in ducats and in escudos. American bullion was normally reckoned in pesos. The American silver peso was valued at 272 maravedís, and the gold peso at 450.

# Chronology

1545  opening of silver mine of Potosí in Bolivia

1553  execution of Servet by Calvin at Geneva

1554  Philip of Spain marries Mary Tudor of England; absent from Spain five years

1555  abdication of Charles V; Philip II as king of Spain (1556)

1557  battle of St Quentin, victory of army of Flanders over French

1558  death of Charles V; death of Mary Tudor; Elizabeth I as queen of England

1559  peace of Cateau-Cambrésis; first big auto de fe against Protestants in Spain

1561  Madrid adopted as seat of royal administration

1563  decrees of Council of Trent, accepted in Spain 1565

1566  image-breaking in Netherlands; Legazpi and his vessels make landfall in the Philippines

1567  duke of Alba with army goes to Netherlands, remains until 1573

1568  death of Don Carlos; outbreak of Morisco revolt in Granada

1571  battle of Lepanto

1572  massacre of St Bartholomew's Eve in France

1578  murder of Juan de Escobedo

1579  arrest of Antonio Pérez and princess of Éboli

1580  Spain invades Portugal

1588  defeat of Spanish Armada

1591  disturbances in Saragossa

1598  death of Philip II; Philip III as king, duke of Lerma as chief minister

1605  publication of first part of Cervantes' Don Quixote

1609  Twelve Years Truce between Spain and Dutch rebels; expulsion of Moriscos commences

1618  outbreak of Thirty Years War; publication of second part of Don Quixote

1621  death of Philip III; Philip IV as king, Olivares as chief minister; renewal of conflict in Netherlands

1623  visit incognito of Charles, prince of Wales to Madrid

1628    Spain goes to war over Mantua; Piet Heyn's fleet seizes Spanish treasure ships

1635    France declares war against Spain

1640    rebellion of Catalonia and Portugal

1643    battle of Rocroi, army of Flanders defeated by French troops; fall of Olivares

1648    peace of Westphalia; independence of United Provinces

1659    peace of the Pyrenees

1660    death of Velázquez

1665    death of Philip IV; Charles II as king, his mother Mariana as regent

1668    independence of Portugal recognised

1677    government coup by Don Juan José, in power 1677–9

1682    death of Murillo

1700    end of Habsburg dynasty with death of Charles II; new Bourbon dynasty with Philip of Anjou king as Philip V

1702    War of Spanish Succession begins

1713    treaty of Utrecht

1714    Barcelona surrenders to Spanish troops; treaty of Rastatt

# Maps

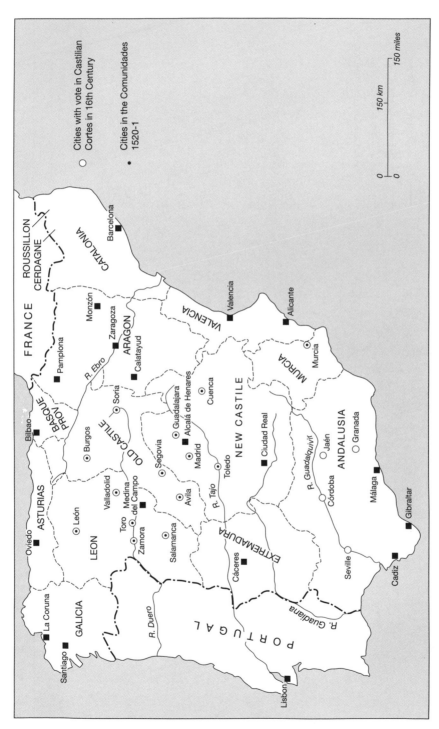

Cities with vote in Castilian
Cortes in 16th Century

Cities in the Comunidades
1520-1

MAP 1  *Spain 1469–1714*

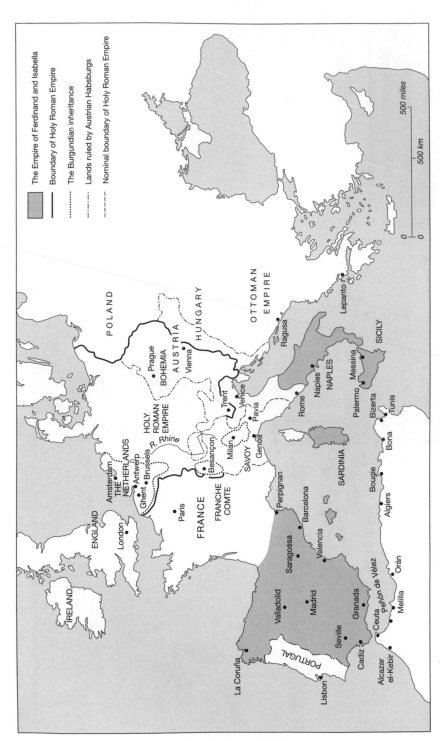

**MAP 2**  *The Spanish empire in Europe – 16th century*

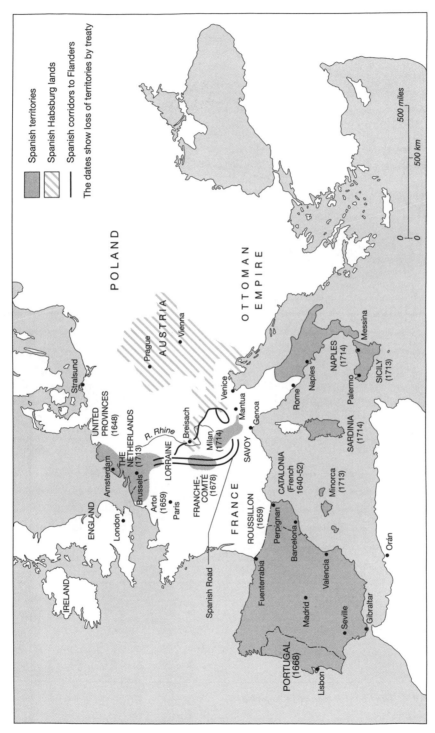

**MAP 3** *The end of the Spanish empire in Europe – 17th century*

**MAP 4** *The Spanish empire in America*

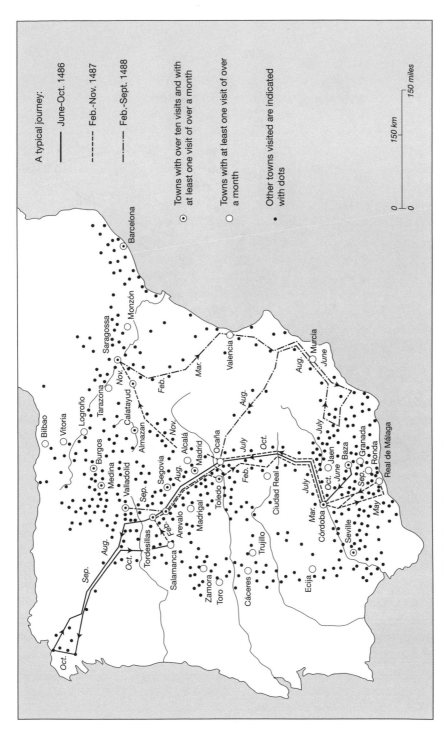

**MAP 5**  *Spanish towns visited by Ferdinand and Isabella*

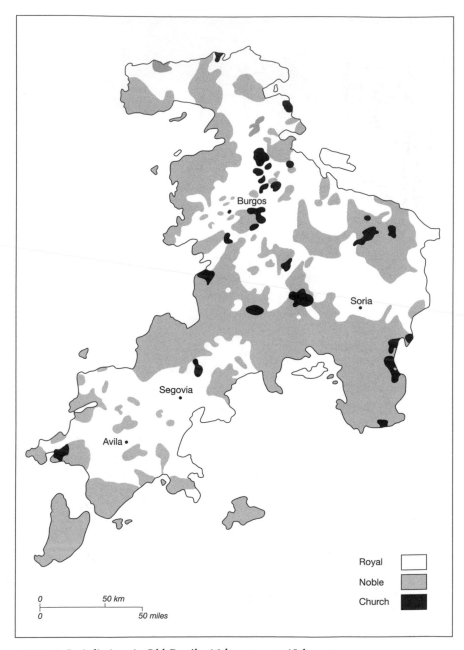

**MAP 6** *Jurisdictions in Old Castile, 16th century to 18th century*

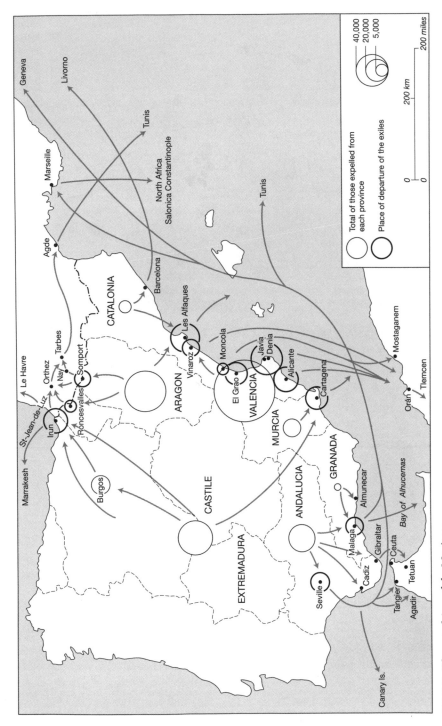

**MAP 7** *The expulsion of the Moriscos*

# Figures

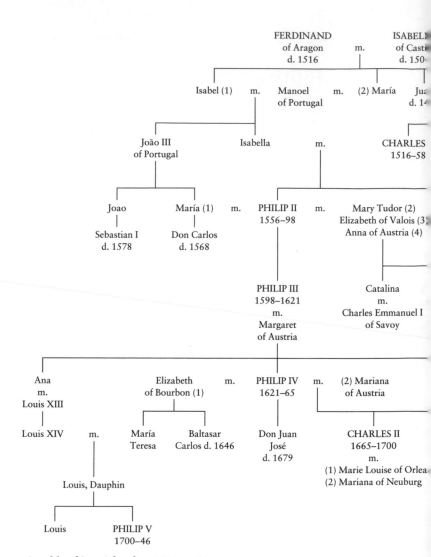

**FIG 1** *Dynastic table of Spanish rulers 1474–1700*

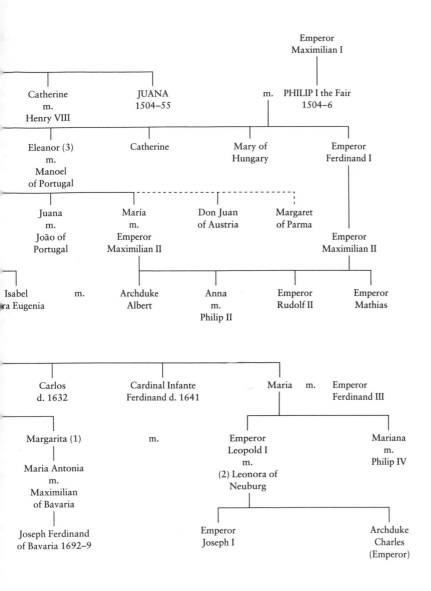

Emperor
Maximilian I

Catherine
m.
Henry VIII

JUANA
1504–55

m.   PHILIP I the Fair
1504–6

Eleanor (3)
m.
Manoel
of Portugal

Catherine

Mary of
Hungary

Emperor
Ferdinand I

Juana
m.
João of
Portugal

María
m.
Emperor
Maximilian II

Don Juan
of Austria

Margaret
of Parma

Emperor
Maximilian II

Isabel          m.
ra Eugenia

Archduke
Albert

Anna
m.
Philip II

Emperor
Rudolf II

Emperor
Mathias

Carlos
d. 1632

Cardinal Infante
Ferdinand d. 1641

Maria    m.    Emperor
Ferdinand III

Margarita (1)

Maria Antonia
m.
Maximilian
of Bavaria

Joseph Ferdinand
of Bavaria 1692–9

m.

Emperor
Leopold I
m.
(2) Leonora of
Neuburg

Mariana
m.
Philip IV

Emperor
Joseph I

Archduke
Charles
(Emperor)

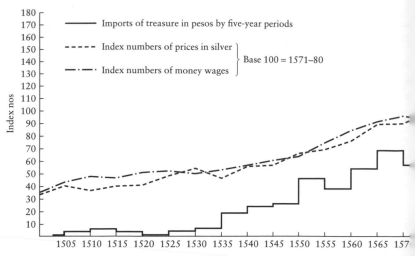

**FIG 2** *Treasure imports, prices and wages in Spain 1500–1650*

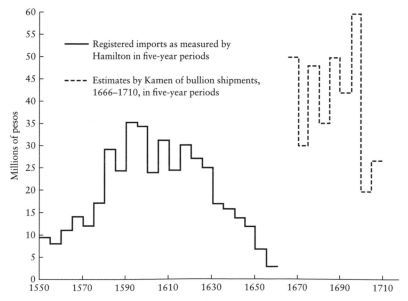

**FIG 3** *Imports of American bullion to Spain 1550–1710*

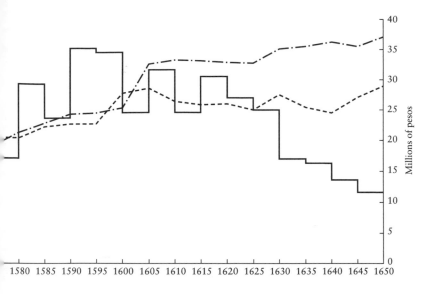

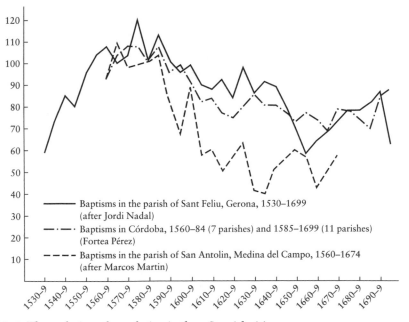

**FIG 4** *The evolution of population in three Spanish cities*

# Prelude

A semi-arid, thinly populated peninsula at the southern extremity of Christian Europe, the Iberian lands had played little part in the life of the continent. In the eighth century they seemed yet more marginal to Europe, after Muslim invaders swept up from north Africa through the straits of Gibraltar and left the imprint of their civilisation on all the lands south of the river Duero and those bordering the Pyrenees. By the tenth century the caliphate of Córdoba was a huge, thriving empire, with a sophisticated administration and culture, active commerce and industry, and an agriculture made more efficient by extensive irrigation. Exotic foods (oranges, rice) entered the Spanish diet; Arabic language and literature dominated culture, even among the 'Mozarabs', the Christians living under Muslim rule. Many Christians, lamented a mediaeval co-religionist, 'know only the language and literature of the Arabs, read and study Arabic books with zeal, and proclaim aloud that their literature is worthy of admiration'. The Jewish minority, although occasionally persecuted, also survived under Muslim rule: as 'people of the book', they were tolerated and became valuable urban artisans and traders. Jewish culture (the language used was Arabic) flourished, its most notable representative being the twelfth-century philosopher Maimonides.

The coexistence or *convivencia* between three faiths and three cultures was an uneasy one, for the Christians and Muslims never treated the faiths under their rule on equal terms. Political alliances, however, were made between religions. The most celebrated medieval Christian hero, the Cid, became in 1094 ruler of the Muslim kingdom of Valencia, proof that two different civilizations could coexist even in the midst of war. Later, when Christians began to conquer Muslim territory in Castile, they continued to advance both through war and through alliances. The so-called 'Reconquest' was never an exclusively religious crusade. Frontiersmen were driven by zeal for land, no less than for religion. Even at the height of the Reconquest, it was possible for Ferdinand III of Castile (d. 1252), who extended Christian rule to the Mediterranean and the Atlantic by conquering Murcia and Cadiz, to title himself 'King of the Three Religions'. Throughout this period, a large Muslim population survived in Christian territory. Known as 'Mudéjars', they were valued particularly for their skill in craftsmanship and the creation of Islamic art for Christian patrons.

By the fourteenth century, Iberia was a complex grouping of societies nurtured in war but aware of the need to coexist. The large land mass of the peninsula, embracing wholly different climates and geography, helped communities with differing traditions to survive in relative isolation. In Aragon, for example, the Mudéjar peasants lived by the drier lands near the river Ebro, which they used for irrigation, while the Christian peasants lived in the rainier mountain lands. Distances between settlements made coexistence easier: a subsequent traveller in Aragon commented that 'one can walk for days on end without meeting a single inhabitant'. Communities survived with strongly local loyalties and culture, linking up with other regions only for trade and, if they were of the same faith, for marriage. In these communities and villages, social acceptance depended on mutual respect, on repute within the local society, on good opinion or 'honour'. Although repute also came to be identified with success in arms and with the Reconquest, it never lost its basic and most important meaning of good opinion within the community of one's kinfolk and one's home region. By extension, there was also a degree of respect between communities, despite the savage clashes of late mediaeval warfare and the bitter divisions of loyalty, lasting from generation to generation, between and even within societies.

With the virtual isolation of the Muslim kingdom of Granada after the last great Reconquest campaigns in the thirteenth century, and the absorption of the Jewish communities into an aggressive, expanding Christian body, the three nations of the mediaeval epoch drifted away from *convivencia*: they began to live apart. Jews, for example, were more and more looked upon as aliens, and in 1391 there were massacres in their ghettos (*aljamas*) in Seville, Toledo, Valencia and other cities. Important sections of the Jewish elite were forced into the Christian religion, where some managed to rise to prominence. At various levels, particularly in smaller communities and towns with long traditions of coexistence, *convivencia* might still survive. A Czech traveller in 1466 was astonished to find that in the household of the count of Haro there were 'Christians, Moors and Jews, and he lets them all live in peace in their faith'. But political and religious developments, particularly in the large cities, were working to undermine mutual respect between the three nations; and only a few were prepared to speak openly in favour of the cultural heritage shared by Christians with their Muslim and Jewish neighbours.

At the very time that the internal traditions of the Spanish realms were being threatened, the subjects of Ferdinand and Isabella were introduced to three heady external ventures. The first of these was association with other kingdoms in a new organism of political cooperation that had long been known generally as 'Spain'. The second was a series of military campaigns that began within the peninsula, directed against the Muslims of Granada, and then beyond the peninsula, against Muslims on the coast of Africa. The final venture involved expansion overseas into the Atlantic and towards the unknown continent of the New World. The last of these proved to be the most innovating experience: the era of discovery uprooted families, created new horizons and affected the stability of traditional society. The attitudes set in motion by these three ventures were so unprecedented that it is difficult to see the epoch as simply an extension of the old Reconquest. Already, it was a new age.

But it was an age that created many more uncertainties than had been experienced during the mediaeval Reconquest. Almost from the beginning there were problematic questions: Should the 'savages' of the Atlantic be enslaved or respected as free men? Was it right to oblige 'barbarians' to accept the true faith? Judging by the differing responses given to these and other questions, there is little doubt that Spaniards were never absolutely sure of their destiny. As Spain extended the sphere of its experience and moved into the modern era, there developed among its peoples serious differences of opinion over the expulsion of minorities, over the colonisation of America, over the war in the Netherlands, over the Inquisition, and indeed over every aspect of their imperial role.

This then is the story of a nation that was caught up unexpectedly into a global role for which it was never adequately prepared and which it made heroic efforts to fulfil, with consequences that altered the face of world civilisation but created deep internal fissures that persisted throughout the period and have continued in some measure down to today.

# CHAPTER 1

# The Catholic Monarchs 1469–1516

## Politics 1469–1516

The accession of a minor, Juan II, to the throne of Castile in 1406 began a period of instability that the great nobles exploited freely. When Henry IV succeeded his father in 1454 they felt strong enough to dispute the king's power and question his choice of successor. The ensuing civil wars (1464–80) came to centre on the problem of the succession. A group of nobles led by Alfonso Carrillo, archbishop of Toledo, supported the rights of Henry's half-sister Isabella, who was recognised by Henry in September 1468, apparently on condition that she marry the elderly king Alfonso V of Portugal. Others, however, led notably by the powerful Mendoza family, supported Henry's infant daughter Juana (b. 1463), known as La Beltraneja because it was rumoured (without any proof, as historians now agree) that her real sire was the king's favourite Beltrán de la Cueva. In search of allies, Carrillo committed Isabella (in January 1469) to marry the son of king Juan II of Aragon, related by marriage to Isabella's supporters the Enriquez family.

The marriage was celebrated in secret on 18 and 19 October 1469 in Valladolid: Isabella was eighteen, her husband Ferdinand, titular king of Sicily, a year younger. It did not seem an auspicious event. Ferdinand, caught up in civil wars in Aragon, had made his way overland to Valladolid in disguise and with only a tiny escort. The couple were cousins and it was necessary to receive a papal dispensation for them to marry. The pope had promised to grant it but dithered; his legate in Castile went ahead and issued the desired permission, which the pope subsequently validated. It was a delicate situation, for there was powerful opposition to the marriage. The king of France, Louis XI, had been hoping to secure

Castile by a union between his brother and Isabella. When Henry IV heard of the event he disowned Isabella and in 1470 recognised Juana as his heir, but his death in 1474 eased the crisis. Isabella was crowned queen of Castile in Segovia on 13 December 1474, the first step in a long upward struggle for the throne. Alfonso of Portugal invaded Castile the following spring, promised to marry Juana, and was recognised as lawful king by a section of the nobility. French troops invaded from the north.

Anarchy returned to Castile. Cardinal Pedro González de Mendoza and other great magnates had in 1473 moved to join Isabella, but in reaction Mendoza's rival Carrillo turned against her, and the powerful marquis of Villena put his strength behind Juana. The resources and energy of Ferdinand proved to be of crucial importance. Over the next few years he helped to collect troops, make alliances and capture towns. Alfonso suffered a reverse at the battle of Toro in March 1476 (the church of San Juan de los Reyes in Toledo was erected in thanks for this victory) and Juana's cause quickly crumbled: by the end of 1476 most nobles had submitted to Isabella. Meanwhile Aragon had troubles of its own. Faced by a revolt in Catalonia (1462–72) against his rule, Juan II began to secure foreign support, most spectacularly through the 1469 marriage of Ferdinand but even more effectively through agreements with Naples and Burgundy (1471). At the end of a short siege, the king in October 1472 entered Barcelona.

The realms of Castile and Aragon were already related dynastically. When the old Aragonese royal house died out in the early fifteenth century, an agreement known as the Compromise of Caspe (1412) placed Ferdinand of Antequera, from a junior branch of the Castilian ruling house of Trastámara, on the throne of Aragon. From this date both kingdoms were ruled by the same dynasty, and a common destiny did not seem impossible. The chronicler Bernáldez recalled that during the 1460s in Castile 'the children took little flags, and riding on willow sticks would say, "Flag of Aragon, flag of Aragon!" And I too said it, many times.' But aspirations to unity were tenuous, in view of the deep differences between the realms.

In the wake of the capture of Zamora and Burgos, and the success against Portugal at Toro, the monarchs summoned a Cortes to meet at Madrigal in April 1476. This assembly of clergy, nobles and municipal representatives was important not only for demonstrating that Isabella had the firm support of the political nation, but also for the fundamental administrative reforms it initiated. The reformed *hermandad*, for example, was organised here. But the civil wars were not yet over, and the court – which had no fixed capital at this period – moved southward with the monarchs to continue the pacification. In this year Isabella sent a demand to the Moorish king of Granada for renewal of tribute, and received the ominous reply that 'we no longer mint gold, only steel'. The queen was certainly troubled by the extent of non-Christian influences in Andalusia. During her stay in Seville in 1477 she was impressed by the testimony of the friar Alonso de Hojeda on the extent of heresy in the region: a direct result was the establishment of a new Inquisition.

France made peace in October 1478, four months after the birth to Isabella of an heir, Juan. The civil wars effectively came to an end when representatives of Castile and Portugal agreed to a peace treaty (Alcaçovas, September 1479) ending hostilities and renouncing all claims on each other. In January that same year Juan II of Aragon died and was succeeded by Ferdinand as king. By the end of 1479, therefore, the title of Ferdinand and Isabella to the thrones of Aragon and Castile was secure. Juana 'La Beltraneja' retired into a convent in 1480 in Portugal, but continued to proclaim her rights until her death in 1530.

In 1480 the monarchs were in a position to make far-reaching decisions on matters of state. A full Cortes was summoned in January to Toledo, where alienated royal property was reclaimed for the crown and *correg-idores* were instituted. In September, at Medina del Campo, Isabella issued the first commissions for the Inquisition to begin its work. Ferdinand at the end of the year summoned the Cortes of Aragon for 1481: he, Isabella and prince Juan spent from April to December 1481 visiting the Cortes and then the cities of Saragossa, Barcelona and Valencia in order to swear to the laws and obtain oaths of loyalty to the prince as heir to the realms. All this activity arose from Ferdinand's scrupulous concern to ensure absolute legitimacy for his and Isabella's rule: already in July 1476 he had sworn at Guernica to maintain the laws of the Basques.

With the restoration of royal authority, the monarchs turned their attention to the Moorish kingdom of Granada. In December 1481 Moors had seized the frontier town of Zahara: this provided the excuse for a counter-attack, and in February 1482 Christian forces captured the town of Alhama. Hostilities developed into the ten-year war that ended with the fall of Granada. Ferdinand assumed active leadership of the campaign, though the slow war did not prevent lengthy absences from the front on business in the north. Early in 1486 the monarchs were first confronted by Christopher Columbus, anxious to explain his projects for exploration. After repeated refusals, Columbus was finally promised financial support from officials of the crown of Aragon (notably Luis de Santángel) and on 17 April 1492 received a commission from Ferdinand and Isabella.

Earlier in 1492 – a year justly famous in Spain's history – two epoch-making events occurred. On 2 January the city of Granada capitulated to the Catholic Monarchs. Then on 30 March, in the same city, the monarchs signed a decree expelling the Jews from all Spain. They spent the latter part of this and most of the subsequent year in the Crown of Aragon, principally in Barcelona. By now foreign policy questions were playing a larger part in state affairs.

The death of Isabella at Medina del Campo on 26 November 1504 threatened the association of the two crowns, since Ferdinand was obliged as a consequence to renounce his title of king of Castile. Isabella's will specified as heir her eldest surviving child, Juana, at the time in the Netherlands with her husband the archduke Philip of Austria. The will also stated that in Juana's absence, or if she proved 'unwilling or unable to govern', Ferdinand could act as regent until Juana's elder son Charles came of age. Both parents may already have been aware of signs of mental instability in their daughter; they were also reluctant to let control of Castile pass into foreign hands. Ferdinand had Philip and Juana proclaimed as rulers of Castile, and confirmed it in the Cortes at Toro in January 1505; but he also made the Cortes confirm his regency. Aware of his weakening hold over a realm where many nobles resented the interference of 'the old Catalan', he strengthened his hand elsewhere by marrying in March 1506 the king of France's niece, Germaine de Foix. The marriage brought him French support and the prospect of a male heir whom he might conceivably also try to set on the throne of Castile. Six weeks later Philip and Juana returned to Castile. Ferdinand met them in June at the village of Villafáfila, north of Zamora. In two hostile interviews, Ferdinand conceded the government to Philip and agreed to withdraw to Aragon. Both men also agreed to exclude Juana because of 'her infirmities and sufferings, which for the sake of her honour are not specified'. Only hours later, Ferdinand protested against the agreement as being injurious to his daughter's rights; he returned to Barcelona and set sail in September for Naples.

Within the month he received news of the sudden death (25 September) at Burgos of Philip, who was only twenty-eight years old. He did not, however, return to the peninsula until the summer of 1507. By then Juana's mind had snapped under the strain of Philip's death: she refused to be parted from his coffin, and in February 1509 retreated with it over the windswept countryside to the isolated fortress of Tordesillas. Cardinal Cisneros, regent from 1506 to 1507, acted in the name of the nobles and invited Ferdinand back to resume the duties laid down by Isabella's will in the event of Juana's incapacity. In October 1510 the king took the oath as governor of Castile in the Cortes at Madrid.

The partnership of Castile and Aragon was now assured; but only by accident. Germaine de Foix's son, born in 1509, survived only a few hours; had he lived, he would have become king of an independent Aragon and the partnership would have evaporated, perhaps forever, an eventuality that Ferdinand must have foreseen. Perhaps to compensate for the fact that both Castile and Aragon would pass to Juana's elder son Charles, Ferdinand lavished attention on Charles's younger brother Ferdinand, who unlike Charles was born (in 1502) in Spain and brought up as a Spaniard.

In the nine years during which Ferdinand was sole ruler of Spain, the realms developed successfully but separately. Aragonese who hoped to see more of their king were bitterly disappointed, for Ferdinand spent virtually all his time in Castile, particularly in Valladolid, now the administrative centre of the realm. It was a logical decision, since Castile was supplying the men and money for the important conquests in Navarre and north Africa, and the expansion into America. Ferdinand took a close interest in the New World, issuing in 1512 the Laws of Burgos, which regulated the exploitation of Indian labour. Aragon was not wholly neglected: general Cortes were held there in 1510, 1512 and 1515.

Ferdinand never entirely recovered from an illness of early 1512. Journeying southwards at the end of 1515 he was overtaken by a further illness and died in the Extremaduran town of Madrigalejo (23 January 1516). Cisneros assumed the regency again, on behalf of Charles of Ghent. It was an extremely unstable situation. Nobles who had been kept in order by Ferdinand took up their arms, but the cardinal proved an able governor. In 1516 he sent troops into Navarre to quell a rebellion and demolish several castles; crushed a plot led by the Mendoza duke of Infantado and other great lords; and in 1517 began the recruitment of a permanent militia of some 30,000 men to act as the core of a royal army. When the hostile nobles demanded on what authority he acted so harshly, he pointed to his militia and cannon: 'these', he said, 'are my authority'. Many Spaniards would have preferred prince Ferdinand as their next ruler rather than the unknown Charles. Uncertainty was heightened by the drift to Charles's court at Brussels of place-seekers, among them many corrupt advisers of the late king against whom Cisneros warned Charles. The relatively peaceful transition to a new dynasty would have been unlikely without the cardinal's firm hand.

# Foreign policy 1469–1516

Soon after the successful battle of Toro (1476), the sovereigns disputed possession of the Canary Islands. In 1479 at Alcaçovas Portugal renounced all rights to the islands, thereby surrendering what was a mere stopping-place to Africa but turned out to be a valuable link with the New World. In the 1480s various Castilian adventurers, among them Alonso de Lugo, were helped by Genoese financiers and Portuguese settlers, and began to occupy the chief islands, of which the three largest (Grand Canary, Palma, and Tenerife) were by around 1500 secured for the crown of Castile.

The enmity with Portugal was succeeded by cooperation and subdued rivalry. Isabella's eldest daughter and namesake was married to the heir of Portugal in 1490, but he died the following year and the monarchs consented to Isabella's marriage early in 1497 to her late husband's cousin, Manoel, the new king of Portugal. The possibility that their issue might inherit the thrones of Spain and so unite the whole peninsula under Portugal was only a distant one, since the Infante Juan was still alive. The latter, however, died in October 1497; it was a bitter blow that prostrated the monarchs. Isabella was brought from Portugal and recognised as heir, but died the year after, 1498; her infant son, the next heir, died in 1500. This unfortunate sequence of deaths left as heir the next child of the Catholic Monarchs, Juana, who had in 1496 married Philip the Fair, archduke of Austria. The couple came south from the Netherlands in 1502 to take the oath of succession: it seemed that fate was conspiring to pass the crowns of Spain to a foreign head.

The partnership of Castile and Aragon committed the former to take part in the traditionally ambitious foreign policies of the Aragonese kings, whose principal enemy at this period was France. Disputes centred on Catalonia's northern provinces of Cerdagne and Roussillon, under French occupation since 1462 and firmly reoccupied by them in 1475. As part of his system of international alliances, in March 1489 in the treaty of Medina del Campo, Ferdinand promised his youngest daughter Catherine to the English heir, prince Arthur; the marriage itself was not celebrated till 1501, because of the extreme youth of both partners. Anti-French in intention, the treaty was intended to help Henry VII of England invade Brittany while Ferdinand marched into Cerdagne. The military intervention was a failure, but France was now turning its interest towards Italy, and ceded both Cerdagne and Roussillon to Spain by the treaty of Barcelona (January 1493).

After the conquest of Granada and the expulsion of the Jews, the Catholic Monarchs moved to affirm themselves on the international scene.

From the 1480s Ferdinand had given occasional help to his brother-in-law, king Ferrante of Naples. Ferrante's father, Alfonso the Magnanimous, had ruled until his death in 1458 over a large maritime empire comprising Aragon, Sicily and Naples, and the three realms continued to have close links despite their division among members of the family. When the French under Charles VIII invaded Italy in force in 1494, pursuing a claim to the throne of Naples, an obvious threat to Aragonese interests was created. It was the beginning of a long era of Franco-Spanish rivalry in Italy.

Charles VIII reached Naples in 1495. Professing indignation at a French occupation that injured the rights of the pope, since Naples was a papal fief (that is, the pope was by tradition its overlord and rulers of the territory accepted their authority from him), Ferdinand made plans to intervene. In 1495 an alliance with the Holy Roman Emperor Maximilian provided for the marriage of Maximilian's son Philip with the princess Juana (1496) and of his daughter Margaret with the Infante Juan (1497). In March 1495 both Spain and the Empire joined a Holy League, which included England, the papacy and other Italian states, against the French invasion: it was one of the great triumphs of Ferdinand's diplomacy. The same month a force of Spanish soldiers, led by Gonzalo Fernández de Córdoba, landed in Naples in order to help the young Ferrante II, who had succeeded his grandfather in January. A remarkable series of victorious campaigns, which led to the expulsion of the French by the summer of 1496, earned Córdoba the title of 'Great Captain' and the gratitude of the pope.

Subsequent peace negotiations between France and Spain, however, served as a cover for schemes of further intervention in Italy. By the treaty of Granada (November 1500) Ferdinand and the new (since 1498) French king, Louis XII, who was now more interested in Milan, agreed to divide the kingdom of Naples, which was by now hopelessly unstable under its fifth king within three years. In the summer of 1501 French troops from the north and Castilians from the south took possession of their prey; but the victors quarrelled and for most of 1503 the Great Captain was occupied in driving the French out, winning notable victories at Cerignola (April) and the Garigliano (December). In March 1504 France finally re-cognised Ferdinand's sovereignty over Naples. The kingdom was granted to him personally by right of inheritance, and remained in all respects independent of Spain. The free hand enjoyed in Naples by his governor, the Great Captain, was soon sharply curtailed by Ferdinand during his visit in 1506–7. The king was deeply concerned about the possibility of a complete separation of Castile (now ruled by Philip I) from Aragon, and was in no way prepared to suffer in addition the loss of Naples, which had been won for him by Gonzalo de Córdoba, whose success and popularity he distrusted. The Great Captain was allowed to retire to his estates in Granada, where he died in 1515. Thereafter Naples was governed through viceroys on behalf of the reunited crowns of Castile and Aragon.

The last major territorial acquisition of Ferdinand was Navarre. For a few years after the death of Isabella, the king's policy inclined towards France, mainly because he feared the implications of a Germanic Habsburg succession. In 1512 a dispute over the succession to Navarre, involving the claims of Ferdinand's wife Germaine de Foix against those of the French-supported Albret family, induced Ferdinand to send in a small army under the duke of Alba. The Navarrese Cortes proclaimed him as ruler, but in 1515, at the Cortes of Burgos, he preferred to associate the kingdom with the crown of Castile while still preserving its formal independence from both Castile and Aragon.

Ferdinand committed Spain to a foreign policy that it pursued through-out the sixteenth century: containment of French interests, domination of the western Mediterranean, repulsion of the Turkish advance. Alliances with England, the Emperor and the papacy were all designed to secure the first of these aims: temporary leagues with France were undertaken only out of sheer expediency, to secure Naples, for example, or to achieve a balance against Habsburg Castile. By the addition of Cerdagne, Roussillon and Navarre, Ferdinand gave Spain security on its northern frontier for a century and a half. In the Mediterranean, where the crown of Aragon had held Sardinia and Sicily since 1409, possession of Naples made the ruler of Spain immediately into the dominant Italian influence and the master, by land and sea, of southern Europe. French interests in Milan were the only serious obstacle to Spanish hegemony. Campaigns against the Turks were less dramatic but none the less frequent. In 1481 Ferdinand contributed seventy ships to the league that expelled the Turks from Otranto; and in 1501 a naval and military force under the Great Captain helped Venice to recover from the Turks the fortress of St George in Cephalonia, off Greece. At home the war against Islam was pursued with vigour in Granada and in north Africa, where the conquests were doubly important for the Catalans, to whom Ferdinand granted trading rights as if to compensate them in Africa for their effective exclusion from direct trade with America.

The foreign policy of the Catholic Monarchs was undeniably aggress-ive. Though the direction and decisions were largely those of Ferdinand, the resources used were principally those of Castile. It was therefore in effect a joint foreign policy, drawing on the one hand from Castile's Reconquest traditions and superiority in men and money, on the other from the active Mediterranean aspirations of the old Aragonese empire. To further their policy the sovereigns made highly effective use of dynastic alliances and diplomatic missions. Dynastic links were forged with the Empire (through Juana) and England (through Catherine); they were the basis of the successful dynastic claims to Naples and Navarre; they also, thanks to the marriage of Catherine's elder sister María to King Manoel in 1500, justified the annexation of Portugal later in the sixteenth century. Only good fortune prevented the whole edifice collapsing when death laid low one heir after another and finally placed the succession on the head of a foreign-born prince, Charles of Ghent.

Ferdinand was one of the pioneers of the European diplomatic system. Previously European rulers had sent out agents and ambassadors on a temporary basis, with a specific mission in mind. In 1487 a Castilian ambassador, Rodrigo González de Puebla, was sent to London: except for one interval, he remained there for over 20 years. Ferdinand in this way extended the practice of resident ambassadors, hitherto common only among the Italian states, to form part of the normal relationship between European states. By the 1490s the Spanish rulers had resident diplomats in London, Rome, Venice, Brussels and in the Holy Roman Empire. The ambassadors were drawn from the class of educated administrators, usually nobles, university-trained lawyers and clergy. Though their salaries were usually paid by the Castilian exchequer, they were recruited from all the nations ruled by the crown and their loyalty was directly to the crown rather than to the territory from which they came. González de Puebla, who arranged the marriage of Catherine of Aragon and promoted the Holy League of 1495, was a former Castilian corregidor and of Jewish origin. In general, envoys were made resident only in states allied to the crown: their expert reports and negotiations helped Ferdinand to build up a diplomatic service which was second to none in Europe, and laid the groundwork for his successes in foreign policy. In spite of its defects – unpaid salaries, poor communications, the absence of any ministers to guide policy – it was of crucial help to the emergence of Spanish power.

In 1514 Ferdinand claimed that 'the crown of Spain has not for over seven hundred years been as great or as resplendent as it now is'. The humanist Nebrija wrote that 'though the title of Empire is in Germany, in reality the power is held by the Spanish monarchs who, masters of a large part of Italy and the Mediterranean, carry the war to Africa and send out their ships, following the course of the stars, to the isles of the Indies and the New World'. Later events would bear out this vision of empire, but much of the claim was, at the time, bluster. For instance, Isabella in her testament asked her successors to 'devote themselves unremittingly to the conquest of Africa and to the war for the faith against the Moors'; but it was principally Cisneros who carried on the Reconquest tradition, with the capture on the north African coast of small towns such as Mers-el-Kebir (1505), the Peñón de Vélez (1508) and Orán (1509). Later, in 1510, a force led by general Pedro Navarro captured Bougie and Tripoli and imposed its 'protection' on Algiers. However, despite his declarations against Islam – the historian Peter Martyr reported in 1510 that 'for him the conquest of Africa is an obsession' – Ferdinand was more concerned with his destiny in Christian Europe. His aspirations to recover Jerusalem from the Turk were probably strengthened by a message in 1515 from a visionary nun, the Beata de Piedrahita, that 'he was not to die until he had won Jerusalem', but they cannot be taken seriously.

Nebrija's pride was in an imperial role achieved largely with Castilian arms. Though Ferdinand's successful policy was conducted primarily in his role as king of Aragon, the effective gains seemed to go to Castile rather than to Aragon. There was a real partnership between the two crowns in foreign policy, but Castile, by dint of its superior resources in population and royal income, came to play the bigger part in an imperial destiny whose origins had been Aragonese.

## Unity and disunity in Spain

The marriage treaty drawn up for Ferdinand and Isabella early in 1469 laid down the basic limits to Ferdinand's future authority in Castile. He was to respect the customs of the realm; all appointments and acts were to be in accord with the queen's wishes; he was to reside in the realm, and pursue the reconquest of land from the Moors; and all public decisions were to bear the signatures of both partners. By the agreement reached at Segovia in January 1475, after the coronation of Isabella, the formal precedence of Castile over Aragon was maintained but greater equality was conceded to Ferdinand: the monarchs' heads were to appear jointly on all coins, they were to dispense justice jointly, the arms of both realms appeared together on seals and banners. The motto which they later adopted – 'Tanto monta, monta tanto/Isabel como Fernando' – emphasised the equal balance between the sovereigns, which Isabella confirmed in April 1475 by granting her husband full powers to act without her in Castile as though she were present.

The marriage did not, and could not, create a new united Spain. In the fifteenth century the word 'Spain' referred, as it had done in mediaeval times, to the association of all the peoples in the peninsula, and had no specific political meaning, any more than the words 'Germany' or 'Italy' had for the peoples of those nations. The writer Diego de Valera, in a work dedicated to Isabella in 1481, wrote that 'Our Lord has given you the monarchy of all the Spains', by which he also meant Portugal. Because of its imprecision the Catholic Monarchs never used 'Spain' in their official title, calling themselves instead 'King and queen of Castile, León, Aragon, Sicily . . . counts of Barcelona . . .', and so on.

Both Ferdinand and Isabella took great care to perfect their political partnership. All their recorded decisions were made in full agreement, even when one happened to be absent; 'for', as Isabella's secretary and chronicler Hernando del Pulgar wrote, 'though necessity separated their persons, love held their wills together'. The love no doubt came under strain, in the contrast of character between the uncompromising, devout and chaste Isabella and the worldly, flexible and frequently unfaithful Ferdinand, whose political deviousness earned him praise in Machiavelli's *The Prince* (1513). The queen's exceptional ability was noted by all contemporaries and served her well in the difficult years of civil war, while Ferdinand's leadership in foreign policy and warfare profited from his greater experience of the world outside Spain.

Beyond the personal union, no attempt was ever made to disturb the complete autonomy of Castile and Aragon, and the achievement of a united Spain was never an objective of the Catholic Monarchs. Minor reforms, such as easing transport of goods between the realms in 1480, or decreeing equality, from 1497, between the three principal gold coins of Spain (the *excelentes* of Valencia and Castile and the *principat* of Catalonia), helped economic exchange. But all the customs barriers between each realm remained fully in force, and their institutions were kept entirely separate.

Differences between the kingdoms of the peninsula must be sought in their mediaeval past. In Castile the weakness of royal authority was caused less by feudal tensions than by the virtual absence of feudalism. The Muslim invasions had destroyed the early mediaeval beginnings of a feudal baronage. Christian resettlement of the Duero valley was begun by small settlers not dependent socially or juridically on any great lord. Constant warfare against the Moors strengthened this evolution of a society of small proprietors who were also obliged, by the insecurity of the frontier, to be armed with a sword and a horse. The authority and lands of the king of Castile advanced during the great Reconquest campaigns, but there was little need for contracts between the crown and the warrior nobles, since these could be rewarded directly from the conquests without having to depend on the crown for reward. The great independent military orders – of Santiago, Calatrava and Alcántara – carved out huge territories for themselves in the frontier lands of New Castile. The 'fief', which created a bond of dependence between warriors and their prince, and which is the institution most commonly associated with 'feudalism', was consequently very rare in Castile.

Castile evolved as a society under arms. By the later Middle Ages the early society of small proprietors was giving way, as the frontier advanced southwards, to one of warlords controlling fairly broad areas of land with a primitive, often pastoral, type of economy and with settlers who accepted protection as 'vassals'. The stagnation of Reconquest from the end of the twelfth century allowed society to consolidate, and political relationships began to take on some of the forms known elsewhere in Europe: the concept of 'homage' by vassals to their lord, for example, was imported from France. At the same time, the kings of Castile tried to extend their influence by granting to select nobles 'immunities' or rights to exercise within their estates virtually royal powers over justice and finance. This made sense for a period when the crown had no bureaucracy of its own, but tended eventually to make the lord's territory or '*señorío*' in practice independent of the king.

The relative absence of institutional feudalism within Castile freed the crown from binding obligations to its vassals, but at the same time gave the nobles considerable autonomy. Royal power therefore necessarily relied on close cooperation with the magnates. This was critically important in times of war, but even in peace the rulers preferred to make laws with the consent of the full political nation in Cortes. Usually they could rely on the support of the Church, which had been under close crown control since the beginning of the Reconquest.

In contrast to an essentially non-feudal Castile, in the east Catalonia experienced full-blooded feudalism because of its position as an outpost of the Carolingian empire in the ninth century. Here by the twelfth century the count of Barcelona was a prince served by feudatories who held territory of him and swore fealty. A baron had vassals who paid homage and fulfilled duties, while he in turn had to protect them. One consequence of this system of mutual obligations was that the political nation, when it met in Cortes, insisted on the prince's contractual duties to protect the laws. There was a correspondingly greater emphasis in Catalonia and the Aragonese lands on the upholding of the constitution.

The crowns of Castile and Aragon thus evolved in different ways, had differing ideals and distinct institutions. The crown of Aragon was a federation made up of the separate realms of Catalonia, Aragon, Valencia, Mallorca and Sardinia. Each realm was governed independently, with its own laws (*fueros*), its own Cortes (composed of the three Estates of Church, nobles and towns; though Aragon also had a fourth Estate, of the gentry), its own language (Catalan was the majority tongue in Catalonia, Valencia and Mallorca), and its own coinage. To the union of the crowns Aragon brought a great imperial and commercial tradition. In the fourteenth century the Aragonese empire, at its broadest extent under Alfonso the Magnanimous (d. 1458), stretched through the Mediterranean as far as Greece. Barcelona, where Catalonia's first maritime code, the famous *Llibre del Consolat de Mar*, was drawn up, became the centre of a trading system with outposts in the Levant and north Africa. During the century a drastic fall in the population of Catalonia, caused by waves of epidemics, precipitated a crisis within the crown of Aragon, which some historians have interpreted as a general decline, though the evidence for this has been convincingly questioned. It is true that Barcelona faced financial difficulties and its inhabitants shrank in number, but this contraction occurred mainly during the civil wars (1462–72), when the city of Valencia expanded in size and took over Barcelona's trade, while Genoese merchants moved in to control sectors of the relatively undeveloped trade of southern Castile. The Catalan population crisis also affected the feudal peasantry; nearly one-third of these were tied to the soil or subject to feudal exactions (the six *malos usos* or 'evil customs'), and were known as 'redemption' peasants (*de remensa*) after the custom obliging them to buy their freedom if they wished to move from their lord's land. When political problems in Catalonia broke out into the revolt against Juan II from 1462 to 1472, the remensa peasants joined the conflict as a way of airing their grievances.

The substantial differences between Aragon and Castile may be considered under six headings. First, Castile was much larger: its land mass was nearly four times the area of the mainland crown of Aragon, with a corresponding superiority in natural resources and wealth. Second, Castile contained nearly 80 per cent of the population of peninsular Spain: with a total Spanish population of under seven million in about 1530, Castile had possibly over five million, while the crown of Aragon had a little over one million, distributed fairly evenly between the three realms. The highest density of population, unlike in modern times, was in the centre and not the periphery of the peninsula. The most sparsely populated realm was Aragon, with little more than five inhabitants per square kilometre, whereas central

Castile had about twenty-one. The three largest cities were in Castile: Seville and Granada, with about 50,000 people each in the 1480s, and Toledo with 30,000. In Aragon the capital cities were Valencia with about 30,000 in 1500, Barcelona with 25,000 and Saragossa with 15,000.

Third, Castile was essentially a united state with a single government: it had one Cortes, one tax structure, one language, one coinage, one administration, and no internal customs barriers. All this, added to its size and population, gave it greater political initiative in the peninsula than Aragon. Castilian unity was, of course, in many ways superficial. The three Basque provinces of Vizcaya, Guipúzcoa and Álava recognised the sovereignty of the king of Castile but were otherwise effectively independent, with their own laws and institutions and with customs barriers that separated them from Castile. The northern realms of the Asturias and (from the early sixteenth century) Galicia had regional governments known as *Juntas Generales*. Elsewhere in Castile local privileges and aristocratic influence often reduced state authority to impotence. Despite all impediments, the crown of Castile experienced no serious obstacles to a long-term extension of its authority over the various autonomous units within it.

Fourth, Castile had larger and more powerful trading structures (most notably, the *Mesta*), which managed the bulk of Spain's external trade and guaranteed Castile's preponderance in any economic association with Aragon. The wool trade, which made the Mesta powerful, also promoted the business of the Cantabrian ports united in the 'Hermandad de las Marismas' ('the marsh fraternity'), an association of seafaring towns comparable only to the German Hanse. Linked with all these was the thriving mercantile city of Burgos. The significant volume of Castile's northern trade, particularly to England, the Netherlands and France, disproves the old image of a backward, non-capitalist and war-oriented Castile contrasted with a commercially progressive Aragon.

Castile, in brief, was a society expanding both militarily and economically. The fifth of the aspects to be noted is its dynamism. By the early fifteenth century Castilian ships and commercial agents were active in the western Mediterranean, where formerly the Catalans had been supreme. Emerging out of the fires of civil war, Castile under Isabella maintained its impetus for change and expansion: the momentous events of 1492 confirmed and extended its primacy.

Sixth and finally, there was a contrast in political systems that tipped the balance of power in favour of Castile. In the crown of Aragon the three Cortes often met simultaneously in the same city (in *Cortes generales*), but in separate sessions; more frequently, they met separately in their own realms. Restrictions on the king's legislative power in Aragon were symbolised by a famous oath that the Cortes in Saragossa are alleged to have taken when swearing allegiance to the king in the sixteenth century: 'We who are as good as you swear to you who are no better than we, to accept you as our king and sovereign lord, provided you observe all our liberties and laws; and if not, not.' The oath probably never existed in this provocative form, but its terms closely reflected the contractual relationship between ruler and ruled. In both Saragossa and Barcelona in 1283 the crown agreed that all future laws must have the approval of the Cortes. The realms of Aragon were a limited, contractual monarchy in which the king at his accession swore to maintain existing laws (commonly called fueros), and could not legislate without the agreement of the Estates (brazos). He was, indeed, subject to the law, according to a later (1622) Catalan claim: 'the laws we have are compacted between the king and the land, and the prince can no more exempt himself from them than he can exempt himself from a contract'. In each of the realms a permanent standing committee of the Cortes, called the Diputación and made up of two representatives from each Estate, supervised the laws and general administration when the Cortes was not in session. The Catalan equivalent, known as the Diputació or Generalitat, became particularly important in the government of Catalonia. The king's ability to raise taxes, to recruit soldiers and to legislate were all severely restricted in the eastern realms.

In Castile, by contrast, although the king usually took care to act through the Cortes, from the fourteenth century onwards it was recognised that the crown had absolute authority ('poderío real absoluto') to make and unmake laws. Ferdinand consequently found his freedom of action in Castile a welcome alternative to the restraints imposed in Aragon. This, no less than his promise to reside in the western realms, explains why in a total reign of 37 years he spent less than three in Aragon proper, only three in Catalonia, and a mere six months in Valencia. During the campaign against Granada he was absent from Catalonia for 11 years, and relied on a new system of viceroys to govern in his place.

It is possible to argue from all this that the union of the crowns may have been unfavourable to Aragon. Not only was the king now an absentee; new conquests, such as Navarre, were added to Castile; new territories, notably America, were made a Castilian preserve; and new imperial institutions, such as the councils and the diplomatic service, were dominated by Castilians. 'Now', Barcelona had announced to Seville in 1479, 'we are all brothers'; but the brotherhood was not destined to be one of equals, and provoked tensions that endured throughout Spain's modern history. The Aragonese were aware of the imbalance: Ferdinand himself reminded the Catalan Cortes in 1495 and 1503 that Castilian resources had paid for the conquests in southern Italy that expanded the crown of Aragon. From another perspective, there may have been fewer imbalances than we think. There was, for example, a profound advance towards co-operation between the crowns in four major areas: in the lengthy war campaign against Granada, in the pursuit of a common religious policy through the Inquisition and the expulsion of the Jews, in a joint military and foreign policy in Italy, and in the acceptance of a shared political control within the territories of peninsular Spain. Despite weaknesses, it was an experiment in collaboration unequalled at that time in Europe.

## The pacification of Spain

The major achievement of Ferdinand and Isabella was to bring peace and order to Spain. Pacification involved more than the restoration of tranquillity: old habits had to be altered, and far-reaching changes were required in political, economic and social life. Pacification was not simply a prelude to reform but also a consequence of it: a long process that took nearly two decades to implement. The triumphal entry of the sovereigns into Seville in October 1477 completed the military stage of the process in Castile. In order to secure the crown of Aragon on the death of Juan II, Ferdinand spent June to October 1479 visiting Saragossa, Barcelona and Valencia and swearing to the fueros. In Barcelona he abolished the military regime of captains-general which his father had imposed, introduced plans for a general restitution of property taken during the civil wars of 1462–72 and summoned a Cortes which sat from 1480 to 1481. In the decree known as the *Observança* he recognised his duty to respect the fueros, and confirmed the powers of the Diputació. This political settlement was only a holding operation, and no effort was made to deal with the grievances of the remensa peasants. Not until another peasant rebellion in 1484–5 did Ferdinand produce the Sentence of Guadalupe, issued in April 1486 when he was in Extremadura. It abolished the 'six evil customs', gave the peasants freedom from their lords and confirmed them in effective ownership of their land; at the same time, a large sum was exacted from them in payment for the Sentence and as a penalty for rebellion. The measure gave the Catalan rural classes a degree of independence and stability, though it failed to resolve the economic inequalities that provoked tensions in later years.

The peace process affected all Spain, not just Castile; hence the import-ance of the tour of Aragon made by the sovereigns and their heir, the Infante Juan, in 1481. Isabella commenced the tour in April by attending the Aragonese Cortes at Calatayud, where Ferdinand issued a decree con-firming her as his absolute equal in all respects. From July to November they were together in Barcelona, where Isabella acted as arbiter in a dispute between the Catalan Cortes and Ferdinand; after this they went on to Valencia and then to Castile. Spain was, like other European countries, still governed by intense local patriotism, and the king and queen were fully aware that their own personal presence was the strongest guarantee of law and order. Although they spent most of their time in Castile, they did not wholly neglect Aragon, and their next important visit was in 1487–8.

If the monarchy of Ferdinand and Isabella had a centre it was located only in their persons and not in any fixed capital city. This fact is crucial to any understanding of their reign. They took care to be present at all times wherever they were required, and in this ubiquity lay the unique con-tribution they made to the strengthening of royal authority. Ferdinand's absenteeism from Aragon had no effective remedy, but he had two meth-ods of maintaining control. He was usually accompanied by a team of Aragonese and Catalan secretaries who despatched the business of the eastern realms. He also relied on viceroys to serve in his place, usually selected from members of his family: Catalonia had viceroys from 1479, Aragon from 1482 (in the person of his 12 year-old natural son Alfonso, archbishop of the see), and Valencia only after 1496, following an earlier rejection of the viceroy in 1482. Castilians, in contrast, benefited from the almost permanent presence of Isabella. Her rudimentary court of advisers and officials was constantly on the move with her for an amazing thirty years, in which time she visited every corner of Castile, both in war and in peace, covering in some years well over 2000 kilometres of terrain. The Catholic Monarchs were the most travelled rulers in all Spanish history, and possibly – with the exception of their successor Charles V – in the entire history of early modern Europe.

The only period when their ubiquity created a problem for government was during the wars against Granada, when the royal council was left to administer the country from Valladolid while the monarchs remained at the battle front in Andalusia. Their personal authority was nevertheless still needed in an emergency such as the 1485 revolt of the count of Lemos in Galicia. When the problem became serious in 1486 the royal pair, who had only just arrived in Córdoba from Medina del Campo, set out again in June, crossed the bleak expanses of New Castile at the height of summer and marched north to Galicia. This extraordinary journey, which was quite comparable to all their other travels, as Map 5 shows, was successful. Thanks to their intervention, Lemos surrendered; but it was symptomatic of the time that he was up in arms again after the queen's death.

The basic ingredient in pacification, then, was the firm use of direct personal authority. It was the essential aspect of the power of the Catholic Monarchs. 'Everyone trembled at the name of the queen', reported a foreign visitor in 1484. Both monarchs were uncompromising supporters of strong authority, but it is meaningless to think of them as 'absolutist', since they had none of the appurtenances of state power: no capital city, no standing army, no bureaucracy, no reliable income, and certainly no theory of absolutism. Only gradually did institutions develop to take over the power they had created. Their concept of sovereignty was mediaeval: the notion of 'lordship' was more relevant than the elevated one of a supreme ruler, and they were referred to as 'Highnesses', not as 'Majesties'. Their authority was assumed to come from God; but it also derived from the community at large, for kings were heads of the body politic and had a duty to care for that body. The chroniclers of the reign place great emphasis on the fact that the monarchs carried out their duties faithfully: 'she was much inclined to do justice', Pulgar wrote of Isabella, thereby reflecting a mediaeval notion of the crown's role. At no time did the queen ever exceed her traditional powers, and even her phrase, 'my royal absolute power', which occurs seven times in her will, was of mediaeval origin and implied no extension of authority.

Isabella did not suffer any disadvantage from her sex: female succession was accepted in Spain, where women normally had full property rights. She recognised nevertheless that the moral authority of two might be greater than that of one, and instructed her chroniclers to report all state acts as being done by 'the king and queen' jointly, even if they did not happen to be together. Dutifully, and with a touch of humour, Pulgar reported that 'the king and queen, on such and such a day, gave birth to a daughter'. There were seven main areas in which the pacification and reform policies of the Catholic Monarchs may be studied: the hermandades, the aristocracy, the municipalities, the military orders, the councils of state, justice, and the Cortes.

## The hermandades

In late mediaeval times several Castilian towns had local peace-keeping forces called *hermandades* or brotherhoods. During the civil wars of the

1460s, those in northern Spain were organised together to preserve law and order. The experiment was so successful that when in 1476 Burgos proposed to revive it in order to protect commerce, the sovereigns took over the idea and persuaded the Cortes of Madrigal to set up a league of the Santa Hermandad, for which royal ordinances were issued in June. It was for twenty years the most significant support of the government. Every city, town and village of over 50 inhabitants was ordered to create a local brotherhood; these were to be leagued together and to send representatives to a central assembly (the *junta general*) that directed policy. Its jurisdiction was over areas outside walled towns; each brotherhood was to be financed by the local population, and had two or more law officers (*alcaldes*) with authority over highway crime and offences against life and property. The first junta general met in July at Dueñas, near Valladolid, in the presence of the monarchs.

The law officers had at their command a small force of armed horsemen who could pursue those accused from one area to another within the territories leagued in the hermandad. They acted both as police and as judges, executing rough and ready justice. Their procedure, commented the royal physician López de Villalobos, 'was so severe that it appeared to be cruelty, but it was necessary because all the kingdoms had not been pacified. . . . There was much butchery, with the cutting off of feet, hands and heads.' 'The Holy Brotherhood', Sancho Panza remarked in *Quixote*, 'has no use for courtesies.' The hermandad was devised to contain and control violence rather than to eliminate it. Indeed, the general policy of the Catholic Monarchs could not have been otherwise, since they were soon to set the entire south of Spain on a war footing, and they actively encouraged all Spaniards to keep arms. A decree of 1495 ordered that 'all our subjects, of whatever rank, should each possess suitable offensive and defensive weapons'.

The scope of the hermandad should not be exaggerated. At Dueñas only eight northern cities were represented, so that in the beginning the organisation covered only those areas that supported queen Isabella against Juana. In December 1476 the Junta decided to extend its organisation throughout Castile, but cities in fact joined only under pressure or when, as in the case of Trujillo in June 1477, occupied by the queen's army. Seville entered the hermandad only after Isabella secured it in July 1477. The achievement of the hermandades was also limited: their forces were large enough to deal only with small disorders, and established law officials disputed their jurisdiction. By the 1480s they were restricted mainly to rural areas.

The organisation was important to the government less for its famous peace-keeping activities than for three other reasons that deserve emphasis. First, by linking the major towns of Castile together in one assembly (the junta), the crown had an unprecedented forum for cooperation and consultation; second, by making the junta agree to establish a militia (originally in 1476 numbering 3,000, under the command of Ferdinand's brother Don Alonso de Aragón) the crown obtained the core of a royal army; third, the crown managed to get from the junta increasingly important sums of money to finance the military effort of the civil war and the Granada campaign. The apparently temporary hermandad of 1476 expanded into a major aid to royal government.

The militia was what the monarchs most prized in 1476. When the Granada wars began, the militia left the localities and operated directly under royal command: in 1483 the Junta voted 8,000 infantry to the crown, in 1490 they raised 10,000 (a quarter of all the infantry under Ferdinand). Cash grants remained modest until 1480, the year when local hermandades agreed to increase their recruitment and those in Galicia and Andalusia agreed to build ships as part of their duties; thereafter they rose sharply. In 1478–9 the crown received 17.8 million maravedís from the junta, in 1485–6 it raised 44 million, and in 1491–2 as much as 64 million. The government's chief tax-farmer, the Jewish financier Abraham Seneor, was in 1488 made treasurer-general of the hermandad, whose officials were now used to collect two of the state's principal taxes, the *cruzada* granted by the pope and the *servicio y montazgo* tax on sheep. These steps suggested that the hermandad had been virtually absorbed, or transformed, into the royal treasury. The junta, moreover, was now a partner in government. Between 1480 and 1498 the Catholic Monarchs summoned no Cortes, a fact often attributed to Isabella's alleged hostility to representative institutions. The real explanation is that during those 18 years the function of a Cortes in Castile was amply fulfilled by the junta de hermandad, which included not only the towns in Cortes but also many others outside it, and was therefore more broadly representative.

The fact that the hermandad was much more than a peace-keeping body tells us why Ferdinand introduced it into other parts of Spain. Active hermandades had existed in the Basque country throughout the fifteenth century, but the monarchs issued new regulations there in 1482. Internal conflicts in Aragon forced Ferdinand to go to Saragossa in November 1487: he ordered a city councillor, involved in a criminal case, to be gar-rotted without trial, and suspended all the elected constitutional bodies in the city. The following month all the cities of Aragon, with the exception of those in Ribagorza, were ordered to join a general hermandad to last for five years; a small armed force was also created. The realm had known hermandades in the past, but this time there was strong opposition from the nobility: the institution was suspended in 1488, then suppressed at the Cortes of 1495. It was a time of intense crisis in Aragon, brought about principally by hostility to the new Inquisition. Ferdinand made no attempt to impose an hermandad on Catalonia, where a comparable institution, the *sometent*, already existed.

## The aristocracy

The 1462–72 civil wars in Catalonia inevitably involved the nobles, but there were few great magnates in the principality and the wars speeded up the ruin of several families, so that only two big noble houses, the Rocabertí and the Cardona, survived into the sixteenth century. Castile, by contrast, was thoroughly dominated by aristocratic families, most of them promoted by the deliberate policy of the early Trastámaras in the fourteenth century. The kings from the twelfth century onwards had granted away the exercise of lordship (*señorío*) over lands that they themselves were in no position to govern. (For a fuller discussion of señoríos, *see* pp. 164–6.) The rise of noble jurisdiction meant the decay of those free towns or *behetrías* that had once been able to choose their own lord; by the fifteenth century peasants in the behetrías were becoming more tied to the soil of a particular lord. Vast tracts of territory were now under the partial or full jurisdiction of great aristocrats, who had immense revenues, thousands of vassals and their own armies. Galicia was dominated by the counts of Monterrey and Lemos, Palencia by the Manriques, León and Zamora by the counts of Luna and Benavente, Salamanca by the house of Alba, Burgos by the house of Velasco, Valladolid by the Enríquez family who were hereditary admirals of Castile, part of New Castile by the Mendoza family, Extremadura by the house of Zúñiga, Andalusia by the Guzmán family. Some 15 families with their various offshoots made up the apex of the Castilian aristocracy in the 1470s. Together they could have overwhelmed the monarchy. This, however, was never their purpose. Like mediaeval magnates, they were more concerned to consolidate their estates, live as beloved patriarchs among their vassals and flex their muscles against their neighbours.

Since the crown was unable to challenge the great Castilian lords directly, Ferdinand and Isabella concentrated on profitable alliances with families like the Mendozas and Velascos, who gave the crown a strong base in the north. Only then was it possible to confront an enemy like the marquis of Villena, Diego López Pacheco, whose immense marquisate stretched from Cuenca down to Almería, covering over 25,000 square kilometres with 150,000 vassals, and producing 100,000 ducats of rent a year. The sovereigns invited Pedro Fajardo, who controlled Murcia like an independent kingdom, to invade the marquisate; and at the same time encouraged revolts against Villena by his vassals. In 1476 the marquisate and all its major towns were ceded to the crown by Villena, who was allowed to keep his title and a portion of his lands. The use of force, the razing of castles, the confiscation of property, were essential to pacification, which from this military point of view was a lengthy process of which only the first stage was over in 1477. During the Granada campaign the sovereigns were able to put the warlike energies of the nobility to profitable use, but even then the 1486 revolt of Lemos in Galicia was proof of a continuing problem. The second stage of military pacification took place after Isabella's death, when Ferdinand was forced once more to take the field against the nobles of Castile. The great nobles of Andalusia, led by the duke of Medina-Sidonia and Pedro Girón, count of Urena, allied in 1507 against the king, who marched south in July 1508 at the head of 4,000 men and crushed the conspiracy.

In Spain, unlike other west European states where the monarchy was also attempting to control the nobility, no aristocratic blood was shed in treason trials. It was the firm policy of Ferdinand and Isabella to recover lost rights and territories for the crown; but to do this they chose the path of compromise and alliance. The first objective was a property settlement that satisfied all parties. At the Cortes of Barcelona in July 1481 alienated royal land was taken back, but this was followed immediately by the settlement of claims between those who had taken part in the civil wars. In Castile during the wars many towns were seized for the crown: in 1477, for example, the marquis of Cadiz was induced to surrender Jérez, and the duke of Medina-Sidonia gave up several fortresses. A broad settlement was agreed at the Cortes of Toledo (1480), where almost all royal lands alienated since 1464 were returned to the crown; alienations made before that date – and they were far greater in number – could be kept. Nobles who collected the royal tax of *alcabala* within their jurisdictions were confirmed in the right: an expensive concession, since the tax was the main source of normal revenue. The 1480 measures were a compromise that bought civil peace by guaranteeing the aristocracy possession of most of their gains over the previous generation.

This was not the end of royal attempts to recover property. The city of Plasencia, for instance, was reclaimed in 1485. The most important assertion of royal control, however, came immediately after the fall of Granada. In 1492 Cadiz was seized from the marquis of Cadiz, who was compensated with new properties and a new title (duke of Arcos); in 1502 Gibraltar was taken from the duke of Medina-Sidonia; and in 1503 Cartagena was taken from Don Pedro Fajardo, who was likewise compensated with other towns. Cadiz and Cartagena, destined to become Castile's biggest naval bases, gave the crown command respectively of the Atlantic and the Mediterranean; together with Gibraltar they guaranteed royal control over Spain's southern coastline.

The pacification of the great nobility turned many of them to quieter pursuits. Their part in the literary culture of the Renaissance was notable. The Velascos, constables of Castile, invested money in a palace in Burgos. The Mendozas did the same in Guadalajara (1480): the architect, responsible also for San Juan de los Reyes in Toledo, was Hans Wass. But in no sense were they disarmed, and indeed the Catholic Monarchs relied heavily on their ability to raise further huge armies to serve in Granada. The cause of Charles V during the *Comunidades* (*see* pp. 77–85) in 1520 could not have survived but for nobles like the count of Benavente and the count of Lemos, who put 2,750 and 1,500 men respectively at the king's command. The crucial difference from an earlier epoch was that the warlike nobility now used their energy in the service of the crown rather than against it or each other.

After the long years of civil strife, it was necessary to reward adherents. The sovereigns helped the process of social mobility in Castile by granting about one thousand patents of nobility (*hidalguía*) between 1465 and 1516, usually for prowess in war. It was the last period in Spanish history when military activity played a fundamental part in the formation of the ruling elite. Ferdinand and Isabella also dispensed new titles generously: a Mendoza obtained the duchy of Infantado in 1475, a de la Cerda the duchy of Medinaceli in 1479, a Manrique the duchy of Nájera in 1482, a Velasco the duchy of Frías in 1492. Despite these honours, and the undoubtedly key position held by the aristocracy in the regime of the Catholic Monarchs, it would be wrong to maintain that the sovereigns handed Castile over to the nobility. Their whole policy was opposed to any extension of noble power. It is significant that apart from a few towns granted for specific reasons (such as the gift of Vélez Blanco and Vélez Rubio to Don Pedro Fajardo in exchange for Cartagena), they seldom created new señoríos. Likewise, the concessions made to nobles who served in Granada have been wrongly presented as a grant of most of Andalusia to compensate for what was lost at Toledo in 1480. In fact the crown retained ownership of most of the territory, but granted certain areas to the aristocracy as '*repartimientos*' or frontier land to be held and defended by the military elite. Señoríos in Granada were created only where there was a mainly Moorish population, and then as a means of control.

Disputes among nobles, particularly over inheritances, could become a serious cause of conflict. To encourage peaceful succession among the great lineages, and also to preserve their economic assets, Ferdinand at the Cortes of Toro (1505) encouraged the use by nobles of the *mayorazgo* or entail, which prohibited sales of land and kept inheritances undivided. Although used regularly in earlier times, the mayorazgo now became the normal way for nobles to consolidate their property.

The taming of the Castilian aristocracy was an outstanding achievement of the Catholic Monarchs: there were no noble revolts in the realm after 1516, unlike in England and France where they continued until well over a century later. The great lords were taken into partnership with the crown and confirmed in their estates and private armies, but were given no extension of privileges. Instead, most of the major cities were taken back into royal control and new state officials were selected from lesser gentry rather than from among the magnates. The absence of any fixed capital or court made it impossible for the aristocracy to congregate together and impose their will on the monarchy, as was to happen in other countries and also in Spain under the Habsburgs. The magic factor holding the disparate personalities of the nobility together was queen Isabella. Praised by every chronicler, both foreign and Spanish, she was not only 'the most feared and respected' (Bernáldez), but also the most universally loved, imposing her will with a unique mixture of 'love and fear' (the phrase used by Castiglione in his *Courtier*, published in 1528) that kept the nobles in place until her death.

## The municipalities

Historians used to affirm that the great towns of Castile became politically and economically weak during the fifteenth century and eventually lost their independence to the absolute power of Isabella and then of Charles V. A closer look shows that changes were not so much imposed from outside as the result of internal evolution. In mediaeval Spain many towns governed themselves through a public assembly (*concejo abierto*, open council) of the propertied citizens. Bigger towns delegated authority to magistrates and municipal officers, who exercised jurisdiction both within the town and over its rural area, jointly referred to as a 'community (*comunidad*) of town and territory'. By the thirteenth century larger towns like Ávila and Segovia in Castile, Calatayud and Teruel in Aragon, were independent 'communities' free of aristocratic jurisdiction. They had proud local traditions, and strict citizenship laws based on qualifications of birth and property. In the late fifteenth century office in the cities was in the hands of a patrician elite who were gentry (*caballeros*) and therefore of noble status; these resisted fiercely any attempt by the higher aristocracy to extend their influence. Struggle for municipal office – as *regidores* or town councillors, and *alcaldes* or law officers – often created serious internal conflict and invited outside intervention. From the fourteenth century, particularly in Castile, the crown realised the importance of controlling the bigger towns and began to claim the right to appoint regidores. In this way cities began to have political rather than communal government, through an *ayuntamiento* (in Castile) or *consell* (in Catalonia and Valencia) rather than a *concejo*. The older system survived for centuries in many regions, but often as an adjunct to the newer town council.

The politicisation of town life was inevitably a reflection of economic changes. Mediaeval towns owned common lands (*propios*) that served as pasture, arable and woodland, and might give economic and therefore political independence. However, when lands fell into the hands of outsiders, the towns became vulnerable to control by oligarchies that had different interests. In the 1440s the outstanding example was Toledo, where internal struggles among oligarchies were the biggest single threat to municipal stability. The civil wars under Henry IV aggravated urban tensions, particularly when the nobles and the patrician elite supported different sides. In Catalonia likewise the disorders created rival factions in the great cities. For most Spaniards the universe within which they lived was no larger than their town and community, the framework of their moral existence and their social aspirations; so that conflicts were not only concentrated on local issues as fought out between rival clans or *bandos*, but transmitted from generation to generation even when the nature of the quarrel had changed.

The Catholic Monarchs adopted a dual policy of pacification in the cities: they intervened as arbiters between factions, and they made concessions to urban oligarchies so as to win their support. Arbitration seems, from the evidence, to have been carried out in a high-handed way, though usually with the support of the disputing parties. The city of Cáceres (Extremadura) is a good example. Weary of its divisions, the queen in

1477 went to Cáceres, suspended its municipal laws, and ordered that the officials should in future be chosen not annually by election but for life by lot. A democratic system, which had in practice led to strife and bloodshed, was replaced by an oligarchic one that brought peace and nevertheless kept power in the hands of the same elite. Ferdinand pursued an identical policy in Aragon. His suspension of the city council and Diputación of Saragossa in 1487 was strongly supported by Alfonso de la Caballería, a leading member of the *converso* elite whose numbers were severely depleted by the Inquisition crisis. When the new council of Aragon was created in 1494, Caballería became its head. The changes being forced through were possible only because of support from a section of the elite. While Ferdinand was in Saragossa at the end of 1487 a deputation of three civic leaders from Barcelona, led by Jaume Destorrent, came to protest about the Inquisition and to discuss other Catalan problems. As a consequence the king became convinced that he needed to reform Catalan politics in order to secure civic stability. In July 1488 he suspended the Diputació, and in November 1490 went on to suspend the city council (*Consell de Cent*) of Barcelona. In both cases he nominated new members: significantly, the nominated head of the consell was Destorrent. Alfonso V had introduced election by lot in some parts of Catalonia where he wished to break the hold of urban oligarchies by enlarging the pool of office-holders. Ferdinand now decreed election by lot for the Diputació in 1493 and the consell in 1498. The system was later extended to the other Aragonese realms.

Few of the municipal changes forced through by Ferdinand and Isabella can be said to have added to royal power. Their effect was rather to confirm the local gentry in power. Election by lot was particularly effective: it is significant that the king refused to introduce the system into Valencia in 1481 because he was already on good terms with the oligarchy. Peace in the cities, the monarchs well knew, was essential to peace throughout the realm. The second essential aspect of their pacification policy, therefore, other than a compromise with the aristocracy, was a compromise and alliance with the urban elites of Spain.

The urban oligarchies were regularly consulted in Castile. If to the various sessions of the Cortes in this period we add the almost annual assemblies of the junta de hermandad between 1476 and 1495, it is possible to say that the Catholic Monarchs consulted their towns more than any other Spanish rulers of the next two centuries. Perhaps even more significant is the fact that they were the only rulers in all Spain's history to visit each and every one of their towns, and to reside in them – as Map 5 shows – for several weeks at a time. This alone does much to explain the profoundly personal nature of Isabella's rule and the immense personal loyalty she attracted. Finally, it is important to observe that the monarchs wished to give financial stability to their towns, which were, after all, the biggest taxpayers. A primary aim of the civic changes in Barcelona in 1490 and 1491 was liquidation of the enormous municipal debt. When the normal tax system was reimposed on Castile in 1495, after the hermandad years, Isabella allowed the towns to collect the alcabala tax by local assessments (*encabezamiento*), independent of control by the government. Local elites consequently felt themselves in control of their own destinies, both political and fiscal.

The crown reserved its right to oversee and intervene in local government. From the fourteenth century it had sent civil governors (*corregidores*) to administer justice in some Castilian towns, but opposition was such that in 1476 the Cortes at Madrigal petitioned that 'in future corregidors not be sent to any city save at the request of its *concejo*'. It was against the crown's interest to do this. At the Cortes of Toledo in 1480 the monarchs accordingly decided, in Pulgar's words, 'to send corregidors to all cities and towns where they did not exist'. Towns were also ordered to build civic centres, 'large, well-constructed buildings in which to hold meetings'. It was a trial exercise and involved no radical departure from past practice. The records show that there were 54 towns with corregidors in 1494, 61 in 1515 and 86 at the end of the seventeenth century. Not until a decree of July 1500 were any detailed regulations issued.

The 1500 rules show that two types of corregidor existed in Castile: judicial officers, recruited from legists (*letrados*) who had studied law for ten years at university; and military (*capa y espada*, cloak and sword) officials, stationed in strategic towns. Corregidors were appointed to 'hear and determine all pleas and causes both civil and criminal', and to supervise justice and public order, notably offences such as gaming, blasphemy, usury and 'public sin'. 'Capa y espada' officials might also supervise military administration. They were appointed initially for two years, but actual practice varied from tenure for only a couple of months to one outstanding case, the famous poet and soldier Gómez Manrique, who acted as corregidor of Toledo for thirteen years (1477–90).

The appointment of a corregidor gave the crown a voice in local affairs but in no way implied a policy of centralisation. Although nominated by the king the corregidors were, in effect, local officials, since their salaries were paid by the city of residence. They might preside over meetings of a town council but were seldom in a position to control its deliberations, and the crown found it far easier to subvert towns by selling the office of *regidor*. Dual loyalty to crown and city must have restricted their initiative, and they were probably most effective in the newly conquered kingdom of Granada. In the Basque provinces the corregidor had a special role as the crown's representative at meetings of the local Cortes, known as *juntas generales*.

Many Castilian cities resented the existence of corregidors, who were a prime target of the Comuneros in 1520. The main grievance was over having to pay their salaries while having little control over their terms of appointment: in 1528 the Cortes complained that 'the salaries of the corregidors have exhausted all the towns'.

## The military orders

In the twelfth century orders of chivalry, military in character but bound by religious vows, were founded to help advance the reconquest of Spain. By the fifteenth century the orders – those of Santiago, Calatrava and Alcántara in Castile, of Montesa and of St John in Aragon – were powerful bodies with extensive ownership of lands, towns and fortresses. They retained only a nominal adherence to their religious duties; in 1540 the knights of Calatrava and Alcántara were permitted to marry, a privilege always enjoyed by the order of Santiago. Each order had a membership of several hundred, and owned large seigneurial estates (*encomiendas*), those of the Castilian orders being concentrated towards the Moorish frontier in the south. By 1616, when sales of encomiendas had reduced the holdings of the Castilian orders by one-fifth, the annual income of the five bodies was as set out in the following table:

| Order | Encomiendas | Value (ducats) |
| --- | --- | --- |
| Santiago | 94 | 308,889 |
| Calatrava | 51 | 135,000 |
| Alcántara | 38 | 114,248 |
| Montesa | 13 | 23,000 |
| St John | 114 | 100,000 |

The Castilian orders under their masters had taken an active part in the turmoil under Henry IV, and Isabella was determined to bring them under her control. Ferdinand was no doubt influenced by his own estimate that the yield of the orders exceeded the revenues of the kingdom of Naples. On the death of the master of Santiago in 1476 there was intensive rivalry for the post: Juan II advised his son Ferdinand to leave the position vacant. In January 1477, when the electors met at Ocana to make their choice, Isabella visited them (the story of her riding three days through the rain to get there seems to be spurious) and advised that the safest solution would be to elect Ferdinand. They respected her view, but continued to elect their current nominee, who held office until his death in 1499, when he was succeeded by Ferdinand. Meanwhile the masterships of the two other orders had also fallen vacant, that of Calatrava in 1487, that of Alcántara in 1494: on both occasions the king was elected for life. In 1523, under Charles V, a papal bull permitted all three masterships to be permanently vested in the crown, which thereby secured an important new field of patronage through access to the encomiendas and revenues of the orders. From 1489 a council of orders began to take over their administration.

## The councils of state

Ferdinand and Isabella were in every sense the last mediaeval rulers of Spain: like mediaeval kings, they administered the realm, dispensed justice and made war, in person. In not a single decisive act of their reign did they proceed through delegated authority. Their ubiquity was, as we have seen, the reason for the respect in which they were held and the authority which they accumulated. Sooner or later institutions had to be created to act in place of the monarchs of so vast a territory, and to help them govern it. The most important of these was the royal council (*Consejo Real*), first created as an advisory body in 1385 and reformed in 1459 by Henry IV, who made sure that eight of its complement of twelve members were legists (*letrados*) qualified in administration. The trend towards letrado government clearly antedated the Catholic Monarchs, who continued it by deciding in June 1480, as a result of discussions at the Cortes of Toledo, that the council should include eight or nine letrados. By 1493 all members of the council were required to be letrados, with at least ten years' study of law at university.

The council evolved into the single most important organ of government in Castile. It was required to meet daily in the royal residence or as near to the monarchs as possible, and was not limited to giving advice but in some administrative matters could act on its own authority. In theory all bishops, grandees and heads of military orders had a right to attend meetings, though without voting; in practice this no longer occurred. The council normally divided into five separate committees (or chambers), according to function. In the first chamber councillors joined select grandees and the king to discuss foreign policy: this was the nucleus of the council of state, which was formed in 1526. In the second chamber the council sat in one of its most important functions, as supreme court of justice of the realm, presided over in its earlier years by the monarchs in person. In the third, the officials of the royal treasury dealt with finance: this ultimately evolved into the council of finance in 1523. The fourth chamber was the council of the hermandad, which survived only to 1498. The last chamber consisted of nobles and letrados from Aragon, Catalonia, Mallorca, Valencia and Sicily: they were formed in November 1494 into a distinct body known as the council of Aragon, presided over by a 'vice-chancellor'.

During the reign other councils took shape. The council of the Supreme Inquisition was founded in 1483, the council of orders in 1489. Apart from the Inquisition, most of the councils had little authority or independence in this period: real power subsisted in the overall royal council, which soon became known simply as the 'council of Castile'. From 1489 the council acquired a 'president' to act in place of the absent and itinerant monarchs: the post was later to become the most eminent under the crown.

The Catholic Monarchs cannot be credited with any originality in their policy over the development of councils. Most of the functions laid down for the council of Castile in 1480, for example, were the same as specified in earlier legislation of 1406. The shape of the councils grew up in response to the evolving needs of the monarchy, and owed nothing to any alleged policy of centralisation. Ferdinand and Isabella made every effort to work personally with the council; but during the war of Granada they were forced to leave it to function independently in Valladolid while they stayed at the front. Far from centralising, the council simply coordinated the work of the various institutions governing a still highly regionalised monarchy, and helped to create the beginnings of a royal bureaucracy, whose growth is demonstrated by the voluminous papers in the archives.

The authority of the councils was based on delegation of royal power, a system long practised in the crown of Aragon, where distances between the Mediterranean possessions meant that the king could not be present everywhere. Ferdinand's absenteeism required, as we have seen, that he delegate his powers to viceroys. The principle of administration through viceroys was thereafter introduced into the Castilian empire, specifically into the American territories. There is absolutely no reason, however, to suggest that the new multiplicity of councils was an imposition of Aragonese practice on the Castilian tradition. The creation of the council of Aragon was devised mainly to help Ferdinand; the other councils were a logical development from Castilian practice.

Although the Catholic Monarchs did not innovate in their emphasis on a letrado bureaucracy, by their preference for lawyers they made letrados into the elite of the Castilian administrative system. Galíndez de Carvajal, himself a councillor, stated that the monarchs appointed 'skilled, prudent persons even though they were of the middle classes'. Diego Hurtado de Mendoza at a later period recalled that 'the Catholic Monarchs placed the administration of justice and public affairs into the hands of letrados, people mid-way between the great and the small . . . whose profession was the law'. Jurists were employed in the councils, in the Chancillerías, in *corregimientos*, in the diplomatic service and in all branches of state administration. Though of modest fortune they were by no means of middling status; almost without exception, letrados employed by the state enjoyed noble rank. They were the essential elements in the transition from the mediaeval government of the Catholic Monarchs to the bureaucratic state of the Habsburgs.

## Justice

Changes in the judicial system were at the heart of the policy of pacification. As elsewhere in Europe, the country was subject to so many conflicting jurisdictions that the crown seldom had a unique claim to control of justice. Although most big cities and much of the countryside were subject to the king's law officers, substantial areas of Spain recognised only the justice of the great lords and of the Church. (Jurisdictions are also examined on p. 164.) There was also a system of commercial law affecting certain trade matters and interpreted by merchant bodies called *consulados*. It was in the interests of the crown to integrate these different jurisdictions into a single system of royal justice, administered from the late fourteenth century in Castile through a permanent court called an *audiencia* or *chancillería*, consisting of about ten judges (*oidores*) and resident in Segovia or Valladolid.

In the earlier part of their reign the Catholic Monarchs continued the mediaeval practice of dispensing justice in person as they travelled around the country. 'That was a golden time and a time of justice', wrote the chronicler Fernández de Oviedo, recalling how the queen had held public audiences in the Alcázar at Madrid, and given free and summary judgment in the presence of her council. 'The humble poor', wrote Bernáldez, 'were weighed along with the gentry, and received justice.' The royal council met as a court twice a week. At the Cortes of Toledo in 1480 the sovereigns recognised the need for a fixed rather than an itinerant judicial administration. Their proposals took shape in the ordinances issued at Medina del Campo in March 1489. By these, the 'audiencia y chancillería' was permanently fixed in Valladolid: it consisted of a president and eight letrado judges appointed annually, and was divided into a number of chambers (*salas*) for civil and criminal cases. A second court was later created with authority over all territory south of the river Tajo: first installed at Ciudad Real in 1494, it became permanently fixed in Granada from 1505. Others were established in Santiago de Compostela, temporarily from 1480 but permanently from 1504, and in Seville, where the mediaeval tribunal was reformed in 1495 and 1525. The courts at Valladolid and Granada, both termed chancillerías after 1494, were considered the highest in rank; appeals from them went to the council of Castile, as the highest court in the land. The lesser tribunals at Santiago and Seville retained the name of audiencias.

In the crown of Aragon each realm had its own audiencia to dispense royal justice. Below the level of these supreme courts, there were throughout Spain a number of law officers in charge of judicial administration. The most unusual of these was the justiciar (*justicia*) of Aragon, an official who in the thirteenth century had been elected by the king in the realm of Aragon to arbitrate in disputes between the crown and the nobility. By the fifteenth century successive Cortes of the realm had invested the justiciar and his court with exalted powers, and made him irremovable from office by the king. The only restriction imposed by Ferdinand in the Aragonese Cortes of 1493 was that in criminal cases the justiciar be advised by five letrados appointed by the crown. Because of its unique independence, the justiciar's court was usually considered to be the guardian of the fueros and liberties of Aragon.

Although in major civil and criminal matters the crown, personifying the state, was the sole judge, with for example sole power to inflict the death penalty, in practice the jurisdiction of the state was confused and frequently disputed. An important step towards winning recognition for royal authority was taken when the Catholic Monarchs entrusted the jurist Alfonso Díaz de Montalvo with the task of collecting and publishing all late mediaeval law codes. His *Ordenamiento*, an enormous work in eight volumes, was ready by the end of 1480; it was published in 1485 as the *Ordenanzas Reales de Castilla* and all large towns were ordered to purchase a copy. In subsequent years more mediaeval codes were published, and in 1503 the lawyer Juan Ramírez issued a collection of the

*Pragmáticas* of the Catholic Monarchs. None of these publications ventured to eliminate confusions in existing laws; an attempt was made by the Cortes of Toro (1505), with the help of jurists including Dr Palacios Rubios, but not until the reign of Philip II was a comprehensive code of Castilian laws drawn up.

## The Cortes

By the end of the twelfth century, a hundred years before other nations in western Europe, the Spanish kingdoms had already developed political assemblies that included not only clergy and magnates but also representatives of the towns. In the fifteenth century all the kingdoms had regular Cortes consisting of three Estates; Aragon was exceptional in having an additional chamber for the lesser nobility. In Castile the principal function of the Cortes was to vote subsidies (*servicios*) to the king for the needs of the state; only to a lesser degree did it intervene to approve legislation. Although all three Estates claimed the right to attend the Castilian Cortes, by the 1450s it was common for only the towns to attend. Under the Catholic Monarchs seventeen Castilian cities had the right to send at least two representatives (*procuradores*) each; Granada was added to their number after 1492.

In the crown of Aragon the parliamentary tradition was stronger, thanks – as we have seen (p. 12) – to the feudal tradition of a contract between ruler and ruled. Ferdinand and Isabella were consequently reluctant to summon Cortes in the eastern realms, where the fueros were a persistent barrier to action. Guicciardini, envoy of Florence at this time, reported the queen as saying that 'Aragon is not ours, we shall have to conquer it over again'. In all, the Cortes of the kingdom of Aragon were summoned seven times, those of Catalonia six, and those of Valencia just once; the joint or general Cortes of all three realms was also convoked three times. Ferdinand apparently felt little need to summon the Valencian Cortes (whose single meeting in 1484 was an extended session that began in Tarazona that year and ended in Orihuela in 1489) because the city of Valencia was already contributing handsomely to his financial needs.

It is frequently claimed that the Catholic Monarchs contributed to the decay of the Cortes in Castile, but the evidence is overwhelmingly against this view. Beginning with the assembly at Madrigal in 1476, they made immense efforts to win the support of all political classes. The Cortes were summoned 16 times between the death of Henry IV and that of Ferdinand: four meetings took place before 1481, twelve after 1498. In the long intervening period, when there were apparently no meetings, the monarchs in fact convened the Junta de Hermandad nearly every year. Thus in practice they had more meetings of representative assemblies than any subsequent rulers of Spain. It cannot be sufficiently emphasised, moreover, that the Catholic Monarchs legislated in, rather than outside, the Cortes. Though only the crown could make laws, it did so in the presence and usually with the consent of the political nation. The continuing importance of the Cortes is demonstrated by the assembly at Toro in 1505 which, in the absence of any effective sovereign (since Ferdinand was now only governor of the realm and not king), issued 83 laws by its own authority; Ferdinand merely ratified the legislation, most of which had been approved in principle by Isabella before her death.

Among the cities of Castile, therefore, the memory of the Cortes of Ferdinand and Isabella was universally favourable. 'The Catholic Monarchs', stated the 13 Cortes cities in the junta of the Comuneros in 1520, 'did and ordered in their Cortes many excellent things for the welfare of these realms.' The towns had become active partners in the government during those years; by contrast, the nobles and clergy tended to absent themselves from meetings whose primary business was to vote taxes from which they were exempt.

## The conquest of Granada

Immediately after consolidating their authority the monarchs turned their attention to Granada. Throughout the century the frontier with the Muslim emirate had experienced regular incidents and attacks, interrupted by uneasy truces and payments of tribute by Granada to Castile. Convivencia was nevertheless still the rule: trade continued, prisoners were regularly exchanged through official mediators, on both sides ballads were composed about the chivalry of frontier heroes. In Granada the emir Abu 'l-Hasan Ali ruled over a territory of some half a million people, a powerful nation but rent by political and clan divisions. The capture of the frontier town of Zahara by Muslim forces in December 1481 provided the excuse for a full-scale campaign by the Christians of Andalusia, who in February 1482 retaliated by seizing Alhama. Over the next ten years the Catholic Monarchs committed all their resources to the struggle.

Civil war among the rulers of Granada helped the Christians. Abu 'l-Hasan's son Muhammad (known to the Christians as Boabdil) rebelled against his father, was captured by Christians in 1483, and agreed to become a vassal of Ferdinand. The emir was in 1485 dethroned by his brother al-Zagal, who was in turn ousted from Granada in 1487 by Boabdil and withdrew into the eastern half of the kingdom, where he held out against the Christians until the end of 1489. By this date most of the territory was conquered and Ferdinand expected Boabdil to surrender Granada to him. When he refused to do so, a long and costly siege of the city (April 1491 to January 1492) was begun. The Moors saw defeat as inevitable; a surrender was negotiated, Christian troops were let in secretly on 1 January to ensure a peaceful handover, and on 2 January 1492 the Catholic Monarchs approached at the head of their army to receive the keys of the city.

The war of Granada was full of episodes in which the gallantry and chivalry of combatants reflected the best ideals of mediaeval warfare. The deeds of Rodrigo Ponce de León, marquis of Cadiz, seemed to recall those of the Cid. But the campaigns were no mere continuation of the mediaeval Reconquest: Christian ideology was now more aggressive, Christian warfare more destructive. The brutal enslavement of the entire population (15,000 people) of Málaga after its capture in 1487 gave hint of a new savagery. For a decade the conflict harnessed the energies of the entire population of southern Spain in providing soldiers, food and supplies: the inevitable state of emergency provoked a huge rise in prices in Andalusia. It was a total effort by one civilisation to subdue another.

It is possible that the complete conquest of Granada was not at first contemplated, but by the end this was certainly the objective. Isabella took only a nominal part in the campaign, leaving the military command exclusively to Ferdinand (she apparently hated bloodshed, and disliked bullfights; after seeing a *corrida* she determined, in her own words, 'never to see one again in all my life'). The monarchy's prestige was enormously enhanced by the war, which took on the status of a European crusade, blessed by the papacy and with volunteers from all over the continent. The pope granted funds and gave Ferdinand a huge silver cross that was carried before the troops. From 1488 many of the soldiers wore crusader crosses on their uniform, and in 1486 the monarchs sought divine aid at the shrine of St James at Compostela. The religious element was deliberately cultivated in official propaganda, though this does not call in doubt the pious motives of the crown. In 1481 Ferdinand declared that his aim was 'to expel from all Spain the enemies of the Catholic faith and dedicate Spain to the service of God'. In 1485 he claimed that 'we have not been moved to this war by any desire to enlarge our realms, nor by greed for greater revenues'.

The campaign encouraged the emergence of a national army. Royal forces were still made up, as in mediaeval times, of soldiers recruited by vassals. Ferdinand's army came from four main sources: the troops of the great magnates (cardinal Mendoza in 1489 supplied 1,000 horse and 1,000 foot); the gentry and their dependants; the militia of the hermandad towns; and soldiers, including Swiss mercenaries, raised by the crown. The forces were regrouped each year at the start of the campaign, so that no permanent standing army existed. Nor were the levies organised or paid on a common basis. Many contingents owed loyalty only to the lord who had raised them, and not to the king; when an attempt was made to deploy elsewhere the soldiers under the duke of Medinaceli, he protested: 'Tell the king my lord that I came to serve him with the men of my household, and that I shall not serve in the war unless accompanied by my men, nor is it reasonable for them to serve without me at their head.'

By 1489, according to Pulgar, 'the host numbered 13,000 horse and 40,000 foot soldiers'. All the organisation was carried out by the crown, which through these long years of conflict established an unquestioned control over the armed forces. The lessons, both logistical and tactical, were put to use in the subsequent wars in Italy, where the commanders Gonzalo de Córdoba and Gonzalo de Ayora adapted their experience of the Granada campaign. In one essential respect the Granada army was superior to all its predecessors: heavy artillery, used regularly from 1487 so that by 1491 the army had over 200 units, was able to demolish mediaeval fortifications and ensured victory over the Moorish towns, which had no cannon. The absence of any significant naval forces was the only weak point in an otherwise overwhelming Christian superiority. The failure of other Muslim powers to come to the help of Granada can no doubt be explained by their awareness that the cause was hopeless. By contrast, the various peoples of Spain forgot their differences in a struggle that contributed, more than any other event of the reign, to a common loyalty to the crown. 'Who would have thought', observed Peter Martyr of Anghiera on the Christian army, 'that the Galician, the proud Asturian and the rude inhabitant of the Pyrenees, would be mixing freely with Toledans, people of La Mancha, and Andalusians, living together in harmony and obedience, like members of one family, speaking the same language and subject to one common discipline?'

The cost of the war could never have been borne by the crown alone, which was able to draw on two extraordinary sources: papal bulls of crusade, and grants by the hermandad. In 1482 Sixtus IV issued a bull of crusade (*cruzada*), granting special spiritual favours to those who contributed to or took part in the Granada campaign. The bull was renewed in subsequent years. Innocent VIII in 1485 made an added concession of one-tenth of the revenues of the Church in Spain: this too was later renewed. The last cruzada granted was in 1491. The total income from the papal grants was enormous: some 800 million maravedís between 1484 and 1492. 'Without such subsidies', reported Guicciardini, 'this king would not have taken Granada.' Over the same period the monarchs were drawing on funds voted by the junta de hermandad: the grants rose from an annual average of 17.8 million maravedís over the years 1478–85, to between 32 and 34.5 million in the period 1485–98; from 1482 to 1490, the crucial war years, the grants totalled 300 million maravedís.

The racial minorities of Castile were forced to contribute to costs; from 1482 to 1491 the Jews paid some 58 million maravedís in special taxes, but the Mudéjars being poorer paid less. To some degree the war also financed itself: the sale of slaves from Málaga realised over 56 million maravedís for the crown. Loans, which were seldom resorted to before 1488 and were taken mainly from city *concejos* and grandees, became important in the closing stages of the campaign. From 1489 to 1491 over 315 million maravedís were borrowed. Since it was impossible to repay such large sums quickly, from 1489 the loans were converted into annuities (*juros*) at an interest rate of 10 per cent: it was the beginning of a national debt. Among those who loaned money were the duke of Medina-Sidonia, 17 million and the Mesta, 27 million.

When Granada fell the event was hailed by an eyewitness as 'the most distinguished and blessed day there has ever been in Spain'; though a Muslim commentator in Egypt saw it as 'one of the most terrible catastrophes to befall Islam'. Ferdinand's triumphant message to Rome, that 'after so much travail, expense, death and bloodshed this kingdom of Granada, which for 780 years was occupied by infidels, has been won to the glory of God, the exaltation of our Holy Catholic Faith, and the honour of the Apostolic See', was echoed by acclamation throughout Europe. A grateful Alexander VI in 1494 (a year when he needed Spain's help against the French) bestowed on the sovereigns the title of *Los Reyes Católicos*.

In legal terms, Granada was not 'conquered'; rather, it agreed on 'capitulations', common in warfare in mediaeval times. The Mudéjars (as they were now called, being under Christian rule) were guaranteed their customs, property, laws and religion; they kept their own officials, to be supervised however by Castilian governors; those wishing to emigrate were allowed to do so. Of the original half million Moors in the realm, 100,000 had died or been enslaved, 200,000 emigrated, and 200,000 remained as the residual population. Many of the Muslim elite, including

Boabdil, who had been given the area of the Alpujarra mountains as a
principality, found life under Christian rule intolerable and passed over
into north Africa.

Reorganisation of the territory was entrusted to Íñigo López de
Mendoza, second count of Tendilla and later first marquis of Mondéjar;
Church affairs were put under fray Hernando de Talavera, Isabella's
Jeronimite confessor who was now created first archbishop of Granada.
Corregidors were appointed to the chief cities and a chancillería fixed
(1505) in Granada. Contrary to what is commonly asserted, the kingdom
was not handed over to the great magnates. Only a few areas, mainly those
with a heavy Muslim population, were granted as señoríos; and even these
gave jurisdiction over justice and taxation rather than over the soil. Towns
granted to nobles rarely had more than 200 vassals, and were more usually
small villages. In 1524 the Venetian ambassador Andrea Navagero noted
that 'except for a few lords, there are no people in Granada with large
incomes'. At the same time, a deluge of landless Christian peasants swept
into the south, most of them from other parts of Andalusia. Some 40,000
immigrants settled in the kingdom over the period 1485–98. The town
of Antequera, which had only 200 families prior to 1480, had 3,500 by
the early sixteenth century. The new peasants assured some continuity in
agriculture, but could not prevent an economic crisis caused by Muslim
emigration and by the collapse of traditional trade to north Africa.

Tensions between the Mudéjars and their new rulers came to a head
over religion. As archbishop, Talavera encouraged conversions by means
of charitable persuasion, respect for Mudéjar culture and the use of Arabic
during religious services. Tendilla, by his scrupulous respect for their
customs, also earned the loyalty of the Mudéjars. Cisneros, who had been
archbishop of Toledo since 1495, was impatient at the slow progress of
conversions and in 1499, when the monarchs were in Granada, asked for
permission to pursue a more rigorous policy. The new phase of com-
pulsory conversion, often with mass baptisms, provoked a brief revolt in
December 1499 in the Albaicín, the Mudéjar quarter of Granada, which
was appeased only through the good offices of Tendilla and Talavera.
Isabella, however, gave her support to Cisneros, who was able to report in
January 1500 that 'there is now no one in the city who is not a Christian,
and all the mosques are churches'.

The fundamental difference of approach between Talavera (d. 1507)
and Cisneros was to have profound consequences for the history of Spain.
The vain protests of Tendilla and Talavera, and the victory of the new
harsh policy in Granada, signalled the end of the old convivencia, the

tradition of mutual respect between the warring civilisations of the peninsula. Isabella and Cisneros were committing Spain, as they already had
done through the recently established Inquisition, to become a society
not of coexistence but of conflict. Ferdinand sympathised with Tendilla's
outlook, and it is significant that for a generation no attack was made
upon the Mudéjars of Aragon. But in Castile there was no mistaking the
trend of the new policy.

The forced conversions precipitated another revolt in January 1500 in
the Alpujarras; it lasted for three months and was put down with difficulty.
Cisneros's view now was that by rebellion the Mudéjars had forfeited all
rights granted by the terms of capitulation, and they should be offered
a clear choice between baptism or expulsion. His personal preference was
'that they should convert and be enslaved, because as slaves they will be
better Christians'. Over the next few months the Mudéjars of Granada
were systematically converted by force; a few were allowed to emigrate.
By 1501 it was officially assumed that the kingdom had become one of
Christian Moors – the *Moriscos*. They were granted legal equality with
Christians, but were forbidden to carry arms and subjected to growing
pressure to abandon their racial culture. A huge bonfire of Arabic books,
ordered by a royal decree of October 1501 and not specifically by
Cisneros, was held in Granada. It was the end of the capitulations and of
Muslim al-Andalus: 'if the king of the conquest does not keep faith,'
lamented the former imam of the mosque at Granada, 'what can we expect
from his successors?'

With Granada apparently converted, Isabella was not inclined to tolerate Muslims elsewhere in her realms. On 12 February 1502 all Mudéjars in
Castile were offered the choice between baptism and exile. Virtually all of
them, subjects of the crown since the Middle Ages, chose baptism since
emigration was rendered almost impossible by stringent conditions. With
their conversion Islam vanished from Castilian territory, and continued to
be tolerated only in the crown of Aragon. By repeating a step that had
already been taken against the Jews, Isabella abolished plurality of faiths in
her dominions but also created within the body of Christian society the
wholly new problem of the Moriscos.

Many Mudéjars had thought that by accepting baptism they would be
left in peace. From about 1511, however, various decrees deliberately
attacked their cultural identity in an effort to confirm their abandonment
of Muslim practice. These measures culminated in an assembly convoked
by the authorities in Granada in 1526, when all the distinctive characteristics of Morisco civilisation – the use of Arabic, their clothes, their

jewellery, ritual slaughter of animals, circumcision – came under attack; to help combat these, it was decided to transfer the local tribunal of the Inquisition from Jaén to Granada.

## Jews and the Inquisition

Of the three great faiths of mediaeval Spain, the Jews were the smallest in number and the most vulnerable. Sporadically persecuted by Christians and Muslims, they none the less coexisted with both in conditions of relative tolerance. By the fifteenth century a rabbi could look back to the distant past and claim that in Castile the Jews 'have been the most distinguished in all the realms of the dispersion: in lineage, in wealth, in virtues, in science'. Excluded by popular anti-Semitism and by state legislation from several aspects of public life among Christians, Jews lived in ghettos (*aljamas*) in the major towns, devoting themselves to specific professions where they could benefit from the private favour of the upper classes. In the early Middle Ages they had been outstanding as scholars and physicians, and continued to be so. Prejudice was directed more against their leading role in finance: in both Castile and Aragon Jews or families of Jewish origin were prominent financiers and tax-gatherers, serving kings, nobles and the Church. Ferdinand in Aragon relied in good measure on financiers of Jewish origin, such as Alfonso de la Caballería, Luis de Santángel and Gabriel Sánchez. Isabella's two most prominent financiers were the Jews Abraham Seneor and Isaac Abarbanel. Among lower-class Christians, there was resentment of those who, by assiduity in trade and finance, seemed to be making profits out of the rest of the population. Many Jews in fact possessed land and became successful peasant farmers, but it did not alter a common perception that they were an urban grouping dedicated to exploiting the townspeople. The chronicler Andrés Bernáldez, parish priest of Los Palacios near Seville, denounced them for being 'merchants, salesmen, tax-gatherers, retailers, stewards of nobles, officials, tailors, shoemakers, tanners, weavers, grocers, pedlars, silk-mercers, smiths, jewellers, and other like trades; none tilled the earth or became a farmer, carpenter or builder: all sought after comfortable posts and ways of making profits without much labour'.

Anti-Jewish violence reached its height in 1391, when massacres took place in the aljamas of Seville, Valencia, Barcelona, Toledo and other major cities, and thousands of Jews were forced to accept baptism. Converted Jews or *conversos* now became a large minority, suspected of insincerity by Christians and distrusted by Jews. Termed 'New Christians' (as Moriscos also were later) but maligned as '*marranos*' (probably, 'pigs'), they were not subject to the disabilities suffered by Jews and consequently rose to high positions in Christian society. Many noble families by the fifteenth century had traces of converso blood, and even great prelates of the Church were of converso descent. Three secretaries of the Catholic Monarchs, including Hernando del Pulgar, were conversos. The common people saw little difference between the new conversos and the old Jews, and their attitude served to foment more anti-Semitism. In Toledo in 1449 civil disorders broke out between Old Christians and New Christians; the leaders of the former, led by Pero Sarmiento, forced through the city council a famous statute (*Estatuto*) excluding all conversos from office in the city. In 1467 further riots confirmed the division of the city into two hostile bands: the Old Christians, led by the Ayala family, and the conversos, led by the Silvas. Similar communal violence occurred in other cities in the 1470s, notably in Córdoba in 1473. Much of the conflict arose out of rivalry between urban elites for political control, but it was obvious that a dangerous phenomenon – antagonism among Christians for reasons of race – had surfaced in Spanish society.

A tract written in 1488 alleged that of all the conversos 'hardly any are true Christians, as is well known in all Spain'. Bernáldez claimed of them that 'the greater part were secret Jews'. There seemed to be good cause for religious hostility. In fact the religious identity of the conversos was often extremely unclear, varying from those who were sincere Christians but retained links with Jewish culture to those who were convinced and secret judaisers. Some, according to Pulgar, 'kept neither one law nor the other' in its entirety. There is abundant evidence that many conversos did not feel obliged to give up all their Jewish background, and in the closely knit community life of the period they continued to respect traditions that appeared compatible with Catholic belief. Purists of both faiths were naturally unsympathetic. Most rabbinical authorities in Spain and north Africa were of the firm opinion that conversos were thorough Christians and in no sense Jews, a view exactly the reverse of that held by Bernáldez and Catholic writers of the time.

Anti-Jewish publicists and preachers, among them the Franciscan fray Alonso de Espina, who exploited his position as confessor to Henry IV to stir up racial hatred, fuelled the controversy. In 1478, when queen Isabella was in Seville, a Dominican prior named Alonso de Hojeda preached to her and denounced the subversion of true religion by false converts within the Church. His testimony was corroborated by that of cardinal Mendoza and Tomás de Torquemada, a Dominican prior from Segovia. Faced by

undoubted evidence of judaising, the Catholic Monarchs applied to Rome
for a bull, granted by Sixtus IV in November 1478, establishing an
Inquisition (in Latin, an 'enquiry') into heresy.

An Inquisition had existed in the crown of Aragon in the thirteenth
century but was now inactive. Castile, on the other hand, had never had
one: the bishops and their courts had so far sufficed to deal with heresy.
The new tribunal was created for an emergency and therefore had unusual
features. Sanctioned by Rome and staffed by clergy, it was essentially an
ecclesiastical body; but all powers over it, such as appointments and
finance, were vested in the crown, making it in practice a state institution.
Possibly because of a wish to proceed with caution, the first inquisitors
were not appointed until September 1480; they began work immediately in
Seville. Created specifically to investigate the religious orthodoxy of conversos, the Inquisition had no authority over unbaptized Christians, and
consequently could not touch the Jews. There can be no doubt, however,
that its purpose was to eliminate Semitic culture from official Catholicism.
According to Pulgar, over 4,000 converso families fled from Andalusia in
the autumn of 1480; 'and since the absence of these people depopulated
a large part of the country', he continues, 'the queen was informed that
commerce was declining; but setting little importance on the decline in her
revenue, she said that the essential thing was to cleanse the country of that
sin of heresy'.

Wealthy conversos of Seville, led by Diego de Susán, plotted armed
resistance, but were betrayed and arrested. They were publicly punished
in *autos de fe*, the first of which was held on 6 February 1481, when six
people were burnt at the stake. The number of judaisers uncovered at
Seville justified the introduction of other tribunals throughout the country.
A further papal letter in February 1482 appointed seven more inquisitors,
all Dominican friars, among them Tomás de Torquemada. By 1492 there
were tribunals in Castile in Ávila, Córdoba, Jaén, Medina del Campo,
Segovia, Sigüenza, Seville, Toledo and Valladolid. In Aragon, Ferdinand
from 1481 began to use the old mediaeval Inquisition to investigate
conversos. Since this tribunal had once been wholly under papal control,
Sixtus IV retained a right to intervene. In April 1482 he protested to
Ferdinand that in the crown of Aragon 'the Inquisition has been moved not
by zeal for faith but by lust for wealth, and that many true and faithful
Christians have without any legitimate proof been imprisoned, tortured
and condemned as heretics'. Ferdinand refused to tolerate any papal
control, however, and eventually in October 1483 a bull was obtained
appointing Torquemada as inquisitor general of both Aragon and Castile,

thereby uniting the Inquisitions under a single head and creating for the first time a body whose authority extended throughout Spain regardless of political divisions. The papacy continued to claim jurisdiction but at every step Ferdinand and the inquisitors blocked interference in what was now a wholly royal and Spanish institution.

As in Seville, there was bitter opposition to the tribunal. In Toledo a converso plot was uncovered in 1484. In the crown of Aragon the introduction of the new institution was seen as a violation of the fueros, and conversos were fortunate enough to gain constitutional support for their cause. A general Cortes was called at Tarazona in January 1484 and the Inquisition was approved in principle. But the Catalans refused to attend, and not until 1487 was the first inquisitor allowed into Barcelona. Even after this, when the first autos were held in the city in 1488, there was profound hostility and protests were sent to the king. 'No cause or interest, however great, will make us suspend the Inquisition', Ferdinand replied. In Valencia the Cortes protested against the violation of their liberties. In the kingdom of Aragon, where conversos had always been powerful, there was armed resistance. 'Those newly converted from the Jewish race, and many other leaders and gentry,' reported the chronicler of Aragon, Jerónimo de Zurita, 'claimed that the procedure was against the liberties of the realm, because for this offence (of heresy) their goods were confiscated and they were not given the names of witnesses who testified against them. As a result, the conversos had all the kingdom on their side.' The city of Teruel refused to accept the Inquisition and acquiesced in the spring of 1485 only when Ferdinand threatened to occupy it with troops. In September 1485 one of the new inquisitors, Pedro Arbués, was murdered in Saragossa cathedral. The murder caused Aragonese opinion to shift against the conversos, and helped the Inquisition to mount a series of autos that destroyed the power of the great converso families in the kingdom.

The early activity of the Inquisition was concerned more with enquiry than with punishment. Thousands of conversos were persuaded to present themselves before the tribunal, and the vast majority suffered 'reconciliation', which in effect covered all types of penalty ranging from imprisonment or confiscation of goods, to a simple reprimand. The impact varied, since in many cities the most prominent conversos were forewarned and managed to escape. The Inquisition at this period was concerned not with 'heresy' in general but only with one variety of it, that involving people of Jewish origin. If someone condemned as a heretic was absent, he was burnt 'in effigy', which meant that a figure representing him was burnt in his place. If a deceased person was revealed to have been a heretic, his remains

were disinterred and burnt. Autos de fe were literally 'acts of faith', celebrated for the edification of the public, at which punishments already
decreed were confirmed in a public religious ceremony; burnings were
not an integral part of the occasion, and were carried out afterwards. The
proportion of conversos actually executed was small (though since the
entire activity of the Inquisition was unprecedented, we cannot minimise
the social impact of its procedures). Most contemporaries offer high
estimates for the number of executions. Andrés Bernáldez estimated that in
Seville between 1480 and 1488 'more than 700 persons were burnt and
over 5,000 punished'. More careful consideration of the available figures
suggests that around 2,000 people may have been executed by the
Inquisition in the whole of Spain in the first 50 years of its activity.

The intensification of pressure on conversos was in addition to and by
no means a substitute for the persecution of Jews. Convivencia survived in
parts of Spain, but official policy seemed now to discourage it. The Cortes
of Toledo (1480) called for previous legislation, that Jews wear distinctive
badges, to be enforced; it was also ordered that aljamas be walled off,
and that Jews not live outside the ghettos. At the end of 1482 a partial
expulsion of the Jewish population from Andalusia was ordered, and from
1483 Jews were expelled from various cities in the south. Jewish witnesses
were made to cooperate in giving evidence against conversos. The
Inquisition, by encouraging Spaniards to identify and denounce judaisers,
gave an enormous stimulus to anti-Semitism, which now became endemic
among both urban authorities and populace. An atrocity story made public in 1491, about the murder of a Christian child at La Guardia (Toledo)
by a group of conversos and Jews who were subsequently burnt for the
alleged crime, fed popular fury. To rid Spain of a people who were also
seen to be supporting conversos in their heresies, Ferdinand and Isabella
on 31 March 1492 issued an edict giving Jews four months to accept
baptism or leave the country.

Out of a likely total Jewish population in Castile of 70,000 and in
Aragon of 10,000, many accepted baptism and others left the country only
to return again, so that the final figure for those who left permanently
could not have been more than about 50,000. The tragic exodus of a
people who were treated as strangers but had known no other home – both
rich and poor, old and young, struggling abroad with the meagre possessions allowed them, cheated and robbed at every stage of their journey
– ended the long history of the Jews in Spain. They went principally to
Portugal (where a forced conversion was decreed in 1497, encouraging
many to come back), north Africa and Italy. Among those who remained

and were baptised was Abraham Seneor, the leading rabbi of Castile and treasurer of the hermandad; he was rewarded with a place on the royal council.

The sultan of Turkey is reported to have said later that he 'marvelled greatly at expelling the Jews from Spain, since this was to expel its wealth'. The quotation comes from a Jewish chronicler of the time, and is probably spurious. In fact the Jews after 1391 were a tiny disadvantaged minority, excluded from the major professions and public posts, and in many areas discriminated against by the law; they took no part in large-scale trade, and limited themselves to a handful of professions and to farming. They paid their taxes mainly to the crown (which ironically stood to lose most by expelling them) but were in no way either a wealthy or a successful minority, and the expulsion of 1492 accordingly seems to have had no serious negative consequences for the country. Moreover, the many who converted in 1492 carried on without interruption all the professional roles formerly fulfilled by Jews, for example in medicine. If its motive had been religious, as the evidence suggests, the expulsion was a total failure, for instead of solving the converso problem it had the reverse effect and at one stroke possibly doubled the number of false converts in the realm.

Despite appearances, the expulsion was not racialist in intention: both Isabella and Ferdinand had Jews and conversos as their closest collaborators and, in 1507, Ferdinand stated publicly that 'we have always had conversos in our service, like any other people, without distinction of persons, and they have served us well'. Nevertheless, the harsh policies represented by the expulsion and the Inquisition soon exposed a serious division of opinion among Spaniards, which expressed itself in various ways and developed eventually into a broad difference between those who still saw Spain as a pluralist society and those who defined it in narrower terms of religion and race. The Inquisition became the central issue in this debate.

The Sicilian inquisitor Luis de Páramo, writing in the sixteenth century, stated that many learned Spaniards, both before and after 1492, thought the expulsion and forcible conversion of Jews to be wrong. The use of force to root out heresy among conversos was likewise condemned by Hernando del Pulgar, who opposed the use of the death penalty, on the grounds that 'exemplary life and teaching of doctrine' were more appropriate methods for dealing with those who had never been properly instructed. Hernando de Talavera was another who felt that discrimination and persecution only confirmed Jews and judaisers in their beliefs. 'He detested', wrote his official biographer and historian of the Jeronimite order, José de Sigüenza, 'the evil custom prevalent in Spain of treating members of the sects worse after their conversion than before it'. The sixteenth-century Jesuit historian Juan de Mariana reported that the Inquisition's use of penitential garments (*sanbenitos*) 'at its inception appeared very oppressive to Spaniards. What caused most surprise was that children paid for the crimes of their parents, and that accusers were not named nor confronted by the accused, nor was there publication of witnesses. . . . Besides this it appeared an innovation that sins of that sort should be punished by death. And what was most serious was that because of these secret investigations they were deprived of the liberty to hear and talk freely. . . . This was considered by some as the most wretched slavery and equal to death.'

Many Spaniards accepted the Inquisition while wishing to reform some of its methods. The case of Diego Lucero, inquisitor of Córdoba (1499–1507), revealed the need for reform. During his term of office he instituted a reign of terror and corruption directed against both conversos and Old Christians: in a huge auto in 1500 he burnt 130 people on charges of Judaism, in 1506 he arrested the members of Talavera's household and accused the old archbishop of being a Jew. In protest at Lucero's excesses the soldier and chronicler Gonzalo de Ayora denounced 'the damages which the wicked officials of the Inquisition have wrought in my land', and led a deputation from Córdoba to see Ferdinand. Cisneros in 1508 convoked a special assembly, including most of the royal council, which sacked Lucero and examined the procedures of the Inquisition, but made no recommendations for change.

Demands for reform of the Inquisition continued with vigour into the next reign. A few concessions were made, such as a limitation at the Cortes of Monzón (1512) on the number of 'familiars', lay officials of the tribunal, appointed in the crown of Aragon. In all essentials, however, the Inquisition remained unaltered. In 1517, rejecting suggestions that the rule of secrecy, which protected the names of witnesses, should be dropped, Cisneros claimed that the Inquisition was so perfect 'that there will never be any need for reform and it would be sinful to introduce changes'. In 1483 the tribunal was given its own supreme council, which directed the work of the Holy Office in its various areas of activity in Spain and later in America. No proper provision was ever made to finance the organisation, which normally had to rely on the income from confiscations; this might and did give rise to abuses, but on the whole did not produce wealth, since most of those accused of heresy were poor.

The expulsion of the Jews from Spain was carried out for religious motives that had long been in the making; the forcible conversion of the

Mudéjars was by contrast an abrupt move. It is very likely that the Catholic Monarchs expected a further programme of evangelisation to produce a nation truly united in religion. This, however, did not happen. Instead, the abandonment of a pluralist society led to the creation within Christian Spain of two great disadvantaged minorities, conversos and Moriscos, which suffered all the disabilities of prejudice but enjoyed few of the benefits of conversion. From the early fifteenth century various official bodies began to discriminate against the New Christians, setting in motion the social pressure for 'purity of blood', *limpieza de sangre*. The university college of San Bartolomé in Salamanca was the first to introduce, in 1482, rules forbidding any but those 'of pure blood' from becoming members. The principal impulse to the spread of this practice was the founding of the Inquisition, which made Spaniards familiar with the image of conversos as a danger to religious integrity and national security. One after another in the 1480s leading institutions adopted statutes of limpieza which aimed to exclude descendants of Jews and Moors: the first religious order to do so was the Jeronimites (1486), the first cathedral was Seville (1515). The Inquisition adopted as its rule (1484) that descendants of those it condemned were ineligible to hold any public office, thereby giving currency to the notion that guilt for heresy remained in the blood generation after generation. It was ordered that sanbenitos of the condemned be exposed in local churches to perpetuate their infamy after their death. The concerted campaign against conversos, presenting them as culturally unclean (not *limpios*) and a stain on the honour of Spain, gathered force in the early sixteenth century and forced them into the role of internal exiles, never entirely at ease in a society into which their forebears had been involuntarily assimilated. However, the drive for 'limpieza' was always limited to small private bodies (colleges, cathedrals), never attained official status in public law and was largely unknown in most of Spain outside Castile.

## The Church and Cisneros

Control of the Church was an explicit part of the pacification programme of the Catholic Monarchs. Like the military orders, the Church was a powerful source of disorder: Alfonso Carrillo, the embattled archbishop of Toledo, was, with a thousand men at his command, 'more a pope than a prelate' in the eyes of one observer, and took the field against Isabella in the battle of Toro in 1476. Like the magnates, the Church had extensive property, though contemporary estimates that it owned a third or a half of national income are without foundation.

Ferdinand and Isabella intended to win back the right, assumed by the papacy in the later Middle Ages, to nominate all bishops and prelates; they hoped to use it to reform Church discipline. In July 1478 they summoned a synod of Castilian clergy to Seville and presented to them for discussion a programme in 17 points touching on relations between the clergy and the crown (Carrillo was still in revolt), reform of the Church and claims against the pope. By consulting directly with their clergy, they secured national support for cooperation with the crown and greater autonomy from Rome. The synod expressed support for reforms including the obligatory residence of bishops in their sees, a demand aimed primarily at papal nomination of foreigners to Spanish benefices. Few measures of reform were attempted in the crown of Aragon, whose Church was independent of that of Castile.

Conflicts between the crown and Rome over nomination to the sees of Cuenca (1482) and Seville (1484) were resolved in favour of the crown. Spanish rulers since the Middle Ages had been granted ecclesiastical patronage in territory they reconquered from the Moors, and the new acquisitions overseas gave the crown a unique opportunity to extend its authority. In 1486 the pope granted the monarchs patronage (*patronato*) over all Church appointments in Granada and the Canaries. Bulls of 1501 and 1508 also granted them an unprecedented patronato over the Church in the New World, where the crown was authorised to appoint and sack clergy, raise taxes and even veto papal decrees. Although the American Church still retained all its basic immunities under canon law, and was subject to the pope, in practice its supreme head was the king. By the end of the reign, the crown was well on its way to controlling the nomination of Spanish bishops (here the only obstacle was the insistence of cathedral chapters on their right to elect), and moreover had full control in the newly conquered territories and in America, as well as over the Inquisition. The gains that the English monarchy was later to achieve through the Reformation were already achieved completely in Spain without any change of religion.

The crown used its initiative in order to choose higher clergy who were pious, celibate, Spanish and university trained. Bishops were required to be resident in their sees, and to encourage reform. The best example of this policy at work was the appointment of Talavera to Avila and later to Granada; but there were notorious exceptions, such as Ferdinand's nomination of his nine-year-old natural son Alfonso to the see of Saragossa. The direct control of state over Church led, in both Spain and America, to the active participation of clergy in political life and a close cooperation between Church and state at all levels.

Ferdinand and Isabella were anxious to achieve political control, but there is less evidence of their concern for any religious reform. The few measures they took in favour of 'reform' were patchy, ineffective and impermanent. The monastic houses in Castile (for the most part Benedictine) suffered from indiscipline, lax observance and freedom from external control. The synod of 1478 had not discussed the problem, but already in the 1480s Talavera had advised the queen to look into disorder and banditry among the monasteries of Galicia. In 1493 the pope issued a bull authorising the crown to investigate all the monastic orders. The Catholic Monarchs seem to have done no more than establish a general right to visit all religious institutions at will: visitors whom they appointed restricted themselves to enforcing rules on residence, separation of sexes and so forth. The real impetus for change came not from the crown but from reforming trends in fifteenth-century spirituality, represented particularly by the foundation (1373) and remarkable success of the Jeronimite order (with its main centre at Guadalupe), of which 49 religious houses were established by 1516. The literature of the Flemish 'devotio moderna' influenced the Jeronimites as well as leading Benedictines such as García de Cisneros (d. 1510), reformer of the Catalan shrine of Montserrat and cousin of the cardinal. The coming of printing helped to spread knowledge of Flemish and Italian piety, and of Spanish works such as García de Cisneros's *Exercises in Spiritual Life* (1500) and the *Life of Christ* (1496) of Francesc Eiximenis (d. 1409).

At the same time there were movements for reform among the mendicant orders, which were split from the early fifteenth century between the traditional 'Conventuals' and the stricter 'Observants'. The Observants gradually gained influence in the three orders – Dominicans, Franciscans and Augustinians – and won the support of the papacy, which in 1497 and particularly in 1517, with the bull *Ite vos*, decreed that the Observants were the sole legitimate branch of each order. Cardinal Cisneros, who happened to be (from 1494) provincial of the Franciscans in Spain, and also an Observant, collaborated fully with the papal directives, which coincided with his own wishes and those of the Catholic Monarchs. The changes enforced on Franciscans in Spain called for stricter adherence to precepts of the order, and abolition of Conventual houses or their merger with Observant friaries. Diego de Deza, archbishop of Seville, began the suppression of all Conventual Dominicans. In both orders the programme was carried through amid bitter opposition, since in all cases the visitors appointed to reform discipline were Observants. Resistance in Aragon, where the Observance was viewed as Castilian encroachment, was particularly strong.

This was in sum the extent of religious change, and nothing remotely resembling a reformation of the Church occurred in Spain. Only the religious orders were touched by renewal, and even then it was a long process that continued into the sixteenth century and bore fruit in the mysticism of Luis de Granada among the Dominicans and Francisco de Osuna among the Franciscans. The religion of the people was unaffected, corruptions among the clergy continued unreformed. Several bishops were conscientious enough to hold assemblies of their clergy at which they tried to improve both priests and people. In Toledo, Carrillo held important synods in 1473, 1480 and 1481, which decreed that priests should learn Latin, wear clerical dress, and preach sermons; at the same time, marriages had to have witnesses, and festivities and carnivals in church were forbidden. Cisneros likewise held a synod in 1497 at which he ordered records of baptisms and Easter communion to be kept. Few, if any, of these measures were enforced. There was a clear gap between pious aspiration and sober practice in a Church where a prelate like Carrillo could enjoin celibacy on his clergy while he himself was known to have two sons: and where the archbishop of Santiago could erect between Zamora and Salamanca a castle dedicated to his mistress, 'del Buen Amor'.

The most outstanding collaborator of the Catholic Monarchs was Francisco Jiménez de Cisneros (1436–1517), Isabella's confessor from 1492, archbishop of Toledo from 1495, regent of Castile from 1516. The personal austerity, extreme religious zeal and unswerving dedication of the cardinal coincided perfectly with the queen's own aspirations. He shared with Isabella an ardent wish to convert the infidel, and his intolerant policy towards the Granada Muslims in 1500 was approved by the queen. Cisneros carried out faithfully the exhortation in her testament to pursue 'the conquest of Africa and the war against the Moors'. In 1505 he supervised the force of 10,000 that sailed from Málaga and captured Mers-el-Kebir. In 1509, relying exclusively on funds from his own see, he personally, at the age of 73, led an army of over 15,000 into Africa and captured Orán. This crusader against Islam – to whom, in his own words, 'the smell of gunpowder was sweeter than the perfumes of Arabia' – was also an enemy of the Jews and is said to have steeled Isabella's resolve in 1492 to expel all Jews from Spain. A strong supporter of religious discipline, he was ruthless in pursuit of unity and order among the Franciscans: scores of Conventuals are said to have fled to Africa or Italy rather than live under his rule. Appointed cardinal and inquisitor general in 1507, he refused, in the face of cash offers (1512 and 1516) from the converso community, to deviate from the principle of inquisitorial secrecy. His most lasting monuments were cultural. He welcomed foreign religious ideas, particularly of a reforming and mystical character, such as those of Erasmus and Savonarola; and encouraged the printing of the devotional works of Savonarola, Vincent Ferrer and Catherine of Siena. He constructed at Alcalá the great new university which opened in 1508 and employed the brightest luminaries of Spanish humanism. Finally, at Alcalá he set in train the preparation of a magnificent edition of the Bible in its four original languages which, begun in 1502 and issued in 1522, became known as the Complutensian (from the Latin for 'Alcalá') Polyglot.

# Finance and the economy

Spain in the late fifteenth century was a poor country with few significant natural resources; as today, it suffered from inadequate irrigation, extremes of climate, bad land distribution, intractable soil. Even more than today, it suffered primitive agrarian methods, poor investment and bad communications made worse by political and customs barriers. The lack of political unity perpetuated economic disunity: the country was divided up into a multitude of small commercial regions which had little contact with each other so that it was not unknown for one province to eat well while its neighbour starved.

Spain's poverty did not make it easy to support an ambitious imperial policy, and the enterprises of the Catholic Monarchs were carried out in conditions of constant debt. Though the crown of Aragon contributed small sums, the bulk of revenue came from Castile, giving it automatic control of all government policy for the whole of Spain. The disruption of the civil wars had reduced Castilian state income in 1477 to the very low figure of 27 million maravedís; the resumption of alienated property in 1480 was of some help, but the Catholic Monarchs were unable to pursue any consistent programme to increase their revenue. Money was raised as and when circumstances permitted, and administered by two members of the royal council who acted as accountants (*contadores mayores*) of the treasury (*hacienda*).

The main source of royal revenue in the fifteenth century was the alcabala or sales tax (*see* p. 21), which produced about 90 per cent of income. Together with other revenue such as the customs, it was collected by tax-farmers (*arrendadores*), since the crown had no tax officials other than those on its own estates. In the course of the reign ordinary tax income rose to 150 million maravedís in 1481, 269 million in 1496 and

320 million in 1510; at the same time extraordinary income rose from
52 million in 1483 to 112 million in 1504. The biggest single enterprise
of the reign, the war of Granada, created special sources of income, from
the hermandades and the papacy, to which detailed reference has already
been made.

Apart from the Granada war which, thanks to papal help, almost
financed itself, most of the projects of the Catholic Monarchs could not be
met by ordinary revenue. In three principal areas – the court, the army and
foreign policy – the assertion of royal authority was an expensive business
in which costs continued to rise. Fortunately, Ferdinand and Isabella had
no fixed court and dressed modestly; 'princes', Isabella told her son Juan,
'should not be lavish in dress'. Even so, the cost of maintaining royal residences and of ceremonial for ambassadors rose from 8 million maravedís in
1480 to 35 million in 1504. The cost of the royal militia and ordinance
rose from 20 million in 1482 to 80 million in 1504; and military expenses
within the peninsula amounted to over 500 million between 1495 and
1504. Foreign wars and royal marriages were exorbitantly expensive: the
first expedition to Naples cost 88 million, the second 366 million; and
arrangements for Catherine of Aragon's journey to England for her marriage cost 60 million. The growing diplomatic importance of Spain was
also a burden: in the last ten years of her reign Isabella spent 75 million
on ambassadors.

Although the Catholic Monarchs survived without major financial
problems, in two respects they bequeathed a negative legacy to their successors. First, from 1489 they began, as we have seen, to pay off their debts
at 10 per cent interest in the form of juros. The annual payments for juros
rapidly became a burden on the treasury: in 1504 the sum payable was 112
million, by 1516 it was 131 million. Second, since they were dependent on
the willingness of their subjects to pay taxes, they were forced into a compromise over their chief source of revenue, the alcabala. The clergy were
made exempt from it, nobles were confirmed in their ownership of local
alcabalas and were allowed to collect it themselves, and the cities were
after 1495 allowed to compound for the tax by paying an equivalent lump
sum (encabezamiento). These important concessions to the governing elite
made the monarchs look elsewhere for new sources of income. They discovered considerable possibilities in the wool trade.

The pastoral industry had always been strong in a Spain where the
moving frontier against Islam was typified more by the roving herdsman
than by the settled farmer. Of the various pastoral groups the largest was
the Mesta, a sheepowners' guild organised in the thirteenth century and

comprising small owners as well as a few great lords and monasteries. Traditionally the crown appointed a judicial officer to the Mesta to settle disputes over the great sheep-walks (*cañadas*) that ran over Castilian territory. Powerful as the Mesta was, it represented the interests of only the migratory sheep (*transhumantes*), whose owners moved their flocks seasonally over the countryside in search of pasture; there were in addition in Castile thousands of non-migratory flocks (*estantes*), whose numbers were plausibly estimated in 1600 as being four times greater than those of the Mesta. Wool, especially the quality wool of the merino sheep, introduced into Spain by the Muslims, was the major non-agricultural industry of Castile and indeed of Spain, crucial to rural economy and domestic textile production, but vital above all to the trading centres of northern Spain and the enormous business enterprise which generated the fairs of Castile and, in particular, the famous fairs at Medina del Campo.

By 1450 Medina was already the financial centre of Castile, and the Mesta was the principal source of its business, with some 2.8 million sheep in its flocks. To strengthen and control this bulwark of the economy the crown in 1500 appointed a member of the council as president of the Mesta, and in 1492 and 1511 new ordinances for it were drawn up by Dr Palacios Rubios. With crown protection and support the Mesta rapidly became a privileged corporation that attracted widespread hostility: in the reign of Isabella alone, the Mesta appears as a party in some 1,100 lawsuits, most of them over disputed pasture. Among privileges granted was one in 1480 that common land dug up in the previous reign be returned to pasture; in 1489 the position and extent of the cañadas were confirmed; and in 1501 a controversial decree allowed the Mesta to occupy land at the low rent at which it had first been leased. Through the Mesta the Catholic Monarchs gained monopoly control of wool, but their main objective was fiscal: control made it easier for them to extend the traditional tax on herds – the *servicio y montazgo* – into a tax on each sheep at pasture, income from which increased substantially during the reign.

The trade in wool, Castile's chief export, was also reorganised. Since the later Middle Ages the main exit route for wool had been towards Bruges in Flanders, but there was also an important trade to England (mainly through Bristol) and France: to all three areas the Spaniards exported raw materials (wool, wine, iron from the Basque country) in exchange for textiles. Castilian merchants, some of them conversos, settled in the ports of Normandy and Brittany, and in Bruges they were one of the biggest foreign merchant colonies. Castilian ships based on the Cantabrian and Basque ports helped to protect the commercial lifeline. The Catholic

Monarchs strengthened the link with Flanders by appointing agents in Bruges and other foreign cities to cooperate with the officials of the Mesta and traders in Spain. From the peninsula the two export centres were Burgos and Bilbao. Although an inland city, Burgos through its merchants controlled the exit of most Castilian wool, and in 1494 a trading body called the *consulado* was created, with a monopoly over trade to northern Europe. Bilbao, the Basque port from which most shipments were made, retaliated by claiming a share of the trade, and in 1511 obtained the formation of its own consulado. A compromise between the cities was reached in 1513, but in turn this agreement was contested by the other northern ports, principally Santander, which never succeeded in attaining the pre-eminence of Bilbao. The rivalry between the Basque port and Burgos continued down to 1558, when a royal decree fixed their respective roles; during all that period Burgos remained Castile's commercial capital, serving the textile industry in Segovia and organising trade not only to Flanders but also to Italy.

The commercial activity of northern Castile and general reliance on the import of textiles in exchange for raw materials, is evidence of a weak industrial base, which the Catholic Monarchs were in no position to remedy. The trading activity, nevertheless, was important enough to controvert (as we have already observed) any presentation of the alliance between Aragon and Castile as being between a nation with commercial experience and one with nothing but a tradition of military activity. It is likewise not helpful to suggest that Aragonese institutions were imposed on the economic life of Castile. The specific evidence for this is the modelling of the consulado of Burgos on the mediaeval consulados of Valencia and Barcelona. But there is no reason to suggest that the guild system was also imported from Aragon: Castile had its own urban guilds, which evolved in the fifteenth century in accordance with the needs of manufacturers in the larger cities. Ferdinand and Isabella had no consistent economic policy, and certainly no intention of introducing Catalan practice into Castile. No joint policy measures were taken to integrate the economic lives of Aragon and Castile, which remained separate and competitive in all respects. Within Castile, the encouragement that the monarchs gave to improving communication and transport no doubt arose from their direct experience of difficulties in their travels across the peninsula. In 1497 they gave privileged status to the carters' guild that had helped resolve transport problems during the war of Granada and now became the *Cabaña Real de Carreteros*. The urgent need for a good postal service, particularly with respect to diplomatic communications with Italy, was remedied by setting up a postal centre in Barcelona; but it was not until the reign of Charles V that monopoly control over the service was granted to an Italian family, the Tassis, that had previously organised the postal system of the duchy of Burgundy.

In Catalonia the economic disruption caused by the civil wars and the remensa rebellions seems to have been checked and reversed, but improvement did not occur before the 1490s. In the great conflict provoked by the Inquisition (1484–7), merchants and administrators fled from Barcelona and trade and finance were affected. Ferdinand nevertheless played a positive role in Catalan recovery, by the agrarian settlement at Guadalupe (1486), changes in the city government of Barcelona (1493–8) and in the city's financial system, and by giving preference to Catalans in the trade with Sicily and Naples and the newly conquered north African ports. Although Valencia city was still, as a German visitor reported in 1494, 'much greater than Barcelona and very densely populated', the Catalans had by now, thanks in part to the ruthless tactics of Ferdinand, overcome their internal divisions; in Valencia by contrast the realm enjoyed a superficial unity which was soon to be exposed by a civil war.

It was at one time believed that the privileges granted to the wool trade, whether to the Mesta or the consulados, were gravely detrimental to agriculture and encouraged producers to favour pasture over arable. The direct consequence, we were told, was famine and a permanent imbalance in the Castilian economy. These claims are wholly untrue. The fact is that, thanks to an increase in population levels from about the mid-fifteenth century, peasant producers looked for more land to grow food, and common lands, wastes and pasture were tilled and sowed. The interest in agriculture was reflected in the publication in 1513 and subsequent enormous success of Gabriel Alonso de Herrera's *Agricultura General*. The agrarian boom extended into much of the sixteenth century. In many communities the ecological balance between pasture and arable appeared to be turning against the former. The Catholic Monarchs were naturally anxious to support a pastoral industry that, taking into account both migratory and non-migratory flocks, supported a very large rural population, was the basis of the domestic textile industry and provided an important revenue both to the traders of Burgos and to the government. As towns extended their arable to meet demand, conflict with pastoral interests occurred. The legislation favouring the Mesta was a reasonable attempt by the crown to prevent disputes over land use; it can be criticised less for this than for its failure to protect the rights of non-migratory flocks. The picture often given, moreover, of migratory flocks being left free to eat up the countryside as they went, is without foundation: not only were the cañadas of carefully defined width, about 75 metres across, but the flocks of the Mesta were expressly prohibited from encroaching on 'the five forbidden things' (*las cinco cosas vedadas*): cornfields, vineyards, fruit crops, hayfields and livestock pasture.

The Catholic Monarchs were in fact anxious to stimulate grain output, since many parts of Spain had to import food in order to survive. The country suffered from unbalanced production: the southern *meseta* of Castile and parts of Andalusia gave good harvests, but by contrast the Cantabrian provinces – Galicia, Asturias, the Basque country – and the crown of Aragon were regular importers of grain. Wheat was the main food crop, with barley and other grain used primarily for animal consumption. Unfortunately, surpluses in one area could not always be sent to other needy areas, thanks to export restrictions and customs barriers. The sovereigns helped rural producers in two ways. First, they decreed in 1480 that all peasants in Castile had the right to change their lords freely, which in theory gave more independence to the rural classes; then in 1486 the Sentence of Guadalupe obtained freedom for the remensa peasants and allowed them to sell the produce of their own lands without restriction. Second, they aimed to abolish all restrictions to grain movement, with the one firm exception that wheat should never be exported to Muslim territory, which up to 1492 included Granada. In 1500 they authorised freer trade in grain, after due payment of export taxes, and expressed the wish 'that our subjects exploit their holdings and work with a greater will in agriculture'. Another decree of 1505 aimed 'to facilitate free trade (of grain) throughout the realm'. When natural disasters struck – a drought in Plasencia in 1488, an epidemic in Vitoria in 1503 – the crown was quick to remit taxes so as to allow production to recover.

In good years exports abroad were permitted. Above all, the needs of the American colonists, who required wheat because it was still a new crop in America, created a major market for Andalusian farmers. More commonly, however, Spain had to import to feed itself: Valencia imported regularly from Sicily, the richest source of surplus grain in the Mediterranean; while Castile imported from England in 1487, from north Africa in 1503 and from Flanders in 1505. Spain's fundamental insufficiency in grain, not any undue favouring of the Mesta, was the cause. The precarious balance in food supplies was threatened above all by population growth. Towards the end of Isabella's reign bad weather also aggravated the crisis. From 1502 to 1507 there were unremitting bad harvests, climaxed by an epidemic in 1507. To stop profiteering and hoarding the Catholic Monarchs in December 1502 imposed a controlled price structure, the *tasa*, on grain. The following year the controls were extended to flour. The tasa proved to be an optimistic and unworkable attempt to control the very complicated Castilian marketing system. The spectre of famine, which was caused exclusively by the weather and not by deficient royal policy, receded but was not exorcised. When Ferdinand returned to Castile from Italy, according to one chronicler, the droughts vanished and the harvest of 1508 was so plentiful that it was called 'the green year,' *el año verde*.

## The discovery of America

Although the conquest of the Canaries brought Spaniards out into the Atlantic, Castile had no distinctive expertise in seafaring. The major achievements of the age in equipment, navigation and shipping were the work of other nations, most notably the Portuguese. It is significant that Christopher Columbus concentrated his search for patronage on Lisbon, but also sought support in other European courts, including France and England, and came to Spain only because of failure elsewhere. His proposal – to sail westwards in order to reach the eastern lands of Cathay and Cipangu – was accepted as feasible, since everyone knew that the world was round. The costs, however, were a clear risk; moreover, Columbus's own credentials were extremely shaky. Scholars have raised doubts about his true name, his nationality, his qualifications and even his religion; at the time he appeared to likely patrons as an obscure Genoese sailor with extravagant expectations.

Rejected by the Catholic Monarchs in 1486, Columbus was given their patronage in 1492 after the intervention and financial help of the Aragonese converso Luis de Santángel, treasurer of the hermandad. The contract promised him, in the event of success, noble status, the title of Admiral of the Ocean Sea, and extensive privileges over the territories he discovered. His three little ships, with a total crew of ninety, set sail from Palos, near Cadiz, on 2 August 1492. After a stop in the Canaries they set out over the Atlantic and made their landfall at Watling Island in the Bahamas on 12 October. Further travel took them to Cuba and Hispaniola; in January Columbus began the return voyage, was forced to put into Lisbon by the weather and arrived at Palos on 15 March 1493.

The explorer at once set out to report to the sovereigns, then in Barcelona. In order to forestall the Portuguese, Ferdinand and Isabella lodged their claim to the new islands with the pope (Alexander VI, a

Spaniard), who issued a number of bulls, one of them the famous *Inter caetera* (1493), confirming the Spanish title. The wording was too vague and too much of a threat to Portuguese discoveries to be acceptable. The Catholic Monarchs negotiated with Portugal and by the treaty of Tordesillas (June 1494) agreed to move the line marking Spanish territory further west; in the event, the line passed through enough of the American mainland to give Portugal its title to Brazil.

The excitement at Columbus's discoveries is reflected in the size of his next expedition, which left Cadiz in September 1493: there were 17 vessels with 1,200 men including 12 missionary priests (unlike the first expedition, which appears to have had none). The intention was to create settlements on the fertile island of Hispaniola, but when they arrived they found that the colonists left there the previous year had been wiped out. The new colony was no success, either: life in the tropics was soon found to be more difficult than expected. Gradually, as further exploration failed to uncover the rich civilisations of the Orient, disillusion set in. There was to be no quick route to Asia, and wealth, apart from some gold and a few slaves, was limited. Columbus, who returned home in June 1496, made two more voyages to America, in 1498–1500 when he touched on Trinidad and the mainland (called Tierra Firme) of South America, and 1502–4 when he scouted the coast of Honduras; but after the first of these he was sent home in irons, and the second was conspicuous by its failure to discover anything significant. He died in 1506, a rich man and still in possession of his titles and honours, but disappointed with the outcome of his endeavours. After his death he did not cease to travel: his remains were transferred from Valladolid to Seville, later to Santo Domingo on Hispaniola, then to Havana (1795) and finally to Seville (1899).

The great admiral had been sustained by a vision that the discovery was part of a divine purpose: in December 1492 he suggested that profits from his voyage might help pay for the liberation of Jerusalem from the Turk. He felt that he had been privileged to discover 'the new heaven and earth foretold by Our Lord in the Apocalypse'. The disappointment at not reaching Cathay failed to dampen the enthusiasm felt by Columbus and his successors for the enormous possibilities offered by the new lands and whatever lay beyond: there were legends of an 'earthly paradise', of the island of the Amazons, of Atlantis, of the seven golden cities. The humanist Peter Martyr of Anghiera, then resident in Spain, drew on Columbus's reports to describe the felicities of what he called a 'new world', *novus orbis*. Spaniards generally referred to the territories as 'the Indies', a perpetuation of the original illusion that Asia lay beyond; but for most

Europeans the name that stuck was 'America', derived from a highly popular account, published in 1507, of the voyages of the Florentine navigator Amerigo Vespucci.

For some 20 years after Columbus's first voyage the Spanish enterprise in America was limited mainly to the West Indies and in large part to one island, Hispaniola, where the New World's first Spanish city, Santo Domingo, was founded in 1496. By 1500 Hispaniola had a white population, exclusively male, of only one thousand. As the number of immigrants increased they ventured outwards in search of two things: slaves, to meet the labour needs in Hispaniola, and land. Warfare, forced labour and epidemic disease began to take their toll of the original Taino inhabitants of Hispaniola: Las Casas was to claim later that three million natives perished between 1494 and 1508. To replace them, the settlers made slaving raids on neighbouring islands: some 40,000 natives of the Bahamas, for example, were transported between 1509 and 1512. In the process the Spaniards also settled the islands: Puerto Rico from 1508, Cuba from about 1511.

It was a restless, savage frontier society, in which there were few white women. Institutions of the Reconquest frontier were adapted to the new conditions. When the Canaries had been occupied, the leader of the expedition, Alonso de Lugo, was appointed *adelantado*, a military office that granted land rights in return for defence duties. The land itself was distributed into *repartimientos* among new settlers. In Hispaniola, by extension, it was the Indians rather than the land who were parcelled out in lots (called repartimientos and later *encomiendas*) among the Spaniards: each *encomendero* was supposed to protect his Indians and instruct them in the faith in return for labour services. The decline in Indians, and the rapid absorption of land by settlers, aggravated the impatience of newcomers, many of whom preferred the easier wealth of gold, of which over 30 tons were sent to Spain from the West Indies by 1520, most of it panned from the mountain streams of Hispaniola.

Gradually the explorers moved on to the mainland. From 1509 small settlements grew up at Cartagena, Santa Marta and other sites. Braver spirits struggled through the dense jungles. One of them, the *conquistador* Vasco Núñez de Balboa, founder of the city of Darien, made his way through the isthmus of Darien and became in 1513 the first European to see the shimmering expanse of the Pacific, on whose coast in 1519 the town of Panama was founded. That year, 1519, was memorable for two other dramatic events that established Spain's imperial destiny. In the spring, Cortés landed on the coast of Mexico and began the epic march that ended with the fall of the Aztec empire. At the same time, five ships left Cadiz, under the command of the Portuguese captain Ferdinand Magellan and with a crew of about 240, in search of a south-west passage which took them across the Pacific and cost them four ships and the life of Magellan; only one vessel, the *Victoria*, commanded by Sebastián Elcano and with 21 survivors on board, limped into Cadiz in 1522. It was the first circumnavigation of the globe.

By 1520 Spain was on the threshold of world empire. Few could have been aware of it, for apart from some gold and exotica, there was nothing to make an impact on the Spanish mind. The historian López de Gómara proclaimed the discovery of America to be 'the greatest event since the creation of the world', but he wrote it with hindsight a generation later, in 1552. In the early years there were only intuitions, as with Talavera's explanation to Isabella of what use Nebrija's new Castilian grammar might be: 'after Your Highness has put under your yoke many barbarian peoples and nations with diverse tongues, they will be obliged to accept our laws and with them our language'. Isabella certainly promoted the laws and usages of Castile in America, which she insisted on reserving for Castile both in the papal bulls of donation and in practical restrictions on emigration. After her death, Ferdinand relaxed the controls so far as to permit Aragonese to emigrate in small numbers. This was eventually confirmed as the right of all Spaniards by Philip II in 1596, but commerce remained confined to the monopoly operating from Seville, in which other Spaniards could participate.

Well before the death of Ferdinand, America began to create conflicts and pose problems whose significance will concern us later (*see* p. 95). The enslavement of Indians, begun by Columbus, was firmly opposed by Isabella, who encouraged the formation of encomiendas and the payment of wages for labour. Abuses in the system, however, led the Dominican friars on their arrival in Hispaniola in 1510 to campaign for the abolition of the encomienda, thereby initiating a great debate on both sides of the Atlantic about the nature of human freedom.

# The emergence of a cultural identity

For both foreign commentators and native scholars, one of the most striking aspects of the reign of Ferdinand and Isabella was its cultural advance. The learning of a previous generation was represented, for example, by Ausias March in Valencia and the marquis of Santillana in Castile (both d. 1458); but their successors, such as Juan de Mena, were already drawing directly on Latin literature in a way that previous scholars had not. In the mid-century, Italy was the centre of active humanism, and it was there that scholars like Juan de Lucena and Alonso de Palencia went, bringing back with them a new appreciation of Latin literature and Renaissance thought. The trend was in both directions: by the 1470s there were Italians teaching in Salamanca, where in 1480 the first chair of Greek in the peninsula was founded. When the scholar Antonio de Nebrija (d. 1522) returned in 1476 from 12 years in Italy, determined to 'uproot the barbarism' of impure Castilian, Renaissance influences were already active in Spain. Famous Italians came in his wake, notably Peter Martyr of Anghiera (who came in 1488) and Lucio Marineo Siculo, professor at Salamanca from 1484 to 1496.

In 1492 Nebrija's Castilian grammar – the first of any modern European language – was dedicated to Isabella and contained the striking claims that 'our language is now at its height' and that 'language has always been the companion of empire'. He asserted that the other peoples of the peninsula would learn Castilian, and that cultivation of Latin was essential, because on Latin 'is founded our religion and the Christian state'. Renaissance humanism put itself at the service of the state, and both Ferdinand and Isabella were strong supporters of the new learning. Latin had to be learnt as an essential prerequisite for service in diplomacy, administration and the Church. The queen herself began to learn Latin in 1482 but seems not to have made great progress. The restricted scope of government at this time, and the absence of a fixed capital city, limited the scope of the new learning to a 'court humanism' rather than the broader 'civic humanism' known in Italy. There were nevertheless important cultural offshoots, principally through the influence of the nobles. The German visitor Münzer recalls visiting a Latin class held by Peter Martyr: 'his students were the duke of Villahermosa, the duke of Cardona, don Juan Carrillo, don Pedro de Mendoza, and many others from noble families, whom I saw reciting Juvenal and Horace. . . . All these are awakening in Spain the taste for letters.' In their turn the nobles in their own courts, notably the members of the Mendoza family, became patrons of Renaissance art and letters. Italian influence was important in art as in literature; it can be seen in, for example, the painting of Pedro Berruguete (d. 1506). But it was by no means exclusive, and the broad mingling of styles in the decorative arts in Spain is clear testimony to the limited impact of the Italian Renaissance and the continuing survival of older forms, notably Mudéjar. Burgundian influences entered from northern Europe, through architects such as Hans Wass and sculptors like Gil de Siloé. The strength, indeed, of Burgundian and Flemish culture extended beyond the arts into devotional literature, a consequence of the close commercial links between Spain and the Netherlands.

The study of classical languages was advanced through the establishment of Alcalá university (1508) and the completion of the Polyglot Bible (1522). All this was necessarily the achievement of a tiny minority of scholars and unrelated to any advances in education or literacy in Spain, so that it is difficult to pass an optimistic judgement on Spain's part in European culture. Apart from Valencia, dating from 1412 but granted university status by the pope in 1500, no places of higher education were founded in the late fifteenth century. Popular traditions persisted, for example in the *Cancionero general* (Valencia 1511), a compilation of fifteenth-century verse; and in the poetry that printing now helped to circulate in the form of chap-books (*pliegos*). Above all, the enduring fame of the *Celestina* (1499), by the writer Fernando de Rojas (who was possibly a converso), helped to confirm the persistence of popular tradition and popular ballads in everyday culture. It is not surprising that Guicciardini in 1512 was unimpressed by the advance made by the Renaissance in Spain. Spaniards, he reported, 'are not interested in letters, and one finds very little knowledge either among the nobility or the other classes, and few people know Latin'.

The first printed book in Spain using movable type was the *Sinodal* issued in Segovia in 1472, though fixed wooden type had been used earlier, as in Sánchez Vercial's *Sacramental* (Seville, 1470). By 1473 German printers were active in Saragossa, and by the 1480s the major Spanish cities had their own presses. In 1480 the Catholic Monarchs abolished all duties on the import of books; but controls over the content of books were reintroduced in July 1502, directed mainly at popular literature. By 1501 over 800 titles had been published in Spain; in the period 1501–20 the total rose to 1,300. In the first period some 10 per cent of titles were in classical literature, in the second about 18 per cent. Even these figures exaggerate the impact of classicism in Spain. Renaissance culture under the Catholic Monarchs was a hybrid growth in which Latin and Italian influences had to struggle, not always successfully, for place.

There is no doubt that the work of Nebrija and others helped to give the Castilian tongue a primacy that was above all the logical consequence of Castile's leading political role. Castilian speech invaded Valencia, Catalonia, Galicia and Portugal. Inevitably, the success of Castilian was achieved at the expense of the other tongues and cultures of the peninsula, not least those of Semitic origin. The Polyglot Bible was one of the last

great achievements involving Hebraic scholarship: thereafter, Jewish
learning came to be despised, and Arabic was no longer encouraged by
the state. The cultural transformation under the Catholic Monarchs was
directly related to the profound social developments taking place in
Spanish society.

# The legend of the Catholic Monarchs

Ferdinand and Isabella came to power in Spain at a time when millenarian
ideas and eschatological visions of the Second Coming of Christ were common coin in Europe. Some Spanish writers reflected this in their eulogies
of the peace achieved after years of civil conflict: the converso *bachiller*
Palma in 1478 claimed that 'the king our lord came to set at liberty the
peoples of Castile . . . out of the slavery from which Christ, and through
him the king, freed us'. The courtly presentation of Ferdinand and Isabella
as Messianic figures took various forms, two common views being that
they would unite the kingdoms and thereafter the whole world under their
sway, and that they would liberate Jerusalem. Although this presentation passed into official propaganda, it was the least of the reasons for the
enormous reputation of the Catholic Monarchs. Pausing one day before a
portrait of Ferdinand, Philip II is said to have remarked, 'We owe everything to him'. Why did the sovereigns retain this unique position in the
minds of Spaniards?

They were, first of all, the last Spanish rulers of Spain; after 1516 the
German Habsburgs and after 1700 the French Bourbons occupied the
throne. In her piety and uprightness, Isabella seemed to represent the best
of Castilian virtues. Both monarchs, in the simplicity and modesty of their
households, contrasted with the extravagance of later rulers; 'on the dress
of the king and the queen', wrote a Flemish noble after visiting them in
Toledo in 1501, 'I shall say nothing, for they wear only woollen cloth'.

Second, by their immense travels throughout the peninsula they were
seen to be participating directly in the government of their subjects: it is
possible that at least in Castile most people saw the king or the queen at
some time in their lives. Never again would Castilians be so directly, and
therefore so well, governed. 'They were monarchs of this realm alone,'
wrote the admiral of Castile in 1522, 'of our speech, born and bred among
us. . . . They knew everybody, always gave honours to those who merited
them, travelled through their realms, were known by great and small alike,
could be reached by all'. Ferdinand and Isabella were still mediaeval
rulers, not 'new monarchs': for them good government did not mean the

imposition of the apparatus of a modern state. Indeed, under the Catholic Monarchs there was no nation state, no new bureaucratic apparatus, no absolute monarchy. Ferdinand wished if anything to strengthen local communities so as to allow them to achieve viable self-government under the tutelage of the crown, and encouraged the view that cooperation with the crown was liberty from oppression. 'Let us', the royal councillor Quintanilla said when urging the towns to accept the hermandad, 'be free men as we should be, and not mere subjects as we are.' Subjects were encouraged, in Pulgar's words, 'to leave the señoríos and come into the royal liberty'. Procuradores to the Castilian Cortes in 1502, 1506 and 1507 were ordered to come with plenary rather than partial powers. Ferdinand realised that without strong, homogeneous, government below there was little hope of control from above. It was accepted, in any case, that the crown had limited powers. In the words of Dr Palacios Rubios, 'to the king is confided only the administration of the realm, not dominion over property'. Even when they were most high-handed in their political actions, the sovereigns ruled with consent, a fundamental component of their style of government.

Finally, the Catholic Monarchs made possible the emergence of a society in which the pluralistic outlook of convivencia was explicitly rejected in favour of the majority culture of Old Christians. The Muslim and Jewish heritage was repudiated, at first only in religion but later also in its other forms and cultural survivals, until the drive against Semitism became a national passion. Ferdinand and Isabella cannot be blamed for this development, since they were in no sense racialist; nor can they even be credited with a passion for religious unity, since the Mudéjars of Aragon continued to survive as Muslims for some 20 years after the death of Isabella. None the less, their religious policy, which undoubtedly had popular support, achieved a superficial consensus at the expense of nurturing beneath the surface tensions and divisions that created within a united Spain a society of conflict.

# CHAPTER 2

# Charles V and Empire 1516–1558

## Politics 1516–1558

The son born to princess Juana of Spain and Philip the Fair in Ghent in February 1500 was named Charles after his great-grandfather Charles the Bold, duke of Burgundy. His paternal grandfather was the emperor Maximilian of Habsburg, his maternal grandparents were Ferdinand and Isabella of Spain: it seemed likely in consequence that he would one day inherit both Spain and the Habsburg lands.

Charles spent his entire childhood in the Netherlands, as did three of his sisters (Eleanor, Isabel and Mary); the other two children of Juana, Ferdinand and Catherine, were born and raised in Castile. When Juana went to Castile to take up her inheritance in 1506, she left her young son behind in the charge of his aunt, Margaret of Austria, who took care of his upbringing and supplied him with tutors. Portraits of the young prince show him to be thin, sickly looking and somewhat ugly, with a prominent nose and a heavy lower jaw, characteristic of the Habsburg family, that protruded slightly so that his teeth did not meet exactly and caused some inconvenience when eating. In the genial atmosphere of the Burgundian court at Brussels, Charles was brought up as a Renaissance prince. Alternating with the pleasures of chivalry and the chase, he was given a solid grounding in statecraft and piety under the guidance of Adrian of Utrecht, an adept of the religious outlook of the 'devotio moderna'. From 1509 his tutor was Guillaume de Croÿ, lord of Chièvres, who kept a firm hand over his charge. Although Charles was not without talent (in languages, for example, he was brought up to speak only French and Flemish, but soon added Spanish and a smattering of German), he relied heavily on his advisers in his early years.

Shortly after the death of Ferdinand the Catholic in 1516, Charles was proclaimed in Brussels as joint ruler, with his mother, of Castile and Aragon. Sailing to Spain the following year, his little fleet was diverted by winds and landed on the wild coast of Asturias on 18 September 1517. From there the royal party had to make a slow and painful journey through winding mountain roads into Castile. Finally, on 4 November, Charles met his mother in her seclusion at Tordesillas: he obtained confirmation of his royal rights, but continued in accordance with the demands of his Castilian advisers to use both their names jointly in official documents. A letter was sent asking Cisneros to come and see him, but the ageing regent died on 8 November, just outside Valladolid, on his way to meet the king.

Charles entered Valladolid on 18 November. His first trial of strength was with the Castilian Cortes, which met there in February and recognised him as king, but in an atmosphere of muted suspicion. Castilians had always preferred as their next ruler the Infante Ferdinand, who was a Spaniard like themselves, had been king Ferdinand's favourite, and enjoyed strong support among a group that later joined in the Comunero rebellion. Charles quickly arranged for his brother to leave for Germany (the prince left Spain on 18 May). On 22 March Charles and his entourage left Valladolid and set out for the crown of Aragon in order to take the customary oath. On 9 May the court arrived at Saragossa and spent the rest of the year in discussions with the obdurate Cortes of Aragon. In June an epidemic of typhus carried off the chancellor, Jean le Sauvage, the second most important man in the court. Charles sent off to Margaret of Austria and summoned one of her advisers, the Piedmontese diplomat and humanist Mercurino de Gattinara, to become his new chancellor in October.

In January 1519, on his way to Barcelona, Charles received news of the death of his grandfather, the emperor Maximilian. In the midst of negotiating with the Catalan Cortes, then, he was drawn into the even more momentous struggle for the Imperial crown. At Frankfurt on 27 June the German electors unanimously chose him as Holy Roman Emperor (the Fifth of his name, but in Spain he was Charles the First). The news was received in Barcelona ten days later and immediately changed all plans. Dropping any intention he may have had to go to Valencia, the new emperor ordered preparations to be made for the court to sail back to the Netherlands. From Calahorra, as he retraced his way back over the peninsula, Charles in February 1520 summoned the Castilian Cortes to meet at Santiago, in distant Galicia, within four weeks. The location was chosen as being nearest to the intended port of departure, Coruña, but evoked rage in the cities of Castile, which eventually convened on 31 March, a bare five days after the arrival of the court in Santiago. Money was reluctantly voted, mainly to cover the costs of the enormous fleet of 100 ships that left Coruña with Charles on 20 May. Already, in central Castile, a revolution had broken out.

Charles's all-too-brief sojourn in Spain was the prelude to a career that, thanks to his new Imperial commitments, made him a perpetual absentee monarch. He now united in himself a greater number of realms than had ever before been accumulated by any European ruler: the entire Burgundian inheritance, centred in the Netherlands; the immense hereditary Habsburg lands, including Austria within the Empire and Hungary outside it; the whole of peninsular Spain as well as its Mediterranean lands, particularly Naples and Sicily; and the continent of America. His duties took him everywhere: at his memorable abdication in Brussels in 1555 he recalled that he had made nine expeditions to Germany, six to Spain, seven to Italy, four to France, ten to the Netherlands, two to England, as many to Africa; and that he had made eleven voyages by sea. He spent one out of every four days of his reign travelling: 'my life', he said, 'has been one long journey'.

It is true that of all his realms he devoted the most time to Spain, a total of some seventeen years, against twelve in the Netherlands and only nine in Germany. But it was also the country from which he was the most absent, an astonishing fourteen years between 1543 and 1556. He was in Spain from September 1517 to May 1520, July 1522 to July 1529 (his longest stay), April 1533 to April 1535, December 1536 to early 1538, July 1538 to November 1539, November 1541 to May 1543, and September 1556 till his death in September 1558. As sovereign of so many states he needed to be present in each of them to maintain his authority; but in the process his repeated absences provoked profound discontent.

Charles's departure in May 1520 was the signal for the revolt of the Comunidades, which paralysed all government in Castile for over a year. Despite the defeat of the rebels at Villalar (1521), it was some time before pacification was complete. After his return in 1522 the emperor made Spain his home for the next seven years, the longest period he spent in any of his dominions. It was perhaps the most successful phase of his entire reign, and Castilians became reconciled to a king who spoke Castilian and governed through Castilians. Furthermore, as he informed the Cortes in 1523, he regarded 'these realms as the head of all the rest (within Spain)', if only because they were becoming a valuable source of revenue.

The seven years were important because Charles used them to settle the government of the country: he reformed the court, reorganised the administration and presided over a significant cultural revival. In practice there was still no capital of Castile, and Charles was an itinerant king. In January 1526, for example, he was in Madrid where he signed the treaty releasing king Francis I of France from captivity. In April he was in Seville, where he married his cousin, the beautiful princess Isabella of Portugal. From May through to the late autumn he spent his honeymoon in Granada, amid the delights of the Alhambra: they were the happiest and most idyllic days of his reign. In December a Cortes was summoned to meet in February at Valladolid, to which the court moved in January: it was there in May 1527 that Isabella gave birth to the future Philip II. These travels within Spain show that Charles had resumed the peripatetic character of the reign of Isabella: he was seen by, and consequently earned the direct loyalty of, Spaniards. This fact is essential to an understanding of how the general suspicion of 1520 was replaced by a good measure of devotion. Catalonia was particularly privileged: virtually all the emperor's comings and goings were through the port of Barcelona, where in April 1535 he assembled the splendid array of forces destined for the siege of Tunis. On the other hand, Valencia benefited least from his presence; his seventeen-day visit to the city in May 1527 began tragically, because the crowds waiting to see him were so great that a bridge collapsed and scores of people died. He visited the city only once again: in December 1542, to have Philip recognised as heir to the throne. In all, he spent eleven years in Castile and just under five in the realms of Aragon.

The court, for all Charles's wanderings in the peninsula, became more sedentary and more distant from the common people. The Cortes pleaded with Charles 'to hold public court certain days in the week as was the custom of the Catholic King', to dispense royal justice; but this never happened. Instead, the royal household adopted the complex and luxurious Burgundian ceremonial, with a huge staff ranging from the high chamberlain to gentlemen of the household and pages. By the end of his reign Charles had 762 persons in his Spanish household, at a cost of 200,000 ducats a year: the figure excludes the households of the empress and the prince. This great number necessarily included most officials of state, since at that time government was inseparable from the household of the king.

Administration in Spain was theoretically under the direction of Gattinara as grand chancellor, but effective control moved more and more into the hands of Spaniards. Of these the most important was Francisco de los Cobos (d. 1547), an Andalusian of humble origins who served in the royal secretariat in Spain and then in 1516 went to Flanders, where he earned the favour of Chièvres and an influential post when the court came to Spain in 1517. When Chièvres died suddenly of plague in Germany in 1521, the emperor began to rely on Cobos, who was also accompanying him, for advice on Spanish affairs. Thereafter the star of Cobos rose while that of Gattinara waned. He became the emperor's chief secretary, in 1529 was appointed to the council of state, and became the king's chief counsellor together with Nicholas Perrenot, lord of Granvelle. Gattinara's death in 1530 confirmed this pre-eminence. Over the next eight years Cobos accompanied the emperor on all his travels, but increasingly deferred to Perrenot in foreign affairs; from 1539 he stayed behind and devoted himself exclusively to the administration of Spain. 'When he is with the emperor', the Venetian ambassador wrote in 1546, 'everything goes through his hands; and when the emperor is absent, in all important matters he is the ruler through the Council and his own judgment.'

Cobos's major contribution was the recruitment and training of a bureaucracy for loyal government in Castile. His senior staff, who included his nephew Juan Vázquez de Molina, and Gonzalo Pérez, who succeeded Alfonso de Valdés as Latin secretary and later became principal secretary to Philip II, were not younger sons of the nobility nor (Pérez excepted) letrados. They were lesser gentry, with an eye on preferment but with a total dedication to the service of the emperor.

Spaniards continued to regret Charles's commitment to northern Europe and the Holy Roman Empire: the theme recurs in every Cortes of the reign. 'Your Majesty's protracted absence from your Spanish dominions', wrote the admiral of Castile in 1531, 'is a thing to which your subjects can hardly reconcile themselves.' They were also unhappy at the use in Spain of the new title 'Majesty'. But after 1521 there appears to have been no significant hostility, and the acceptance of Spaniards in the court (Charles selected Spanish clergy as confessors, for example) placated opinion. Spaniards became eligible for foreign honours: from 1516 ten places in the famous Burgundian Order of the Golden Fleece were reserved for them, and the first members were invested at Barcelona in 1519. The Spanish language began to be used together with French and Latin in correspondence and administration, and Charles learned to speak it perfectly. At a famous address to the pope and cardinals in Rome in 1536, he rebuked a French prelate who criticised him for speaking in Castilian: 'do not', he said, 'expect me to speak any other language but Spanish, which is so noble that it should be learned and understood by all Christian people'. The refusal to speak French, his own tongue, was a gesture of anger directed against the French king, who had just declared war. It did not give any special status to Spanish, which was never again used by Charles in an international assembly, and French always remained his preferred language.

After the suppression of the rebellions of the 1520s, the reign remained singularly bare of great events. The emperor's fleeting visits to Spain were notable only for the rapid summoning and dissolution of the Cortes in each realm. After 1529 the empress Isabella was regent of Spain, acting with the advice of the archbishop of Toledo, cardinal Tavera, president of the council of Castile. She died in 1539, when Philip was only 12 years old. After a short interval, the prince was in May 1543 appointed regent, to act with the advice of Tavera, the duke of Alba, and Cobos. At the same time Charles prepared, in his own hand, two Instructions for his son. One, the 'Confidential' Instruction, outlined the personal and political ideals he wished his son to follow; the other, a 'Private' Instruction, was a report on the principal advisers he had left with Philip. Commenting on Tavera and Cobos, Charles wrote: 'Though they are the heads of rival cliques, nevertheless I decided to appoint them both, so that you might not be left in the hands of either one of them.' This careful balance of interests, which Philip later adopted in his own government, helps to explain the apparent absence of conflict in the governmental affairs of Charles in Spain.

When Philip had to go to the Netherlands and Germany (he left in October 1548 and returned in May 1551) his place was temporarily taken by the archduke Maximilian, Ferdinand's son, who came to Spain to marry Philip's sister Maria. Philip resumed the regency again from 1551, but interrupted it in July 1554 to go to England for his marriage to Mary Tudor; in the interim his sister Juana, widow of the king of Portugal, acted as regent. For the prince it was to be an eventful absence: he came back from it as king. Charles returned to the peninsula in September 1556, having divested himself of Spain and its associated territories, though not yet of the Holy Roman Empire.

# Foreign policy 1516–1558

In 1519, shortly after Charles's election to the Imperial throne, Gattinara wrote to him: 'Sire, since God has conferred on you the immense grace of raising you above all the kings and princes in Christendom, to a power hitherto possessed only by your predecessor Charlemagne, you are on the path to a universal monarchy, you will unite Christendom under one yoke.' The idea of a universal monarchy was by now commonplace, part of the fund of concepts shared by politicians, poets and humanists; but the extent of Charles's possessions seemed to give substance to the idea. 'Under this most Christian prince', wrote his Latin secretary Alfonso de Valdés, 'the whole world may receive our Catholic Faith and the words of Our Saviour will be fulfilled: *fiet unum ovile et unus pastor.*' Years later, after the battle of Mühlberg, the poet Hernando de Acuña continued the refrain in looking forward to

*una grey y un pastor sólo en el suelo . . .*
*un monarca, un imperio, y una espada*
*(one flock and one shepherd on earth; one monarch, one empire,*
*one sword).*

There seems little in Charles's own actions or declared motives to lend weight to these aspirations towards an 'imperial idea'. His enemies, led by France, certainly suspected that he had dreams of world dominion; but he firmly denied this before Paul III and the cardinals in 1536: 'There are those who say that I wish to rule the world, but both my thoughts and my deeds demonstrate the contrary.' He was in any case never wedded to a fixed view of his role: as he grew in experience, so his ideas and likewise his advisers changed.

Even had he wished to create a strong, unified 'empire', Charles lacked the means. Nothing held his diverse territories together except a common loyalty to him as their ruler. He was in reality 'emperor' only of the lands included in the Holy Roman Empire: elsewhere he ruled individual territories as king, or duke, or count. Even in Germany the title of emperor gave only limited authority; Charles's power rested more securely on the hereditary Habsburg lands in the east, and the provinces (the Netherlands, Franche-Comté) that made up the Burgundian inheritance, to which he was deeply attached and treated almost as a family holding. Because all these territories had no common institutions, Charles was forced to improvise. The one great obligation on him, to rule personally in each of his dominions, was of course impossible to fulfil; and he appointed, as we shall see, regents or viceroys from members of his family.

In order to have a central consultative body Charles appointed dignitaries from several parts of the monarchy to his council of state, a largely honorific body that by 1526 was composed mostly of Spaniards. In practice Charles himself coordinated business, with the help of advisers and a small secretariat. Chièvres at first, and then Gattinara until his death in 1530, dominated his counsels. The highly efficient work of Cobos, who enjoyed the title of secretary of state and was answerable for Spain, Italy and the Indies, pointed the way to a regional division of responsibilities. When Nicholas Perrenot de Granvelle (d. 1550) replaced Gattinara, he was accordingly put in charge of affairs in northern Europe, where the paperwork was done in the French language. The Venetian ambassador concluded in 1546 that 'the emperor has two principal counsellors, Cobos and Granvelle, who transact all the business of all his states'; but this underestimates the enormous personal labour of Charles in the field of diplomacy and above all in war. There is every reason to blame the emperor's ill health and early abdication less on his inordinate appetite and recurrent gout than on the heavy burdens of office.

Imperial policy did not coincide entirely with the interests of Spanish foreign policy. The Protestant struggle in Germany seemed too distant to touch Spaniards directly, and the Cortes was (as in 1527) willing to finance war against the Turks, but not when the Turks were on the Danube. Though the great international conflict between Habsburg and Valois coincided exactly with Spain's old quarrel with France, in Italy that was being rapidly resolved in favour of Spain, and the extension of the feud to northern Europe was a departure from traditional Spanish interests. Spaniards consequently continued to be critical of Habsburg policy; only when Charles took up the struggle against Turkish expansion in the western Mediterranean was he seen to be reverting to the interests of the peninsula, and to the crusading ideals of Isabella and Cisneros.

The rivalry with Francis I of France took place over three issues: Navarre, which Ferdinand the Catholic had annexed in 1512 and which France claimed; the old duchy of Burgundy, with its capital at Dijon, which had been annexed to France since 1477 but which Charles persistently claimed as his birthright, 'notre patrie' as he described it in his Instructions to his son, and where he desired to be buried; and Italy, where all parties disputed control of the strategic duchy of Milan. Charles's election as emperor, against the rival candidature of Francis I, intensified the conflict between the two monarchs, which at times took on the character of an intense personal quarrel, culminating in his celebrated chivalric challenge before the pope in 1536, that 'in order to avoid the deaths of so many people', all his quarrels with Francis 'would be better resolved person to person with swords, capes and daggers . . . on land or on sea, in a closed field or in front of our armies, wherever he chooses'.

Hostilities began in 1521 with a French invasion (timed to coincide with the Comunidades) of Navarre: this ended in June. Thereafter the struggle was centred on Italy, where early in 1522 the cardinals elected as pope cardinal Adrian of Utrecht, Charles's old tutor, regent and inquisitor general of Spain, and the only Dutchman ever to be elevated to the see of Peter. England, the papacy and Italian princes were drawn into an international alliance against France. This stage of hostilities ended with French invasions of Milan in 1523 and 1524, but on 24 February 1525 the French army, commanded by Francis I himself, was decisively defeated outside Pavia. It happened to be the emperor's birthday: the triumphant Charles, at the time in Madrid, became host to the imprisoned king of France, who in January 1526 signed the treaty of Madrid, ceding Burgundy as the price for his freedom.

Safely back home, Francis I refused to carry out the unrealistic terms of the treaty. He was supported by England, by the new pope Clement VII (Adrian had died at the end of 1523) and the Italian princes. In May 1527 a vengeful Imperial army, made up largely of German mercenaries under the command of Francis's enemy the constable of France, Henry of Bourbon, descended upon Rome and sacked the Eternal City. Alfonso de Valdés used the occasion, in his *Dialogue of Lactancio and an archdeacon*, to vindicate his master and attack the corruption of the Church; but there was universal horror at the outrage. Profiting from this, Francis led his troops into Italy again and laid siege to Naples. Fortunately for Charles, at this juncture (1528) the all-important mercenary naval force under the Genoese admiral Andrea Doria defected to him and remained thereafter firmly in his service. The pope was no more in favour of French than of Spanish hegemony in Italy; and England was beginning to trouble the papacy with requests for the divorce of Henry VIII from Catherine of Aragon. Emperor and pope came together in common interest, and Francis by the peace of Cambrai (August 1529) was forced to agree to their terms.

In effect Charles was left in control of Italy, while France was confirmed in Burgundy. The peace ended an epoch in Charles's policy. Till that date his chief preoccupations had been in the Mediterranean; henceforth, despite further wars in Italy, his commitments lay in the north with the rising tide of the Reformation. When he left Barcelona for Italy in July 1529, he cut his hair short, in deference to the style now common in western Europe. Those of his entourage who were likewise obliged to cut their hair (long hair was traditional in Spain) wept when they did so. The conflicts of the next 15 years in Italy – terminated by the peace of Crépy in 1544 – did little to disturb the equilibrium achieved at Cambrai. Charles's achievements were brought to a suitable climax amid pomp and ceremony at Bologna where, on 23 February 1530, he received from

Clement VII the iron crown of the Lombards; and on the following day, his birthday, was crowned Holy Roman Emperor.

Rivalry in the south was only interrupted, not terminated, by the death of Francis I in 1547. In 1540 Charles had meanwhile conferred on his son Philip the duchy of Milan, a fief of the Empire. It remained thereafter under the control of the Spanish crown, which appointed a viceroy to govern it. The new French king, Henry II, came to power when Charles in northern Europe was at the most vulnerable stage of his career. By active alliances with the Lutheran princes of Germany, and with the Turks (who had, since their unsuccessful siege of Vienna in 1529 – Charles was there in 1532 – continuously threatened the Hungarian frontier), Henry succeeded in imposing intolerable and expensive pressure on the emperor. The German situation deteriorated rapidly. Despite his convincing victory over the Lutherans at Mühlberg (April 1547), his miserable and humiliating failure when besieging Metz (1552–3) convinced Charles that a different hand was required at the helm.

In 1536 the emperor had claimed that 'my intention is not to war against Christians, but against the infidel'. This was no more than a traditional ritual invocation. The policy of Ferdinand the Catholic had been, according to his secretary Pedro de Quintana, to have 'peace among Christians, and war against the infidel'; and in 1513 the poet Torres Naharro had called on the king to 'impose peace among Christians'. Charles's statement was in part directed against France, whose links with the Turks were common knowledge. He was none the less committed to the anti-Muslim struggle, which he saw as a divine mission; and in 1519 in Barcelona described it as 'the thing most desired by us in this world, in which we intend to employ all our realms'. For once, Spanish sympathies coincided entirely with his; but it was not until after 1529, when the north African ruler Khayr al-Din Barbarossa seized from Spain the island fortress of the Peñón of Algiers, and a Spanish fleet of eight galleys was defeated off Ibiza, that vigorous action was taken.

Charles now had two extra advantages in the war against the Turk: the winning of Andrea Doria for the first time gave Spain a regular naval force; and in 1530 the Knights of St John of Jerusalem, expelled by the Turks from Rhodes in 1522, established themselves in Malta. Doria in 1532–3 led a naval expedition that, with the help of Spanish troops and a naval contingent under Spain's leading naval commander Álvaro de Bazán, seized Coron and Patras in Greece. Barbarossa, however, continued to dominate the western Mediterranean. Charles thereupon organised the famous 1535 expedition against Tunis. The Spanish units under himself and Doria sailed from Barcelona to the general rendezvous at Cagliari: in all the huge fleet comprised 82 galleys and some 300 transport vessels with 10,000 Spaniards and twice as many from other nations. In July the fortress of La Goleta and then the city of Tunis itself were captured, and handed over to the ruler dethroned by Barbarossa, Muley Hassan, to hold as the emperor's vassal. Barbarossa escaped and made his way to Istanbul, where he took command of naval operations in the eastern Mediterranean.

The two decades after Tunis, however, saw a slow deterioration in Christian power, due primarily to Charles's prior commitments in northern Europe. A gigantic international expedition based on collaboration between Doria, Venice and the pope, and foreshadowing the great Lepanto enterprise a generation later, had a half-hearted engagement with Barbarossa off the Greek coast in September 1538. A more determined effort was made by Charles himself in October 1541, against the city of Algiers. A force almost as large as that which had taken Tunis, and including in its ranks Hernando Cortés, was however denied success by a terrible storm that wrecked the fleet and forced the Christians to withdraw. It was the emperor's last attempt to stop the infidel. Barbarossa died in 1546 at the age of 80; but the erosion of Spanish power went on at the hands of the pirate Dragut. The Muslims took Tripoli in 1551, the Peñón de Vélez in 1554, Bougie in 1555. By the end of the reign the Spanish presence in north Africa was limited only to Melilla, Orán, Mers-el-Kebir and La Goleta.

Disappointed in all other areas of his foreign policy, the emperor could still hope for success in his native Netherlands, whose territory he had appreciably extended over the years by the annexation of Tournai (1521), Artois, Utrecht, Groningen and Gelderland (1543). To give some unity to what were called 'the Seventeen Provinces', in 1548 he reorganised all the territories into one administrative unit within the Holy Roman Empire. At the same time, by a Pragmatic Sanction he made his family the heirs by primogeniture to each of the provinces. The otherwise fragmented territory thus took on the semblance of a nation state, which in the emperor's absence was governed first by his aunt Margaret of Austria and then from 1531 by his sister Mary of Hungary.

The Netherlands (and with them the rest of the Burgundian inheritance, including Franche-Comté) were of all his possessions closest to the heart of the emperor. He felt bound to them by ties of family and sentiment, and spent more of his reign there – 12 years – than in any other part of his monarchy after Spain. His attachment explains why he decided to bind the Netherlands to Spain when he divided up his territories, and why he charged Philip to preserve them as a sacred trust. In fact there were also sound practical reasons for Charles's attitude. Situated at the confluence of Europe's trading routes, secure in possession of an extensive range of heavy and light industry, served by the great capitalist metropolis of Antwerp, the Netherlands were the most flourishing region of his empire and the most capable of contributing to his financial needs.

The progress of Lutheranism, and its alliance with hostile political interests in northern Europe, caused Charles the greatest anguish. In Germany his policy was frustrated by the princes and he was driven into compromise. In the Netherlands, by contrast, he began to introduce an Inquisition (1522) and from 1525 published severe edicts (*placards*) against Lutheran and Anabaptist heretics, culminating in the introduction of the death penalty for all heresy in 1550. 'What is tolerated in Germany', he wrote to Mary of Hungary, 'must never be suffered in the Netherlands.' Political dissension in the provinces – notably the revolt of Ghent in 1539, which Charles personally suppressed – was likewise firmly controlled.

After 1545 the Catholic initiative in religious affairs in Europe passed to the Council of Trent and the papacy; the emperor in Germany was forced into compromise settlements such as the 1547 religious truce or Interim and the 1552 military peace of Passau. To protect the Burgundian lands against France and the threat from Germany, Charles turned to England, which he had long hoped to bring into the Habsburg orbit. The marriage of Philip and queen Mary of England (July 1554) was intended to associate England with the defence of the Netherlands, and Spain with the re-conversion of England to Catholicism.

The emperor's disappointments in Germany were climaxed by his failure to take Metz from the French (October 1552–January 1553). He handed over German affairs to Ferdinand, who eventually achieved a settlement in the peace of Augsburg (September 1555). Charles was seriously unwell. Gout and recurrent insomnia – he would spend his sleepless hours taking his collection of clocks to pieces and putting them together again – aggravated his moods of intense depression: 'he spent long hours sunk in thought and then wept like a child', reported one observer in 1553.

His decision to abdicate and leave the government in younger hands was put into effect at the solemn assembly of the Estates General in Brussels on 25 October 1555. Philip came over from England expressly for the ceremony. In a moving speech that reduced his audience to tears, the emperor outlined his labours, his successes and his failures; he then resigned the Netherlands to Philip. Three months later he formally abdicated from all the Spanish dominions, and in March 1556 Philip was proclaimed king in Valladolid. Further instruments handed Franche-Comté to Philip. In September Charles also renounced the Empire, but the formal abdication and election of Ferdinand did not take place until May 1558. He took ship for Spain from Vlissingen on 17 September, landed at Laredo and made a slow progress southwards to the residence that was being prepared for him beside the Jeronimite monastery at Yuste in Extremadura. Throughout his retirement he continued to correspond widely and to take a vigorous interest in affairs. He died on 21 September 1558; twenty-six years later his remains were transferred to the tomb expressly prepared by his son at the Escorial.

# Spain and revolution 1517–1522

Uncertainty, faction and local revolts continued after the death of Ferdinand the Catholic and during Cisneros's brief regency. The proclamation of Charles in Brussels began a drift there of Spaniards (like Cobos) anxious to ingratiate themselves with the new ruler; in Spain, on the other hand, many supported the rights of queen Juana and looked to prince Ferdinand as her successor. Divisions of interest and loyalty in Castile, which Isabella had helped to conjure away, began to surface again. To strengthen internal security, Cisneros put into effect a plan for a citizen militia of 30,000 men, raised among volunteers from each region of Castile and financed mainly by the cities. The project would have made the crown militarily independent of the grandees, who consequently used their influence to provoke resistance in the cities. An insurrection in Valladolid, which quickly spread to other towns, forced Cisneros in February 1517 to drop the plan.

Spaniards representing opposing groups which the Catholic Monarchs had done little to reconcile now contemplated the new dynasty with a mixture of unease and hope. In the flourishing commercial city of Burgos the merchants who profited from the voluminous wool exports to Flanders could expect further favours; their success, however, was resented by the towns of central Castile, whose fragile textile industry, centred in Segovia, was threatened by foreign cloth imported in exchange for wool. This difference of economic interest became acutely important during the Comunidades. Likewise many who had failed to achieve a reform of the Inquisition by Ferdinand the Catholic or Cisneros placed their hopes in the chancellor Jean le Sauvage, who seemed sympathetic to their views.

The first contact between the king and his kingdom, at the Valladolid Cortes in February 1518, was by no means unfavourable. Charles was not looked upon as an alien. After all, Castile had only recently had a Burgundian ruler – Philip I – and Castilians were anxious to accept their new sovereign; but they were cautious. Juana was still queen, they reminded him, with superior rights. As king he had certain powers, but also certain duties. 'Most powerful lord,' they said bluntly, 'you are in our service (*nuestro mercenario es*)'; word for word, it was a repetition of a claim that the Cortes at Ocaña had made to the weak Henry IV in 1469. The Holy Inquisition must be reformed so that 'the wicked be punished and the innocent not suffer'. The export of bullion must be stopped; only Castilians must hold public and Church posts. He should learn to speak Castilian, the better to understand his vassals and they him. In return for a promise to preserve their rights, the Cortes recognised Charles as king and granted him a subsidy (servicio).

The installation of pro-Burgundian advisers and of Flemings in official posts quickly disillusioned Spaniards. Over the next few months opposition focused on three main complaints: excessive taxation, the appointment of foreigners to office and the absence of the king. On the first, there were reactions immediately after the Cortes in February. The procuradores from León who had voted for the servicio were denounced as 'traitors' on their return. Objections to foreigners were even more vigorous. Chièvres and his friends received and distributed honours as though they were in a conquered country. To avoid breaking his promise not to give offices to foreigners, Charles issued them all with letters of naturalisation, a transparent and widely resented subterfuge. Scores of lucrative posts were granted to the Flemings. Some, like Charles's own physician, and his tutor cardinal Adrian, received bishoprics. Laurent de Gorrevod, a Savoyard, received the whole of Yucatán and Cuba as a fief, and in August 1518 was granted the first substantial licence to trade black slaves to America. Chièvres was granted immensely profitable sources of income and the right to nominate to all vacant posts in America. The appointment that most stirred public opinion, however, was that of Chièvres's nephew, Guillaume Jacques de Croÿ. Already a cardinal and bishop of Cambray, now at the age of 17 in 1518 he was appointed to the richest see in Spain, the archbishopric of Toledo which Cisneros had just vacated (it was a brief tenure: Croÿ died of illness in Germany in 1521).

The grandees of Castile were outraged. Some, such as the hereditary admiral of Castile, Fadrique Enríquez de Cabrera, and the constable of Castile, Íñigo Fernández de Velasco, expressed open dissent. The nobles nevertheless were divided by clan feuds and found it difficult to make common cause. The major cities of Castile – Burgos (the constable's own city),

Córdoba, Seville – were split between factions allied to rival nobles. In Toledo the rivalry was particularly bitter between the Ayala group of families and those related to the Riberas and Padillas. These family feuds, crucial to an understanding of events in some cities, were in others often superseded by more overriding interests: in Toledo the regidor Hernando de Ávalos found that his hostility to Chièvres took him into alliance with Juan de Padilla, a regidor from the rival clan.

The king's very rapid passage through Castile (Valladolid was the only major city he visited), his departure for Aragon in March, and his equally fleeting return before taking ship at Coruña, seemed to show contempt for his Castilian inheritance. The election to the Empire and the placing of his Imperial title before his Spanish one, suggested that Spain was to be relegated to a minor role. Where Charles had, like kings of Spain before him, been addressed as 'Lord' or 'Highness', it was required that he now be titled 'Majesty'. The cumbersome new form of address – 'Sacred Catholic Caesarean Majesty' – was rejected by the city of Toledo, which petitioned that the king 'keep the title hitherto used'.

Before his departure Charles spent nine months in Saragossa and a year in Barcelona; in neither city did he clash with local privileges. In Castile it was different. Discontent within the cities broke out in the autumn of 1519. Toledo sent letters to all the other cities in the Cortes, asking them to meet over common grievances, and received several replies in favour. In Valladolid angry sermons were preached from the pulpits against the Flemings. In Salamanca a group of leading friars drew up a list of in-structions for their procuradores to the Cortes summoned by Charles to Santiago: 'adjourn the Cortes ... stop offices going to foreigners ... do not agree to any servicio the king may request ... the Comunidades must not be mis-governed, the king's duty is to govern them by his presence, not by his absence'. That crucial word, 'Comunidades', meant no more than the communities, the towns, of the realm: but now it began to take on a more fateful ring. When the Cortes opened on 31 March 1520 under the presidency of Gattinara and Pedro Ruiz de la Mota, bishop of Badajoz, the latter tried to urge on the delegates the unique mission of their nation in Charles's empire: 'his fortress, his treasure, his sword, his steed ... is Spain'. The assembly – from which the cities of Toledo and Salamanca absented themselves – was unimpressed. The Cortes adjourned and met again in April at Coruña: in a stormy session and after intense pressure the government managed to obtain a servicio, but the vote was narrow: nine cities, mainly those which stood to profit from the wool export trade, complied and were finally joined by three more.

A month before the emperor left Spain, Toledo was in revolt. Its regidores, including Pero Laso de la Vega (kin to the Mendozas and brother of the poet Garcilaso) and Juan de Padilla, aided by Padilla's wife Maria Pacheco (daughter of the second count of Tendilla and sister of the soldier and scholar Diego Hurtado de Mendoza, a firm supporter of Charles V), took over leadership of a broad and popular communal movement, expelled the king's corregidor in mid-April, and proclaimed the Comunidad. In Segovia in May one of the procuradores who had voted for the servicio was seized by the mob and murdered; similar riots occurred in other cities. In Burgos, by contrast, the situation was kept under control when the constable accepted leadership of the Comunidad. Toledo in June summoned all the Cortes cities to a meeting, but only four were represented at the first session of the Santa Junta de Comunidad at Ávila in August. To dissuade further opposition the government, led by Adrian of Utrecht as regent, decided to punish Segovia for the murder of its procurador, and sent an army against it. The Comunidad at Segovia, led by Juan Bravo, appealed for help: in response Toledo sent a force under Padilla. The royalists sent a detachment to Medina del Campo to seize the artillery there and prevent it falling into rebel hands; when Medina resisted, the troops, possibly by accident, set off a fire that burnt down half the town (21 August 1520).

The shock of the fire destroyed what remained of the authority exercised by Adrian and the council. Towns that had remained aloof now sent delegations to Ávila. Adrian was forced to pay off his army. A week after the burning of Medina, the embattled leaders of the Santa junta, accompanied by Padilla and his men, were ushered into the presence of queen Juana at Tordesillas. They recognised her as 'Your Majesty', but they themselves were now the real power in Castile.

September and October 1520 were the zenith of success for the Junta at Tordesillas. Padilla and Bravo at the end of September went to Valladolid, where they arrested the members of the royal council and detained Adrian. Of the eighteen cities in the Cortes fourteen were now represented in the junta, Murcia being the last one to join; only the four Andalusian cities – Seville, Granada, Córdoba, Jaén – were absent. The revolution in Castile was not restricted to the Cortes cities: throughout the country the word 'Comunidad' provoked uprisings and stirred idealism. There were repercussions in Guipúzcoa; in Extremadura the cities of Cáceres, Plasencia and Ciudad Rodrigo supported the Junta; in Andalusia there was support in several towns including Seville, Jaén, Úbeda and Baeza; in New Castile the movement was strong around Toledo; and in Murcia it won over

Cartagena, Lorca and other towns. The heart of the revolution remained nevertheless in the north, in Old Castile; attempts by Segovia to proclaim that 'we are all together for the sake of the whole of Spain' found little response. This fairly narrow base of support was constantly endangered by the intense localism and particularism of the Spanish towns, which looked with suspicion on demands that did not reflect their own direct interests. Beyond exploiting the crisis to settle old feuds, or to displace local rivals, many provincial communities refused to commit themselves to the Junta.

Because a clear majority of the Cortes towns were represented, and the new procuradores were elected on a popular vote, the Junta felt that it represented the authentic voice of the nation. The Comunidad was, moreover, not an exclusively urban movement but enjoyed extensive support among the peasantry of Old Castile. 'When my villages rose', commented the constable, whose estates were around Burgos, 'I could not find a single reliable man throughout my lands'. In addition to popular support, however, the Comuneros needed the help of the powerful grandees, and they never got it. The aristocracy certainly detested the Flemings and lamented the king's absence: the count of Benavente declared that 'the laws must be observed, and so I am ready to support the cities'. Cardinal Adrian commented perceptively that such support from nobles was 'for fear lest their tenants rise against them'. Some were equivocal, like the Mendoza duke of Infantado: 'if I do anything against Chièvres, it should not be taken as if it were against Your Majesty'. In Andalusia the great lords refused from the first to collaborate, and because noble power was at its strongest there the south never rallied to the Comunidad. In 1520 the Mendoza marquis of Mondéjar, brother of María Pacheco, crushed incipient revolts and in 1521 organised the League of La Rambla, a broad alliance of Andalusian cities and nobles hostile to the Castilian junta. The rebels, finally, could not count on the queen: Juana encouraged them, but was cautious enough never to put her signature to any document.

What did the Comuneros wish to achieve? They made their principal demands at Tordesillas in November 1520, by which time they had accepted Charles as king because they were unable to get any decision out of queen Juana. They asked that Charles return to Spain, that he exclude foreigners from his entourage, that he marry soon, that the Cortes be given a major role in government and meet automatically every three years, that the expenses of the new court and administration be reduced, that the alcabala be cut to its 1499 level and collected not by tax-farmers but by the towns, and that the export of wool be controlled. None of the demands was revolutionary: all reflected in some degree the style of government of the Catholic Monarchs, whose reign lingered in the memory of Spaniards as the ideal by which subsequent rulers must be judged. Charles was therefore asked to 'act in everything like the Catholic lords, king Ferdinand and queen Isabella'. For the Comuneros the new reign was a deviation in three ways: for ever-present native monarchs it substituted an absentee foreigner, for a Spanish regime it substituted one of aliens who despised Castilians and treated them 'as Indians', for an empire based on the Mediterranean it substituted one centred in the north. Castile through the Comuneros was rejecting Europe, as in many ways it continued to do in subsequent generations.

Disagreement arose less over these demands than over the growing radical tendencies, both inside and outside the junta, that exposed the perennial tensions in Spanish society. Some towns were accused of wishing to abolish the monarchy and follow the Italian ideal by setting up independent city-states in Castile. It was suggested that all taxes be suppressed, or that rich and poor be equally liable to pay. 'We were all born free and equal', argued fray Alonso de Castrillo in his *Treatise on the state* (1521), maintaining that government must rest on the consent of the governed. Constantly there were demands for 'liberty': in 1521 Valladolid, the most radical of the cities, urged the peasants of the Tierra de Campos to defend 'your liberty . . . and be treated like men not like slaves'. The uneasy alliance between towns and nobles was threatened by popular revolts against seigneurial dues: the first known uprisings were at Madrigal in June 1520 and Dueñas in September. In a village near Palencia the parish priest promised that 'by the end of this month there will be no more nobles'. Apocalyptic prophecies circulated through the countryside.

The radical threat split the movement. On 3 September 1520 Charles had appointed the constable and the admiral as co-regents with Adrian. Early in November the city of Burgos, which had always been conservative in its views, withdrew from the junta; the split encouraged the regents to begin collecting troops. At this stage Antonio de Acuña, the fiery sixty-year-old bishop of Zamora, who had supported the Comunidad from the beginning, placed himself at the orders of the junta, bringing with him three hundred of his priests armed to the teeth. Negotiations began between the admiral, who shared many of the aspirations of the Comuneros, and the junta. 'They say', the admiral commented, 'that they seek liberty: so do we. They say they want our laws observed: so do we. . . . If then we all seek the same thing, why the quarrel?' By now the nobles were convinced of the drift to revolution: the junta was reported as claiming 'that they are above the king and not he above them'.

'Our war', observed the admiral gloomily, 'is against immortals to whom there is no end.'

On 5 December in a surprise attack the royalist forces, consisting mainly of the grandees and their armies, seized and sacked Tordesillas, secured the queen and captured some of the junta. Two months later, however, the Comunero army under Padilla won a convincing victory at Torrelobatón, and began negotiations. Troop movements continued, and on 23 April 1521, near the village of Villalar, the superior cavalry of the Castilian aristocracy crushed the forces of Padilla, wearied by a long march and torrential rain. Padilla, Juan Bravo and their comrade Francisco Maldonado were captured, tried and executed that very day. When Bravo protested at the summary procedure Padilla said, 'My beloved Bravo, yesterday we should have died fighting like gentlemen, today let us die like true Christians.'

A single battle could not extinguish the movement. Northern Castile was secured for the aristocracy, but Toledo now became the centre of the struggle, ably led by María Pacheco and with forces commanded by the bishop of Zamora. Royalist troops were diverted by the French invasion of Navarre. At the end of May Acuña was apprehended: imprisoned in Simancas, he tried to escape in 1526 after murdering his gaoler and was promptly tried, tortured and executed on the orders of Charles. Finally Toledo agreed to capitulate, and in February 1522 María Pacheco fled to Portugal, where she died in 1531.

The repression was harsh, but ceased after Charles returned to Spain. By All Saints Day 1522, when he signed a general pardon, 22 rebels had been executed; 293 more, drawn mostly from the urban elites, were excepted from the pardon, but there were no further executions. All the cities participating in the revolt remained untouched in their privileges; this clemency, followed by other concessions and a limited amnesty in 1527, gave the king a strong basis for reconciliation with his subjects.

The defeat of the Comuneros was a permanent blow to the political pretensions of the cities. Ironically, over the next few years all their major demands were put into effect: the Cortes, for example, did meet regularly, to renew the servicios; and in 1525 and 1534 the collection of taxes was granted to the towns. But Charles made it perfectly clear that the cities were to play no part in government. Who then gained from Villalar? The grandees, whose enormous military power had helped to save the government, were confirmed amply in their social position and seigneurial privileges; but they were denied any increase in political power, which thereafter rested firmly in the hands of the crown, the true victor of Villalar.

At the very time that the Comunidades shook Castile, a major rebellion broke out in Valencia, but never made common cause with the Comuneros, clear evidence of the divisive localism in Spain. In 1519 a representative of the artisans' guilds in Valencia, Juan Llorens, went to Barcelona to ask the king's permission to recruit a brotherhood (*germanía*) or militia to defend the coasts against Barbary pirates. On receiving authorisation from Chièvres the guilds in December set up a council of thirteen and proposed remodelling Valencia's constitution to reduce the privileges of the nobles and set up a city-state like Venice. The arrival in April 1520 of a new viceroy, the Mendoza count of Melito, provoked clashes between the nobles and the guilds, which now appropriated two of the six places on the Diputación of Valencia. The germanías proceeded to wrest control of the major cities from the authorities. In July 1521 Melito responded with armed force but was soundly defeated. Llorens, killed in battle in this month, was replaced by Vicent Peris, a radical leader whose policy and violence alarmed the moderate section of the germanías. Melito's elder brother the marquis of Zenete came to the viceroy's help and proved more successful, reconquering Valencia city in October. Peris was eventually caught and executed in March 1522. Resistance continued under the leadership of a millenarian figure called *El Encubierto* (the hidden one), rumoured as being (a chronicler reports) 'he of whom men spoke in past times, who is to come into the world to chastise tyrants and succour the peoples'. A general pardon for the rebellion was finally published by the new viceroy, Germaine de Foix, in December 1524, after the ferocious execution of hundreds of rebels.

Unlike the Comunidades, the germanías were from the beginning a clear class conflict between urban groups – bourgeois and artisans – and the aristocracy. Unlike the Comunidades, they occupied the entire kingdom, and spilled over into Murcia (which however later joined in the repression, under the leadership of Pedro Fajardo, first marquis of Los Vélez) and into Mallorca (where a violent germanía took over the whole island, under the eventual leadership of Juan Colom, and was not crushed until March 1523). Finally, unlike the Comunidades they were inspired by bitter antagonism to the Mudéjar communities, some of which were sacked, while the Mudéjars as a whole were terrorised into forcible mass baptisms that theoretically freed them from their lords and served in this way as an attack on aristocratic power.

The revolutionary period from 1517 to 1522 was not, of course, precipitated solely by the Habsburg succession. Charles's mistakes had served rather as a trigger to unleash the conflicts, both political and ideological, latent in Spanish society: in that sense these were years, not only in Valencia but also in Castile, of outright civil war. The inter-communal and inter-family splits would persist for generations: between towns, between *barrios* (quarters) in the same town, between great nobles, and even in the council of State, where in 1578 an angry admiral of Castile claimed that descendants of Comuneros dominated affairs. Charles V did not easily forget the crisis, nor did his son: when Philip was rebuked for harshness over a case of sedition in Ávila in 1591, he retorted, 'Was this not the town where Henry IV was deposed, and where they favoured the tyrant Juan de Padilla?' As in every civil war, fears bred myths. 'It is common knowledge in Spain', declared archbishop Siliceo of Toledo a generation later, 'that the Comunidades were incited by descendants of Jews.' The constable in 1521 explicitly informed the king that 'the root cause of the revolution in these realms has been the conversos'. Though factually incorrect, these claims underline the importance to Spaniards of a conflict that was seen to be not merely rebellion against the king but the consequence of dark forces working to subvert society.

Victory at Villalar established the Habsburg succession in Spain and set the country on a path radically different from that which the Catholic Monarchs had followed and the Comuneros had espoused. But it would be a mistake to regard it as a triumph for absolutism. Like the Catholic Monarchs before him, Charles sustained his authority over the aristocracy and the towns only by collaborating with them and making it unnecessary for them to claim more power than they already had. If there were no further revolts by the privileged classes in Spain it was because their interests were directed to lucrative careers in the rapidly expanding court and bureaucracy of the worldwide monarchy. There was likewise no triumph of Europe over Spain, which remained stubbornly impervious to foreign influence, absorbed only those Flemish and Italian currents that had already penetrated into the peninsula and actually succeeded in Hispanising the emperor himself.

# Administration and empire

The enormous number of territories governed by Charles, from central Europe to the Pacific, were not an 'empire' in the old sense of lands acquired by conquest. Spaniards, in particular, preferred to call the lands associated with Spain a 'monarchy', by which they meant an association of independent states united only by obedience to the same dynastic ruler. Because each realm had its own separate laws and institutions it was impractical to devise a common central administration. Policy was necessarily decided at the centre, in the early 1500s through chancellor Gattinara and then after his death through Charles alone. Imperial administration was always on the move, with no fixed centre other than the person of the emperor, who was usually accompanied by his secretaries and advisers.

Charles respected the autonomy of his kingdoms and made no attempt to impose political or fiscal unity. To preserve his personal links with the more important realms he employed members of his family as governors or viceroys. In Spain Germaine de Foix, widow of Ferdinand the Catholic, was (in 1523) made viceroy of Valencia; and during Charles's own absence the empress Isabella governed Spain. In Germany his brother Ferdinand was (from 1521) given charge of the Habsburg lands and in 1531 secured succession to the Imperial throne by being elected king of the Romans. In the Netherlands Charles's aunt Margaret of Austria (1518–30) and then his sister Mary of Hungary (1531–55) ruled. Elsewhere a number of viceroys ruled the non-Castilian territories in Spain, Italy and America; but each of them was required to act in liaison with a new system of administrative councils based on Castile.

It was logical that Charles, like the Catholic Monarchs before him, should choose Castile, with its strong royal traditions and superior resources, as the centre of his monarchy. On the initiative of Gattinara, a complete overhaul of royal administration was undertaken and a number of innovations made which formed the framework of Habsburg rule in Spain. The king governed through several councils, some advisory and some administrative. Of the former, which were the higher in rank, there were two. In 1526 a council of state was set up, consisting of Gattinara, Henry count of Nassau and five leading Spaniards, 'to discuss the most important matters concerning the government of Spain and of Germany'. In practice Charles seldom used it and preferred to work through Granvelle and Cobos. After the emperor's abdication, however, the council became the supreme organ of government in the Spanish monarchy; it was staffed primarily by grandees and had special responsibility for foreign policy as well as the power to oversee decisions of the other councils. From about 1522 a council of war, which ended up simply as the council of state sitting under a different name but with distinct officials, helped to coordinate the military obligations of the crown. Both these councils had obviously been created to meet the new obligations of empire.

The administrative councils, on the other hand, were inherited or adapted from the legacy of the Catholic Monarchs. The principal organ of government was the royal council of Castile, with about 12 members, all letrados, whom Charles like his predecessors preferred rather than grandees. It was the highest administrative body – 'the support of my realms', Charles termed it – and also the supreme court, to which cases could be appealed from the high courts (chancillerías and audiencias). In 1588 a subsidiary administrative body, the chamber (*Cámara*) of Castile, was created to help its work. The council was also an advisory body that tendered advice to the king on a broad range of matters. As Castile's part in the direction of the monarchy increased, the responsibilities and size of the council grew: by 1588 there were sixteen members, by 1691 twenty.

Of the other councils, the Inquisition (1483), military orders (1489) and the cruzada (1509) dated from the epoch of the Catholic Monarchs; the last two were eventually made subject to the council of Castile. In 1523 a new council of finance (*Hacienda*) was created by Gattinara, although its direction was entrusted to his rival Cobos; modelled on the council of finance in Flanders, it included Henry of Nassau among its three members: by 1525 all the members were Spaniards. The new council was closely associated with that of Castile, since it managed the finances of the realm; but it also came to handle the accounts of much of the monarchy.

As the Spanish empire expanded the task of governing distant territories became more difficult. The formation of the council of Aragon by Ferdinand in 1494 provided a model for the councils concerned with a specific territory. The council liaised between central government and the viceroys, discussed public policy and acted as a supreme court of appeal. The first new territorial council created under Charles was that of the Indies, in 1524, with jurisdiction over American affairs. In 1555 under Philip II the Italian states, which had till then been represented on the council of Aragon, were allotted a separate council of Italy. This development would not have been necessary under Charles, whose travels brought him into touch with all his European possessions. Philip's residence in Spain, by contrast, forced the creation of a territorial council for Flanders in 1588.

Spain continued to have no fixed capital under Charles. Although administrators tended to work from Valladolid, councils were obliged to move around with the king, whose absences abroad robbed the system of a focus, so that considerable credit must go to Cobos for guaranteeing an efficient administration that laid the basis of a reliable bureaucracy in Castile. It was also Cobos who between 1543 and 1545 arranged for administrative papers to be deposited in the fortress of Simancas, conveniently near Valladolid, and thus created the beginnings of the official state archive.

The initiative gained by Charles after Villalar was not in practice very great, and led to no significant changes in government. The new councils were still largely advisory bodies, whose deliberations were presented to the government in the form of reports (*consultas*) that the crown was never obliged to accept. It is true that they oversaw a very wide range of business, but they were seldom in a position to implement policy, mainly because Spain lacked any network of administrative officials responsible to the central government. This was even more true overseas, in America, where the repeated orders of the council of the Indies were seldom obeyed or put into effect. The daily government of Spain therefore continued as it was before Villalar, with essential continuity of political life and institutions being maintained by the local nobility and gentry, many of whom were royal corregidors of the towns but did not feel they were there to promote the crown's power.

It was essential for the king to keep in touch with the political elite, and this meant consulting the Cortes. The Cortes of Castile met fifteen times in the reign (seldom, it is true, for more than three months at a time). In Aragon the general Cortes met six times at Monzón, while the regional assemblies met twice in Catalonia, once each in Aragon and Valencia. In every case the Cortes were summoned primarily to vote taxation. Provided money was forthcoming, Charles never curtailed their freedom of speech or restricted their proceedings only to financial matters. The voluminous records of their meetings are clear proof that the crown accepted a free interchange of ideas with its subjects. The defeat of the Comunidades extinguished any hopes among the cities for a bigger share in government, but changed little in the status of representative institutions.

The limited role of the Castilian Cortes was recognised by the assembly at Valladolid in 1544, which asked not to be summoned more often than once every three years 'because of the great costs and expense'. The king was willing to make concessions. In the Cortes of Toledo (1525) he allowed the assembly to elect two procuradores as a standing committee, on the model of the Diputación in the crown of Aragon. He also conceded to most cities that their taxes be paid by an encabezamiento rather than through the tax-farmers, an arrangement that was adopted firmly by a later Cortes in 1534. In 1527 the king took the unusual step, not practised since 1480, of also summoning the nobles and clergy to the Cortes at Valladolid. This extraordinary meeting was brought about by Charles's need to finance his Hungarian campaign; but the privileged orders were adamant that any servicio from them might set a precedent and prejudice their freedom from taxation, so the king went away empty-handed. All three Estates were not again summoned to a Cortes until the assembly at Toledo in 1538, when the main business was again finance. The Estates were obliged to meet separately, to avoid collusion. The government's main request, for a new excise tax (*sisa*) on food, was rejected by the nobles and towns; the latter were willing only to vote a further servicio. Dismissing the grandees curtly from the Cortes, the president of the council, cardinal Tavera, said: 'Your lordships are not required any longer: each of you can go home or where you will.' It was the last time that nobles and clergy were ever summoned to a working Cortes, since their presence was superfluous to its primary function of granting taxes.

Public opinion was slow to adjust to the emperor. The contemporary historian Sandoval reports that once, while hunting in the Montes region of Toledo, Charles got lost and fell into conversation with a peasant who did not recognise him. The old man said that he had lived to see five kings in Castile. When Charles asked which of these was the best and which the worst, he replied that Ferdinand the Catholic was certainly the best and the present king the worst. Pressed to explain, he said that the king had abandoned his wife for foreign parts, had carried off with him all the treasure of Spain and the Indies, and that he was ruining the peasants with taxes. Spaniards by mid-century seemed to have gained remarkably little from the reign of the great emperor. No significant conquests were made for Spain in the Mediterranean, since the famous occupation of Tunis was intended above all to give Italy more security. Spain's real interest was in securing Algiers, but the attempt ended in disaster. The enterprise across the Atlantic in the New World was one in which the state played only a small part. Meanwhile in Europe the soldiers of Castile had an auxiliary rather than a principal role in the major events of the Reformation and the Italian wars.

There was, all the same, an unmistakable growth of sympathy for the emperor and pride in his enterprises. There were inevitably some complaints – about the emperor's absences, about the high cost of the royal court – but the new Habsburg regime made no radical changes in political life, there were no rebellions after 1520, and apart from the Turkish threat peninsular Spain enjoyed peace and tranquillity for the rest of the reign. By showing that he was genuinely concerned for the welfare of Spain, and by actively employing its officials, clergy and soldiers in aspects of European policy, Charles weaned Castilians away from their isolationism. The Spanish presence began to be felt in northern Europe, and Spanish ways and culture penetrated the jungles of central America. At the end of the emperor's reign, in 1555, the apocalyptic voice of a Franciscan friar in

Mexico, Toribio de Motolinía, appealed to him to 'bring about speedily the fulfilment of the Fifth Monarchy of Jesus Christ, which is to embrace the whole earth and of which Your Majesty is the head'.

## Finance and empire

In theory each of the emperor's territories should have been self-supporting; in practice, he accumulated commitments, such as the fight against heresy in northern Europe, and the struggle against the Turk in the Balkans and in Africa, that grew to international dimensions and forced him to draw on the resources of all his states. In the early years he relied heavily on the wealthy Netherlands and then on Italy for finance. In the 1530s, however, the Netherlanders began to complain that, among other things, they were paying for the conquest of Italy; the tax revolt of Ghent in 1539 was a warning to Charles. It was easier to tax Naples, where there was no strong parliamentary tradition to oppose the crown. The kingdom gave him 1.75 million ducats for his armies in 1525–9, and large sums in subsequent years, so that by 1540 the Spanish viceroy was protesting that further claims would be 'to squeeze juice from a stone'. It was at this stage, in 1540, that the emperor admitted to his brother Ferdinand that 'I cannot be sustained except by my realms of Spain'.

This was an astonishing development. Though large in size, Spain was a relatively poor country. Charles himself had observed in 1523, when the new council of Finance was being set up, that government debts in Castile 'amount to far more than I receive in revenue'; and all the income for 1524 had already been spent. How then did Spain come to be the emperor's chief financial support? There were essentially two reasons: unlike the Netherlands, Castile and its Cortes had little constitutional resistance to higher taxation; and, above all, Charles could draw on the wealth of the Indies. The new Spanish council of finance gave valuable support to the king. It had two major objectives: to coordinate the work of the existing accounting departments (*contadurías*) set up at the Cortes of Madrigal in 1476, and to act as a treasury of receipt for state income. The first was more attainable than the second, since in practice income was often paid directly from source to outlet without ever appearing in official records, so that financial statements of the period were habitually incomplete.

The Spanish crown had four main sources of revenue: Castile, Aragon, the Church and America. The least fruitful of these was Aragon, whose fueros limited both the amount of tax payable to the crown and the uses to which the money could be put. From the six general Cortes at Monzón – in

1528, 1533, 1537, 1542, 1547 and 1552 – Charles is estimated to have received no more than an average of 500,000 ducats for each five-year period.

The Church was officially exempt from taxation but because of its great wealth was always held to be under an obligation to contribute to state expenses. By the sixteenth century the clergy in Spain were in some ways even more heavily taxed than laymen, being forced to pay not only regular impositions (the *tercias reales*, *subsidio* and *cruzada*) but also extraordinary grants (*donativos*). The tercias reales, granted to the crown in the thirteenth century, were two-ninths of the substantial income that came to the Church in tithes (which in 1623 in Castile alone were estimated by the Cortes to produce seven million ducats). The subsidio was a proportion of Church income throughout Spain, conceded to the king by the pope. It was first paid in 1519, and thereafter only at irregular intervals according to Charles's needs: the next levy, in 1532, realised 372,000 ducats; another in 1536 realised 212,000; and finally one in 1551 produced 500,000. Not until 1561 was the subsidio made a regular levy, by agreement between Philip II and Pius IV: its value then was fixed at an annual 420,000 ducats. The cruzada, from which the Catholic Monarchs benefited, was payable by both laity and clergy. It was preached from the pulpits like any other indulgence, and then purchased by the faithful for two reales in Castile and somewhat more in Aragon. Later it was extended beyond the peninsula to Sicily, Sardinia and America. Between 1523 and 1554 it brought in an average of 121,000 ducats a year. The three military orders of Castile, which enjoyed ecclesiastical status, had their property and revenue confirmed to the crown in May 1523 by Adrian of Utrecht, now pope as Adrian VI. The king's income from the masterships (*maestrazgos*) of the orders was, however, soon assigned to bankers for expenses in Germany. The first administrators of the maestrazgos were the Fuggers, who took it over from 1525: by the 1530s the crown was receiving an annual 146,000 ducats. When to these is added occasional revenue from donativos, vacant sees and other sources, it can be seen that the Spanish Church was a major contributor to royal finances.

Whereas Charles in Aragon was dependent on the Cortes for revenue, in Castile most taxes were extra-parliamentary, thereby reducing the need for the king to rely on the Cortes. The most important of the ordinary taxes of the crown – all of them indirect, and not personal – was the alcabala, which originated in the fourteenth century. It was a general tax on all sales (later in the century settling to 10 per cent of value) and was payable by all laymen, whether noble or not. Its broad scope meant that, together with the tercias, with which it was normally reckoned, it accounted for over three-fourths of crown revenue in Castile. Normally the yield of the alcabala should have risen with inflation. But since 1495, when Ferdinand and Isabella had first allowed some towns to compound for a sum equivalent to the alcabala yield (a system known as encabezamiento), demands grew for the practice to be made more general. Finally Charles conceded to the Cortes at Madrid in 1534 that the alcabala and tercias be thenceforth paid by encabezamiento, though the system took two years to put into effect. Once a global sum had been agreed, the Cortes were able to oppose increases in its size; the real yield of the taxes therefore fell. Between 1536 and 1548 the yield of the encabezamiento, representing the bulk of Castilian taxes, rose by only 2.5 per cent, whereas that of other taxes rose by 27 per cent.

In 1550 the total value of the ordinary taxes of Castile was 1.25 million ducats: of this the encabezamiento represented about 70 per cent. The balance came mainly from customs duties of various sorts, including the almojarifazgos in Andalusia (the duty at Seville was known as the almojarifazgo mayor) and those levied at the puertos secos or customs posts on the frontiers with Aragon, Navarre and Portugal, as well as from other dues such as the servicio y montazgo tax on sheep and silk taxes in Granada.

Thanks partly to the decline in the value of the alcabala, Charles's ordinary revenues failed to keep pace with inflation: between 1536 and 1553 the overall yield rose by only 21 per cent, whereas prices rose by a third in Old Castile and a half in Andalusia. The government was obliged to resort to the Cortes, which cooperated generously. In 1523 the Cortes of Valladolid voted a servicio of 400,000 ducats, to be paid over three years and levied directly on taxpayers; subsequent assemblies even agreed to extraordinary servicios in addition to the regular three-year grant. In the course of the reign the yield from servicios more than tripled, from about 130,000 ducats a year in 1524 to 410,000 in 1555. In effect the servicios were now a regular tax, and augmented ordinary income by about one-third. This development had two important consequences for the social history of Castile. In the first place, set beside a reduction in the real value of the alcabala it meant a substantial shift from indirect to direct taxation. Secondly, since people of noble rank (hidalgos), representing well over a tenth of the population, were exempt from direct taxation, it moved the fiscal burden from the privileged classes to the ordinary taxpayers (pecheros). Upper-class officials, themselves exempt, were responsible for levying the tax and tended to let its weight fall on those least able to resist. The Cortes, it must be said, attempted to establish some equity: in 1541 it stipulated that the rate should vary from 117 to 155 maravedís per pechero, and in 1551 that the levy should vary 'according to the property of each taxpayer'. In practice, as the trend in the fiscal system seemed to be moving in favour of personal taxation, there was a corresponding attempt by people to buy privileges of hidalguía which would make them exempt.

The last of the major sources of revenue was America, which under the emperor began to pour a torrent of bullion into Europe. The receipts, as registered on arrival in Seville, have been measured by Earl J. Hamilton. Up to about 1530, amounts coming to the crown were small. From 1536 to 1540, however, receipts averaged 324,000 ducats a year and generally kept rising. From 1546 to 1550 the average was over 382,000 ducats a year, and from 1551 to 1555 it was 871,000 a year. The total of bullion coming for the crown between 1516 and 1560 was some 11.9 million ducats, or about 270,000 ducats a year. This was by any standards a very handsome sum. In addition to it, Charles managed to obtain a further 3.5 million from seizures of contraband and private bullion. Though much larger sums were to come later for Philip II, there can be no doubt that the American bullion reaching the emperor's treasury – well over 15 million ducats – was of significant help to his finances.

Up to 1530 nearly all the precious metal coming to Spain was gold, drawn primarily from the Caribbean islands. Thereafter the trend was to silver, after the development of the rich silver mines of Bolivia (Potosí, 1545) and Mexico (Zacatecas, 1548, and Guanajuato). The crown at this time drew about half its American income from the *quinto* or royal fifth, which was strictly levied on all bullion produced; and half from American taxes, and customs duties such as the *almojarifazgo mayor*, introduced in 1543 and representing 5 per cent of value.

Thanks to the rapid growth in the emperor's commitments, all these resources together were insufficient to remedy a constant deficit. By 1534 the government had spent most of its revenue for the next six years. The position worsened with each successive – and expensive – campaign; the siege of Metz in 1552 cost over two million ducats, for example. In February 1544 Charles was told that his budget needs for the year came to 2,375,000 ducats, and the available cash to only 750,000. In March prince Philip reported to his father: 'There is a deficit of 3,135,000 ducats, and we do not know from where or how to meet it, since income from the Indies is committed for several years.' Various emergency expedients were adopted: titles of hidalguía were sold, silver coming from America for private individuals was seized (as mentioned above), from 1545 public offices began to be sold in small numbers. Royal land, which the Catholic Monarchs had been so concerned to secure for the crown, was alienated: sales of land belonging to the military orders realised 1.7 million ducats for the crown between 1537 and 1551, one of the biggest purchasers (for 192,000 ducats worth) being Francisco de los Cobos.

The only sure way to balance the budget, however, was to borrow. Borrowing by the state was done through *juros*, which Ferdinand and Isabella had already begun to exploit. Yielding an interest at this period of up to 7 per cent, juros were annuities which repaid loans out of the ordinary revenues and thereby in effect mortgaged a good part of state income. In 1522 their repayment consumed about 36 per cent of normal revenue, the proportion rising to 65 per cent by 1543 and 68 per cent by 1556. By the end of the century the juros had become a sort of national debt in which all social classes invested, with serious social consequences that will be examined later (*see* p. 263). The greater burden of debts, however, was not in Spain but overseas. In order to obtain money rapidly, and transfer it easily from one part of Europe to another, Charles made use of the various bankers who did their business through the international trade centres at Burgos, Antwerp and other towns. A contract (*asiento*) would be agreed in Spain for a banker to advance cash elsewhere. He in turn would issue 'bills of exchange', to be paid abroad by a colleague, specifying the place and date of delivery. The sum paid back to him by the government would include an extra sum – in effect, interest – for the costs of the transaction. In the early years Charles's bankers were principally German (Fugger, Welser), but Italians later became important. As money became more difficult to find, the interest charges paid by the crown rose from 17.6 per cent in the 1520s to a horrifying 48.8 per cent in the 1550s. The asientos concluded during the reign are set out in the table that follows, according to the analysis made by Ramon Carande.

| Period | No. of asientos | Ducats borrowed | Interest (%) | Ducats repaid | Bankers (%)* |
|---|---|---|---|---|---|
| 1520–32 | 101 | 5,379,053 | 17.6 | 6,327,371 | G48, I37, S15 |
| 1533–42 | 86 | 5,437,669 | 21.3 | 6,594,365 | G47, I41, S12 |
| 1543–51 | 183 | 8,397,616 | 27.8 | 10,737,843 | G34, I30, S27, F9 |
| 1552–6 | 132 | 9,643,869 | 48.8 | 14,351,591 | G24, I51, S9, F16 |
| Total | 502 | 28,858,207 | 31.7 | 38,011,170 | |

* G: German, I: Italian, S: Spanish, F: Flemish.

The figures show clearly the emperor's mounting financial crisis, the desperate resort to loans even at crippling rates of interest (the rate charged by the Genoese after 1552 was 67.4 per cent), and the growing hold of foreign financiers on the Spanish treasury. Since all the loans were made on the security of the Castilian crown, Charles had set in train two developments of fundamental importance for the history of Spain. First, it was Castile rather than any other realm of the crown that had to bear the cost of empire; second, foreign financiers were now in place to dominate sections of the Spanish economy for over a century. In this reign German financiers were, in repayment for their services, permitted to buy offices, lands and juros, and were granted administration of the three military orders and the mercury mines at Almadén.

Spain's preponderance in Europe was clearly not based on superiority either of wealth or of arms. With limited resources at its disposal, the country had been elevated to an imperial role through the accident of inheritance; and the financial effort to keep it there created a heavy burden that the Castilian pechero felt unable to support. The rising scale of debt, and the enormous proportion of revenue absorbed by juros, forced Philip II in one of his first acts as king to try to make a clean start. In April 1557, while in London, he decided to suspend all payments from the Castilian treasury: the decree for this was issued in June. All outstanding debts were consolidated into juros at an interest rate of 5 per cent. The move was not a bankruptcy, since the crown still had considerable credit and was also able to pay cash to the Fuggers, who distrusted Castilian juros. Moreover, the juros were a desirable investment and many bankers re-sold theirs at premiums of 50 per cent or more. But confidence was shaken, and the Spanish monarchy never shook off the legacy of debt bequeathed to it by the emperor.

# America

The news of the circumnavigation of the globe by the *Victoria*, brought personally by Elcano to Charles in September 1522 at Valladolid, confirmed the emperor's belief in his own world destiny. Not only had his subjects now traversed the entire East Indies, normally the preserve of Portugal, but in that same month Charles also decided to confirm Hernando Cortés as captain-general of the realms of New Spain.

Cortés had commanded an expedition from Cuba that landed on the site of Vera Cruz in Mexico with about 600 men, 16 horses, 6 pieces of artillery and a few Indians. With these he set out in August 1519 on the historic march that ended two years later in the fall of Tenochtitlán, capital of the mighty Aztec empire. His success inaugurated on mainland America the great age of the conquistadors. Of these the best known was Francisco Pizarro, who in 1524 began a number of expeditions southwards from the Pacific port of Panamá. During his third expedition, in 1531, he stumbled on Inca territory, and in 1532, at the head of about 160 men and several horses, captured the Inca emperor. The fall of the Aztec and Inca empires was not, of course, achieved solely by this handful of men. Cortés would not have triumphed but for the inestimable help of tens of thousands of Indian allies who revolted against Aztec rule and made possible the long siege and eventual capture of Tenochtitlán. In Peru Pizarro did little more than disrupt the Inca empire, which after the murder of Atahualpa pro- duced other Incas to carry on the struggle against the Spaniards for another 40 years. The heroism of those who established Spanish rule in America was inevitably determined by self-interest: Francisco de Orellana, who left Quito in 1539 and spent nearly two years journeying down the entire length of the Amazon river, was typically more concerned with riches than exploration. Greed, as the Aztecs soon realised, was the dominating motive of the white man.

This was hardly surprising. The pioneers in America were not nobles, who took no part in early settlements and conquest, but poorer Spaniards of all conditions, many of them soldiers and sailors unemployed after the wars in Granada and Italy had come to an end, others young and hardy men of limited means, including many hidalgos (like Cortés) and illiterate labourers (like Pizarro) who looked to America to better their fortunes. Though the early adventurers were mostly of low extraction, they did not lack skills: nearly half of Pizarro's men could read and write, and by 1560 in Peru a tenth of all Spaniards were artisans trained in Spain. Up to 1559 about 35 per cent of all licensed emigrants to the New World came from Andalusia, and over 50 per cent from Extremadura, the two Castiles and León. Most emigrants were drawn from the provinces of Seville, Badajoz, Cáceres and Toledo: Extremadura, with only 7 per cent of Spain's popula- tion, supplied 17 per cent of emigrants prior to 1580. Rural misery was an obvious reason for emigrating: thousands of peasants saw in America a hope of escape from feudal lords, heavy taxation and the harsh struggle for survival. Las Casas reports meeting in Castile in 1518 four hidalgos who wished to go to America in order to have their sons 'grow up in a free world', and a couple of farmers who wished 'to leave our sons in a free and pleasant land'. By mid-century urban expansion, and with it urban poverty, began to contribute increasingly to the outflow: up to 1580 some 31 cities, led by Seville and Toledo, accounted for 45 per cent of licensed emigrants to America. Women were no more than 5 per cent of emigrants prior to 1519; by the 1550s they were some 16 per cent and then in the 1560s their numbers rose dramatically to over 28 per cent of licensed emigrants. Total figures for the exodus across the Atlantic are problematic: the documentation for registered migrants is deficient, and illegal emigration was substantial. Working simply from the number of passengers each ship could have carried, it has been suggested that up to 150,000 Spaniards crossed to America before 1550; for the whole century the figure could not have exceeded 250,000. The figures are unreliable, and need to take into account that very many also returned to Spain.

America became for Spain a frontier society, where violence was the rule and wealth the prize. Caribbean gold was the first attraction: 'I came here to get gold', protested Cortés when he first arrived in Hispaniola in 1504, 'not to till the soil like a peasant.' In reality, motives were more complex. Though wealth always seemed important, for many the adventure and excitement of the environment in the New World was an irresistible lure. 'For twenty years', said the adventurer Diego de Mexía, 'I have sailed seas and traversed lands through different climates, altitudes and temperatures.' 'When in ancient or modern times', exclaimed a conquistador of Peru, Francisco de Jérez, 'have there been such great enterprises of so few against so many, through so many lofty climates and vast seas and endless lands, to conquer the unseen and unknown? Who can equal those of Spain?' Brought up in Spain on romances of chivalry, notably the *Amadis of Gaul* (1508), many young men saw legends coming to life in America. As the vision of Tenochtitlán burst upon the eyes of Cortés's men when they entered the valley of Mexico, 'it seemed', the conquistador Bernal Diaz wrote later, 'like the enchanted things told of in the book of Amadis, and some of our soldiers wondered whether it was not all a dream'. Orellana claimed to have met Amazon women on his voyage, thereby giving the great river its name. California was named after an island in Garci Ordóñez de Montalvo's chivalric novel *Las Sergas de Esplandián* (1510).

At the same time the ideology of Reconquest Spain, a stern and militant Catholicism, permeated the entire enterprise. Every expedition had its priest, every conquistador commended his cause to God. 'We came', Bernal Diaz observed, with a nice sense of priorities, 'to serve God and His Majesty, . . . and also to get rich.' Throughout the conquest there was a clear consciousness of a sacred mission to civilise and convert the natives. The conquistadors displayed it with characteristic brutality and helped to fix in the Indian mind a burning hatred for the cruel faith of the Christians.

As the savage epoch of the conquistadors (to about 1540) merged into the more orderly period of settler rule, wealth was seen to consist less in gold than in the more enduring riches of the soil and the abundant labour force of Indians. As in mediaeval Spain, where the advancing Reconquest had resettled the land among a potentially hostile population, Spaniards in America aimed both to colonise and to control. The new encomiendas on the mainland, however, repeated the devastation already caused in the West Indies. The Dominicans, in Hispaniola since 1510, were the first to awake to the tragedy, and began a campaign against the encomienda that led to its partial reform in the Laws of Burgos (1512). One encomendero at least was converted to the cause; at the age of 40 he gave up his encomienda (1514), joined the Dominican order (1522), and devoted the rest of his life to the liberation of the Indian. His name was Bartolomé de las Casas (d. 1566).

From their arrival in America in 1510, the friars of the mendicant orders set the pace and determined the objectives of Spain's religious mission. Products not of the reformed post-Reformation Church but of the spirituality of the Observance and of Renaissance humanism, they came to America with a burning millenarian zeal and carried out an astonishing programme of conversion that had no precedent in the history of Spain or indeed of Europe. The first large number of Franciscans (among them three Flemings) arrived in Mexico in 1524, significantly in a group of 'twelve' to symbolise Christ's apostles. They were followed by the other regular orders and last of all, after the mid-century, by the Jesuits. For many it was a unique opportunity to create a Christian continent unpolluted by the corruptions of the Old World. The Indians were seen as 'noble savages', 'of such simplicity and purity of soul that they do not know how to sin', according to the Franciscan Jerónimo de Mendieta; 'very simple, without evil or duplicity', according to Las Casas. Consonant with this optimistic view, they demanded full personal liberty for the Indians in order to bring them peacefully and willingly into the Church. Schemes were operated (by Las Casas in Venezuela in 1520, by the bishop of Michoacán, Vasco de Quiroga, in Mexico in 1534) to create communities where the Indians could live as free Christians. Quiroga's scheme was copied from Thomas More's *Utopia* and was therefore the first historical example of a Utopia in practice. Since some two-thirds of the bishops appointed to America under Charles V were from the religious orders, it would seem that their visionary schemes had a hope of success.

The struggle to preserve the Indians was one on which the interests of clergy and crown coincided. The latter, in addition to the issue of prin-ciple (queen Isabella had been opposed to Indian slavery), did not wish the native population removed from royal jurisdiction. The settlers, on the other hand, relied entirely on labour exploitation for their profits and held that the Indians in the Caribbean were no better than beasts. The division of opinion on both sides of the Atlantic began a controversy of some 40 years' duration that proved to be the first of the great debates over Spain's imperial role. In 1516 a special commission of Jeronimite friars set up by Cisneros went to Hispaniola to take evidence from the earliest settlers as to whether the Indians were capable of living as free beings, that is like Spaniards. The evidence, and the commission's judgement, went against the Indians; but the debate had only just begun. During the Comunidades the city of Valladolid, where the influence of the friars was strong, petitioned that 'since the Indians are Christians they should be treated as such and not as slaves'. The discovery of the high culture of the Aztecs did little to change the bulk of settler opinion, but Cortés himself tended to the view that Indian slavery was wrong. Opinion polarised between those, like the historian of America Fernández de Oviedo and the humanist scholar Juan Ginés de Sepúlveda, who regarded the Indian as an irrational savage in need of civilising; and those, like most of the friars working in America, and Las Casas himself, who felt that Indians were in no way inferior to Spaniards. While conquistadors and settlers ruthlessly and heroically extended the frontier of Spanish occupation, the controversy went on. The defenders of the Indians were in effect calling in question the very presence of Spain in America by their denunciation of the encomienda and of Spanish cruelty, and their proclamation of the equality of the Indian. The Franciscan Mendieta and the Dominican Las Casas both agreed that God had given America to Spain not for conquest or exploitation of silver but exclusively for the salvation of Indian souls.

Thanks to his enormous influence at the court of Charles V, Las Casas was able in 1542 to obtain the passing of the famous New Laws. It was the year that the Cortes in Valladolid petitioned the emperor to 'remedy the cruelties which are committed in the Indies against the Indians'. The New Laws were epoch making: they decreed the abolition of the encomienda and the liberty of all Indian slaves in America. But it was another matter to try to enforce them, and in Peru they provoked a bloody revolt of settlers. Despite this failure, Las Casas retained the confidence of the crown, which in 1550 sponsored a historic debate in Valladolid, where the elderly 'Protector of the Indians' and Sepúlveda were invited to present their respective cases before the royal council. Charles V took the step, unparalleled in any empire before or since, of ordering all further conquests in America to cease until the justice of the Spanish position could be clarified. The famous confrontation achieved little of value, since the conquests were resumed. But Sepúlveda's treatise was forbidden publication, while Las Casas was permitted in 1552 to publish his inflammatory *Destruction of the Indies*, which bitterly attacked the whole Spanish conquest. He went on, moreover, to enjoy the highest support. His friend and fellow Dominican, Philip II's tutor Bartolomé de Carranza, took up his cause and defended it in a special meeting of officials in London in 1554. Thanking him, Las Casas reminded Carranza that the debate was so important that it should be held not in some dark corner of England but in front of 'the whole of Spain', with the emperor and court present.

By this time the labour structure in the Indies was collapsing, not under the pressure for reform but under the impact of demographic catastrophe. As Spaniards penetrated the remote territories they brought with them new viruses, particularly smallpox, to which the natives had no immunity and which caused devastating epidemics. The unaccustomed labour obligations (for Las Casas, 'the greatest evil which has caused the total destruction of those lands . . . is the encomienda'), the wholesale disruption of communities, the cruelties of the Spaniards (the Franciscan Motolinía, one of the 'twelve' who came to Mexico in 1524, gave a grim catalogue of mines where you could not walk for the bones of dead Indians and where the skies were darkened by scavenging vultures), all had their effect. In central Mexico the Indian population declined rapidly from a possible 25.2 million in 1518 to 2.65 in 1568 and just over one million in 1605; in Peru a pre-conquest population of about nine million fell to some 600,000 in 1620. As the workforce shrank, the encomiendas became impractical, so the authorities stepped in and organised a system, known in Mexico as the repartimiento and in Peru by the pre-Spanish term *mita*, whereby available labour was leased out to estate owners for limited periods.

By the 1550s, when the age of silver production was dawning, Spain and America were beginning to make a fundamental impression on each other. Spain was about to alter the human, animal and biological geography of the New World. In the human sphere, the introduction first of new diseases and then of labour systems shifted the balance of life firmly against the Indian and in some areas made the indigenous population extinct. To replace the deficiency, from 1518 licences were issued for the import of black slaves, initially from Christian territory and then later from west Africa; it was the beginning of the most prolonged and tragic racial transplantation in history. By the 1560s there were more blacks than whites in Hispaniola, Mexico city, Lima and throughout Spanish America. Las Casas was one of the first to recommend that black labour be introduced; he was also the first to condemn the new slavery, arguing 'that it is as unjust to enslave negros as it is to enslave Indians, and for the same reasons'.

In the animal sphere the first settlers were obliged to import their own horses for transport and their own pigs for meat, since America lacked any beasts of burden (other than the humble llama in Peru) and most domestic animals. Over the years Spanish vessels brought to the New World all the animals a farmer deemed essential: cattle, mules, fowl, dogs. Three animals in particular changed the history of America: the horse, which helped the conquistadors in battle and enabled them to cross great distances; and the sheep and cow, which in their thousands occupied the plains and semi-deserts, bringing profits to colonial farmers but depriving Indians of land for their food and thus creating an ecological crisis and an epoch of recurrent famines. Wherever cattle went, the Indian died; it was a stark and simple equation. In the biological sphere, finally, a revolution was initiated by the introduction, among a mass of other plants and fauna, of three foods considered essential to a native of the Mediterranean: wheat, vines and olives. By the end of the century wheat, hitherto unknown, was the most widely cultivated crop in the New World.

In the long run, Spanish culture made its mark on the language, religion and architecture of the New World, though at all levels the Spanishness was modified and enriched by Indian art and custom. By contrast, the impact of America on Spain was surprisingly muted. The first generation of explorers was, like Cortés and many others, ready to admire the achievements of the Aztecs and Incas; but as the vision of an earthly paradise receded the more stolid colonial mentality, with its overtones of racial superiority and cultural arrogance, took over. There was nothing, it seemed, to be learnt from the inhabitants of America, though some of their produce filtered back to Spain. Plants like the tomato and potato slipped unobtrusively into the Spanish diet; maize began to be grown in the Cantabrian provinces and by the seventeenth century was a staple food; tobacco spread as a habit and became a lucrative state monopoly. From the 1490s there was evidence in Andalusia of what they called 'the French disease' (syphilis), which was said to have its origin in America.

The New World was important less for its direct than its indirect impact: it brought wealth (we shall examine this shortly), it stimulated enquiry and it promoted social mobility.

For a Castile with no history of exploration or empire the stimulus given by the voyage of the *Victoria* and the conquest of the pre-Columbian world was crucial: the events created a new confidence and an ideology for domination. The light of experience, tested by Castilian eyes and hands, was creating knowledge and falsifying the ancients, claimed the historiographer royal, López de Gómara. For the historian Fernández de Oviedo, America was the greatest intellectual adventure of all time, yielding up secrets unknown to all the old learning: 'what I speak of cannot be learnt in Salamanca or Bologna or Paris'. The fruits of the enquiry stimulated by America can be seen, in America itself, in the monumental scholarship of the Franciscan Bernardino de Sahagún, whose *History of the Things of New Spain* was a compilation of the entire culture of Mexico; and, in Spain, in the thought of the Dominican professor of Salamanca, Francisco de Vitoria, whose study of the Indian problem enabled him to develop principles on the relationship between peoples that created a framework for international law and the rights of man.

The opportunity for advancement was perhaps the main appeal of the New World. Few were as fortunate as Cortés, who in 1529 became a marquis, with the grant of an immense territory in Mexico comprising more than 20 large towns and villages and upwards of 23,000 Indian vassals. America offered none the less a unique avenue to freedom for the poor and oppressed of the Old World, among them people of Jewish origin. By the later sixteenth century the number of conversos in America, most of them of Portuguese origin, was enough to make the inquisitor in Lima, seat of the first Inquisition in America (1570), comment that 'there are twice as many of them here as in Spain'. Spaniards brave enough to risk the long passage to America – a sea voyage averaging between one and six months – and the harsh struggles of the frontier, might make their fortunes and then possibly return home, as half of Pizarro's men did, with their wealth. A brother of St Teresa returned in the 1570s, astonished his neighbours by assuming the title 'don', and bought an estate near Ávila for 14,000 ducats. Little is yet known of the impact which these returning '*indianos*' had on their home communities, though the transformation of Trujillo by the wealth of the Pizarros is testimony to one great success story. By contrast, most emigrants who prospered in America from the availability of land preferred to settle there and call their families over: such were the tailor in Mexico pleading with his cousin in 1576 to 'leave that wretched country, because it is only for people who have a lot of money', and the mill-owner's wife from Puebla in 1589 asking her brother in Seville to come over from 'that poverty and need which people suffer in Spain'. The free economy in the colonies, moreover, offered endless opportunities to the farmer and entrepreneur: commerce in America, stated a Peruvian merchant in 1636, 'is so esteemed that he is not considered honourable who does not trade or contract as best he may'.

# The economy and the price revolution 1500–1560

After the ravages of the Black Death in the fourteenth century and other epidemics in the fifteenth, a final great onslaught swept over the peninsula with the plague of 1507–8. But in Castile from the late fifteenth century and in Toledo even from mid-century, population levels rose. In Andalusia there was a spectacular increase, caused initially by the southward land rush during the resettlement of Granada, and then by the early stages of the American enterprise: the population of Lower Andalusia rose from 355,000 to 517,000 between 1534 and 1591, and Seville tripled its population within a generation from 33,000 in 1534 to 95,000 in 1561. For a full half-century after 1508 there were no major checks to growth other than regional crises such as in Andalusia in 1521 and Valencia in 1530. Census figures show that within this period most towns expanded: between 1530 and 1561 the population of Cadiz rose from 3,300 to 6,000, that of Burgos from 8,600 to 21,700, that of Salamanca from 13,400 to 25,200. Between 1530 and 1580 the total population of Castile in both town and countryside probably increased by some 50 per cent. Higher population levels had two important long-term consequences: there was a rise in demand, particularly for food, which began to push up commodity prices well before the discovery of America; there was also greater pressure on land use and on grain supplies, obliging Spain to become a regular importer of wheat.

The agrarian problem was, as we have seen, not solved by the Catholic Monarchs. Rural producers attempted to meet growing demand, but with primitive and inefficacious methods that earned the condemnation of Herrera in his *Agricultura General* (1513). Critics like Juan de Arrieta in 1578 singled out the use of mules instead of cows as a major reason for poor production. Increase in output came then not from technology but from harder work, from conversion to arable of common land (*tierras concejiles*) and public land (*tierras baldías*), and from a preference for crops over pasture: all these trends could be found in the Valladolid country-side as early as 1503. Sustained growth, however, was impossible without further investment. It was here that America made its contribution.

Between 1503 and 1600, according to the estimates of Earl J. Hamilton, 153,500 kilograms of gold and 7.4 million kilograms of silver reached Spain from America, an enormous addition to the bullion reserves of Europe. Some 66 per cent of the gold and only 8 per cent of the silver had arrived before 1560, but it was enough to make an impact on Castile, where prices doubled in the first half of the century. Contemporaries attributed the price rise to a number of reasons, principally speculation by foreign traders. In 1556 Martín de Azpilcueta suggested that imports of treasure might be responsible: 'in Spain, when there was less money, goods and labour cost much less than after the discovery of the Indies, which flooded the country with gold and silver. The reason for this is that money is worth more where and when it is scarce than where and when it is abundant.' Other writers, like the Frenchman Bodin in 1568 and Tomás de Mercado in his brilliant *Suma de Tratos* (Seville, 1568), arrived independently at the same conclusion. In recent times the causal connection between American bullion and Spanish inflation was most persuasively argued by Hamilton. The pace of price inflation, it seemed to him, closely followed the level of gold and silver imports (*see* Figures 2 and 3). In its essentials the argument is valid, but needs to be qualified by other considerations. Price series used by Hamilton are not always typical for their areas, and there are significant variations in some regions from the steady price rise his graph presents. His data for bullion imports, moreover, are only of registered treasure and take no account of the large quantity of smuggled metal, which may have been as little as 10 per cent of registered values for the early period (as Hamilton suggests) but was certainly very much higher by the late century. Finally, any attempt to relate imports to prices must take account of whether the bullion actually entered the country, and whether the credit created by bullion was a far greater stimulus to inflation than the metal itself. Any crude equivalence between imported metal and a price rise needs to reckon, for example, with the fact that the inflation rate was much higher in the early sixteenth century, when little bullion had entered Spain, than later in the century.

There were in the early century three principal and inter-linked generators of inflation, which provoked a much steeper proportionate rise than in the late century when bullion imports were at their peak: the three were population pressure, the discoveries and bullion imports. To the demand created by expanding population within Spain was added the demand from colonists in America for food and manufactures. Andalusian farmers exported to the New World and received silver in return. Imported treasure gave merchants more cash to invest in trade, and gave manufacturers more money to invest in production. A veritable boom hit the Castilian economy, principally in Andalusia where between 1511 and 1559 the price of wheat rose by 109 per cent, of oil by 197 per cent and of wine by 655 per cent. When he toured Spain in 1526 the Venetian ambassador Navagero took a close look at economic activity in Castile. There were, he reported, three major centres of activity: Granada, Seville and Valladolid. In Valladolid, there were 'many artisans of every sort . . . and this abundance of activity is caused by the presence of the court'. In Granada, the silks 'sell very well throughout Spain, but are not as well made as in Italy'. From Seville, centre of a thriving Andalusia, 'they send to the Indies all their wheat and wine, as well as doublets, shirts, trousers, shoes and similar items, which until now they did not send but from which they get enormous profits'. In northern Castile the business world was also thriving, but on the basis of exporting raw materials and importing manufactured goods. In Medina del Campo, he wrote, 'most of the business is in bills of exchange', in Burgos 'most of the inhabitants are merchants and rich, trading not only in Spain but throughout the world'.

The characteristics and consequences of the boom are discussed below (*see* pp. 108–9). For consumers, the consequence of inflation was a fall in living standards. Although the annual price rise was small, the phenomenon of a regular increase was unprecedented and therefore revolutionary. 'Today', wrote Alonso de Herrera in 1513, 'a pound of mutton costs as much as a whole sheep used to, a loaf as much as a sack of wheat.' 'Thirty years ago', wrote Mercado in 1568, 'a thousand pennies was something, today it is nothing.' In a less flexible economy than ours is today, with large sections of the people, both labourers and landlords, subsisting on traditionally fixed incomes, the impact of creeping inflation could be catastrophic. In the region of Valladolid, wages managed to rise between 1511 and 1550, but by less than 30 per cent; meanwhile, the price of wheat rose by 44 per cent, of mutton by 41 per cent, of wine by 64 per cent. For those who earned money for only part of the year (which was true of most seasonal labourers), or who had more mouths to feed in the family, the lag in wages could be disastrous. A study has been done for those years, on building labourers in Valencia, measuring their wages against a cost-of-living index composed of various consumer items; the results show an ever-widening gap between low income and high prices. Since only a minority of Spaniards owned their own plot of land or their own house, rent levels must also be considered. Some examples from Valladolid (where the presence of the royal court helped to push up prices) show that land rents between 1530 and 1555 rose by over 86 per cent, and house rents by up to 80 per cent.

Inflation of course hit all classes and not just wage-labourers. Clergy on fixed stipends, nobles whose income from their vassals was in cash rather than kind, all suffered. In 1581 the Italian engineer Antonelli, on contract to Philip II, stated that in Spain 'the prices of goods have risen so much that nobles, gentry, commoners and clergy cannot live on their incomes'. The price revolution had a corrosive effect, weakening those sections of society with traditional incomes, but benefiting those able to adapt to and profit from the new situation: it therefore became a primary cause of social change.

Complaints against the rising cost of living were made in most of the Cortes of Charles V. Higher prices, the continuing export of raw materials, and the import in their place of foreign goods that competed successfully against dearer Spanish articles not only in Spain but also in America, posed a balance of payments problem. Merchants sought the wealth of the Indies in Spain. The export of raw materials was not new; the novelty lay in the rising tide of foreign manufactures that flooded in to meet the demand created by bullion. 'Foreigners who bring merchandise to these realms must give a surety to take back merchandise and not money', demanded a procurador in the Cortes of 1548; 'Spain has become an Indies for the foreigner', claimed another in the same session. Meanwhile the bullion continued to pour out of Spain. Much of it was taken out illegally through trade channels, hidden among other commercial items; the Venetian envoy Soranzo claimed in 1556 that in this way there entered France every year from Spain up to 5.5 million gold crowns. Other quantities left quite legally, as payment for goods traded to Spain. Finally, by far the largest amounts were exported by the Spanish state to pay for foreign policy commitments. Already in the 1530s Charles V was transporting bullion out of Spain to Antwerp to pay for material supplied by the Netherlands, and to reimburse foreign bankers.

From 1515 to 1551 the Cortes petitioned on 12 occasions for a ban on exports of bullion. The theme was taken up again in 1558 in a memorandum presented to Philip II by a royal official, Luis Ortiz. Ortiz reasoned that precisely because of the great amount of bullion coming to Spain, foreign manufacturers introduced their goods into the country in order to take out silver. The high price levels gave them good profits and impeded competition from domestic industry. Raw materials exported by Spain came back as foreign manufactures: 'things have reached such a state that even the pig-iron exported to France comes back soon as ironmongery. Goods are now so expensive in these realms, because they come from foreign lands, that it has become a scandal. Foreigners now treat us worse than Indians.' Ortiz argued that real wealth came not from the ability to purchase trinkets from foreigners in exchange for silver – hence the reference to Indians, whom the Spaniards had themselves exploited in this way – but from labour and higher output.

The effect of the price rise provoked by bullion was felt most sharply in the south: 'a thousand ducats', Mercado commented, 'are worth more in Castile than in Andalusia'. In 1503 a House of Trade (Casa de la Contratación) was set up in Seville, and the port was given a monopoly over trade to America that lasted till 1680. Seville had already been the principal point of departure for voyages: the choice was given added force by its role as entrepôt for the produce of Andalusia, and by the favourable situation of the south-west coastline relative to the winds and currents required for the Atlantic crossing. Though the city was a hundred miles from the sea, the river Guadalquivir was freely navigable and at the river's outlet a cluster of ports, principally Cadiz and Puerto Santa María, co-operated in the monopoly. In 1524 a council of the Indies was created to supervise all matters relating to the government of the New World. The merchants trading from Seville were incorporated into a consulado (1543) modelled on that of Burgos.

At the accession of Charles V America became for a brief while prey to the Flemings. Though the notorious profiteers were excluded after the Comunidades, in reality Castile continued to depend heavily on foreigners for capital to invest in New World enterprises. There had long been a colony of Genoese traders in Seville; they were now well placed to invest in and profit from the developing transatlantic exchange. From 1524 to 1538 the emperor tried to repay his foreign bankers, mainly Germans, by granting permits to trade directly to America: the Welsers undertook, for example, to colonise Venezuela. Over the same period a number of other Castilian seaports, both on the Cantabrian coast and in Andalusia, were allowed to trade directly. These expedients, motivated by the crown's lack of money to invest in America, ceased after 1538: from that date the monopoly was limited to the Seville complex. It is however not true, as often supposed, that Catalans and other subjects of the crown of Aragon were excluded from the commerce. Though Charles in 1522 rejected a petition by Barcelona for permission to trade directly, Aragonese were allowed to emigrate to America, and Catalans and Aragonese could be found in Seville trading freely from 1524 onwards. The monopoly was never a narrowly exclusive one. From the late century a few foreign merchants, usually long domiciled in Seville, were granted naturalisation and allowed to trade directly; many other foreigners did business openly through Castilian agents; and other areas of Spain participated in varying degrees in the enterprise. The northern ports of Spain, for instance, built some 80 per cent of the ships used on the Atlantic crossing in the period 1520–80.

# Social change in an age of inflation

The price revolution in Spain changed both fortunes and status. Profits from agriculture and cash from the Indies helped to stimulate social mobility. At the end of the sixteenth century about 10 per cent of Castile's population claimed to have noble status (*hidalguía*), ranging from the Basque provinces where virtually everybody was an hidalgo to Andalusia where under 1 per cent were. The outward sign of noble status was exemption from direct taxes, a privilege highly desirable in itself and which attracted many to purchase nobility. An hidalgo by birth or purchase, however, was only the lowest rung of the ladder of ranks in the noble estate. Above hidalgos came the higher grade of *caballeros*, normally identified by the possession of property and including the bulk of the urban or local nobility; among them also can be classified those who held encomiendas of the military orders. In the crown of Aragon the caballeros were the most numerous and influential section of the noble class; in Catalonia (where they were called barons) and Valencia they dominated the second chamber of the Cortes, and in Aragon they were privileged to have their own chamber (of caballeros or infanzones) in the four-chamber Cortes. At the very top of the ladder, finally, came the titled nobility (*títulos*) and the grandees (*grandes*).

Because it had not been mediaeval practice in the crown of Aragon or the Basque lands to grant territorial titles, only in Castile did an extensive titled aristocracy come into existence. Charles V in 1520 divided the upper Castilian nobility into two categories: ordinary títulos (there were then 35) and an elite of 25 grandees, whose privileges were purely honorific (they could keep their hats on in the royal presence, and were addressed by the king as 'cousin'). A titled aristocracy developed gradually in the crown of Aragon, but in the course of the century its leading members (notably the dukes of Cardona in Catalonia, Híjar in Aragon and Gandía in Valencia) gravitated towards the court and married into the Castilian noble elite.

Traditional status qualifications were still absolutely essential for acceptance into the noble Estate; chief among them were military service, possession of public office and service to the state (in law, finance and trade). By the end of the fifteenth century people with some of these credentials constituted the ruling class throughout Spain. The urban elite was made up of caballeros whose way of life might sometimes have seemed 'bourgeois' but who in terms of accepted status were 'nobles'. It was still a relatively mobile society where several avenues of access to noble rank were available and where there were few rigid distinctions between social orders. The mediaeval policy and outlook of the Catholic Monarchs reinforced this openness. Between 1465 and 1516, as we have seen, they granted about a thousand new hidalguías, mainly for service during the years of war. By choosing lesser gentry for public service as secretaries, judges and corregidors, they moreover showed their willingness to encourage talent and to reward it with status. The 1505 law on *mayorazgos* aided the process of social mobility by enabling gentry to conserve their property from one generation to the next, and thus to found dynasties. A typical case is Rodrigo Ronquillo, who became famous as a royal judge in the Comunidades. A successful career enabled him on his death in 1552 to found a small mayorazgo comprising his home in Arévalo, with some land near by, and a juro worth 100 ducats a year. From these small beginnings sprang one of the great bureaucratic families of the seventeenth century.

America and the Seville trade were the most striking cause of social advance. Traders of all nations, led by the Genoese, flocked to the Andalusian ports. Among Castilians who invested in the commerce was the banking family of Espinosa. Some merchants became fabulously rich, like Juan Antonio Corzo, allegedly the wealthiest man of his time, who in 1597 left a fortune of 1,600,000 ducats. The aristocracy were not slow to recognise the possible benefits: the dukes of Medina-Sidonia and Medinaceli, each with a seaport on their estates, were among those who exploited their agrarian resources and participated in trade. Bulk and seaborne trade was accepted as fully compatible with noble status, Spanish practice here being no different from that of other nations. By the late century trade in Seville was frequently controlled by aristocrats:

*Es segunda maravilla*
*un caballero en Sevilla*
*sin ramo de mercader*
(*it is yet another wonder to see a nobleman in Seville who does not also trade*)

commented Ruiz de Alarcón.

The rise in prices at home, and the emergence of new fortunes derived from commercial success or from America, both quickened the pace of mobility and revolutionised social values. 'We no longer consider the virtue of a gentleman', lamented the historian Diego Valera, 'but rather how wealthy he is'. Another contemporary, Dr Villalobos, denounced 'the modern need for unending sums of money'. 'In these times', wrote Pérez de Guzmán, 'he is noblest who is richest.' Cervantes was later to comment that

*Ya no se estima el valor*
*porque se estima el dinero*
*(money is prized rather than worth).*

By then it was also commonly felt that too much mobility threatened the stability of the state: in Lope de Vega we find the view that

*la perdición*
*de las repúblicas causa*
*el querer hacer los hombres*
*de sus estados mudanza*
*(states are destroyed through men wishing to change their status).*

In fact, when mobility within the upper classes was discussed money was seldom mentioned. The broad range of nobles who were rising to prominence through non-military means preferred to emphasise two aspects: 'virtue' in the sense of loftiness of soul (or intellectual ability) and proven service to the crown, and the exclusive power of the prince to create 'nobility'. This conception of rank, which reflected the interests of the letrado hierarchy of Castile, tended to play down the hereditary element and to argue that the elite must be continually regenerated by men of honour whose virtue was recognised and rewarded by the state. True nobility must also maintain a proper lifestyle. Juan de Arce Otalora, graduate of a *colegio mayor* at Salamanca and later a judge of the chancillería of Valladolid, published his *Summa nobilitatis* in 1553. He traced his noble lineage to 1441, and himself founded a dynasty of public servants who gave distinguished service to the crown. His book stated that 'it is the law and custom that those who do not live nobly do not enjoy the privileges of nobility': wealth, in other words, was essential to maintain status.

The newer concept of nobility was challenged by all those whose status was sanctified by tradition. For them, nobility was based essentially on lineage and (an important consideration for those without titles) on common repute. In reaction to the proliferation of new nobles created by the state, some theorists in the sixteenth century began to emphasise that ancient blood and heredity, rather than 'virtue' or recent wealth, were the guarantees of true nobility. This was also the period when the anti-Semitic statutes of limpieza de sangre began to gain some acceptance in specific Castilian institutions, with the result that 'pure' blood also tended to become a prerequisite for obtaining a noble title. In this way, status struggles among the elite in the early sixteenth century developed along two lines:

the hereditary aristocracy clung to an exclusive blood concept of rank and claimed to despise the newer elite of lawyers and merchants, and there was open discrimination against the entry of people of Jewish origin into the elite.

Much of the status conflict was, however, a sham, as we can see by the many people of lowly origin who were accepted into the ranks of the nobility. By the seventeenth century it was recognised frankly that money had to play a part in the formation of an elite, as shown in the well-known lines of Lope de Vega:

*No dudes que el dinero es todo en todo,*
*es príncipe, es caballero, es hidalgo,*
*es alta sangre, es descendiente godo*
*(doubt not that money is all in all: it is prince, knight, noble, ancient*
*blood, Gothic ancestry).*

Even people of Jewish origin could rise socially, and in many respects the insistence on 'blood purity' was also a sham. The highest bodies in Church and state condemned the cathedral of Toledo when in 1547 it attempted to exclude conversos from holding office. In practice there continued to be constant discrimination against people of distant Jewish origin, who often found it difficult to better themselves because of the demand that they should demonstrate their 'purity'. But such demands were used very selectively, were not employed in the greater part of Spain and were often resorted to less out of racial prejudice than out of the attempt to eliminate political rivals.

The conflict between concepts of nobility persisted throughout the early modern period, but it is not clear what effect it had on the composition of the elite, whose evolution was firmly controlled by the crown. The exclusion of the aristocracy from the constitutional arena after the Cortes of 1538 was a blow of only limited impact, since in practice the great lords continued to exercise their influence without interruption in the towns and estates under their control. More important was the creation of a fixed court and seat of government (Valladolid from 1544, Madrid from 1561), which obliged the nobles to reside at the centre of power if they hoped for preferment. Although the aristocracy undoubtedly profited from the agricultural output of their lands in the early century, they seem at the same time to have committed themselves to outdoing each other in expenditure. The relatively peaceful reign of Charles V, when Spain was not directly at war on its own account, confirmed the unwillingness of young nobles to risk their lives in battle when it was possible to enter the state bureaucracy

in order to exercise power; the military reformer Diego de Salazar in his
*De re militari* (1536) claimed that 'the military estate is decayed and has
forgotten its former calling'.

The bulk of complaints against undesirable mobility during the price
revolution was directed at the middle orders. 'Many tax-paying farmers',
stated the Cortes of Valladolid in 1518, 'obtain privileges to be hidalgos
and free of taxes, which is very damaging to the villages'. The city of Seville
in 1598 claimed that 'the persons who attempt to buy hidalguías and civic
offices are merchants and businessmen'. Mobility in both countryside and
town was a recognised fact: the Spanish bourgeoisie (a term used here for
the entire middle sector involved in the professions and in making wealth)
was an active, thriving minority, whose success was in no way dislocated
by the expulsion of the Jews in 1492. Under the Catholic Monarchs,
Castilians controlled the bulk of their own internal trade (the wool towns,
the fishing ports); and since the Genoese at first had little hold over the
wool trade to northern Europe, Castilian merchants were to be found in
Antwerp, Rouen and Nantes. Burgos, centre of the trade, produced merchant families (some of converso origin) like the Maluenda, the Miranda,
the Salamanca, the Bernuy. In Medina del Campo, Simón Ruiz expressed
his wish to pursue 'honourable commerce' (*negocios honrados*). The
participation of such men in commerce invalidates the opinion, voiced by
Guicciardini on his visit to Spain in 1512 and since echoed by many historians, that 'Spaniards do not dedicate themselves to trade because they
consider it dishonourable'.

There was in reality no formal obstacle to commerce in Spain. The
humanist Juan Luis Vives recognised that 'vita est in pecunia, in quo
Hispani magnifice insaniunt', an opinion mirrored by Jean Bodin's view in
1568 that 'the Spanish people have no other occupation' but commerce.
The widespread acceptance of wealth when acquired honourably made it
compatible with high social status. 'Working and sweating in order to
acquire property in order to maintain *honra*', as the writer Luis Mexía put
it, was perfectly reconcilable with traditional values. In the seventeenth
century Lope de Vega made one of his characters state that

*habéis de saber*
*que en cualquier mercader*
*es honra tambien la hacienda*
*(you must know that for any merchant money is honourable).*

'Riches, for the most part, may lead to nobility', conceded fray Benito
de Peñalosa in 1629. In practice, then, the bourgeois plied his profession in

a manner which least offended the common opinion (i.e. repute, honour) in his community, and was able to climb socially if he did not breach any accepted norms. Where he managed to break through into big enterprise, as in Burgos with wool or in Seville with the Indies trade, social success became a complement to economic success. Since capitalism was never decried in Spain, it is not surprising to see that nobles likewise took an active part in American commerce. The expansionist period of the sixteenth century was one of considerable triumphs for the Castilian bourgeoisie. If the success was followed by failure, the reasons must be sought less in a change of ethical attitudes than in a change of the economic situation.

It was argued against the aspiring bourgeois that work, particularly manual or 'mechanical' work, disqualified him from attaining noble status. Claims like this normally arose out of status conflict among the urban elites, and were an attempt to restrict mobility. In 1548, for example, the Cortes petitioned that those with 'public shops' be excluded from city government; in 1558 they petitioned the reverse, that those already in city government be forbidden to trade. The requests point to a struggle between different views of the work ethic. Further evidence comes from Luis Ortiz, who in 1559 suggested 'that laws discriminating against mechanical workers be repealed, and others be passed granting them honours and position, as in Flanders and other countries'. The contradiction in attempts to argue that nobles should not work, or that those who worked should not become nobles, is revealed by a case in San Sebastián in 1582. When a prospective member of the order of Santiago was accused of having worked at a 'mechanical trade', various witnesses deposed that 'all the citizens of San Sebastián, even if hidalgos, have mechanical trades and live by them'. The candidate obtained his membership (hábito), which could not be denied him since in the Basque country the older tradition of work as honourable still survived.

The means whereby the middle class rose were the same as elsewhere in Europe: profits from the soil, investments, tenure of office. The prerequisites for advancement in Spain, however, were only three: a good income, a respectable position in society and the presumption (often, as we have noted, ignored) of freedom from Semitic blood. Without all three it was difficult to rise in Spanish society. Sometimes nobility might be achieved in as little as one generation: a diarist in the early seventeenth century in Catalonia sneered at those 'who the day before yesterday were peasants, yesterday merchants and today caballeros engaged in commerce – and all in the space of thirty years'. Hostility to the newcomers was foreseeable:

the Cortes in 1592 protested against 'persons of inferior quality', in 1639 against 'persons of lowly condition'. At the upper level some bourgeois could, like the Salamanca family of Burgos, succeed in producing distinguished administrators of the crown; at the lower level they reinvested their profits in long-term and secure assets, such as land, juros or censos.

*Censos* (called *censals* in the crown of Aragon) were loans issued by individuals or municipalities, who were repaid in annuities until the extinction of the debt. In the 1520s, when capital was still scarce, the interest rate on censos in Castile varied from 12 to 15 per cent; as more money entered the market, the rate fell to between 7 and 11 per cent in 1535–40 and to 7 per cent in 1563. The agricultural boom created a demand among peasants for improvement in their landholdings: in Valladolid, for example, peasants were the biggest class of borrowers. The accounts of the Valladolid notary Antonio de Cigales show that in 1576–7 over 51 per cent of his borrowers were peasants, 10 per cent were artisans, 13 per cent office-holders and 3 per cent nobles. The immediate impact of censos was beneficial: they injected much-needed capital into the countryside, and provided resources for all types of development. Lenders found that both censos and juros were a profitable investment, and both soon featured in the disposition of many bourgeois fortunes.

The principal casualties of the price revolution in Spain were the lower orders and the poor. The population increase of the late fifteenth and early sixteenth centuries strained economic resources and crowded the towns. In a period when full, regular employment was not the norm, and labourers earned part-time cash as sowers in spring or harvesters in the autumn, unskilled earners had no reliable source of income to combat the rise in prices. An increase in vagrant beggars was one of the earliest signs of the growth of mass poverty: the Cortes in 1518 petitioned that 'the poor should not wander through the kingdom, but each one should beg in his own town'. The aim was to aid only the local poor, and exclude outsiders, but these drifted to the towns anyway. In Segovia in 1561 a sixth of the population was registered as poor, in Valladolid about one-fifth and in Trujillo as much as one-half. The majority of the indigent appear to have been women and children: in Segovia 60 per cent of the adult poor were females, in Medina del Campo 83 per cent. Those on regular wages were equally liable to suffer the ravages of inflation. In Valencia a building worker's wages sufficed for living costs in 1500–15, but by 1568–75 they covered only a third.

Vagrancy provoked problems of law and order. Charles V restricted beggars to an area within six leagues' radius from their home towns, and only those with permits could beg. Under Philip II this method of control was centred on the parish. The parish priest had to issue begging licences, each parish created officials to superintend the poor, and an attempt was made to register all vagrants. The licence system never worked successfully and there were periodic moves to ban begging completely. The humanist Juan Luis Vives was the first European writer to outline a new approach to poor relief in his *De subventione pauperum* (1526). Hospitals must be set up to take the poor off the streets, he wrote, and relief must consist 'not in mere almsgiving, but in all the ways by which a poor man can be uplifted'. Implicit in this approach was the conviction that the Christian state had a duty to maintain its less fortunate citizens and that the task should not be left to private charity. Juan de Medina in his *Plan of poor relief practised in some Spanish towns* (1545) also outlined a scheme to abolish begging and hospitalise the sick and needy; and in the same year Domingo de Soto published his *Considerations on the poor*.

The wandering poor were augmented by gypsies, who made their first appearance in western Europe in the late fifteenth century. In Spain the first recorded law against them was in 1499. In 1525 the Cortes of Toledo petitioned that 'the Egyptians not wander through the realm, since they steal from the fields and destroy orchards and deceive people'. It was the start to a long history of persecution. A more direct consequence of the new age was the spread of colonial slavery. Traditionally most slaves in the peninsula had been Muslims, casualties of the Reconquest. Their numbers were greatly increased by the victorious campaign against Granada, and the subsequent wars of Cisneros and Charles V in north Africa, together with constant conflict by sea, made the slavery of Muslims a permanent feature of life in the sixteenth century. When the age of discovery began, Iberian slavery shifted its focus from the Mediterranean to the Atlantic, from Muslim to African slaves. 'The American trade', a Flemish observer reported in 1655, 'has given new life to the institution of slavery in this country, so that in Andalusia one sees few servants other than slaves'. Black slavery in Spain was thus an extension of the American experience. By 1565 Seville was estimated to have 7.4 per cent of its population as slaves, mostly black. Most of these were employed as household servants, a luxury to be found mainly in the seaports, and in the households of great nobles and clergy.

In a well-known letter of May 1545 prince Philip informed the emperor that 'with what they pay in ordinary and extraordinary taxes, the common people are reduced to such utter misery that many of them go around naked. And the misery is so universal that it is even greater among the vassals of nobles than among Your Majesty's, for they are unable to pay their rents since they lack the means; and the prisons are full'. Although the impact of taxation was to be much heavier in Philip's own reign, there is no doubt that the frequency of the new taxes was creating problems in the rural areas, where the bulk of the population lived and where the social crisis was at its most intense. If the injection of bullion had managed to revitalise agriculture and change its techniques, then rising production would have coped with the inflation rate and higher taxation. In fact, investment in agriculture merely maintained production levels, and most silver seems to have been used for extending vineyards (to meet American demand) and developing the fisheries. By the end of Charles's reign the commercial sector had certainly grown but the excess capital passed away from the rural communities; and in provinces like La Mancha, Ciudad Real and Jaén, where production was inadequate for subsistence and pro-vided no surplus with which to pay taxes, poverty became ineradicable.

The tax burden, of which the Cortes complained repeatedly, was more a symptom than a cause of distress. Inflation in an underdeveloped country, as modern experience has shown, can be catastrophic unless there are structural changes in the economy. No adequate changes occurred in the Spanish countryside, and the benefits of the price rise were restricted to specific sectors – foreign trade, finance – whose growth was superficial and transitory and tended to promote a wealthy elite at the expense of the real producers in the country, the peasants. For these the century of inflation was scarcely a blessing. Since 1480 the peasant in Castile had been legally free. However, most 'peasants' were in fact day-labourers (*jornaleros*) and did not own or rent any land: in New Castile at this time jornaleros were some 70 per cent of the rural population. Landowning peasants were more common in the north of Spain; but in many areas, notably Galicia where the holdings were tiny and subject to heavy rents called *foros*, they were unable to gain an adequate living from the soil. The dues that a peasant had to pay on the produce from his land could be heavy. In New Castile in the 1570s land rents absorbed between one-third and one-half of a peasant's harvest, and were by far the heaviest burden. Taxes and tithes would each account for possibly another tenth, and seigneurial dues would be a further fraction. In addition to these expenses, a peasant would need enough left over from his produce to feed his family, to set by for the next harvest, and to sell in order to obtain cash for pur-chases and debts. A village near Toledo complained in 1580 that 'after paying the rent, nothing was left'. It is not surprising that the Cortes in 1598 complained that 'everything tends towards the destruction of the poor peasantry and the increase in property, authority and power of the rich'.

The steady rise in taxation through the century was prompted, as we have seen, by foreign policy needs, but was clearly a consequence of the price revolution. The requirements of state finance increased at higher than the inflation rate: between 1554 and 1566 the budget doubled from just under three million ducats to nearly five and a half. The Castilian pechero was called upon to pay. Ironically, those who really profited from the inflation, namely the merchant elite and the landlords, often escaped the burden. Though taxes became far more burdensome in the next century, already the gap between rich and poor was widening inexorably.

# Humanism and empire

Upon the accession of Charles V Spain became committed to a bold confrontation with Europe. A political dimension was now added to the existing cultural links with Italy and the Netherlands. The momentary rejection of northern Europe by the Comunidades did little to impede the entry of some elements of Renaissance humanism.

In 1517 Cisneros had unsuccessfully invited Erasmus to visit Spain. The cardinal's university at Alcalá represented a promising focus of humanism in the peninsula. Its first chancellor, Pedro de Lerma, had studied at Paris, Nebrija was (as Erasmus wrote to Luis Vives in 1521) its 'principal ornament', and among its professors were the converso brothers Juan and Francisco de Vergara. In June 1524 Vives wrote to Erasmus that 'our Spaniards are also interesting themselves in your works'. Significant support for the Dutch humanist came from the archbishop of Toledo, Alonso de Fonseca, and the inquisitor general, Alonso Manrique de Lara. When Erasmus's *Enchiridion* was translated and published (1526), the translator claimed that 'at the emperor's court, in the cities, in the churches, in the convents, even in the inns and on the highways, everyone has the *Enchiridion* in Spanish'. In reality the reception of Erasmus and of humanism in general was often lukewarm, and there was considerable hostility from clergy who resented Erasmus's attacks on the mendicant friars. The religious orders prevailed on Manrique to hold a debate in Valladolid in March 1527 to decide whether Erasmus's works were heretical or not, and when the conference was suspended without any decision it was seen to be a victory for the Erasmians. In December Charles himself wrote to Erasmus, assuring him that 'we shall always hold your honour and repute in the greatest esteem'.

The support given to Erasmus indicated an 'opening' to broader horizons, and to a cultural outlook shared by officials like Charles's Latin secretary Alfonso de Valdes, clerics like cardinal Mendoza, aristocrats like the marquis of Villena, intellectuals like the Benedictine Alonso de Virués. However, it was at all times a minority movement, with very little impact outside court circles, and most influential only during the emperor's stay in Spain from 1522 to 1529. During those years the fruitful cultural links with the Netherlands were represented not only by Erasmus, but also by a distinguished Spaniard, the philosopher Juan Luis Vives. The case of Vives revealed one of the difficulties that separated peninsular from European culture. Born in Valencia of converso parents who continued to practise their Jewish religion in secret, Vives at the age of 16 was sent by his father to study abroad in Paris (1509), a year after the death of his mother in an epidemic. His life and brilliant career were thereafter based in the Netherlands. After Nebrija's death in 1522 Vives was invited to occupy his chair at Alcalá, but refused. Family circumstances combined to make Vives a permanent exile from his homeland: in 1520 his father was arrested by the Inquisition as a judaiser and burnt alive in 1524; four years later his long-dead mother was also prosecuted and her bones disinterred and burnt. Witness in his own person of the peculiar problems faced by scholars in Spain, Vives was well qualified to write to Erasmus in 1534 that 'we are going through times when we can neither speak nor be silent without danger'.

By that date the humanist dawn in Spain had been shattered by a number of independent developments that found their focus in Erasmus. First, the beliefs of a group of mystical illuminists (*alumbrados*) provoked the Inquisition to look closely at religious views that appeared to be subversive. Second, the rise of Lutheran ideas in Germany seemed to threaten the Church, and some of the theologians at Valladolid in 1527 saw little difference between Erasmus and Luther. Finally, the disgrace of the inquisitor general Manrique in 1529 and the departure from Spain that year of the Erasmian court, left the humanists without effective support in high places. Through the 1530s the tide moved against them: the decade closed with the deaths of Vives (1540), and of Juan de Valdés (d. 1541, twin brother of the emperor's secretary) who had fled to Italy in 1530.

Spanish culture returned in part to its Mediterranean base. From 1544, when the Italianate poetry of Juan Boscán (d. 1542) and Garcilaso de la Vega (d. 1536) was published in a single posthumous volume, the success of Italian influences was assured. Unlike the earlier style, this period was not one of slavish imitation. Spanish writers used Italy as a starting point for a more universal approach, more in accordance with the horizons of the Habsburg monarchy. Bartolomé de Torres Naharro, who lived in Naples, and Gil Vicente, who was Portuguese by origin, both chose to write in Castilian, as though in fulfilment of Nebrija's view of the imperial role of language. In the theatre new work was created through the Sevillan Lope de Rueda (d. 1565). Above all, the cosmopolitan novel *Lazarillo de Tormes* (possibly composed in the 1520s, but published in 1554) began a genre that influenced the literature of all western Europe.

As we have seen, Spain's commitment to the Renaissance was neither extensive nor profound. The court humanism of the Mendozas, of Nebrija, never succeeded in superseding the popular culture represented on the one hand by the *Celestina*, on the other by romances of chivalry. For Spain the early sixteenth century was the quintessential age of chivalry, marked by the publication of the romances *Amadis of Gaul* (1508) and *Esplandián* (1510), which came out in several editions and together with their numerous imitators flooded the literature market. Between 1501 and 1650 a total of 267 editions of chivalric novels were issued, two-thirds of them in the early sixteenth century alone: every cultured person had them in his library. They formed the staple escapism of ordinary Spaniards at home and the campfire reading of adventurers on the American frontier. No one was more surprised than the conquistadors when they saw the legendary novels come to life in distant Mexico: to Bernal Díaz, the enterprise in which he took part was a valiant expedition like that of Roland against the heathen. The chivalric tradition was not, of course, simply a literary fancy. It survived from the Reconquest ethic, and had taken the form (in 1434) of the famous *passo honroso* at Santiago, when Suero de Quiñones and his knights defended the name of their ladies against all comers. The same chivalric ideal was active during the wars in Italy under Gonzalo de Córdoba, notably in 1503 when the French chevalier Bayard, the famous knight 'sans peur et sans reproche', fought a combat with ten other Frenchmen against eleven Spanish knights outside the walls of Trani. The greatest perpetuator of the chivalric myth, however, was Charles himself, who introduced into Spain the courtly ritual of Burgundy and the pageantry of the Order of the Golden Fleece. The emperor also laboured under the curious illusion that war could be conducted as a series of chivalric encounters: hence the challenge he issued to Francis I in 1528 (from which he was dissuaded by a sensible Spanish grandee), and the even more celebrated challenge he issued in the pope's presence in 1536 when he offered to settle all quarrels with Francis 'person to person'. On grounds both of literary merit and of the need for public order (because of deaths caused by duelling), public authorities in Spain disapproved of the romances and in 1555 the Cortes petitioned that they be banned.

Some of the finest writing of the early century arose out of the experience of empire and took the form of histories. The great chroniclers of the Catholic Monarchs (Hernando de Pulgar, Diego de Valera, Bernáldez) were followed under Charles by equally outstanding writers (Sandoval, Santa Cruz); but a new dimension to historical studies was opened up by the world vision of the Habsburg monarchy. Charles encouraged the development by adding to the established post of chronicler royal in Castile corresponding posts for Aragon (occupied by Jerónimo de Zurita) and the Indies. America was the most fruitful inspiration: among its historians were Antonio de Herrera, Gonzalo Fernández de Oviedo, Bernal Díaz del Castillo and López de Gómara. Their work was a small part of the adventure that propelled Spaniards into the mainstream of enquiry in geography, navigation, engineering and medicine.

The cultural advance of the Spanish elite was promoted under Charles V in an unexpected way: by an increase in the bureaucratic needs of the state. The development was already foreshadowed under the Catholic Monarchs by their insistence that members of councils and chancillerías should be letrados with at least ten years' training in law. The ideal of a king's servant skilled in Latin and literature as well as in war – represented in *The Courtier* by Castiglione – encouraged public acceptance of higher education. At the local level, towns with money available opened grammar schools: by 1490 the town school in Madrid was described as a place 'where all the sons of caballeros and of leading residents of the city learn'. At the topmost level new universities were founded: in 1450 there had been four main 'estudios generales' in Spain (Salamanca, Valladolid, Huesca, Lérida) but from the reign of the Catholic Monarchs onwards several more were founded, twenty in the course of the sixteenth century, the most outstanding being Cisneros's at Alcalá (1508). At the same time within each university a number of colleges were created, 38 over the period 1500–63 alone. The most distinctive of these colleges were the *colegios mayores*, small institutions (of about 20 to 30 places) which were open only to mature students, theoretically of 'poor' origin, and which enjoyed considerable privileges. Of the six colegios mayores, four were at Salamanca (founded between 1401 and 1521), one at Valladolid (1484) and one at Alcalá (1508). They became the major recruiting ground for Spain's emergent bureaucracy. Many Spaniards still preferred to educate themselves abroad, primarily in the Spanish college at Bologna, founded in 1369, and in the medical faculty at Montpellier or the theological faculty in Paris. Aristocrats, likewise, preferred to be educated privately, though lesser nobles attended the public universities. Education now began a phase of expansion in Spain, and the state chose to draw its officials from university graduates, trained now to become the elite not only of Spain but of its world empire as well.

## Reformation and reaction

The mystical trends in fifteenth-century Spanish Catholicism gave birth to a Franciscan school of spirituality supported by Cisneros and expressed most clearly in Francisco de Osuna's *Spiritual ABC* (1527). Adepts, known as *recogidos*, believed in the possibility of the 'taking up' of 'God into the soul and the soul into God'. About the same time another group of mystics was active in Guadalajara: known as *alumbrados* ('enlightened') or *dejados* ('abandoned', i.e. to God), they also had Franciscan members but were largely a lay group consisting of Isabel de la Cruz, Pedro Ruiz de Alcaraz, the widow María de Cazalla and her brother, bishop Juan de Cazalla. The group were all of converso origin and met regularly in the palace of the Mendoza duke of Infantado who, like the marquis of Villena, was a sponsor of spiritualising movements. A similar circle of alumbrados was active in Valladolid, under the leadership of the *beata* (holy woman) Francisca Hernández, who attracted into her group Bernardino Tovar, brother of Juan de Vergara, and the Franciscan friar Francisco Ortiz. Most of the alumbrados were conversos, which may have reflected a tendency for religious Spaniards of Jewish origin to escape from formal into spiritual Catholicism. Some have seen in the movement a direct rejection of orthodox Christianity. Although the first denunciation against the alumbrados occurred in 1519, it was not until Lutheran influences penetrated Spain that the first moves were made against them.

As late as 1520 Luther had not been heard of in Spain, and the first Spaniards to come into contact with his teachings were those who accompanied the emperor to Germany. Some of these, seeing in him only a reformer, were favourable to his ideas. By early 1521 Lutheran books, translated into Latin, were using the Flanders trade route in order to enter Spain. The first ban on them was issued by Adrian of Utrecht, in his role as inquisitor general, on 7 April 1521. In view of the Comunero revolt, the political no less than the religious implications of Luther were taken seriously in Spain. Books continued to arrive at all the major ports in the peninsula, but the Inquisition was vigilant: a vessel seized at Pasajes from the French had its hold full of books 'of writings by Luther and his followers'. In Burgos Bernardino Tovar was able to purchase Lutheran works imported from Flanders. By 1524, it was reported from the court, 'there is so much awareness of Luther that nothing else is talked about'.

In this new context the tenets of the alumbrados attracted attention. Isabel de la Cruz and Alcaraz were arrested, and on 23 September 1525 Alonso Manrique issued an edict listing exhaustively the errors of the alumbrados. Arrests went on sporadically over the next few years: Isabel and Alcaraz appeared in an auto de fe in 1529, the year that Francisca Hernández and Ortiz were also arrested in Valladolid; finally in 1532 María de Cazalla was also taken into custody (her brother the bishop had opportunely died in 1530) and appeared in an auto in 1534. Though all these personalities suffered severely at the hands of the Inquisition, none of them ended their days in prison or at the stake, as heretics normally would have done.

The fact is that though the beliefs of the alumbrados were strongly opposed to Catholic practice and were in a formal sense heretical, it was impossible to identify them as a 'sect'. They were above all a protest movement against the world they lived in, and their tenets were a loose amalgam of ideas borrowed, some from Franciscan piety, some from the Lutherans, some from Erasmus, to whose writings they later developed an affinity. Lutheranism as a substantial heresy was alleged in the trials of the Erasmian Diego de Uceda (1528) and María de Cazalla, but in neither case was the issue pressed. There was, in short, no indigenous Lutheran movement in Spain, no native heresy (like that of Wycliffe in fifteenth-century England) on which the German ideas could build. Though there was widespread interest in the country about Luther's views, an effective ban on the import of certain books prevented any direct information being diffused. Two or three people were burnt at the stake as self-confessed 'Lutherans' – one such was Juan López, disciple of Isabel de la Cruz, burnt in 1530 – but their Lutheranism consisted of little more than adherence to vague beliefs they assumed to be in accord with those of Luther.

The significant reaction in Spain was not then against heresy but against Erasmus. The arrest of Francisca Hernández in 1529 was followed by that of Bernardino Tovar. To defend herself, the beata implicated both Tovar and his distinguished brother Vergara, denouncing them as Lutherans. In 1529 Juan de Valdés, twin brother of Alfonso, had published his *Dialogue of Christian Doctrine*, which was immediately attacked by the Inquisition despite the testimony of Vergara and others. The controversy over the book took so dangerous a turn that in 1530 Valdés fled to Italy, just in time to avoid trial. In June 1533, finally, Vergara was arrested: it was a shock move that changed attitudes to foreign ideas. Secretary to Cisneros and later to Fonseca, professor at Alcalá and the most eminent humanist in Spain, Vergara was a personal friend of Erasmus and had spent two years with him in the Netherlands. Accused of sympathy for the alumbrados, Luther and Erasmus, he admitted that many Spaniards in Germany had once admired Luther but maintained that for himself 'there can be nothing more abominable than Luther and his opinions'. Acquitted of any charges of heresy, he was obliged to disavow his errors in an auto de fe at Toledo in December 1535 and was confined to a monastery for a year. Other eminent Erasmians now faced the tide of repression. Alonso de Virués, chaplain to Charles V, was arrested in 1533 and confined in prison by the Inquisition of Seville for four long years, though he pleaded – in vain – that Erasmus had never been condemned as unorthodox; his release was eventually secured by the emperor and he was appointed bishop of the Canary Islands. Leading lights of Alcalá University, like its librarian Miguel de Eguía (1533), its former rector Mateo Pascual (1537) and its former chancellor Pedro de Lerma (1535), were prominent victims of the campaign against Erasmus. Lerma left Spain after his sentence and chose to teach in Paris; his nephew Francisco de Encinas, famous in the history of European Protestantism as Dryander, claimed that in Lerma's home city of Burgos people were so alarmed by the case that those who had sent their sons to study abroad recalled them at once. Erasmus and the new human-ism were being identified with the German heresy, and for some the only protection was dissociation.

In December 1533 Rodrigo Manrique, son of the inquisitor general, wrote bitterly from Paris to Luis Vives, on the subject of Vergara's impris-onment: 'You are right. Our country is a land of pride and envy; you may add, of barbarism. For now it is clear that down there one cannot possess any culture without being suspected of heresy, error and Judaism. Thus silence has been imposed on the learned. As for those who have resorted to erudition, they have been filled, as you say, with great terror. At Alcalá they are trying to uproot the study of Greek completely'. Erasmus saw his friends in Spain being silenced one by one. His last surviving letter to that country is dated December 1533.

The gradual extirpation of Erasmus's ideas was a national phenom-enon: in Valencia, for example, the converso humanist Pedro Juan Oliver, who had studied in Paris and knew Erasmus, was in 1528 excluded from a chair. The death of inquisitor Manrique in 1538 removed one of the last protectors of Erasmus in the peninsula. The astonishing aspect of these years is that Protestantism failed to materialise in Spain, despite the regular infiltration of books and ideas. In part this is explicable by the fact that heterodox tendencies, such as the continuing illuminist and mystical traditions, were never explicitly concerned with points of doctrine, and moved subtly towards Lutheran positions – such as belief in justification by faith alone – without ever formally rejecting Catholic dogma. The importance, above all, of the Inquisition cannot be exaggerated: Spain was the only European country to possess a national institution dedicated to the elimination of heresy; by its vigilance and by coordinating its efforts throughout the peninsula, the Inquisition may have checked the seeds of heresy before they could be sown. In the 1540s, therefore, the only Spaniards to come directly into contact with Lutheranism were those in foreign universities (at Louvain, for example, where Philip II was shocked by the views of some of the Spaniards in 1558; or in France, where Servet was educated); those accompanying the emperor's court in Germany; and those who, with the opening of the Council of Trent (1546), were obliged to read Lutheran books in order to combat the errors in them.

In Spain the region most vulnerable to the penetration of foreign ideas was Seville, centre of international commerce. As archbishop, Manrique encouraged the appointment of scholars from Alcalá as canons and preachers of the cathedral. One of these, Juan Gil or Egidio, was in 1549 nominated by Charles V as bishop of Tortosa, but the appointment was quashed when Egidio was accused of heresy and in 1552 made to retract ten propositions. He died in peace in 1556. Times were changing, both in Spain and in Seville. In 1546 the city obtained a new archbishop who also became inquisitor general, Fernando de Valdés, a ruthless careerist who saw heresy everywhere. In 1556 Valdés objected to the appointment as cathedral preacher of Constantino Ponce de la Fuente, an Alcalá humanist and converso who was chaplain to Charles V in Germany between 1548 and 1555. His writings were examined for heresy, he was arrested by the Inquisition in 1558 and died in its cells two years later. By this date the small Protestant community in Seville had been exposed. Numbering perhaps no more than 130 in all, they included the prior and members of the Jeronimite monastery of San Isidro and several nuns from the convent of Santa Paula; in 1557 several members of San Isidro managed to flee abroad, among them Casiodoro de la Reina.

Meanwhile, in northern Castile, another circle of Protestants had come into existence. The founder was an Italian, Carlos de Seso, who had been turned to Protestantism by reading Juan de Valdés. His missionary zeal soon converted an influential and distinguished circle, of noble status and with some converso origins. The most eminent of the converts was

Dr Agustín Cazalla, who had been to Germany as chaplain to Charles V and had also accompanied Philip there. Cazalla was influenced by his brother Pedro, parish priest of Pedrosa, near Valladolid, and with him the whole Cazalla family, led by their mother Leonor de Vivero, fell into heresy. Their beliefs were no simple extension of the illuminist or Erasmian attitudes of the previous generation. In their clear rejection of purgatory, of the mass ('a worthless sacrifice, since that of Jesus Christ alone sufficed', claimed a priest in the group), and other Catholic dogmas, the Valladolid heretics were true Protestants.

The Seville group was exposed in 1557, when Juan Ponce de León, eldest son of the count of Bailén, was arrested together with others for introducing books from Geneva. His chief accomplice was Julián Hernández, who had spent a considerable time in the Reformed churches of Paris, Scotland and Frankfurt, and specialised in smuggling Protestant literature into his native country. The Inquisition collected information and in 1558 made a wave of arrests including the whole Cazalla family (April) and Constantino (August). Fernando de Valdés set a merciless repression in train. At the top, it is worth noting, the real instigator of the harsh policy was not Philip, who is often associated with the drive against heresy but was in fact absent during most of it; it was his father Charles V. Seeing the rise in Spain, and in the very capital, Valladolid, of a contagion that had destroyed his health in Germany, the emperor, in a famous letter of May 1558 to the regent Juana, demanded that nothing should stand in the way of an immediate application of the death penalty to all the heretics involved. 'It must be seen', he wrote, 'whether they can be proceeded against as creators of sedition, upheaval, riots and disturbance in the state; they would then be guilty of rebellion and could not expect any mercy'. From now on, heresy was to be treated not simply as an offence against God but as something far more serious: an offence against the security of the state.

From 1559 to 1562 a series of spectacular autos de fe virtually extinguished Protestantism in Spain. The two autos at Valladolid in May and October 1559, and those in Seville in September 1559 and December 1560, followed by two more in April and October 1562, eliminated the groups. Protestantism never again succeeded in taking root in Spain. A couple of hundred Spaniards were suspected of the heresy in the course of the late sixteenth century, but fewer than a dozen were actually burnt for it in those years.

A direct result of the crisis of 1557–8 was the decision to protect Spain against foreign ideas. Action against heretical books was not new. In 1502

Ferdinand and Isabella had introduced the licensing of books, and in 1521 Adrian of Utrecht had banned the works of Luther. Other countries were also beginning to issue controls, leading the Inquisition in 1551 to produce an Index of prohibited books based on one issued in the Netherlands five years earlier. In September 1558 a new edict was issued by the regent Juana in collaboration with Valdés. For the first time, it stipulated the penalties of death and confiscation of goods for introducing books into the country without permission and for printing or circulating material, even in manuscript, without licence. Control of all licences and printing was vested firmly in the council of Castile, but the Inquisition was permitted to operate a parallel system of censorship through its indices of forbidden works. The edict was followed by the issue in August 1559 of the first native Index of the Spanish Inquisition, in which the principal casualty was Erasmus, whose works now began to be prohibited. Many Spanish clergy criticised the criteria adopted by the Index, since books by well-known religious authors featured among those condemned. In particular, the Jesuits reacted angrily to the fact that the most notable member of their order in Spain, Francisco de Borja, had a book forbidden. The system of outright condemnation of books was not repeated thereafter, and new principles of control were adopted from the 1570s.

When Philip II returned to Spain in September 1559 he put into effect further attempts to protect Spain against the Reformation. In November he ordered that subjects of the crown of Castile studying or teaching abroad, apart from those at specific colleges in Bologna, Rome, Naples and Coimbra, should return home within four months. The order did not apply to subjects of the crown of Aragon. A high proportion of Spaniards was therefore not affected by the measure, and it would be wrong to imagine that the king was trying to seal the country off from foreign influences. Castilians themselves did not bother to obey the order, and many continued to go abroad to colleges of their own choice. The law was not applicable to clergy, who also continued to study abroad, especially in Germany and Italy. Meanwhile, students in the rest of Spain went where they wished and suffered no restrictions until the end of the century.

The erection of barriers against the Reformation did not mean that Spain was rejecting Europe. The rejection of international perspectives in favour of national ones was a policy common to other countries such as England. The consequences were foreseeable, especially in the world of learning. Of a sample of 228 Spanish scientific authors who flourished in the early sixteenth century some 11 per cent had been professors in foreign universities and 25 per cent had studied abroad; after 1560 the proportion was negligible. However, a universal monarchy such as Spain could never opt for a policy of isolation. With its constant international obligations, Spain was committed to fostering the regular movement of trade and of men (inevitably, soldiers) into and out of the peninsula, and this continued with no interruption. The restrictions of 1559, then, were temporary rather than permanent crisis measures. They were applicable only to Castile and not to the crown of Aragon, which inevitably robbed them of much of their efficacy. Whether inefficient or not, the measures may have helped to save Spain for Catholicism. The influence of Erasmus was extirpated and Protestantism in the peninsula was strangled at birth. The question, which still provokes debate, is whether in the process damage was not done to the nation and its culture.

# CHAPTER 3

# Philip II and the power of Spain 1556–1598

## Politics 1556–1598

### The king

Philip II was present in Brussels when his father resigned to him the government of the Netherlands (October 1555) and of Spain itself (January 1556). International matters, principally his marriage to queen Mary of England and the war against France, kept him in northern Europe. In August 1557 the army of Flanders, led by the duke of Savoy and the count of Egmont, crossed the frontier into France and inflicted a crushing defeat on the French at St Quentin. Philip arrived in time to congratulate his generals, but failed to follow up the advantage; negotiations began and were interrupted by the death of Mary in November 1558. Eventually peace was agreed at Cateau-Cambrésis in April 1559, one of the conditions being the marriage of Philip to the daughter of Henry II of France, Elizabeth of Valois. The king sailed from the Netherlands in August 1559 and landed at Laredo in September.

He never left the peninsula again. Domestic politics lapse into relative quietness during the reign, so that events seem to depend more than usual on the personality of the king. Philip, however, was no less dedicated to the problems of internal government than to the weighty issues of foreign policy.

Aged 28 at his accession, he was already an experienced ruler, having been regent for his father intermittently since 1543. His fair hair and blue eyes betrayed his Habsburg origin, but no ruler could have been more Spanish. Brought up in Castile and trained by excellent tutors, he preferred Spaniards as advisers and spoke only Castilian fluently, though he had a working knowledge of Latin. Pensive by disposition, and always reluctant to rush into decisions – hence the tag of 'Prudent King' – he had a deep sense of duty which governed both his personal and public life. His stern side was what foreign ambassadors saw and reported, and Philip cultivated the public reserve expected of a king; but his relaxed and affectionate private side emerges clearly in his correspondence. Above all, the Catholic religion gave him comfort and conviction. He was four times married: in 1543 to the Portuguese princess Maria, who died two years later giving birth to Don Carlos; in 1555 to Mary Tudor, who was eleven years older than he; in 1560 to Elizabeth of Valois, who was only fifteen at the time and who bore him two daughters; finally in 1570 to his niece Anna of Austria, twenty-two years younger than he, who in six years gave birth to five children and died in childbirth of the sixth.

There is no doubt that his father was the ruling influence on his life. In his Instructions of 1543, which were meant to be a code of conduct for the prince's first regency, Charles commended him to serve God, uphold the Inquisition, suppress heresy, dispense justice and hold the balance between his advisers. He also urged him to pay particular attention to finance, 'upon which the success or failure of my policies depend'. He must never recede from an inch of territory, and should maintain integrally the inheritance given by God: a policy carried out stubbornly in the Netherlands, which Philip like his father considered his patrimony. There was basic continuity of political policy from Charles through Philip, though the latter obviously reacted differently to specific problems. The instruction he is supposed to have left for his son in 1598 (and which appears to be spurious) shows much the same preoccupations as those of his father: religion, justice, peace. His desire to find a suitable resting place for the emperor's remains was the principal reason for building the gigantic monastery-palace of El Escorial, begun in 1563 in the hills north of Madrid under the personal direction of the king, and not completed till 1584.

## The 'first ministry' 1556–1579

The first major problem of the reign was the succession. Don Carlos early on showed signs of being mentally unstable and the king was forced to exclude him from affairs of state and any position of authority. The prince had several violent fits, engineered bizarre plans to escape and even plotted against his father. Finally, in January 1568, Philip ordered him to be arrested and confined; an action taken, as he explained to the pope, 'with sorrow and grief, since he is my only son and first born'. Six months later

Don Carlos died in confinement. Not until 1571, with the birth of Anna of Austria's first son, was a male heir secured; he, and two more brothers, died within a few years, the only male survivor being the fourth son, Philip.

The 1560s were difficult years, with the treasury struggling under the shadow of the bankruptcy of 1557. Philip's government in Spain was headed at the top by the council of state, shorn since 1559 of its non-Castilian members. The council's chief secretary until his death in 1566 was Gonzalo Pérez, a priest who may have been of converso origin; thereafter the post was divided between Gonzalo's son Antonio as secretary for the south and Gabriel de Zayas for the north. True to his father's policy of allowing differing views to develop, Philip tolerated a conflict of opinions, not always with fruitful consequences. The chief rivals in the council of state were the king's long-standing friend the Portuguese Ruy Gómez de Silva, and the duke of Alba. Ruy Gómez, created prince of Éboli and duke of Pastrana, married into the powerful Mendoza family, headed by the duke of Infantado, and thereby became linked with a clan of nobles from the highest grandee families, the Zúniga, Velasco and Guzmán. Fernando Álvarez de Toledo, third duke of Alba and Philip's most distinguished general, was head of the house of Toledo and had similar powerful connections. The division in the council between these two – a normal rivalry between clans, of the sort common both at government and local level – also extended to the secretaries, Antonio Pérez being allied to Éboli and Zayas to Alba.

Differences between the groups, as with all political factions, arose primarily out of a struggle for power. Given the complex problems that faced the Spanish monarchy, there were occasionally issues on which some took a hard line: Alba, as Charles V had warned Philip, was inclined to be authoritarian. Historians have long ceased to categorise one group – Alba's – as the 'war' party, or its opponents as the 'peace' party. Nor, as we shall see, is it possible to distinguish any real difference of approach to constitutional problems. The problem over which the factions took most issue was the revolt of the Netherlands, which precipitated the famous affair of Antonio Pérez.

Immediately after Philip's return to Spain in 1559 he began a massive effort to put the country into an adequate state of defence: Turkish expansion in the 1560s inevitably made foreign policy the first concern of government. At the same time difficulties in the Netherlands were brought to him in person when the count of Egmont arrived in Madrid in February 1565. From this period Spain was burdened by a dual commitment to northern Europe and to the Mediterranean, and the numerous mistakes made by Philip in his dealings with the Netherlanders can in part be blamed on priority given to affairs in the south. Aware, none the less, of his obligations, the king made preparations to visit Flanders in 1567. He was dissuaded from this by Alba, and in 1568 two personal crises – the death of Don Carlos in July and then of Elizabeth of Valois in October – forced him to remain in the peninsula, where on Christmas Eve a major uprising of the Granada Moriscos began.

The death of Ruy Gómez in 1573 made Antonio Pérez effective head of the Éboli faction at court. A contemporary noted that Pérez 'climbed so high that His Majesty would not do anything save what the said Antonio Pérez marked out for him'. Philip depended heavily for advice and policy on this brilliant and sinister young man whose fortunes were linked with those of Ana de Mendoza, princess of Éboli, the beautiful one-eyed widow of Ruy Gómez. Pérez's arm stretched as far as Flanders, where the king's half-brother, the famous Don Juan of Austria, was acting as governor. Don Juan's personal secretary, Juan de Escobedo, had been a protégé of Pérez, who expected to be kept reliably informed of the plans and ambitions of the governor of the Netherlands. Don Juan's proposals for policy in the north, however, were at variance with government intentions in Madrid, and Pérez and Escobedo soon found themselves opposed to each other on a number of issues. Philip in turn was wary of the ambitions of his half-brother, the victor of Lepanto. Suspicious of the way his plans for Flanders were being blocked by Madrid, Don Juan sent Escobedo to Spain in 1577 to make enquiries. On his arrival at the court it appeared to Escobedo that Pérez had been duping Don Juan and presenting his case in an unfavourable light to the king. He apparently issued threats against Pérez, accusing him rightly or wrongly of a liaison with the princess of Éboli, and of betraying state secrets. But Pérez had already managed to convince Philip that Escobedo was the malign influence in the affairs of Flanders and hinted to the king that the only solution was to eliminate Don Juan's secretary. In March 1578, as it turned out, hired assassins murdered Escobedo in a street in Madrid.

Popular rumour instantly pointed to Pérez as the assassin, and Escobedo's family, aided by Pérez's rival the king's private secretary (from 1573) Mateo Vázquez, demanded justice for the murdered man. No action was taken, clearly because the king himself was unwilling to move against Pérez. In the spring of 1579, however, Philip was sent the private papers of Don Juan, who had died the previous October. On reading them Philip discovered that Pérez had deceived him and that his brother and Escobedo were guiltless of the imputations against them. He encouraged Vázquez to make a secret enquiry into Pérez's actions in office, and determined to make a clean sweep of his ministers.

Since his return from the Netherlands in 1573 the duke of Alba had been active in the councils at Madrid, but in 1579 was placed under house arrest for letting his son make an unauthorised marriage, and was called back to duty only to undertake the invasion of Portugal. His disgrace in 1579 was followed by Philip's decision to place the direction of affairs in the hands of the Burgundian Antoine Perrenot, cardinal Granvelle, who had been withdrawn from the Netherlands in 1564 but had since served the crown with distinction in Italy. On 28 July 1579, the very day that Granvelle reached Madrid, Pérez and the princess of Éboli were arrested.

## The 'second ministry' 1579–1598

Granvelle, 62 years old in 1579, was the only non-peninsular statesman ever to hold government office in Habsburg Spain after the reign of Charles V. He brought with him Juan de Idiáquez, a career diplomat who had served in Italy and now took over both secretaryships of State. Granvelle's formal position was president of the council of Italy, but in practice he took over most aspects of foreign policy. His special interest in northern Europe created differences with Castilian advisers and with the king, but the years of his ministry coincided with a markedly successful phase in Spanish fortunes, including the victories of Alexander Farnese in the Netherlands and, within the peninsula, the annexation of Portugal.

In the summer of 1578 king Sebastian of Portugal, Philip's nephew through the marriage of his sister Juana to prince João, and ruler of his country since the age of three (1557), led an international army out into the deserts of Morocco in an ill-conceived design to carry the crusade into Africa. His forces were annihilated at the battle of Alcázarquivir in August. He himself was never seen again, which led in later years to the recurrent story that he had survived and would return one day to claim the throne. His great-uncle, cardinal Henry, was proclaimed the next king; but as he was vowed to celibacy, and both ill and senile, the question of the succession remained unresolved. Philip II had the satisfaction of knowing that he had the strongest claim, through his mother Isabella; but there were numerous other claimants, including the duchess of Braganza and Antonio, prior of Crato, a bastard nephew of cardinal Henry. To prepare the ground for his cause, Philip sent as ambassador to Lisbon his Portuguese adviser Cristóbal de Moura. Opinion among the Portuguese upper classes was favourable to his cause; 'all the best people here are in favour of

Spain', reported a correspondent of the Fuggers in February 1580. In a special Cortes convoked by cardinal Henry, the nobles and clergy supported Philip, but the towns were opposed, and favoured the claims of the prior of Crato. Henry died in January 1580. When it became clear that Antonio would not accept the various compromises offered him through Moura, invasion emerged as the quickest solution. In June 1580 an army of 37,000 crossed the frontier under the command of Alba; at the same time a fleet under the marquis of Santa Cruz set out from Cadiz. The prior of Crato was proclaimed king by his supporters, who counted on help from foreign powers; but the rapid capture by Spain of Setúbal and Lisbon (accompanied in each case by excesses on the part of the soldiery, whom Alba tried vainly to restrain) settled the issue definitively. Antonio of Crato fled, and continued until his death in 1595 to call upon French and English help to liberate Portugal.

Despite the violence of the invasion, the terms on which Portugal surrendered to Philip make it plain that there was no 'conquest'. In April 1581 he met the Portuguese Cortes at Tomar, swore to observe all the laws of the realm, and was recognised as king. In November 1582 he swore to uphold a broad range of Portuguese privileges. He promised to reside as much as possible in Portugal; a council of Portugal was to be formed on the model of other regional councils; Portuguese alone were to hold office in the realm and in their empire, which would continue to be administered without any interference from Spain; the viceroy in Lisbon was to be either Portuguese or a member of the royal family; and customs barriers between Portugal and Castile would be abolished (they were restored in 1593). In effect, the country retained all its liberties and autonomy. It had been absorbed into the crown on the same realistic terms that Ferdinand and Isabella had merged their respective realms, and the only thing it shared with the rest of the peninsula was a common sovereign. Peninsular unity had been achieved, Roman 'Hispania' restored: from this time, his biographer Cabrera de Córdoba remarked, Philip called himself king of 'Spain'.

The king took readily to the Portuguese. He tried to speak the language, his maternal one; he enjoyed the fresh, clean air of Lisbon, and toyed with the idea of moving his seat of government there (Granvelle favoured it, but the Castilian grandees were uniformly hostile). In all he spent over two years in Portugal (December 1580 to February 1583). They were possibly the most relaxed years of his reign, and it was from his residence overlooking the Tajo that he penned the famous letters to his daughters Isabella and Catalina: 'here at Almada' (in June 1581) 'where I have a very pretty but small house, and from all the windows you can see the river and Lisbon and the ships and galleys', and later from Lisbon (April 1582) 'how much pleasure I get from your letters and the news you give of Aranjuez, and what I most miss is the singing of the nightingales, which I have not heard this year, since this house is far from the countryside'.

His absence raised serious problems in Madrid, where Granvelle had been left in control since Philip's departure in March 1580 to join the army in Extremadura. Granvelle being a supporter of a vigorous war policy in the north of Europe, his emphasis on the affairs of the Netherlands caused disagreement with Castilians who were more worried about security in the Mediterranean. Shortly after Philip came back in 1583, the experienced diplomat Juan de Zúñiga y Requesens, younger brother of the late commander in the Netherlands, returned from Naples and became the focus of opposition to the cardinal; he was also made governor to prince Philip. Granvelle's star began to wane, and the king came to rely increasingly on Cristóbal de Moura for advice. When he died in September 1586, aged nearly 70, the cardinal felt isolated and disillusioned.

In the autumn of 1585 the king, overburdened by paperwork, agreed to allow some administrative matters to be discussed not in full council but in an informal committee that met in the evening, before dinner, and was consequently called the *Junta de Noche*. The committee consisted of Zúñiga (d. November 1586), Moura, Idiáquez, the count of Chinchón, and Mateo Vázquez as secretary. Idiáquez dealt with foreign policy, Chinchón with Aragon and Italy, Moura with finance and Portuguese affairs, Vázquez with Castilian affairs in general. Their deliberations were meant to speed up and not be a substitute for council government. The new grouping, which was active to the very end of the reign (Vázquez died in 1591 and was replaced by Idiáquez's cousin Martín de Idiáquez), has been called Philip's 'second ministry'. It did not consist of great nobles but of experienced administrators from the lower nobility, who were for the most part free of the clan alliances that split Éboli and the house of Alba; this made it possible for men like Moura and Idiáquez to work together. But there was another fundamental difference between the two generations. Granvelle and his aristocratic predecessors, notably Alba, had direct knowledge of European war and peace and related this to their own vision, one essentially inherited from Charles V, of Spain's role in the world. Philip's later ministers, although experienced and well trained (Idiáquez continued the traditions of Granvelle), were inclined to judge international policy from the fixed viewpoint of the peninsula; and the king, it seemed, shared their views. Serving soldiers were particularly vociferous critics of this, and blamed the Armada defeat, for example, on the civilian planners. 'Things must go ill', a leading general and councillor of state – Hernando de Toledo, natural son of Alba – told the Venetian ambassador in 1589, 'when all decisions are made by those with no experience': he added that Moura had never been outside the peninsula, and Idiáquez had never been in battle.

The accumulating problems of government reached their apogee in 1596, the year of Philip's last big bankruptcy and the first ominous year of the plague that devastated Spain for some five years. After settling the problems of Aragon in 1591, Philip began to cut down his work commitments and ceased to travel any distance; he now suffered from recurrent poor health because of gout, and arthritis tended to confine him to his chair. From the end of 1595 state business, as well as the signing of papers, was assigned more and more to the infante Philip. One of the king's last major decisions was the granting of autonomy to the southern Netherlands, in a measure signed by the infante in May 1598. The Netherlands were to be ruled jointly by the infanta Isabella and by the king's nephew archduke Albert of Austria, who were married in Valencia in April 1599. In the summer of 1598 Philip managed to travel to the Escorial, where he died on 13 September at the age of 71, after a long and painful illness.

# Foreign policy 1559–1598

In policy and outlook Philip was the direct heir of his father, though there were substantial differences between the two over detail and method. For both, the war against heresy and against the Turks was fundamental, 'peace with Christians and war against the infidel' being a principle repeated ritually since the days of the Catholic Monarchs. The priority given by Philip to religion, however, was never absolute. It would be an error to judge his policy solely by the statement he made in 1566 through his ambassador in Rome, informing the pope that 'I would prefer to lose all my dominions and a hundred lives if I had them, because I do not wish to be lord over heretics'. The declaration was made specifically to impress the pope, who at that time was criticising the king for doing nothing to control heresy among his subjects in the Netherlands.

The division of the German from the Mediterranean lands by Charles V created major problems of adjustment for Spain. The emperor had been able to draw on German credit, soldiers and princes to back up his continent-wide strategy. Philip, by contrast, was obliged to build Spain up into a world power almost from scratch; with what success we shall see presently. Fortunately, the monarchy as bequeathed by Charles –

essentially, the empire of the Catholic Monarchs together with the Burgundian inheritance and Milan – seemed to have ample resources, and the diplomatic service as developed under the emperor was the finest in Europe. Even so, after the peace of Cateau-Cambrésis Spain was far from being an aggressive power. The Venetian ambassador observed (1559) that Philip's aim was 'not to wage war so that he can add to his kingdoms, but to wage peace so that he can keep the lands he has'.

From 1559 to 1566 Spain's history was concerned almost exclusively with the Mediterranean. In the north the marriage with Elizabeth of Valois assured an understanding with France which Philip did his best to maintain. France, however, had problems. Rivalry between the Guise party and the Huguenot nobles, rapidly destabilised politics there and led in 1562 to the massacre at Vassy, which in turn precipitated a generation of civil war. Though they were leaders of the Catholic interest, Philip distrusted the Guises, who were led by the duke of Guise and the cardinal of Lorraine. The dynastic ambitions of the Guises centred on their kinswoman Mary Stuart, queen of Scots, queen of France in 1559 as wife of Francis II and Catholic claimant to the throne of England. A union of the three nations under Stuart and Guise rule could seriously threaten Spain's security. Philip therefore emerged as protector of the English queen, blocking attempts by Rome to excommunicate her in 1561 and 1563. By this date the Protestant nature of Elizabeth's admin-istration was becoming clear, and there was a further threat in a possible alliance between the English and the French Protestants. Spain objected to English intervention in the early stages of the French civil wars, and in a famous meeting at Bayonne in 1565 Elizabeth of Valois and Alba pressed on Catherine de' Medici the need to act more firmly against heresy in France.

These were years of Turkish military activity in the western Mediter-ranean. A Spanish expedition to recapture Tripoli, led by the duke of Medinaceli and admiral Gian Andrea Doria, was caught in 1560 on the island of Djerba: 28 galleys were sunk and 10,000 troops were forced to surrender. The disaster forced Philip into a complete overhaul of his forces, which enabled him to react positively to the next major Turkish onslaught, the siege of Malta in 1565. Heroically defended by the Knights of St John, two of the island's fortresses held out from May to September until relieved by a Spanish force. Hailed as a significant victory, the relief made it possible for Philip to turn his attention to the growing problems of the north.

During his visit to the Netherlands (1555–9) Philip had had first-hand experience of the independent spirit of the 17 provinces and the ambitions of their nobility, led by William prince of Orange. Disputes in the government, which was directed by Philip's half-sister Margaret duchess of Parma, divided the nobles against the professional administrators headed by Granvelle. In 1564 the king agreed reluctantly to Granvelle's dismissal, but opposition then centred on the proposal to reform the episcopate of the Netherlands by creating more bishops and strengthening the heresy laws. Egmont returned from a visit to Madrid in 1565 with the impression that Philip had agreed to relax the persecution of heretics, but the king had never even entertained the possibility. Early in 1566 the higher aristocracy went on strike by resigning their offices, and a group of the lower nobility (many of them Calvinist in sympathy, whom an official denounced as 'beggars') demanded religious freedom and the suppression of the Netherlands Inquisition (established by the pope in 1522 at the request of Charles V). The baron de Montigny was sent to Madrid in the summer of 1566 to try and obtain concessions from Philip over toleration of dissent, and over the role of the chief nobles in the Brussels government. Though the king made a few concessions, they were overtaken by events. In August mobs of Calvinists ranged through the major cities of the Netherlands, desecrating churches and smashing images.

A military solution became inevitable. Alba left Spain in April 1567 and took the Spanish Road to the north, arriving in Brussels in August at the head of 10,000 troops. Counts Egmont and Hornes were arrested, and executed a year later; William of Orange fled the country. A special tribunal called the Council of Troubles (nicknamed the 'council of blood' by Netherlanders) judged those detained: well over one thousand people were executed over the next few months. In Spain Montigny was arrested and eventually garrotted in October 1570 in the castle of Simancas, after a secret trial. The king intended to visit the country to complete the pacification but this never materialised.

Spanish occupation of the Netherlands stirred the fears of both people and government in England, and in 1568 relations between England and Spain approached breaking point, first with a clash between Sir John Hawkins and Spanish vessels in the harbour of San Juan de Ulúa (Vera Cruz) in Mexico in September, and then with the provocative seizure in the Channel of the duke of Alba's pay-ships by Elizabeth in November. Philip II was also profoundly preoccupied with the Don Carlos problem and the Morisco uprising at the end of the year. The sudden turn for the worse of his relationship with all the major powers, including France, made 1568 one of the most critical years of his reign.

The death of Suleiman the Magnificent in September 1566 has been taken to mark the end of the great period of Ottoman expansion, but the military threat to the Christian west continued to be very real. Spain felt the menace most directly through the wars in Granada in 1569–70, which forced it into military conflict in the Mediterranean at the very time that new and potent quarrels were emerging in the north. Awareness of Spain's overstretched capacity made Alba refuse to exploit the situation in England, allowing the northern earls there to rise hopelessly against Elizabeth in 1569. Spanish attention was now almost wholly absorbed with the Turks, whose threat to Cyprus galvanised Venice and the pope (Pius V) into organising a Holy League, agreed upon in May 1571. Spain was given command of the planned expedition, appointed Don Juan of Austria as commander and paid a substantial proportion of the costs. On 7 October the two great fleets encountered each other in the gulf of Lepanto, off Greece; there were 208 Turkish galleys against 203 Christian. On the Turkish side the commander, Ali Pasha, was killed; nearly all the galleys were destroyed or captured; and there were 30,000 casualties and 3,000 prisoners. The Christians lost 15 galleys and 8,000 dead. It was a resounding victory whose glory echoed through Christian Europe but failed to check the Turks, who a year later put another similar fleet to sea.

Though there was a continuing commitment to the Mediterranean (Tunis was briefly re-occupied by Don Juan in 1573), for the next few years from 1572 to 1579 Spain was sucked relentlessly into the maelstrom of the Netherlands. Alba's proposal to impose a new tax, the 'tenth penny', aroused universal protest and fortified the opposition of those, both Catholic and Protestant, who wished to see their country free from foreign occupation. In April 1572 the 'Sea Beggars' were turned out from England, where they had taken refuge from Alba, and returned to seize the port of Brill, which became a base for patriotic resistance against Spain. The rapid success of the largely Calvinist Beggars in winning the northern provinces and electing William of Orange as their leader, opened the second and most decisive phase of the revolt of the Netherlands. In France the influential voice of admiral Coligny, the Huguenot leader who was now prominent in the royal council, called for French intervention in support of the rebels. The massacre of St Bartholomew in August 1572, engineered by Catherine de' Medici for domestic reasons, conveniently removed Coligny and the threat from France.

The failure of Alba to stem rebel successes in the Netherlands forced Philip to recall him in 1573 and appoint Luis de Requesens. A new policy of moderation was tried. Its failure, and Requesens's death in March 1576, was followed by the appointment of Don Juan of Austria as governor. But the Spanish government declared a bankruptcy in 1575 and was unable to pay its soldiers in northern Europe. As a result the troops mutinied and in November 1576 sacked the great commercial city of Antwerp at a cost of some 8,000 lives and a great amount of property. This 'Spanish Fury' confirmed the resolution of the 17 provinces, assembled at Ghent in the States General, to decide their own destiny. That same month they negotiated a general peace (the Pacification of Ghent), and demanded of Philip that he accept the current religious position and withdraw all Spanish troops as the precondition for a settlement. Don Juan was forced to accept and in February 1577 issued a Perpetual Edict and withdrew the army. The Calvinists, however, failed to respect the religious truce. In retaliation Don Juan recalled the army under Alexander Farnese, prince of Parma, and in 1578 at Gembloux defeated the army of a Netherlands now wholly united in revolt under William of Orange. Don Juan died in October and was replaced by Farnese: the affairs of the north were now in chaos.

From 1579, with the change in ministry at Madrid, fortunes improved. Granvelle gave his full support to the programme of Farnese, who in May 1579 by the Union of Arras won over the southern Catholic provinces to a firm alliance with Spain and in June captured the rebel fortress of Maastricht. (The northern provinces formed the Union of Utrecht under the leadership of Orange; in 1581 they eventually renounced the sovereignty of Philip II and for a brief while elected the duke of Anjou as their ruler.) Successes in the Netherlands were complemented by the successful annexation of Portugal. Spain at the end of 1580 could feel it was at the height of its imperial power. The city of Manila in the Philippines was firmly settled, viceroy Toledo had overcome Inca resistance in Peru, expeditions were moving up from Mexico into what is now the southern United States, in the La Plata area the city of Buenos Aires was refounded (1581). From 1580, with his outpost on the Atlantic at Lisbon, Philip II turned Spain away from the Mediterranean at the same moment that the Turks turned away from western expansion. Conflict continued sporadically but total Christian–Muslim confrontation came to an end. The king now devoted all his resources to the wholly new aim of making Spain an Atlantic power, one that would be capable of protecting the bullion routes from America, restraining the ambitions of England and returning the Dutch rebels to obedience.

Diplomatic activity for the rest of the reign was centred on northern Europe. English involvement in Drake's piratical expeditions, in the schemes of Antonio of Crato, and in Dutch affairs, made Philip more amenable to negotiating with Mary Queen of Scots, a virtual prisoner in England since 1568. In consequence, ambassador Bernardino de Mendoza was expelled from London in January 1584 for implication in the Throckmorton Plot. In July 1584 William of Orange was murdered (he had been outlawed by Philip in 1580), a month after the death by consumption of Anjou. The Dutch rebels were left without an internationally recognised leader. Meanwhile Farnese's army swept victoriously through the central Netherlands: in March 1585 he recovered Brussels and in August Antwerp; all the major cities were now back in Spanish control. To make sure that France would not intervene again, Philip at the end of 1584 had recognised the importance of the Guises and the Catholic League by coming to a secret agreement whereby they would support the Catholic cause in the Netherlands in return for Spanish subsidies. Then in May 1585 he warned off England by seizing all English ships in Spanish ports in retaliation for English piracies. The move angered English opinion and enabled Elizabeth to advance to a position of open war. In August 1585 by the treaty of Nonsuch she agreed to send some 6,000 men under the earl of Leicester to help the Dutch. A fleet of 25 warships was also entrusted to Drake, who began by attacking Vigo and then went off to the West Indies where he sacked Santo Domingo and Cartagena.

Philip now agreed with his advisers that a direct invasion of England was necessary. A key feature of the plan was to have been the proclamation of Mary of Scots as queen; but her negotiations with Spain were exposed in the Babington plot (1586), which led inexorably to her execution in 1587. The preparations for the 'enterprise of England' went ahead despite continual setbacks. In February 1588 the appointed admiral, Santa Cruz, died and was replaced by the duke of Medina-Sidonia. Quite apart from battle logistics the success of the great Armada depended on two things: the ability of Farnese in the Netherlands to provide a deep-water port where the galleons might take on the army of Flanders and supplies; and the immobilisation of France so that it could not interfere in the Netherlands while Farnese's men were in England. The second condition was soon met. Backed by Spain, the Guises took over Paris in the Day of Barricades (May 1588) and made Henry III in effect a prisoner of the Catholic League. 'The French king will be unable to assist the English in any way', Bernardino de Mendoza wrote with satisfaction to Philip II. The first requirement proved disastrous. The juncture between Medina-Sidonia's galleons, when they sailed up the Channel in July, and the troops of Farnese never took place. English and Dutch vessels patrolled the shallow waters through which Farnese had hoped to get his men out on barges; his army was pinned down. At sea the galleons were rapidly outnumbered and then out-gunned by the English who, with the help of fire ships and the wind, forced the Armada to flee into the North Sea and return to Spain around the coasts of Scotland and Ireland. About 40 out of 68 vessels were destroyed, perhaps 15,000 men perished. A Spanish contemporary considered it to be a disaster that: 'lost us respect and the good *reputación* among warlike people which we used to have'. It was not the end of Philip's resources. He sent a fleet against the port of Brest in 1596, and another armada against England in 1597; but both were scattered by the weather. The Armada defeat encouraged Henry III in France to act against the duke and cardinal of Guise, who were assassinated on his orders; though he himself was murdered in August 1589 by a mad monk. This left Henry, king of Navarre, a Protestant, as heir to the throne.

'The affairs of France', Philip wrote to Farnese in 1589, 'are at this moment the principal thing'. The dominant view in Madrid was that a Protestant king of France would inevitably help the Dutch rebels, and that the best way to preserve the Netherlands was to help the Catholic League by invading France. There was bitter opposition to this strategy by Farnese and other advisers both in Brussels and Madrid. As time proved, they were right, for military intervention in France seriously prejudiced any chances of success in the Netherlands. In 1590 Farnese crossed into France with the army of Flanders and relieved Paris, then being besieged by Henry of Navarre; other Spanish troops marched into Brittany and Languedoc. But by 1591 the situation, far from improving, began to worsen. Expenditure on war had reached an all-time peak. A revolt broke out in Aragon, fomented by Antonio Pérez, and Philip had to raise an army in Castile to deal with it. Then in Holland the Dutch found a new and able commander, Orange's son Maurice of Nassau, who during the absence of the Flanders army in France launched a vigorous campaign in 1591 and captured several major towns.

Farnese died in December 1592, the last of Philip's great generals. In 1593 Henry of Navarre abjured his heresy and became a Catholic. The conversion won him the support of many Catholic nobles and of the pope; it also swung French Catholic opinion in favour of a national rather than a Spanish king. With most of France behind him, Henry IV in 1595 declared war against Spain and in 1596 brought England and the Dutch into alliance with him. Philip II had the most powerful war machine in the world, but it was unable to stem the tide moving against Spain. A small incident is illustrative: in June 1596 the earl of Essex,

Antonio Pérez's patron in England, led a daring surprise attack on the port and city of Cadiz, which was sacked and held effortlessly by the English for 17 days.

By now the campaign in the Netherlands, where the governor from February 1596 was Philip's nephew the cardinal-archduke Albert of Austria (formerly viceroy of Portugal), had ground to a halt. The failure of the 1596 armada to Ireland helped to bring Philip's financial system crumbling down: in November he declared a bankruptcy. Peace was essential. In May 1598 the treaty of Vervins ended the war between France and Spain. In the same month the plan to make the Netherlands autonomous under Albert, whose vows as cardinal were to be waived so that he could marry Philip's daughter Isabella, was put into effect.

It is plausible to maintain that Philip II's entire foreign policy was defensive. In 1586 he himself argued to the pope that 'I have no reason to allow myself to be ambitious for more kingdoms and estates'. But the requirements of defence meant that first in 1560 and then in 1580, in the Mediterranean and in the Atlantic, he was obliged to elevate Spain into a superpower, as the only way to maintain worldwide security. Once the Spanish system had been created, force and therefore aggression became an integral part of it, though there is no acceptable evidence or plausible reason to suggest that the king had expansionist dreams. Religious and dynastic considerations always remained fundamental, with the qualification that the king had his own view of what 'religion' entailed. When Philip disagreed with the papacy and France it was precisely because he felt their policies would not best serve the universal Church. At no point is the importance of the religious element clearer than in the Netherlands revolt, where all efforts at compromise with the Dutch ran into trouble because the Spaniards insisted on preserving the exclusive position of Catholicism.

## The debate on the Netherlands

Perhaps the most disputed public issue of the Habsburg era in Spain was policy towards the Netherlands. The debate was far from being restricted only to the king's advisers or to factions in his councils. It was in reality a broad public discussion, conducted in part through the Cortes which voted the money for Philip's policy, in part through the soldiers and officials with direct knowledge of the Netherlands, in part through writers who reflected sectors of opinion. It reveals much of the king's methods of government that he himself encouraged the debate. Anxious to clarify the options available to him, Philip relied on various, and sometimes contradictory, sources of advice.

It has been traditional to suppose that policy for the Netherlands was dictated by the preferences of the Alba and Éboli factions in Madrid, the one for 'war', the other for 'peace'. Available documents in reality provide no evidence that either party had a consistent policy on the Netherlands, or that the differences between them could be reduced to simple formulations. Certainly Alba's was not simply a war party. Like all professional soldiers the duke wanted a quick, clean military solution. He thought that this was possible in Flanders, just as he later thought it was not possible in England and so opposed the 'war' policy of Granvelle and those who counselled an invasion. In any case, Philip II never delivered himself wholly into the hands of any of his advisers. Even while giving Alba an apparently free hand, he accepted offers of alternative policies from correspondents in Italy, Spain and the Netherlands itself. Granvelle, while viceroy of Naples (1571–5), was one of those who insisted that the real solution lay in the king: 'if Your Majesty had decided to follow the duke to the Low Countries *without an army*, in order to issue a general pardon, those parts would have experienced neither repression nor war'.

To monitor the progress of Alba's programme, Philip employed as his correspondent in Flanders the distinguished humanist Benito Arias Montano, who was in Antwerp to discuss the production of a new Polyglot Bible with the printer Christophe Plantin. Montano supported Alba's military measures, and pointed out to Philip that Spain must remain in the Netherlands for three main reasons: to protect religion, to participate in trade and for strategic purposes – 'from these states one can keep Germany at bay, constrain France and bind England'. It was Alba's failure to find an acceptable pacification policy that eventually disillusioned Montano, split Spanish opinion and provoked the second stage of the revolt in 1572. In February 1573 Montano wrote prophetically to Gabriel de Zayas that if Spain's policy were not altered, 'I see clearly an unending problem, unbearable expense and the loss of innumerable lives, both theirs and ours'.

In June Montano sent to Philip detailed proposals for an alternative policy. There must be clemency and a general pardon, and Netherlanders must govern equally with Spaniards. 'The arrogance of our Spanish nation here is insupportable', he wrote; many Spaniards 'have begun to call this sort of behaviour "reputación" '. It was an indictment by a Spaniard of the developing hubris in Spain's imperial role, the fear to compromise lest it be seen as loss of face, loss of reputación. In October, Philip sent Montano's proposals to Luis de Requesens, the serving governor of Milan whom the king now appointed to replace Alba. At the same time Philip wrote to Montano that his proposals were 'valuable'. He also informed Requesens that 'the problems of the Netherlands have been complicated by the differing reports I have been sent. As I do not know the truth of the matter I cannot suggest a remedy'. As soon as Requesens arrived in Brussels he had several long meetings with Montano. The new policy was to be based on a general pardon, mutual discussion and the integrity of Netherlands institutions.

At precisely the same time Requesens was in touch with another Spaniard, who was also a correspondent for Philip II. This was the Valencian humanist Fadrique Furió Ceriol, who had left Spain in 1549 and in 1559 published at Antwerp his *Council and Counsellors of the Prince*, dedicated to Philip. In 1575 Furió produced a group of proposals, called *Remedies*, which he presented both to William of Orange and to the king. Going much farther than Montano, he suggested that Spanish troops should be withdrawn completely, though with certain guarantees; that all religious persecution should cease; and that the laws of the Netherlands be confirmed. In substance, these were the principles of the 1576 Pacification of Ghent, accepted reluctantly in 1577 by Spain.

The policy put into effect in the Netherlands between 1573 and 1577 was no preserve of the Éboli faction. In the government committee that met at Aranjuez in 1574 to discuss the problem, it was agreed by all that 'the Flemings in their liberties are like the Aragonese, and to take away their liberties and impose on them a tribunal of blood, is hard to bear and difficult to justify'. One of the most influential proponents of compromise in Madrid was the representative in Spain of the States General, Joachim Hopperus. Don Juan of Austria supported the initiative, and wrote to Philip in 1577: 'Your Majesty should be firmly convinced of one thing that is deeply rooted in the minds of both the good and the bad: both desire freedom of conscience'.

Both Arias Montano and Furió were born (in the same year, 1527) and died in Spain. Though profoundly Spanish, both drew deeply from their experience of the Netherlands, where Montano spent eight years, Furió somewhat more. Their unprecedented influence on the policy of the world's most powerful state was a high point for post-Erasmian political humanism in Europe. Furió from 1556 was a friend and disciple of the Basel humanist Castellio, and became a convinced supporter of freedom for all faiths. Montano, while remaining externally a Catholic, experienced an interior conversion towards a more spiritual religion, based on his contacts with the Family of Love sect in the Netherlands; there is no proof that he became a Familist, but he subsequently communicated many of his spiritual ideas to his disciple fray José de Sigüenza, librarian of the Escorial.

The solution they attempted through Requesens was wrecked by rebel distrust, by government bankruptcy, by Requesens' own death in March 1576 and by five consecutive mutinies in the Spanish army of Flanders leading to the sack of Antwerp, the 'Spanish Fury', in November 1576. The appointment of Don Juan promised to continue the initiative, and the Perpetual Edict of February 1577 put into effect the substance of Furió's proposals; but again circumstances forced Spain back into a military solution. Furió returned to Spain that year; Montano had gone back in 1575.

Official policy after 1577 tended to lay more emphasis on the war against Calvinist heretics, and less on the legitimate grievances of the Netherlanders. This was in clear contrast to much of the advice Philip had received in the previous decade. In 1573, for instance, he had informed Requesens that some of his advisers 'say that religion is of little importance: the real causes are the bad treatment the natives have suffered'. The division of opinion, whether to castigate the Netherlanders as rebels or as heretics, continued to be an active one. In 1578 the king was advised from Italy not to impede a solution by presenting them as heretics: 'in all the public statements so far made by the Flemings, they have always shown themselves as Catholics'. Behind this type of opinion lay an unease that seems to have been felt also in the peninsula. Many Spaniards (Requesens in Flanders in 1573 had claimed '*most* Spaniards here') – and no doubt the Portuguese too after 1580 – considered the constitutional demands of the Netherlanders to be just, and saw Alba's presentation of them as heretics as an attempt to mask the real issues. What Montano had seen as 'arrogance' in Flanders could be experienced also in the peninsula. It was ominous that a French diplomat priest, touring the peninsula in 1582, met many people who 'felt that the cause of the States of the Netherlands could be justified had heresy not become mixed up in it'. Philip's apparent disregard for the nobility of Flanders struck a jarring note among the local nobility of the non-Castilian provinces, excluded from what they deemed a proper share in the government of their own country. In 1587 the Diputados of Aragon complained to Philip that whereas the Aragonese had once enjoyed government office, 'now we are deprived of all these goods and favours'. When the events of 1591 occurred in Saragossa, the Aragonese count of Morata warned: 'if Your Majesty does not provide a remedy at once, we will have another Netherlands'.

There was, moreover, disagreement among Spaniards with the foreign policy implications of the war in Flanders. Throughout the Habsburg regime in Spain, from 1517 to 1700, a small but growing body of Castilian and indeed Spanish opinion opposed the commitment to the Netherlands as a deviation from Spain's proper sphere of interest, which was deemed to be what it had been in the time of the Catholic Monarchs – the Mediterranean. Added to this opposition, the heavy cost to Spaniards in money and blood, foretold by Montano, helped create a profound crisis of conscience. 'Why', protested a procurador in the Cortes at Madrid in 1588, 'should we pay a tax on flour here in order to stop heresy there? The Catholic faith and its defence belong to all Christendom: if that is what these wars are for, Castile should not have to bear all the burden while other realms, princes and states just look on'. The protest was more marked in the Cortes of 1593, when one procurador called for an end to the war against the Dutch heretics: 'if they want to be damned, let them!' By the end of the century the debate over the Netherlands had reached the sombre stage where official policy was almost entirely at variance with informed opinion.

Philip was aware of the cost in money. The war, he admitted in 1578, 'has consumed the money and substance which has come from the Indies', since Flanders regularly required more bullion than the plate fleets brought. Between 1566 and 1654 the crown sent at least 218 million ducats to the Netherlands for expenses, but received only about 121 million from America. The cost in men was certainly high, though not as high as Francisco de Quevedo suggested in the 1630s: 'we have sacrificed more than two million men, for the campaigns and sieges of the Netherlands have become the universal graveyard of Europe'. Not surprisingly, writers in the seventeenth century were overwhelmingly hostile to the war effort. In 1624 an official of the council of the Indies wrote: 'if the Dutch wish to remain in unbelief, why should we have to pursue such a harmful and ruinous war that has lasted for sixty-six years? Christ never ordered conversions by force of gun, pike or musket'. 'Nobody doubts', summed up the distinguished bishop Juan de Palafox in 1650, 'that the wars in Flanders have been the ruin of this monarchy'.

## Philip II and the crown of Aragon

The biggest constitutional crisis of the reign was the revolt in Aragon in 1591. Since the union of the crowns the kingdom of Aragon had preserved its fueros intact, and developed its own separate institutions. An overwhelmingly rural society of noble landlords and sheep-owners on one side, and a depressed peasantry made up partly of Moriscos on the other, it had little active political life. Though the king had considerable powers – only he could summon the Cortes, wage war and nominate all higher officials – custom and feudal survivals, exemplified in the legendary 'If not, not' oath (see p. 15), limited his power to interfere in domestic affairs. Of particular importance also was the office of the judge known as the justiciar, whose court could not be overruled even by the king. In common with Catalonia and Valencia, the two other peninsular realms of the crown of Aragon, the kingdom of Aragon posed two distinct types of problem to the king. In the first place the inflexible concern of the realm for its laws or fueros, which protected the privileges of the ruling elite, tended to impede all political change and at the same time restricted the ability of the crown to raise money or troops. Royal absolutism could therefore make no advance. By the same token, feudal authority survived: Aragon was the only realm in the peninsula (other than Catalonia before 1486 when the Sentence of Guadalupe under Ferdinand the Catholic had liberated the peasants) where the lords were recognised to have an 'absolute' power over their vassals, in the sense that they could punish or kill them without any recourse to the law. In the second place, the extreme independence of localities, towns and noble territories; the rivalry between families and clans for local office and influence; the growing social problems and poverty of the period; all combined to create levels of conflict that surfaced most commonly in banditry. Without any strong royal authority capable of intervening, banditry became in the sixteenth and seventeenth centuries the predominant form of lawlessness throughout the crown of Aragon.

Philip was confronted by the fueros at the very start of his reign, in 1556 when the viceroy of Aragon was accused in Saragossa of a contrafuero and the Cortes met in emergency session without royal summons. The crown compromised and the crisis passed. Though it was once mistakenly believed that Philip neglected his realms in the crown of Aragon and seldom visited them, the truth is that he went there for several extended stays, and the months that he spent there added up to a total of more than three years. His first important trip as king was in 1563, when he opened the general Cortes at Monzón (during his reign only one regional Cortes, that of Aragon in 1592, took place). During this visit he swore to the fueros in Saragossa and then did the same in Barcelona and Valencia in 1564. This was followed by a long absence. He did not return until 1585, when again he opened a general Cortes at Monzón and attended the wedding in Saragossa of his daughter Catalina to Carlo Emanuele duke of Savoy, accompanying her subsequently to Barcelona and then returning to Castile via Valencia in 1586. It was a very long stay, lasting 14 months in all. The visits were always occasion for complaints to be presented, particularly against officials of the crown. The Aragonese, for example, resisted attempts by the king to purchase for strategic reasons the county of Ribagorza bordering France; it was a matter that led to further complications arising out of the prevalence of banditry.

Many bandits enjoyed protection from local nobility, and the crown could not intervene to ensure law and order because its powers were limited. 'In the three kingdoms of Aragon, Valencia and Catalonia', reported the Venetian ambassador Tiepolo in 1567, 'where His Majesty does not have absolute power, the most atrocious crimes are committed and travellers have no security because those parts are everywhere infested by bandits, but the inhabitants will not allow the king to intervene except in conformity with their traditional constitutions'. A high proportion of rural lawlessness involved Morisco bandits, who were particularly active in the period after the 1569 Granada rebellion. In 1582, for example, Philip felt obliged to send 18 companies of infantry into Valencia to defend the coast against a possible rendezvous between north African corsairs and Morisco dissidents. It was a clear contra-fuero and there were bitter complaints in the Cortes of 1585. In Catalonia there was a grave risk of collusion between bandits and the French; and in 1569 the viceroy, succumbing to the tensions of a period of crisis, ordered the arrest of the Diputats of Catalonia on a suspicion of collusion with Huguenots. There were daring attacks on the convoys of silver sent from Madrid to Barcelona for transportation to Italy, an entire shipment being captured in 1587. Banditry was of course also common in Castile, but Castilian brigands frequently chose to flee to the eastern realms where royal justice was weaker.

The lawlessness endemic in the feudal society of Aragon could be seen at all levels in the county of Ribagorza, a territory of some 230 villages belonging to the duke of Villahermosa near the border with France. Because of the county's strategic importance the crown tried to take it over in 1554 with the consent of its vassals, who hated their lord; but the move was blocked by an appeal to the justiciar's court. Subsequent attempts to take it over were led by the count of Chinchón, Philip II's chief adviser on Aragon. Chinchón had a personal motive for intervening: his sister-in-law had been murdered (on a charge of infidelity) by her husband the count of Ribagorza, Villahermosa's son, and Chinchón was instrumental in having the culprit executed for the crime (1573). Both personal and political enmity thus opposed the Villahermosa family to the crown. For lack of money to compensate the duke, Philip II dropped plans to annex Ribagorza and in the Cortes of 1585 granted him full possession of the county. This, however, provoked serious disorders that eventually forced royal troops to intervene. The discontented vassals rebelled against their lord, and in retaliation the duke in 1587 launched a surprise attack and murdered their leaders. There were strong protests in Madrid, led by Chinchón. At the same time the Christian vassals of the mountain area, the *montañeses*, exploited the disorder to direct raids against the Morisco peasants of the plains: an incident at Codo in 1585 was followed in 1588 by a massacre of Moriscos at Pina. Unable to tolerate this situation any longer, the king in 1589 sent in Aragonese troops to pacify the county, and in 1591 incorporated Ribagorza into the crown.

The case of Ribagorza shows that the fundamental political problems in Aragon arose within Aragonese society and were not caused by the crown. This was also true of the events of 1591. In 1588 Philip sent as a special envoy the Castilian count of Almenara, through whom he hoped to have closer control over affairs in Saragossa. The appointment, which contravened the fuero that officials must be native Aragonese, was presented to the justiciar's court and obtained approval. Almenara was in practice superseding the incumbent viceroy, and in May 1590 was sent out again from Madrid with extra powers that made it likely he would become the next viceroy.

By then Aragon was already in turmoil. In April 1590 Antonio Pérez escaped from prison in Madrid and made straight for Aragon, where he claimed the right to be tried by the justiciar's court and thus put himself out of the direct reach of royal justice. Philip had no wish to expose himself to the procedure of the court, where his status would be that of any common plaintiff. Pérez, on the other hand, used the court to publicise sensational allegations involving the king in the murder of Escobedo, and at the same time encouraged sections of the nobility and the guilds to believe that the appointment of Almenara was part of a scheme to undermine the fueros.

The Pérez affair became identified with the cause of the 'liberties' of Aragon. In order to get Pérez out of the hands of the justiciar and into a more amenable court, Philip made the Inquisition in Madrid trump up charges of heresy against the fugitive. Armed with these, the Holy Office in Saragossa went to the justiciar and demanded that Pérez, as a proven heretic, be surrendered to their jurisdiction. The transfer of Pérez on 24 May 1591 from the justiciar's prison to the cells of the Inquisition in the

Aljafería palace, provoked a major riot. Mobs attacked the justiciar and
beat and stabbed Almenara, who died of his wounds two weeks later. They
then triumphantly bore Pérez back from the Aljafería to the justiciar's
prison. The popular mood was firmly on the prisoner's side: a second
attempt to move him back to the Aljafería, on 24 September, provoked
a similar riot.

With the support of the council of state, Philip had since early
September been preparing to restore order by force. In mid-October he
sent a warning to all the nobles and cities of Aragon that he was going
to send in an army. The rebels in Saragossa, led by Diego de Heredía,
Juan de Luna and others, thereupon seized the city's armouries and distributed arms. With these, they prevailed upon the Diputación to support
resistance, and persuaded the new justiciar, Juan de Lanuza, who at 27
had just (in September) succeeded his father in the hereditary office, to
declare that any invasion by the Castilian force was a contra-fuero. In
effect, this was to declare war against the king. A council of war was
set up, but most of the nobles refused to join it: exceptions were the duke
of Villahermosa and the count of Aranda. Letters were sent throughout the
kingdom to coordinate resistance, and pleas for support went to Catalonia
and Valencia.

At the end of October Philip II was preparing to send in his army
of 14,000 men and 25 pieces of artillery. On 2 November he issued a
statement that the force, commanded by Alonso de Vargas, was marching
not against Aragon but against France; that only the leaders of the troubles
would be punished; and that 'my wish has always been that the fueros
be maintained'. Vargas and his forces entered Aragonese territory on 8
November. There was extreme tension on both sides, in the royal army as
well as in the towns through which it passed, but there was no conflict of
any sort. All the cities in Aragon – with the exception of Teruel – refused
to sympathise with the rebels. The Diputació of Catalonia limited its help
to interceding with the king. Vargas entered Saragossa peacefully on
12 November, a day after Pérez had fled north to Béarn and the rebels had
dispersed. There was no revolt of any sort in Aragon, nor any use of force.

It seemed that a compromise might be reached, but in December a
handwritten order from the king, which had been approved by ministers
in Madrid, ordered the summary beheading without trial of the justiciar.
The general amnesty issued in January 1592 excluded 22 people: among
these were Villahermosa and Aranda, who were taken to Castile where
they died mysteriously in prison within a few months. On 19 October
1592 Heredía, Luna and other rebels were publicly executed; the following

day a huge auto de fe with over 80 penitents was held by the Inquisition, as if to celebrate the royal triumph. Philip's harshness to the rebels was in part motivated by the serious threat from France, which Pérez used as his base to organise an abortive invasion of Aragon in 1592.

Constitutionally, Philip was a model of moderation; he no doubt had in mind his mistakes in the Netherlands. In any case, the solid refusal of the nobles, cities and people of Aragon to support the riots in Saragossa, and the complete absence of resistance to the invading army (against which the justiciar and Heredía had been able to muster only 2,000 men), demonstrated that no rebellion had occurred. The Aragonese Cortes sat from June to December 1592 at Tarazona and accepted – not without opposition – the constitutional changes proposed by Philip, who made a special journey from Madrid to attend the final sessions. The justiciar would henceforth be removable by the king; a majority vote rather than unanimity would suffice for each chamber of the Cortes, except in fiscal matters; the king was allowed to choose non-Aragonese as viceroys. Royal authority had therefore made some gains, but these were concurred in by the ruling classes, who feared the greater dangers resulting from rebellion, particularly when there was danger of an invasion by the French. The growing fears of Morisco agitation were likewise stilled by a royal order of 1593 ordering all Moriscos in the kingdom to be disarmed.

# Absolutism in theory and in practice

The regime of Philip II in Spain has frequently been described as 'absolutist'. We may examine the validity of this term in three main areas: the king's own methods of government, the common opinion of contemporaries and the structure of the Spanish state.

## What was the role of the king in government?

Philip II did not bequeath, either in word or in writing, any reflections on the duties of his office, so that it is difficult to assess the standards he set for himself. There is no doubt that he was utterly devoted to the service of his subjects, for whom he felt responsible directly to God. 'Your principal object', he instructed a viceroy in 1559, 'must be to work for the community which is in your charge, so that it may live and rest in full security, peace, justice and quiet'. In practice, royal government could never be wholly personal, for the king needed advice from experts and required servants to carry out his orders. 'The king can govern well', runs a statement in the apocryphal testament to his son, 'only through good ministers. If you cut yourself off from the advice of your best ministers, and disregard it and run matters alone, you would appear a very foolhardy king, an enemy of the well-being of your subjects'.

Though dependent on his ministers, Philip never let himself fall into their hands (the great exception, possibly, was Antonio Pérez). Like other sixteenth-century monarchs, he was obliged by custom and political necessity to employ grandees in the principal and most lucrative posts. But, also like them, in day-to-day administration he preferred those of lesser rank, partly because they were more qualified, partly because they relied wholly on the crown for remuneration. Through assiduous service, such men became crucially important to the administration. In the 1550s Philip relied on Francisco de Eraso, a Navarrese who had served Charles V and who by 1559 was secretary to six of the councils and a member of two more. In the 1560s the rising star was Diego de Espinosa, a humble letrado who became president of the council of Castile (1565), inquisitor general (1566) and cardinal (1568). The count of Chinchón described him in 1566 as 'the one man in all Spain in whom the king places most confidence and with whom he discusses most business'. Thereafter, as business became more complex, the team helping the king expanded. After 1572, when Espinosa died of a stroke, the cardinal's secretary Mateo Vázquez de Leca attached himself to the king and became Philip's indispensable private secretary. But over the same period the king was also dependent at a policy level on Antonio Pérez and his successors, notably Moura and Idiáquez.

Regardless of the help available from bureaucrats like these, Philip insisted that all decisions must be made by himself alone. This meant that all significant papers, whether *consultas* from the councils or petitions from the public or administrative documents passing through the hands of his secretaries, were meant to come to him for deliberation or signature; he would write his comments or decision, where necessary, in a virtually indecipherable scrawl. The volume of paper crossing his desk was enormous: in May 1571 alone, 1,252 separate memoranda had to be dealt with by the king. Philip's insistence on bearing this burden did not arise solely from dedication to duty. He seems to have had little confidence in his ministers, and never trusted them to make decisions alone. To make sure that he himself decided correctly he consulted others extensively and pored for hours over their memoranda. All this slowed down the executive process, as Philip's colleagues and contemporaries were well aware. In 1560 Gonzalo Pérez complained that 'decisions are taken so slowly that even a cripple could keep up with them'; and in 1565 he commented that 'His Majesty makes mistakes and will continue to make mistakes in many matters because he discusses them with different people, sometimes with one, sometimes with another, concealing something from one minister and revealing it to another; it is little wonder that different and even contradictory decisions are issued'.

Pope Pius V wrote impatiently to Philip that 'Your Majesty spends so long considering your undertakings that when the time to perform them comes the occasion has passed'. The criticism fails to take into account the heavy responsibility borne by the king. His two great enemies, as we shall have occasion to refer to later, were space and time: if information reached him too slowly he was in no position to make a viable decision. In good conditions, Madrid was four days away from Seville and Lisbon, ten days from Brussels, two weeks from Milan, nearly four weeks from Rome and possibly six from America. When the information was inadequate or contradictory, Philip was perhaps right in refusing to commit himself. This enabled him, for example, to pursue a flexible policy in the Netherlands with Requesens and Don Juan. It also, of course, aggravated the frustration of his subordinates. A correspondent of Alba informed the duke in 1571 of Philip's activities: 'it is the same thing that Your Excellency knows and has experienced: papers and more papers, and more of them every day'. The well-known image of Philip II as a 'paper king' is all too true. Even after the appointment of a competent private secretary such as Mateo Vázquez, he could not cope with the quantity of business, 'these devils my papers' as he once called them. The complaints about overwork occur throughout his correspondence. 'I have not been able to contact you today', he scribbled to Vázquez in March 1576, 'because I have had to get through my papers and have had to sign at least four hundred signatures; but tomorrow I shall try'. Charles the warrior king was in Philip transformed into a bureaucrat: 'what his father had acquired with the sword', as the historian Merriman observes, 'Philip proposed to preserve with the pen'.

It would be wrong to conclude from this that there was too little devolution of responsibility and that all power was centralised in the king. Under Philip the monarchy was in transition from personal rule to bureaucracy, and royal power was much weaker in practice than may appear. At the level of executive power, however, there is no doubt that the king was in sole command. All Philip's councils, for example, were purely advisory: he could reject their recommendations and make his own decisions. The Cortes of Castile were likewise subordinate. 'If I so wish', Philip is said to have informed them in 1555, 'I shall annul without the Cortes any laws made in the Cortes; I shall legislate by decree and abolish laws by decree'. Philip almost certainly made no such statement (he was not even in Spain that year), and it would have been out of character (as well as politically foolish) for him to have done so. Like his predecessors, he was permitted absolute rights of life and death over every citizen in the interests of state security, but never exercised the right alone. In two of the most criticised political executions of the reign, that of Montigny and the justiciar of Aragon, Philip acted with the written advice and support of his ministers. In his so-called testament to his son, the following statement is attributed to the king: 'Never condemn a man to death except unhappily or unwillingly, forced by the demands of justice and the necessity for law and order'.

His medical adviser one day criticised Philip for 'sitting forever over your papers, from your desire, as they say, to seclude yourself from the world'. Happy and affectionate within his family circle, Philip presented a colder image to his subjects and to foreign diplomats. There is no doubt that he disliked being a public person, and he certainly lacked the common touch with which biographers have tried to credit him. The most striking monument to his reign, the great monastery-palace of San Lorenzo del Escorial, on which he lavished over six million ducats, seems to epitomise his lonely eminence. Begun in 1563 under the Neapolitan architect Juan Bautista de Toledo and then continued by Juan de Herrera, the building was conceived in part as a mausoleum for Charles V, in part as a Jeronimite monastery. Yet the king was very far from being a prisoner of the Escorial, which he did not begin using until 1571 and which was not completed until 1584. His normal routine was one of movement: an annual ritual of hibernating in Madrid (which he fixed as his seat of government in 1561 when it had barely 20,000 inhabitants), then moving out in spring to the Escorial or Aranjuez, returning to Madrid in June, then moving out of the summer heat to his palace of Valsain 'in the Segovia woods', or to the Escorial.

A persistent legend, determined to present Philip as a narrow-minded anchorite, maintains that he immersed himself in Castile because it was the only place he understood. It is worth recalling that the king was in reality the most travelled ruler of his day. In the period that he governed Spain, before his accession to the throne, he spent fourteen months in England, a year and three months in Germany and five years in the Netherlands. After he became king, he spent two years and four months in Portugal (1580–3), and three years in the crown of Aragon (for meetings of the Cortes, in

1563–4 and 1585–6, and to Aragon alone in 1592). The intensity of work inevitably tied him down to central Castile, where his travels were limited to the area marked out by the royal palaces. But he also managed to make one visit to the south of the peninsula, to Córdoba and Seville in 1570 to supervise the end of the Granada wars. The visits were not enough to undo an impression that his subjects began to have of him, as a distant and impersonal ruler. In contrast to the Catholic Monarchs, whose power and reputation had rested on close contact with all their peoples, Philip II began the important and highly negative move of distancing the monarchy from its subjects. He is credited with saying, in his so-called testament, that 'travelling about one's kingdom is neither useful nor decent'. He may not have said it, but his style of monarchy reflected the sense of the phrase. There is no doubt that the failure of Philip and his successors to keep in personal touch with their subjects weakened the hold of the Habsburg monarchy over the hearts of the people of Spain.

## What did Spaniards think about absolutism?

As recently as the Comunidades, strong feelings had been voiced against the use by Charles V of the title 'Majesty', which some felt to belong only to God. Not surprisingly, and despite the image of Philip as an absolute despot, sixteenth-century Spain lacked any doctrine of extreme royal power and even produced the most eloquent anti-absolutist theorists of the age.

'Absolute power' was clearly stated in several Castilian Cortes of the fifteenth century to be a characteristic of monarchy, but seems to have implied little more than an affirmation of the king's sovereignty, that is his position at the head of the law. The influence of Roman Law, with its belief that the prince was 'free from' (*ab solutus*) control by the laws, could however be found occasionally, as in the 1453 claims by the king (Juan II) that he was 'sovereign lord with no superior in temporal matters' and that he was 'free (*soluto*) and not bound to keep oaths or promises'. As jurists began to define a concept that was coming to be accepted in other countries, they refined their views. Juan Ginés de Sepúlveda in the mid-sixteenth century defined a kingdom as being one 'in quo rex summan habet rerum omnium potestatem' ('in which the king has supreme power'). The crown and its judicial agents were concerned to emphasise the extraordinary position of the monarch in the body politic. Likewise Charles V in his testament of 1554 laid claim to 'supreme jurisdiction'. In Spain as elsewhere these claims must be taken as part of the process by which legists were attempting to give the state complete autonomy from other jurisdictions, notably that of the Church. Spanish theory was perfectly consonant with that of foreign Catholic writers, such as Bodin, on the transcendent authority of the crown.

In principle there was no difficulty in accepting the notion of 'absolute' power. The authority of the crown, according to the Cortes of Toledo in 1559, 'is by its nature indivisible'; sovereignty resided only in the crown or, as a fourteenth-century Spanish formula put it, 'in uno regno, unus rex' ('one kingdom, one king'). Both cities and nobility in the late fifteenth century tended to support this view, which promised to save the country from disorder. It was in his role as lawgiver that the king gave clearest evidence of sovereignty. Charles V had authorised further codification of the laws: this task was completed by the council of Castile under Philip and a code was issued in 1569. The *Nueva Recopilación*, as it came to be called, confirmed the emergence of the crown as the source of law; and the Cortes in 1592 conceded that 'the making of laws has always been part of the supreme jurisdiction of the prince', though it preferred the laws to be made in Cortes rather than out of it.

It is well known that in territories of Spain not governed by Castilian law, the power of the king was restricted and was considered to be regulated by a contract between crown and subjects. A clear statement of this view, already referred to briefly, was made by the Diputació of Catalonia in 1622: 'In Catalonia the supreme power and jurisdiction over the province belongs not to His Majesty alone but to His Majesty and the three estates of the province, which together possess supreme and absolute power to make and unmake laws. . . . These laws we have in Catalonia are laws compacted between the king and the land, and the prince can no more exempt himself from them than he can exempt himself from a contract'. In reality the contrast between a 'free' crown of Aragon and an absolutist Castile has often been overdrawn, and it is important to recognise that in Castile too there were recognised limits to royal 'absolutism'.

The king could, in the first place, be cited before ordinary courts in private litigation, even though he was the fount of law and justice. Legists like Castillo de Bobadilla in his 1597 *Política para corregidores* (Policy for corregidors) accepted this, as did Philip II himself. A contemporary tells us that during a dispute between the crown and a subject he instructed the judge: 'Take note . . . in case of doubt, the verdict must always go against me'. State or royal law was not yet supreme in Spain: important areas of jurisdiction were still catered for by local customary law, by seigneurial law and by Church law. The crown was obliged to respect these distinct spheres of authority, and there were considerable restrictions on its power to act. In the second place, the king had in theory no power over the private property of subjects. We have already quoted Dr Palacios Rubios's dictum that 'the king is entrusted solely with the administration of the realm, not with dominion over property'. This basic principle was repeated time and again by legists (with very few dissentients; one such, Pedro de Valencia, argued that the crown had a right to 'supervise' property in the public interest). It was of great constitutional importance, as we can see from the conclusions drawn by Juan de Mariana: 'The prince has no right whatever over the goods of his subjects. . . . It follows that the king cannot impose new taxes without the prior consent of the people'. Mariana got into trouble when he later denounced royal manipulation of the coinage as an attack on the property of subjects. In the third place, the crown was held to have no right to alienate its own property. Stated in the fourteenth century, and repeated firmly by the Cortes at Madrigal in 1476, the principle was pressed on Charles V at the Cortes of Valladolid in 1523, and accepted for example by the legist Diego de Covarrubias in 1556. The crown from Charles V onwards repeatedly violated the principle by selling off property, but always obtained either the permission of the pope or the agreement of the Cortes before doing so and thereby seemed to recognise its limitations in law. Finally, the king was bound to respect the 'laws of the realm' or fundamental laws. The concept was most clearly expressed by Mariana in his *De rege* (On the King) of 1599. He distinguished between revocable laws made by the prince, and public laws (particularly on religion, the succession and taxes) that could be changed only with the full consent of the people. In 1572 Jerónimo Osorio argued that 'fundamental laws' were binding on the king. Much of this theorising may have borne little relation to a real world in which the crown often – and almost exclusively for financial reasons – interfered with the property rights of its subjects, but it can be argued that under Philip II such acts (seizure of private bullion, for example) were limited in scope and were specifically recognised to be exceptional.

As part of their effort to fortify the theory of kingship, legists rejected the feudal right of rebellion, recognised by Magna Carta in England and by the mediaeval Partidas in Spain. As early as 1440 the Cortes of Valladolid declared that 'those who resist the king, resist God'. Most writers under the Catholic Monarchs would have agreed with Hernando del Pulgar's view that 'only God can punish kings'. In Spain, this tradition was balanced by a no less freely recognised tradition that the interests of the prince

and the people were identical, and that the people were therefore obliged
to render advice and criticism if necessary. Philip II in 1559 asserted that
'the community was not created for the prince, but rather the prince was
created for the community'. This was another way of saying that the ruler
must observe the laws of the realm, a principle that in any case Charles V
had urged on his son in 1543 and had personally heard expounded in
Salamanca in 1528 by the legist Martin de Azpilcueta on the theme, 'the
realm belongs not to the king but to the community, and authority in it
belongs by natural law not to the king but to the community'.

In Spain, therefore, the humanist cult of the prince – represented for
example by Antonio de Guevara's claim that 'we are obliged to obey
princes in everything' – failed to predominate, and all through the sixteenth century, in a monarchy that many foreigners regarded as 'absolute',
two surprising features can be seen. First, there was a total absence of
the cult of monarchy. The kings of Castile were an exception in Europe,
since they consciously rejected many of the symbols of power used by
monarchies outside the peninsula. They did not consider their office
sacred, did not claim (like the rulers of France and England) any power
to heal the sick, and enjoyed no special rituals at the time of their birth,
crowning or death. The imagery of magical royal power, common in other
monarchies, was notably absent in Spain. The rulers of Castile from
Isabella to Philip II and beyond, evolved no coronation ceremony and no
cult of personality. From the 1580s Philip II toned down Burgundian ritual
at court and reverted to simpler Castilian practice; at the same time, he
ordered that courtiers and ministers address him simply as 'Sir' instead of
'Majesty'. The court portraits of Sánchez Coello give vivid evidence of this
more austere style. Second, remarkably free discussion of political affairs
was tolerated, and public controversy occurred on a scale paralleled in few
other countries. The great debate initiated by Las Casas carried on into
the reign of Philip, under whom new controversies broke out over the
Netherlands, over the cult of limpieza, and over the fate of the Moriscos.
The historian Antonio de Herrera confirmed that such free discussion was
essential for otherwise 'the reputation of Spain would fall rapidly, for
foreign and enemy nations would say that small credence could be placed
in the words of her rulers, since their subjects were not allowed to speak
freely'. At the same time the new tradition of *arbitrismo* (*see* p. 251) was
initiated by memorials such as that of Rodrigo de Luján to Cisneros in
1516, and of Luis Ortiz to Philip II in 1558.

Seen in this context, there was nothing startling about the anti-
absolutist writings of the Spanish 'monarchomachs' (a word used in the

sixteenth century for those who favoured limiting the powers of kings), who were principally from the Jesuit order – Luis de Molina, Juan de Mariana, Francisco Suárez. It is significant that their discussion of the right to resist was directed against foreign rulers and they did not see the need to apply it at home. Mariana's *De rege*, available freely in Spain, was condemned in Paris by the *Parlement* and burnt by the public hangman (1610). Suárez's *Defensio Fidei*, which attacked absolutism in England, was likewise condemned in Paris (1614). Moreover, the government allowed them and a large school of other theorists to develop political doctrines that redefined royal power in a non-absolutist and more democratic sense. Mariana specified that 'the king must be subject to the laws laid down by the state, whose authority is greater than that of the king', and Cristóbal de Anguiano even elevated the rights of conscience: 'the subject is obliged to obey in accordance with his own conscience and it is unlawful for him to do anything against it'. Many of these democratic writings flourished, it is true, in the following reign; but they were never considered subversive and were permissible – indeed, influential – opinions within the rich variety of Spanish political thought.

## Was the Spanish state absolutist?

The day-to-day restrictions on royal power are perhaps the clearest evidence that 'absolutism', if it existed in peninsular Spain, was more a legal fiction than a political reality; and that the elaborate systems of the political theorists should be treated with considerable scepticism. In the crown of Aragon and in Navarre, which had active parliamentary systems, the ability of the king to raise money or make laws was subject to the approval of the Cortes. In the Basque provinces, which were virtually self-governing republics within Spain, royal authority was so nominal that in Vizcaya the king had the status only of a feudal lord ('king in so far as he is lord of the land', the law stated).

Though the king lived in Castile, he made no attempt to Castilianise Spain, and the various realms of the peninsula continued to enjoy the complete autonomy that they had enjoyed under the Catholic Monarchs. Philip was always conscious that he had to respect the laws of each kingdom, and said so specifically when he explained his political principles to the Portuguese in 1580. 'Though Aragon and Castile have a single ruler', he assured them, 'they are not united, and remain as separate as they were when they had different rulers'. By the same token, he did not create a capital city for Spain. He chose Madrid in 1561 to be his seat of government, but it functioned as capital only for Castile. The other kingdoms had their own capital cities.

Though limited in other realms, was the king's power more extensive in Castile? The image of a 'paper king' suggests an actively centralised monarchy, but this is to ignore the very severe restrictions placed on government in early modern Spain. In the first place, an immense proportion of Spain was not under royal jurisdiction: in 1600 about two-thirds of its 4,600 towns and one-half of its 15,800 villages and hamlets were in private control (*señorío*), but only 22 of its 148 cities. The significance of this is discussed below (*see* p. 164). Second, the lack of a centralised state bureaucracy, either in judicial matters or in finance, made it impossible to secure firm control over the administration. The king in Castile had no civil service to help him collect taxes, which were normally farmed out; he had no police force (except in Madrid) to maintain law and order; he had no standing army. To govern his provinces the king relied utterly on the cooperation of the ruling elites: local oligarchies, great lords and clergy. If order was maintained in Castile it was not through force or tough government, but exclusively through a good working relationship between the local communities and the crown. The sixty-six corregidors active in Castile under Philip were symbols of royal authority and occasionally the cause for conflict with towns, but their task was to liaise with local government rather than to dominate it or extend royal power. Spain, in short, had neither the machinery nor the structure of absolutism. To remedy the lack of a lower bureaucracy, Philip attempted to collect information on a large scale with the help of his corregidors. In 1566 he gave orders for the further deposit of papers in the state archive at Simancas, and later established an archive for the Indies in Seville. The council of Castile in 1575 began an ambitious census of the population and economy, in the so-called 'relaciones topográficas', but the survey was completed only for New Castile. At the same date the council of the Indies conducted a similar census for America, but succeeded in surveying only New Spain.

The Cortes of Castile, finally, exercised tangible restraints on the crown. The 36 procuradores of the 18 cities met 12 times during the reign (1558, 1559–60, 1563, 1566–7, 1570–1, 1573–5, 1576–7, 1579–82, 1583–5, 1586–8, 1588–90, 1592–8), the main business each time being finance. The Cortes were no longer an active partner in legislation; it was accepted that any decrees made by the king in Cortes had the full vigour of law, and the assembly's role was restricted to petitioning. Nevertheless, the Cortes of Philip II cannot be dismissed as an irrelevancy. They remained the principal forum for political discussion and criticism of the government: their repeated protests against expenditure, economic policy and (in 1593) the war in the Netherlands, could not always be ignored. Moreover, the increasing reliance of the crown on servicios which by definition were grants of the Cortes rather than direct taxes, ironically gave the assembly more of a say in financial matters than it had possessed under Charles V. This explains the anxiety of the government, from the 1560s onwards, that procuradores should come armed with plenary powers from their cities, and not be able to postpone voting grants on the pretext that they did not have the authority. The argument over these powers reached its height with the creation of the grant of *millones* in 1590, certainly the most hated tax of the entire Habsburg era and one over which the government was forced into repeated negotiations with the Cortes.

# Bureaucracy and absolutism

Looking back from the reign of Charles V to that of Isabella, the historian Fernández de Oviedo remarked that 'since God took away this blessed queen it is harder to deal with the servant of a secretary than it was in those days with her and her council'. The emergence of a unified monarchy and a fixed centre of government, the added obligations of empire, all made necessary the growth of a new bureaucracy, which seemed however to interpose a barrier between crown and people.

The preference of the Catholic Monarchs for letrado officials was backed up by measures to improve their training. In 1493 they ordered that 'no letrado can hold any post in our tribunals nor in any town of our kingdom unless he has a notarised document certifying that he has studied common or civil law for a minimum of ten years at a university'. The decree strengthened existing practice and identified the universities more closely with state requirements, thereby stimulating the demand for higher education. At their peak in the 1580s the Castilian universities had an annual intake of about 20,000 students, most of them from the cities and from the hidalgo class. Fewer than a third of these survived to take a degree: most of those who did went on to staff the worldwide bureaucracy of Spain's empire.

The universities did not enjoy a high level of culture. The humanist content in their courses disappeared during the early century, giving way to an emphasis on career subjects. At Salamanca in 1555 Latin grammar still attracted over 35 per cent of matriculations and Greek 1 per cent; by 1595 only 9 per cent of students took Latin, and it had been 30 years since anyone studied Greek. By contrast, in 1595 as many as 57 per cent now preferred canon law, and another 16 per cent took civil law; nearly three-fourths of all students were now taking courses that promised them a career in the bureaucracy of both Church and state. University graduates, particularly those from the elite colleges (the *colegios mayores*), increasingly monopolised senior administrative posts, and in turn the universities, from being places of research and learning, decayed into training grounds for letrados. Faculty chairs became stepping stones to high office, some changing their holders almost every year. Academic studies declined in importance, and universities fell behind the standards commonly accepted elsewhere in Europe. The universities were fortunately not the only repository of learning in Spain. There were several *estudios generales* which gave higher education but could not grant degrees. Above all there was the educational impulse of the religious orders, led by the Jesuits, who founded their first college (later a university) at Gandia in 1547, and by the end of the century probably had over 10,000 students in their schools in Castile alone.

As in other European countries, higher education became essential in order to pursue a career in public service. State service, whether in the Church or abroad in the empire or at court – *iglesia o mar o casa real* – gave an income but even more surely gave status and thereby completed the process of social ascent for sons of merchants or farmers, and sons of minor nobility. The search for office became a rising tide that Philip managed to satisfy by offering government posts for sale. In Castile the upper bureaucracy consisted of two wings. One was a letrado hierarchy of university-trained jurists, who tended to monopolise professional posts in the law courts, the Church, the upper administration and the government councils. The other was a 'capa y espada' ('cloak and sword') wing of officials with noble status and a military background, who served in peace-keeping, war, diplomacy and on the council of state. Since 'capa y espada' posts required no formal qualification, they became vulnerable to sale by the government, which from 1540 began to alienate offices both in Spain and in America. The biggest volume of sales was in Castilian local government: by 1600 alienated municipal offices accounted for three-fourths of the total value of all posts sold.

The letrado hierarchy was recruited by preference from Castile's three main universities at Salamanca, Valladolid and Alcalá. Of 103 judges appointed to the high court of Valladolid between 1588 and 1633, only seven did not come from them. Within this elite, there was an even narrower elite. The six colegios mayores (*see* p. 120) at these universities developed into favoured institutions from which the administrative elite of Castile, whether serving in universities or the Church or in councils of state, was drawn. *Colegiales* were given preference over *manteístas* (ordinary university graduates) when appointments were made. In the sixteenth century well over half the members of the high courts of Granada and Valladolid, and of the council of Castile, were colegiales. In the seventeenth the proportion was nearly two-thirds for the courts, nearly three-fourths for the council. The elite became self-perpetuating as sons followed fathers into the colegios mayores and thence into the chief administrative posts of the country.

The evolution of the universities into a recruiting ground for the bureaucracy of Spain had a serious consequence. Professors accepted chairs only as a prelude to administrative office. Certain academic subjects decayed rapidly: Hebrew at Salamanca had only one student in 1555, the last year it appeared on the matriculation books. In 1578 the chair of mathematics there had been vacant for three years. The state, moreover, could not fail to exercise control over a body that was responsible for training its officials. The government began to issue decrees regulating university procedure in salaries, dress, textbooks and examinations; and in 1623 the state began appointing professors. It was believed at one time that higher education suffered because Spain reverted to medieval theology and dogmatism. That was only one factor, since the fact is that theology also declined in popularity. By the seventeenth century, at Salamanca and Valladolid law students outnumbered theologians by over twenty to one. Spain was following a course common to other west European nations, integrating university studies with the needs of the state.

Although the new breed of jurist administrators formed a 'robe nobility' comparable to that of other countries, there were no visible status distinctions between them and the old nobility. This was because most letrados were already of hidalgo or noble origin, and the colegios mayores also attracted aristocratic students, so that even children of grandees were prepared to take up office-holding careers. In 1586 the jurist Castilla y Aguayo affirmed that it was 'easier to study in college than to go to battle', signifying that for many nobles it was an acceptable alternative; 'they say that there was once an age of gold, now there is an age of letters'. A crucial development was Charles V's decision at the Cortes of Madrid in 1534 to exempt from direct taxation those with doctorates from the universities of Bologna, Valladolid and Salamanca (and later, Alcalá). Tax exemption in this context implied noble status, which immediately confirmed the privileged social position of letrados. The privilege was confirmed for jurists in the crown of Aragon in 1553.

The bureaucratic expansion of the sixteenth century should not be exaggerated. There were possibly not more than 500 senior letrado posts in Castile under Philip II. Adding other letrado posts and the much larger number of capa y espada positions, in both Castile and America, the total would possibly not exceed 2,000. The administrative expansion did not contribute to any significant expansion of royal power, and Philip II managed to limit the number of personnel in the central councils during most of his reign. Only after about 1590, when his control loosened, did both the size and the salaries of the councils increase and continue to rise for most of the seventeenth century.

The recruitment of officials helped in some measure to Castilianise the Spanish empire. Senior posts in the judicial and administrative tribunals of America and, after 1707, of the crown of Aragon, were reserved for those who had been educated at the colegios mayores and the leading Castilian universities. It naturally created resentment among the qualified elite of the non-Castilian realms.

## Crown and aristocracy: the problem of señoríos

To observers in the sixteenth and seventeenth centuries the most obvious restriction on royal power was the area of the country not controlled by the king. In the province of Salamanca, for instance, 63 per cent of the territory and over 60 per cent of the population fell under noble jurisdiction, 6.5 per cent of land and 6 per cent of population under ecclesiastical jurisdiction. The situation was similar throughout Spain. In Valencia, according to one official, 'the king has only 73 large and small towns, and over 300 are seigneurial'; in Aragon the crown in 1611 had jurisdiction over only 498 of the 1,183 centres of population, with nobles and the Church in roughly equal control of the remainder.

The most striking feature was the power of the great lords. The Velasco constables of Castile controlled 258 towns and villages in Old Castile; the Mendoza duke of Infantado controlled nearly 800 towns and villages and nominated over 500 public officials throughout Spain. Some of the noble holdings were virtually independent states, huge concentrations of territory where the only writ recognised was that of the lord: in the seventeenth century the estates of the duke of Osuna in Andalusia and the duke of Gandía in Valencia were typical of these. Ironically, the crown itself had been the chief contributor to an increase in noble power.

The señorío was in principle a delegation of jurisdiction by the crown to an individual. In the twelfth century, when most señoríos in Castile and

Aragon originated, the crown sought to build up strong allies to help reconquer and repopulate new territory. It therefore delegated functions without surrendering sovereignty. Señoríos fell into two main categories: 'territorial' lordships, where the land was actually owned and the population therefore bound by tenancies; and 'jurisdictional', a much larger category which developed mainly in the fourteenth century, where the lord was granted rights to administer justice, collect taxes, nominate officials and enlist men for the king, but did not own the land. Many older señoríos were both territorial and jurisdictional: in the hands of the great nobles, these developed over the centuries into great estates or 'latifundia'.

Ferdinand and Isabella favoured their nobility in several respects, but opposed granting away royal land and jurisdiction. The few señoríos they created were mostly in compensation for land taken away; for example, they gave the towns of Serón and Tixola to the marquis of Villena after the wars in Granada. In the sixteenth century, however, under Charles V and Philip II, there was a significant extension of the seigneurial regime in Castile, contrary to the trend in much of western Europe. Three trends put more land in noble hands: the process of social mobility, since rising gentry bought land and secured it with an entail (mayorazgo); expansion into royal and common lands, where a noble with simple jurisdiction would secure ownership of the land and so obtain territorial rights as well; and the economic problems of individuals, towns and the crown itself, all of whom put land on to the market in an attempt to meet expenses and pay debts.

The role of the crown was particularly important. From the 1530s Charles V received papal permission to sell estates of the three military orders. The sales realised nearly 1.7 million ducats for the treasury between 1537 and 1551; most purchasers were nobles intent on enlarging their holdings. The precedent was followed in 1551 by further papal permission, this time to sell Church land; but Charles was reluctant to act on it. His son felt no such scruples, and made regular sales from a number of sources to help cover state debts. *Baldíos*, or communal lands which technically belonged to the crown, were one fruitful source: beginning in 1557, sales reached their peak in the 1580s, and occurred mainly in the south of the peninsula. Philip during his reign gained about 4.8 million ducats from these alienations. The extensive sale of Church land, however, was one of the most remarkable aspects of the policy of the Catholic king. Supported by papal bulls, Philip II fell upon the property of the Church. In 1574, for example, he was given permission to sell Church towns to a value of 40,000 ducats a year, and alienated about sixty-nine towns within five years. Some consequences can be seen in the census returns for New Castile in 1575. Between 1516 and 1575 eighty towns in this area were transferred to noble jurisdiction, representing an increase of 43 per cent in the number of señorío towns in the region.

Many merchants and letrados benefited from the sales. In 1548 Charles V sold the Andalusian town of Benamejí to the financier Diego de Bernuy; the regent Juana sold the town and region of Estepa, once a property of the military orders, for 550,000 ducats to the banker Adam Centurión; Philip II in 1575 sold the town of Cantillana for 150,000 ducats to the Corsican merchant Juan Antonio Corzo, who had made his fortune in the Indies. In 1581 Philip incorporated into his royal domain the large estate of La Guardia in Toledo province; he then immediately sold it to a member of the royal council, Juan Cristóbal de Guardiola, whose family a century later obtained a marquisate to complete the process of mobility. The great nobles were also prominent purchasers: the fortune of the duke of Pastrana, whose income in 1600 was 80,000 ducats a year, was based in large part on towns and land that had previously belonged to the Church or the crown. The duke of Medina-Sidonia in 1576 paid 150,000 ducats to buy five estates to incorporate into his immense holdings near Cadiz.

The extension of the seigneurial regime, the consolidation of noble estates and the rise of latifundia in the south of the peninsula, where most new señoríos were created, received their decisive and perhaps final impetus in the sixteenth century. Though many more señoríos continued to be created in the seventeenth century, they were jurisdictional (the so-called 'sale of vassals') rather than territorial. An increase in noble power was not the only consequence of sales. Many towns managed to buy back municipal lands that they had lost, and recover control over their own administrative offices. The result was an increase in the political and economic 'liberty' of local communities, which looked to the crown for support. The sale of towns thus had two parallel consequences: on one hand, the cession of authority by the crown to the aristocracy, and on the other, the recovery of autonomy by villages that felt their future lay with a strong king rather than with the nobility.

# The mechanics of imperialism: the Spanish system

Spain's empire appeared to be at the peak of its power under Philip II, but it also had serious deficiencies that were made worse by growing debt and constant war. The king was acutely aware of problems; writing from Spain to Granvelle in 1559 he commented that 'it is absolutely impossible for me to help you, or even in this country to satisfy the most trifling needs'. The immense extent of his territories made it difficult to be in touch with events, and the space-time factor remained an insuperable barrier. From 1870 the British could govern India effectively by telegraph; Philip however had no way of conquering distance. Delays in communication held up decision-making and frustrated action. How could the king take any urgent counter-measures if, as happened in 1586, he heard of the sacking of Santo Domingo by Drake only three months after the event? The monarchy in Europe was no more accessible than America. Though Brussels might be only ten days from Madrid by letter, in 1575 Requesens was complaining that he had not heard from the king for three months. In 1567 it took the duke of Alba four and a half months to move his personnel from Spain to the Netherlands. The distance to America, of course, posed exceptional difficulties, since the voyage from Spain varied between 39 and 175 days, and the route back took from 70 to 298 days. To get to Manila in the Philippines the voyager from Acapulco would have to allow four to six months: it was a trip which, according to a seventeenth-century historian who did it, 'is enough to destroy a man, or make him unfit for anything as long as he lives'.

Efficient communication – post, transport, diplomacy – was essential to ensure control. The postal system, still controlled by the Tassis family, remained a government monopoly but from 1580 was also made available to those of the public who could afford the high rates. Transport received particular attention after the choice of Madrid as centre of government in 1561: Philip intended to improve the entire road and river network of the peninsula. When the Italian engineer Antonelli came to Spain in 1559 he proposed to construct a network of canals. Philip obtained grants from the Cortes to make the Tajo navigable as far as Toledo, a proposal that would have connected Lisbon with the heart of Castile; but the scheme eventually collapsed. The diplomatic service improved thanks to the collaboration of conscientious agents, such as Bernardino de Mendoza, whose terms as ambassador in England (1578–84) and then in France (1584–91) played a key role in the international policy of the 'Prudent King'.

A successful imperial policy depended on the ability to deploy men and money when and where required. Contact and interchange between different parts of the empire was crucial because Castile had too small a population and was economically too underdeveloped to operate an imperial programme from its own resources. Properly speaking, Spanish imperialism was really a vast exercise in international cooperation between

Spaniards, Italian soldiers and financiers, German soldiers and bankers, Flemish merchants, and innumerable people of varying profession and nationality who stood to gain from service under Europe's one super-power. If the different components of the structure failed to cooperate properly, Spanish power became vulnerable and could be paralysed. This was shown most clearly in troop movements. Under Spanish rule the duchy of Milan became a flourishing armaments centre and a prime recruiting ground; it was also the vital strategic link between the Mediterranean and northern Europe (*see* Map 3). From Milan – it was the route taken by Alba in 1567 – the army would take the Mont Cénis or the Little St Bernard pass into Savoy and then strike north through Franche-Comté and Lorraine till it reached the Netherlands; this was the famous 'Spanish Road'. To go east the troops would take the Valtelline and Engadine corridors through the Swiss territory of the Grey Leagues (called in French 'Grisons'), then follow the river Inn towards the Empire and the Habsburg hereditary lands. Both these vital routes depended heavily on the goodwill of surrounding states. From 1568, when English naval activity made the Channel – Spain's third major route to the north – unsafe, Philip was forced back on to the two land routes from Milan, making control of northern Italy an absolute essential of Spain's foreign policy, and freedom of movement through the Rhineland and the Alpine passes crucial. By the early seventeenth century Savoy had become a client of France, rendering the 'Spanish Road' unusable: Spain was reduced to dependence on the single lifeline of the Valtelline.

Deployment of money was also highly vulnerable: the seizure of the duke of Alba's pay-ships in 1568 forced Philip to turn to the land route through France, employed from 1572 to transport large quantities of bullion to the Netherlands. The French civil wars soon made the route insecure, so that after 1578 the government preferred to send money over-land to Barcelona, thence by sea to Genoa and so to the Low Countries or Germany. This became the main channel through which American silver poured into the Mediterranean in the 1580s; from Italy the coin was traded against foreign imports and made its way to the Levant and Asia. The Madrid to Barcelona route was however also at times rendered insecure by bandits who, in 1587 and again in 1613, made spectacular raids on the bullion.

The bulky transport of coin was fortunately not always necessary. As Philip wrote to Requesens in 1576: 'the surest and swiftest method of sending you money is by bills of exchange'. The regular use of bills and of the asiento system, which survived each royal bankruptcy, kept the wheels of imperialism oiled. To operate this system of credit the government relied on an international network of financiers of all nations, upon whose services Charles V had already drawn extensively. From 1516 to 1556 the Fuggers and other German financiers were the chief collaborators of the Spanish crown; from 1557 to 1627 (the dates refer to state bankruptcies) it was the turn of the Genoese, who in fact had been active since the first decade of the century. Thereafter, following the decline of Antwerp and the collapse of the Genoese fairs at Piacenza in Italy, the state was drawn into negotiations with Portuguese converso financiers whose credit was in part based on the new centre of international capitalism at Amsterdam.

America provides the most revealing insight into the successes and failures of Spanish imperialism. In theory Castile exercised absolute domination over its New World territories, both in state and in Church matters. A council of the Indies was set up in 1524 with a president and eight councillors; it had supreme jurisdiction and was the only source of law, since no lawmaking bodies or representative assemblies were allowed to exist in America. In the course of the early sixteenth century the crown began to impose its authority on lands that in practice had been developed by conquistadores or missionaries. For this the council worked through audiencias and viceroys. In America, the audiencias were administrative and judicial tribunals; the first was set up at Santo Domingo in 1511, and there were ten in America by 1550. There were two viceroys, one for New Spain, first appointed in 1535, and one for Peru, beginning in 1542. Most senior bureaucrats were appointed directly from Spain, partly to enhance control but also to provide career outlets for office-seekers from Castile. Control over trade was likewise in theory quite rigid. Shipping was normally restricted to the monopoly port of Seville for departure and arrival, and all vessels and goods had to be registered and discharged there. Because of the dangers of the Atlantic crossing, both from weather and from enemies, it became the practice for ships to sail out together in fleets in the spring, and return together in the autumn. One group, the *flota*, was destined for New Spain; the other, the *galeones*, traded to the coasts of South America and Peru.

The astonishing ability of a poor country like Spain to maintain control over America for three centuries must be balanced against the fact that in four fundamental respects this control was illusory. First, the Spaniards never managed to occupy more than a tiny fragment of the vast dimensions of the New World, and 'control' was limited to a few coastal areas and centres of settlement. Their efforts were spent exclusively in clinging on to the little that they had. Second, space-time obstacles made it essential to devolve decision-making upon officials who lived in America. It was accepted that officials could appeal to the medieval principle of 'I obey but do not comply' (*Obedezco pero no cumplo*) in order to suspend legislation that they thought inappropriate. Viceroy Mendoza of New Spain, for example, suspended the operation of the New Laws of 1542 on these grounds. At the same time Spain allowed control of the townships, the chief centres of government in America, to drift into the hands of settler oligarchies. Sale of office in America by Philip II confirmed this trend. By the early seventeenth century much of the reality of political power rested with the creole (*criollos*, American Spaniards) elite of the New World. Third, Spain had little or no military power to defend its American possessions. There were no regular Spanish forces deployed there before the 1760s, and local militia (usually, black slaves) were the only organised defence force. Naval power was non-existent, making possible the famous raids by Francis Drake in the 1580s. Only after this decade did Spain, advised by the engineer Antonelli, begin to fortify the ports and maintain naval patrols in the Caribbean and on the Pacific coast. It was, however, an expensive exercise and therefore soon discontinued, with the consequence that Caribbean territory remained an easy prey to foreign aggression in the seventeenth century. Fourth, the trade system, which in theory was a monopoly operated from Spain, was rapidly taken over by foreigners. Since the demand from American settlers for manufactured goods and textiles could not be met from Spain's limited industrial potential, the items were imported into Spain and then re-exported to the New World. From the 1570s, when some American centres were producing their own goods, demand for Spanish produce fell even further, though the demand for higher-quality foreign textiles was maintained. The result was disastrous for Spanish industry. 'Foreigners are doing the trading', commented Tomás de Mercado in 1571, 'and wealth is disappearing from the realm'. 'All the trade', complained a Seville merchant in 1578, 'is in the hands of Flemings, English and French'. By its inability to exploit the American market from its own resources, Spain condemned itself to becoming an entrepôt for foreign merchandise travelling to the Indies. This had a long-lasting impact on Spain's economy.

# The cost of empire

Spain became a great power in its own right only under Philip II. Under the emperor there was no substantial Spanish army in Europe. Spanish troops acted only as contingents in a larger force: they constituted, for example, less than a fifth of the army that sacked Rome in 1527, less than a sixth of the 40,000 serving Charles in Germany in 1546. Beyond these campaigns there were small detachments in various locations, principally the African forts, and from 1536 there was a *tercio* in Milan. The relatively small military establishment underlines the fact that the monarchy bequeathed to Philip had come into existence less through conquest than through inheritance. Even in America, as we have seen, there was little conquest by the famous conquistadors, who inevitably owed their successes to the help of native allies. The naval lifeline to America was likewise pioneered not by the crown but by private enterprise: there were no royal ships on the Atlantic route in the early century.

The limited role of Spain in the emperor's enterprises is in sharp contrast to its substantially new role under Philip. By imposing on Spain the Burgundian territories and other obligations, Charles forced it to take on leadership of an empire that neither its military nor its economic capacity had earned. Philip was well aware of the problem. After the early years, when weaknesses in border defence were already apparent, the government suffered its first major shock on the home front with the Granada revolt (1568–71), which exposed its military failings. Castile, it then appeared, had no militia; the towns lacked armouries; the coasts were ill-defended. 'Not even when the country was conquered by the Moors', complained an officer in 1575, 'was Spain in its present state. There are no horses, no weapons, nor anyone who knows how to handle them'. A serious programme of fortifications was begun, especially on the vulnerable Levant coast, where defence expenditure increased fivefold between 1577 and 1611. But in many vital respects the country was poorly equipped. For example, four-fifths of the firearms used to repress the Granada revolt were imported.

From the time of its entry into the Netherlands conflict Spain was compelled to upgrade itself dramatically into a major world power. The challenge of war was new, in the sense that till then wars had been distant ones which did not put a strain on manpower. 'As a result of the peace that has reigned here for so many years', said the council of war in 1562, 'the exercise of arms and the habits of war have greatly diminished'. Improvements were attempted in the system of recruitment, and the number of men under arms soared. Under Philip II about 9,000 men a year on average were recruited from Spain; in crisis years (such as 1580) the total could rise to 20,000. Between 1567 and 1574 nearly 43,000 men left Spain to fight in Italy and the Low Countries, at the very time of the Granada revolt. The Flanders army increased from a defence force of 13,000 in

1570 to a full-scale army of 67,000 in 1572. In 1580, when an army of 46,000 was on duty in Flanders, another numbering 37,000 marched into Portugal. In the one year 1587 it was estimated that throughout his dominions Philip II had over 100,000 men (of whom only a small proportion were Spaniards) in his pay. Military expenditure rose accordingly: the money spent on Spain's internal forces tripled between 1578 and 1594, armament spending tripled between 1581 and 1595. The treasury could not bear the burden, and wages were therefore unpaid. Reports in 1599 from all over Spain speak of troops starving and in rags. There were regular desertions; in the African forts, men fled and joined the Moors; in the Peñón de Vélez in 1596 troops had not been paid for four years.

The growth of the navy was equally dramatic. In the first half of the century Spanish naval activity was limited exclusively to the Mediterranean, where no significant naval force existed prior to 1528, when the Genoese admiral Andrea Doria contracted to serve Charles V. By the 1530s there were four galley squadrons available to Spain: the galleys of Spain (ten in 1535); Doria's Genoese ships (twenty in 1539); and those of Naples (nine in 1568) and Sicily (about twelve), financed by those realms. For reasons of cost, the government normally preferred to own only a small number of galleys directly, and to operate the rest through contracts (asientos) with men who were simultaneously entrepreneur and commander, such as Andrea Doria in Genoa or Alvaro de Bazán in Spain.

The disaster at Djerba in 1560 made the rebuilding of naval power in the Mediterranean an urgent priority, and a massive construction programme was begun. Between 1560 and 1574 about 300 galleys were built, at a total cost of over 3.5 million ducats: Philip now had under his command a naval force perhaps four times greater than his father had possessed. The growth in sea power can be measured in the great expeditions mounted by Spain: to the Peñón de Vélez in 1564 with 93 galleys, to Tunis in 1573 with 107 galleys. Between these dates there was the enormous contribution to Lepanto in 1571: for this Spain paid two-thirds of the costs, supplied one-third of the galleys and 40 per cent of the men.

The acquisition of Portugal was just as decisive in naval as in military affairs. The importance of maintaining the sea route to the Netherlands, and the increase in Protestant privateering in home waters and in the Indies, were already matters of concern: in 1570 a fleet of eight ships under Pedro Menéndez de Avilés had been formed to protect American trading lanes. Unfortunately further action was impossible, because Spain had no navy of any sort on the high seas. Immediately after 1580 a committee in Lisbon initiated a costly new programme that represented

Spain's emergence as an Atlantic power. By 1587 Philip was maintaining 106 ships in the Atlantic: from 1594 the force was known as the Armada of the Ocean Sea. This revolutionary move enabled Philip to commit himself fully to the battle of the Atlantic, and represented a decisive shift away from the Mediterranean. The defeat of the Invincible Armada in 1588, far from destroying Spanish power, increased the determination to achieve maritime supremacy, as shown by the further armadas launched in 1596 and 1597, the latter with 98 ships and 17,000 men. The navy was given its own secretariat in 1586 and its own administration in 1594, and at the same time there was a substantial increase in soldiers and sailors attached to the galleons. Between 1580 and 1598 the average annual total of men in the naval and land forces serving the crown of Castile rose from 20,000 to 50,000.

Because most troops were deployed abroad the peninsula itself was never completely secure, and the English were imaginative enough to exploit the weakness. Daring raids were made on Vigo by Drake in 1585 and 1589, and Cadiz was attacked on two spectacular occasions in 1587 and 1596. Spanish losses in the last of these were estimated at 20 million ducats, and a witness of the devastation lamented that 'no powder, no swords, no weapons of any sort' were available for defence. The vulnerability of Spain helps to place in perspective the real sources of the country's new war capability. The peninsula's limited industrial and demographic potential could never have provided by itself a firm basis for imperialism, which was rendered possible only because each part of the empire contributed on a scale that often dwarfed that of Spain. In the Mediterranean the naval contribution was always predominantly Italian. Of the 93 galleys at the Peñón in 1564, 63 were Italian; and except for that one expedition all the great campaigns – Djerba, Malta, Lepanto, Tunis – were fitted out in Italy and were largely Italian in composition. In the Atlantic the Portuguese were an important constituent of all the armadas. With manpower the picture was the same. It is doubtful if Spain had more than 20,000 of its own natives serving abroad in any one year, and auxiliary contingents were drawn primarily from Germany and Italy. Of the 67,000 troops under Alba in the Netherlands in 1572, for example, 57,000 were non-Spaniards; of the 35,500 under Farnese in 1588, only 5,000 were Spanish.

Though other nations might contribute men, arms and vessels, the cost of course fell mostly on Spain, and it was crippling. As each new theatre of war opened up, expenses mounted. The number of asientos negotiated annually with financiers rose steeply in the 1560s, to 21 in 1566 and 50 in

1567. Before 1566 the total annual military expenditure of Castile in Spain, the Mediterranean and Flanders never reached two million ducats; in the 1570s it was over four million; by 1598 it was estimated at ten million. The single most expensive campaign was the Invincible Armada, which cost ten million. But in the long run the greatest drain on finances was the war in the Netherlands, a conflict that eventually drew in both England and France and brought the Spanish treasury to its knees. Between 1567 and 1586 the government sent an average of 1.5 million ducats a year to Flanders, in all some thirty million; the total by the end of the century was some eighty million, though in the 1590s the bulk was being spent less on the effort within the Netherlands than on related areas (in 1590–1, of two million sent to Flanders, three-fourths was diverted to the war inside France).

In 1550 under Charles V the total ordinary revenue of Castile had been only 1.25 million ducats. How then did the government manage to meet the phenomenal cost of its new imperial commitments? At first every effort was taken to make each theatre of war self-financing. The Italian states contributed generously to all the Mediterranean campaigns: for Lepanto, to take one example, they paid 400,000 ducats where Spain paid 800,000. In the Netherlands, however, apart from a brief while in 1570–1 when Alba managed to meet most of his costs locally, the possibility of a self-financing campaign rapidly vanished. Moreover, as the balance of war moved towards the Atlantic, it was unlikely that the Italians would participate willingly in a conflict that appeared not to concern them. To an objection from the council of Italy in 1588 the king explained that 'except in the most urgent cases, it is not the custom to transfer the burdens of one kingdom to another, but since God has entrusted me with so many, and since in the defence of one all are preserved, it is just that all should help me'.

Inflation remained a major enemy of state finances. As early as 1561 it was reported that Philip was 'making more and more economies, desiring to provide for the future'; and in 1563 the government adjusted the interest rate in its favour. Of the four main sources of revenue enjoyed by Charles V, the crown of Aragon continued under Philip to be the least important. The Church, by contrast, increased its contribution. From 1561 the subsidio became a regular tax. Then from 1567 the papacy granted the excusado, theoretically the income from property in each parish but usually paid as a global sum by the Church. Together with the cruzada, these taxes were known as the 'Three Graces' and were paid by the whole Church throughout Spain, not merely in Castile. Their yield increased fourfold in the course of the reign, to over 1.4 million ducats a year in the 1590s. There were also other lucrative revenues tapped from the Church. Some of the income of bishoprics was taken: these *pensiones* eventually amounted to one-third of all episcopal revenues, or about 270,000 ducats a year. The crown also claimed the right to exploit vacant sees, and notoriously enjoyed the revenues of the see of Toledo during the long imprisonment of archbishop Carranza. Taken in conjunction with the many other contributions made by the Church, such as the *tercias* and the sale of lands and towns, it is likely that by the 1590s ecclesiastical sources provided well over one-fifth of government income. This confirms the complaint of a bishop in 1574 that over half the revenue of the Church was being taken by the state. It underlines moreover the unique degree of control over clerical income by the Catholic king (there was no parallel to it even in Protestant countries), and the way in which a theoretically tax-exempt body was in fact financing the state.

Since there were obstacles to raising money in the fuero provinces, the burden of imperial costs fell mainly on Castile. After his return to Spain in 1559 the king began to increase the level of taxation in Castile. As a consequence, income from the encabezamiento, customs duties and other taxes nearly tripled between 1559 and 1577, over a period when the price level rose by only 25 per cent. The Cortes were induced to concede higher levies by a threat to return to direct imposition of the alcabala, but from 1577 the higher rates failed to bring in the anticipated revenue, and the government had to reduce the levy by one million. Over the next 20 years tax income stagnated at about its 1580 level, while inflation continued to rise. This suggests that the Castilian taxpayer was unable to pay more. The financial crisis caused by the defeat of the Armada in 1588, however, persuaded the Cortes in 1590 to grant a special new subsidy of eight million ducats, to be collected every six years and to be paid in addition to the servicios granted every three years. Known as the millones, this new imposition was levied on four basic foodstuffs (meat, wine, oil and vinegar) and became widely hated since it struck at the very means of subsistence. It gave the impression, moreover, that yet another burden had been placed on the taxpayer, when arguably it did little more than restore to the crown what it had lost by the fall in tax income since 1577. A subsequent increase in the millones in 1596 did nothing to endear the tax to the public.

Inefficient collection, and mortgaging of revenue, rendered much tax income insecure. Fortunately, America was now beginning to pour out its treasures, with the development of Potosí in Bolivia and Zacatecas and Guanajuato in Mexico. In the first half of the century bullion for the crown

had averaged 220,000 ducats a year; by the 1560s this sum had quadrupled; and by the 1590s it had increased twelvefold. It was derived not
only from the royal *quinto* or fifth, but also from American taxes such as
the alcabala, customs duties and the cruzada. The total officially received
by the government during the reign came to over 64.5 million ducats. In
addition, large sums were seized from private traders, particularly in 1566
(when 400,000 ducats was taken), 1583 and 1587, the owners in each case
being compensated with juros. The total seized in this way during the reign
amounted to eight million ducats. In the best years American bullion represented little more than a fifth of all state income, but its real importance
lay in the fact that it was hard cash, guaranteed to arrive year after year
and internationally negotiable, thus creating an invaluable fund of credit.

The needs of the monarchy were so pressing that Philip had to resort to
special expedients, which were accepted at first as exceptional but later
became regular practice. Sales of common lands (baldíos) reached their
peak in 1587, when they brought 357,500 ducats to the treasury. Sales of
towns reached their peak in 1582, when they produced 407,870 ducats.
The sale of jurisdictions ironically also involved the alienation of revenue,
because in many of the towns the new owner was granted jurisdiction over
the alcabala. Between 1560 and 1598 this benefited the crown by 665,500
ducats from sales, but the long-term loss in revenue was incalculable.
There were two other highly important fiscal expedients: sales of nobility
and sales of office. Privileges of hidalguía were offered for sale from 1552,
but only 72 hidalguías were actually sold over the period up to 1599,
showing that this was not a popular way to achieve noble status. Sale of
office was far more successful: the practice began in about 1540 but
reached its peak under Philip II. Most sales were made in cities and towns
where oligarchies wished to tighten their control over political life. In one
year alone, 1567, the crown obtained 270,000 ducats from this source. In
addition to such measures the king also asked his nobles and clergy for free
gifts (*donativos*) and loans: in 1591, for example, the Castilian nobility
were asked for a loan of 800,000 ducats.

Philip II's total annual income from regular sources more than tripled
between 1559 and 1598, from about three million to 10.5 million ducats.
Over the same period the burden on the ordinary Castilian taxpayer
increased by some 430 per cent, at a time when nominal wages had risen
by only 80 per cent. Castile under Philip was therefore suffering not only
a price revolution but a tax revolution as well. Up to about 1580 the tax
rise may have been possible to support because of increased agricultural
output, but thereafter the burden was undoubtedly heavy.

Despite all the effort and financial sacrifice, at no time did Philip succeed in raising enough cash to cover his expenses, and the state had to declare 'bankruptcies' in 1557, 1560, 1576 and 1596. The second suspension, in November 1560, was a short-lived attempt to pay off debts in juros, still at 5 per cent, on the House of Trade at Seville. Creditors, however, preferred their annuities to be drawn on the government rather than on one of its agencies. The treasury managed to survive through the 1560s even though interest payments for juros were at a staggering level and continued to rise sharply at each bankruptcy: in 1565 payments took up over 84 per cent of income.

When Philip came to the throne in 1556, over two-thirds of ordinary state income was already mortgaged at source, normally to holders of juros. Since no government of the time ever aimed to balance income and expenditure neatly – an operation rendered impossible anyway by imprecise accounting methods – budget figures for the reign are seldom reliable. All that is certain is that debt accumulated as imperial costs rose, leading in April 1574 to a calculation by the acting head of the council of finance, Juan de Ovando, that current debts were some 74 millions ducats and the year's income only 5.6 million.

These desperate straits, which provoked outspoken criticism in the Cortes of November 1574, encouraged Philip to suspend payments again in September 1575. The decree was deliberately calculated to break the stranglehold of the Genoese on Spanish finance: 'they have destroyed our incomes and our way of life', a Spanish financier commented. The measure helped the emergence of native Spanish financiers, among them Simón Ruiz of Medina del Campo and Juan de Maluenda of Burgos. But the sack of Antwerp by Spanish mutineers in 1576 forced the crown back into the hands of international financiers: only their credit could rescue the treasury. In December 1577 Philip issued the *medio general*, a compromise agreement which cancelled the September 1575 decree and promised to pay off the Genoese partly by creating juros, partly by selling jurisdictions. The continuing civil wars in France, which disrupted trading at the big banking centre of Lyon, likewise obliged Philip to negotiate bullion transfers through the Italian banking centre, dominated by the Genoese, at Piacenza.

Philip attempted once again, by the suspension of November 1596, to free himself from the Genoese; this time he resorted to Portuguese converso financiers. The Genoese hurriedly came to terms, promised to advance further sums at the very low interest of 10 per cent and in return obtained another medio general (November 1597), which created seven million ducats of juros. The reign ended with an endless spiral of government debt, as more and more of its income sources became pledged to the payment of annuities. A state juro debt of 36 million ducats in 1557 had increased by 1598 to 85 million; at this latter date interest payments exceeded 4.6 million a year, in contrast to the annual 349,000 ducats paid at the accession of Charles V. Between 1516 and 1598, therefore, juro payments had increased by 1,326 per cent; in the emperor's reign the increase was 250 per cent, in that of his son it was 528 per cent.

## The economy 1530–1580

In the middle years of the sixteenth century Spain was basking in the warm sunshine of success. The government was in debt, but this was common in all western European states. By contrast, thanks to income from America and its own key position in the European political system, Spain was enjoying an unprecedented expansion. Population increase was a major stimulus to economic activity, by creating demand for food and services. The arrival of bullion raised inflation levels and prices, but it also increased profits and boosted trade and production. More money was in circulation, and as a consequence the rate of interest tended to fall.

The most visible evidence of expansion was the boom in agriculture. Under the pressure of more mouths to feed, uncultivated land was put under the plough. In the countryside around Valladolid during the 1550s, arable increased at the expense of pasture. In the rural areas of Segovia a modest population increase, of 24 per cent between 1531 and 1591, pushed up production levels: common lands were converted to arable, hill slopes were deforested, land sales increased. 'Even the wilderness disappeared', wrote Florián de Ocampo in 1552, 'as everything in Castile was dug up for sowing'. In the valley of Bureba, north of Burgos, an area covering some thousand square kilometres, output between about 1560 and 1580 expanded by 26 per cent in wheat, 51 per cent in wine and 54 per cent in rye.

Industry expanded over the same period. The chief woollen manufactures were at Segovia, Toledo and Cuenca, with lesser centres at Ávila, Córdoba, Baeza and Úbeda. In 1552, according to a report by the Cortes of Castile, 'it was striking to walk the length of Segovia and Cuenca and see the application, with everyone working in the production of wool'. American and Castilian money was invested in the enterprises, which served the demands of a growing population at home and a settler class abroad. The outstanding centre was Segovia, which by about 1580 had some 600 looms and produced about 13,000 pieces of cloth a year. In the years before 1520 a domestic system of manufacture was common here, but as output increased a factory system became more normal after 1570. In silk the principal area of production was the kingdom of Granada, where hundreds of Morisco communities cultivated the silkworm as their sole cash crop.

The boom in Castile was a temporary phenomenon. Food output increased solely because more land was put under the plough, not because the yield per acre had been raised. After mid-century, demand from America fell off, and demographic crises in Spain began to check population growth. In 1557–8 there was an epidemic accompanied by poor harvests; in 1565–6 a general epidemic caused 16,000 deaths in Saragossa and mortality elsewhere in the north of the peninsula; in 1580 an epidemic in the western regions carried off queen Anna and caused 35,000 deaths in Lisbon; in 1590 an epidemic in Catalonia caused 11,790 deaths in Barcelona. The change can be seen vividly in the communities of Bureba. During the plague of 1565–6 some villages lost half their population, and in the decade after 1586 the whole area lost about one-fifth of its people, many simply through emigration because of financial hardship.

In the very sectors where profits were most quickly made and investment was therefore highest, that is in the raw wool and textile markets, there were disquieting signs that Castile was losing control over its own destiny. The boom period was the last successful epoch of Castile's own bourgeoisie, a small group of merchants and financiers whose fortunes were concentrated in northern Castile and linked to the international wool trade. Their business was conducted principally through Medina del Campo (whose trade fairs were the biggest in Spain in mid-century), and Burgos, chief exit for wool and seat of the powerful consulado. From these cities a network of connections reached out to other trading and manufacturing cities: to Bilbao and Santander on the northern coast, Barcelona and Alicante on the east, to Cuenca and Seville, and above all to the textile cities of Toledo and Segovia. Among the Castilian capitalists who thrived in these years were the traders Maluenda, Bernuy and Curiel of Burgos, and Simón Ruiz of Medina del Campo, best known of them all because his family papers have survived. So long as the dimensions of Spain's trading system remained as they were in the early century, these native capitalists were capable of playing an important part.

Castile, and with it Spain, was however moving more and more into a larger world system. The three great outlets for Burgos wool were Flanders, Italy and France, in that order of importance. The Flanders market was particularly important, absorbing about 60 per cent of Spain's total wool output. The Netherlands also supplied Spain with Baltic wheat, naval supplies and textiles, a cogent reason for Spain to keep hold of the rebellious provinces. Control over external trade was exercised principally by merchants in Antwerp and Genoa, the chief foreign ports used by Spain and Europe's most advanced centres of financial capitalism, with which Spanish traders could seldom compete. Castile was in this way only one component, and by no means a dominant one, of the international credit system described by Tomás de Mercado in his *Suma de Tratos* (1568). The fairs at Medina, Mercado wrote, were 'attended by people from all parts, from Seville, Lisbon, Burgos, Barcelona, Flanders, Florence, to deal in insurance or exchange: a mountain of paper, for you see almost no metal but only bills'. Mercado saw clearly that Spain was a junior participant; even for trade to America, he said, 'to take out insurance you had to do so in Lisbon, Lyon and Flanders, because of inadequate insurance in Seville'. The initially weak position of Spain's capitalists was rapidly undermined in the sixteenth century by three main developments. The enormous expansion of the American trade created a capital market in which Castile's role became much smaller; the extension of Spanish imperial commitments created a demand for credit which Spain's financiers alone could never satisfy; and the permission given to foreign financiers from 1566 to export silver from the peninsula, encouraged them to view Spain less as a country in which to invest than as one from which metallic wealth could be easily extracted through trade.

From the late 1560s these developments changed Spain from a country that might have become rich through its imperial connections and its access to America, into a nation whose economic fate was dictated by international capitalism. The American market and the vulnerable Spanish market attracted manufactured goods into the country. 'The debit of Castile in European countries became greater than its credit', reported Mercado, 'in respect of the many goods which entered from all parts for internal consumption and the Indies trade'. He criticised 'our senseless subjection to foreigners in giving them control of all the most important things in the country, something that informed people have lamented for many years. The best properties are theirs; the biggest estates, the bulk of the kingdom, are in their hands'. The most glaring example of foreign control was the commerce of Seville. As merchants of all nations realised the potential of direct investment in American trade, Andalusia became a hub of international activity. From about 35,000 people in the 1480s, Seville increased to over 50,000 in 1533 and about 120,000 in the 1590s, making it for a while the largest city in the peninsula, with a population level it maintained until the epidemic of 1647. Between 1562 and 1608 the number of vessels on the Indies route increased by 176 per cent, the volume of their tonnage by 238 per cent. With the new surge of bullion production from Potosí and Zacatecas, the quantities of silver entering Seville tripled between the 1560s and the 1590s. Italian, Burgundian, French and other foreign merchants began to dominate the thriving business community:

*Toda España, Italia y Francia*
*Vive por este arenal*
*Porque es plaza general*
*De todo trato y ganancia*
*(all Spain, Italy and France depend on these shores, the marketplace of all trade and profit)*

wrote Lope de Vega of the life of Seville. The economic life of late sixteenth-century Castile, though generated in part by native resources in wool and agricultural produce, was ultimately fuelled by American bullion and international finance's interest in that bullion. The boom in Seville, like the credit boom in Medina and Burgos, was triggered more by external investment than by internal success. Seville's trade flourished, but most of it was in foreign goods; bullion poured back to Spain, but most went to alien merchants. Castile was in this way ushered into a period of superficial prosperity which had few roots in its own resources and which perceptive observers quickly recognised to be a delusion.

## The Moriscos in the sixteenth century

After 1502 the Mudéjars in Castile were officially Christianised as Moriscos, but in Aragon they were left unmolested until forcibly converted in their thousands during the germanías in Valencia in 1520–2. Forced baptisms were usually regarded as invalid, but the authorities after 1522 were reluctant to let the new Moriscos revert to their old religion. Early in 1525 the Inquisition ruled that the baptisms were valid. It now seemed incongruous to tolerate unconverted Mudéjars elsewhere in the crown of Aragon. Though many Aragonese nobles resisted interference with the religion of their vassals, steps were taken to persuade the latter to convert. Eventually, in November 1525, Charles V issued a decree ordering the conversion of all Mudéjars of the crown of Aragon in Valencia by the end of the year and elsewhere by the end of January 1526.

From 1526 the Muslim religion no longer existed in Spain: all Mudéjars were now Moriscos. Writing to the pope in December that year, Charles V admitted that 'the conversion was not wholly voluntary among many of them, and since then they have not been instructed in our holy faith'. Considerable efforts were subsequently made to evangelise the new 'converts'. Among the prelates leading the campaign was the humanist Antonio de Guevara, who laboured in both Valencia and Granada. At the same time the activities of the Inquisition were restricted. In 1526 the Morisco leaders of Aragon obtained from the crown and from inquisitor general Manrique a secret concordia or agreement by which, in return for 40,000 ducats and submission to baptism, the Moriscos would be free from prosecution by the tribunal for 40 years and be permitted to retain some of their customs. The concordia was made public in 1528, the year when the Aragonese Cortes at Monzón petitioned the emperor to prevent the Inquisition prosecuting Moriscos until they had been instructed in the faith. The concern of the nobles in the Cortes had an explanation: the Moriscos were their tenants and enjoyed their protection. During the Cortes at Monzón in the years 1533, 1537 and 1542 loud complaints were raised against attempts by the Inquisition to confiscate land from Moriscos, since that would have been to deprive the real owners, the feudal nobility. Attempts by the government to disarm the Moriscos, as in Valencia in 1563, were also resisted. In the kingdom of Granada, where there was no such protection for the converts, events took a different turn.

In occupied Granada the Moriscos were some 54 per cent of the total population, the highest ratio in the peninsula. Direct pressure of land-hungry Christians on a free Morisco people created tension between the two communities and provoked grievances in at least three major respects. First, as part of the process of land settlement after the conquest, Moriscos were required to present proofs of the title to their land. Those unable to present a title were fined, and if they could not pay the fine their lands were sold. In this way some 100,000 hectares passed into the hands of Christian officials during the period 1559–68 alone. Second, attempts were made to take over the principal industry of the Granada countryside, silk production. The worst abuses were committed through the illegal import from neighbouring Murcia of raw silk, which was cheaper because it was less heavily taxed. The imports undercut and ruined the Morisco producers. The third and most deeply felt of all the grievances arose out of the religious programme. Many officials, who felt that the cultural customs of the Moriscos were the principal barrier to conversion, encouraged petty persecution and active social discrimination. Finally in 1565 the clergy met in synod in Granada and advised the king that the old policy of patient evangelisation should be replaced by one of radical repression. Moriscos, they said, should in future be forbidden the use of their language, their dress, their literature, their dances and their traditional rites. Their houses should be regularly inspected; judicial officers must be stricter; children should be brought up away from the influence of their parents. A royal decree giving effect to these proposals was published in 1567. The Moriscos petitioned against it and one of their leaders, Francisco Núñez Muley, wrote a memorial outlining the grievances of his community: 'every day we are mistreated in every way, by both secular officials and clergy, all of which is so obvious that it needs no proof'.

The authorities for their part were alarmed at the security threat posed by the Moriscos. It was well known that the governments of Morocco and Turkey were in contact with them. Prophecies circulating in the villages foretold the conquest of Spain by Islam. Morisco bandits were active throughout the eastern part of the peninsula, and north African pirates were welcomed into the coastal areas. As a result attempts were made to disarm the population, but with limited success. Two generations of tension exploded finally into the revolt that began on Christmas Eve of 1568.

The rebellion, which held out successfully for two years and was led initially by an official who gave up his name of Hernando de Córdoba for the Muslim one of Aben Humeya, drew its support primarily from the villages of the Alpujarra district, where silk production was concentrated. It gained little support from the Muslim quarter of Granada, the Albaicín. Numbering only 4,000 at the beginning, the rebels by 1569 amounted perhaps to 30,000, the bulk of the adult Morisco population in the region. With Spain's best troops away in Flanders under Alba, the threat to internal security was serious. At the height of the campaign, nevertheless, the royal armies under Don Juan of Austria as commander-in-chief were able to muster some 20,000 men. It was a ferocious war, with massacres on both sides. Particularly notable was the resistance put up against Don Juan in February 1570 by the town of Galera. When it fell all its 2,500 inhabitants, including women and children, were slaughtered; the town was razed and salt poured over it. Philip II's concern arose not least from the support given to the rebels by the Turks, and from the realisation that if the Moriscos of Aragon and Valencia were also to rise, the very existence of Christian Spain would be threatened. In 1570 the Venetian ambassador reported widespread panic in Valencia. In the event the help received by the Alpujarra Moriscos – some 4,000 Turks and Berbers fought among the 25,000 insurgents in spring 1570 – was not enough to turn the tide. The sultan was more preoccupied with the conquest of Cyprus, the Algerians with their reconquest of Tunis: both these were achieved in 1570.

Even before the end of the rebellion the government had decided on a brutally simple solution to the Granada problem: the uprooting of whole sections of the population. A decree of 1 November 1570 gave it effect. Within the month over 50,000 Moriscos were forever expelled from their homeland and resettled in Castile, western Andalusia and Extremadura. Possibly a quarter of these died from the harsh conditions of their departure. Over the whole period 1569–73 it is likely that some 80,000 were driven out, and expulsions continued well after these years, as in 1584. Taking into account the further impact of deaths and refugees, the kingdom of Granada may have lost up to 120,000 people. It was a province laid desolate. Some 50,000 Old Christians, most of them from elsewhere in Andalusia, were resettled on Morisco land; but they lacked the agricultural techniques of the previous cultivators and the Jesuit Pedro de León, who worked among them, criticised them as shiftless people completely lacking in the moral quality of the old Moriscos. A third of the 400 towns and villages vacated remained empty, and the overall level of population in the province fell by 28 per cent between 1561 and 1591.

For both Moriscos and Christians the sixteenth century was a period of cultural confrontation. This was aggravated by the Granada expulsions, which brought into many Castilian communities a Morisco presence they had not hitherto known. Where Castile had about 20,000 Mudéjars in 1501, by the end of the century there were over 100,000 Moriscos. Castilians began to share the community tensions that had so far been restricted to the south and east of the peninsula. One of the last vestiges of cultural coexistence and tolerance was the romance *Abencerraje y Jarifa* (1565), a story of love between Christian and Moor, which even when it was written was at variance with social reality. Throughout the peninsula uneasy coexistence was disturbed by regular violence and fears of violence. Morisco banditry became more extensive, particularly in Valencia, and there were cases even around Valladolid. From 1585 to 1588 the conflicts in northern Aragon between Old Christian montañeses and Morisco peasants flared into massacres. As hostility increased in the majority community, so did racial antipathy.

At no time in all this period did the religious effort slacken: missions were preached, schools founded. Juan de Ribera, the prelate who became archbishop of Valencia in 1568, initiated schemes to make work among Moriscos more congenial to the clergy, and founded a college for Morisco children. For the 43 years that he held this see, Ribera made every effort to attend to the needs of the Moriscos. There was also religious coercion, directed mainly by the Inquisition. From 1526 there had been an Inquisition in Granada, transferred from Jaén. Its activity, like that of other tribunals, was relatively mild in the early century. From mid-century, and in particular from the late 1560s, it intensified its work. In the three-quarters of a century preceding their expulsion, Moriscos were the principal victims of the Inquisitions of Granada, Saragossa and Valencia. In the 12 autos de fe held in Granada between 1550 and 1580, Moriscos were over 78 per cent of the accused. In the tribunal of Saragossa between 1560 and 1614, they made up 56.5 per cent of the accused. They inevitably hated the Holy Office, perceiving it as 'presided over by the devil and informed by falsehood'. In 1542 the Cortes at Monzón claimed that Moriscos were fleeing abroad 'because of the fear they have of the Inquisition'. Afraid of losing their vassals, the lords persuaded the Inquisition to compromise. Accordingly, in 1556 the Moriscos of Aragon agreed to pay an annual tax to the tribunal of Saragossa, on the condition that those brought to trial would suffer no confiscation of property. The Moriscos of Valencia made a similar agreement in 1571.

Though a few Moriscos were assimilated and became genuine Christians, most remained in conflict with the established faith. In Granada and Valencia Arabic was still spoken, circumcision was common, and Muslim clergy, the *alfaquis*, circulated among the people. In Castile and much of Aragon, by contrast, coexistence with the Christian community had diluted traditional practices, and the survival of Islam owed more to community solidarity and verbal transmission of customs. In general, Moriscos were strongly repelled by the doctrines of the Trinity and the divinity of Jesus, and felt extreme repugnance at the sacraments of baptism, penitence and the Eucharist. Much of their hostility became directed specifically at the figure of the priest, who was their principal contact with Christianity. Priests were the primary targets of the rebels in the Alpujarra uprisings. All the outward practices of Islam were still kept: prayers, the great fast of Ramadan, ritual ablutions, prohibition of foods.

The fundamental issue for Christian clergy was whether converts should also be required to jettison the broad range of completely different cultural habits. There were basic differences in the method of killing animals, in diet, in hygiene (the synod of Guadix noted in 1544 that 'it is suspicious to take baths, especially on Thursday and Friday night'), in festivities (the *zambra* dance), in dress and in language (the form of Castilian spoken by Moriscos was known as *aljamía*). In 1538, a Morisco of Toledo was arrested by the Inquisition and accused of 'playing music at night, dancing the *zambra* and eating couscous', all prima facie evidence of heresy. While demanding that Moriscos shed all these cultural traits, however, Old Christians refused to make corresponding concessions, and continued to discriminate against them at every level. The statutes of limpieza de sangre were applied against them, as they had been against Jewish conversos. After 1552 Moriscos could not normally become familiars of the Inquisition, after 1573 they could not enter the priesthood. A tiny minority managed to enter private professions, notably as doctors; apart from this, nearly all were denied access to public position and thus to status. Many turned to commerce and industry. While the bulk of the Moriscos of the crown of Aragon were depressed peasantry, there is little doubt that many in Granada and Castile were of comfortable means, and some were very rich. In remoter areas they were able to build up thriving communities. The most striking of these was Hornachos (Extremadura), a flourishing and almost entirely Morisco town with 4,800 inhabitants in the 1580s. Its real estate was valued at 122,300 ducats and in 1590 it purchased its own jurisdiction from Philip II for 30,000 ducats. Tolerated by its neighbours solely out of fear, in 1610 the town emigrated in its entirety and regrouped itself in Salé in Morocco.

By the end of the sixteenth century social and religious tensions seemed to have rendered assimilation or coexistence impossible. Among some Morisco communities there were, particularly in the year 1577, strong millenarian hopes of liberation. In these circumstances the security threat took on sinister proportions. The evidence of banditry, of piracy and of contact with the Turks and the French Protestants, was incontrovertible. The most disturbing aspect of all was the rapid rate of increase in the Morisco population. In Granada the continuing rise in their numbers was the chief reason for the expulsions of 1584. In Aragon there had been 5,674 Moriscos in 1495 but in 1610 they were 14,190, a fifth of the total population. In Valencia the result of censuses made in 1565 and 1609 suggested that the Old Christians increased in number by 44.7 per cent and the Moriscos by a remarkable 69.7 per cent, a difference explicable in part by the tendency of Morisco girls to marry at a younger age than Old Christians.

Various extreme solutions were proposed, such as removing all children from parents, forbidding marriages or even castration (suggested by Martin Salvatierra, bishop of Segorbe). The view that finally obtained most support was for expulsion. In Lisbon in 1581 Philip II convened a special committee to discuss the matter, and in September 1582 the council of state, after carefully weighing all the factors and interests involved, formally proposed a general expulsion. The Church and the Inquisition supported the decision. International events, and considerable opposition from the nobles of Valencia, delayed action for a quarter of a century; but the peace of Vervins in 1598 at last opened the way to implementation.

## Spain and the Counter-Reformation

Philip II's authority was possibly more complete over the Church than over any other institution in Spain. There was no single 'Spanish Church' (though we shall continue to use the term here): the clergy and bishops in the crown of Castile, normally headed by the see of Toledo, were separate from those of the crown of Aragon, who met under the leadership of the see of Tarragona. In numbers and wealth, the Spanish Church was the third largest in Christendom after those of Italy and France. At the end of the sixteenth century, after a reorganisation of dioceses carried out by Philip, there were in Castile five archbishops and thirty bishops, and in the crown of Aragon three archbishops with fifteen bishops. Subject to these was a clerical population in 1591 of some 40,000 secular priests and 50,000 religious of both sexes. On this basis clergy were little more than 1.2 per cent of the total population, but the distribution was extremely uneven, with a heavy concentration in the major towns and very few in remote rural areas.

The Catholic Church in Spain had, without any upheaval comparable to the Reformation in northern Europe, achieved a position of almost complete independence from Rome. The crown already controlled the Church in Sicily through an eleventh-century privilege called the 'Monarchia Sicula', by which the king himself acted as papal legate. Then in 1504 and 1508 two papal bulls granted the 'Patronato Real' or full royal patronage over ecclesiastical finance and appointments in the New World, with the result that the Church in America became directly subordinate not to the Spanish bishops but to the crown alone, and its affairs were dealt with in the council of the Indies. In Castile, royal claims were voiced in a lecture by the rector of Salamanca university in 1487: 'Provisions made to churches in Castile and León by the vicar of Christ are null without the consent of our kings.' After several sharp conflicts the right to nominate all prelates was confirmed to Charles V by the pope in September 1523. Thereafter the crown controlled all important offices in the Church in both Castile and Aragon; by extension, it could also dispose of much revenue. Clergy in dispute could still exercise their right to appeal to Rome, but the many royal decrees restricting this were eventually confirmed by one of October

1572, which forbade any foreign jurisdiction over Spaniards in ecclesiastical cases. As a result the pope was virtually deprived of any juridical authority in Spain, and the crown became absolute master of the Church. To justify this situation, unique in the Catholic world, jurists evolved a doctrine of 'regalism', which asserted that the crown alone controlled Church affairs.

Thanks to its uninterrupted evolution over the centuries the Spanish Church was powerful and wealthy, but the distribution of wealth was very uneven. Its holdings in land were smaller than often thought, perhaps one-sixth of Spanish territory by the end of the seventeenth century, usually with full jurisdiction. Donations and wise investments in the course of the sixteenth century created wealth in other areas: by the late seventeenth century Church institutions owned one-third of urban property in Seville, over half in Saragossa, and three-fourths in Madrid; at the same time they were usually the largest group of investors in municipal bonds (censos) throughout the country. At the upper end of the scale some sees and monasteries were fabulously rich: there were prelates who controlled cities (Palencia, Santiago), castles and extensive estates. The richest see in Spain, Toledo, had an annual revenue in 1519 of over 66,000 ducats, controlled some 1,900 benefices, exercised jurisdiction over 19,000 vassals and commanded a score of fortresses; a hundred years later its annual income was over 200,000 ducats. This picture is modified if we remember that possibly a third of most episcopal income was spent on charitable welfare, that the state took a high proportion of revenue and that the wealth was not typical: in 1534 about 40 per cent of the sees in the peninsula had incomes of 5,000 ducats or less. Extremes of wealth and poverty, uneducated clergy and extensive abuse of clerical status were commonplace in the sixteenth-century Spanish Church and underline the fact that no significant reform had ever been undertaken. Not until the reign of Philip II was a determined effort made to restructure and reinvigorate Spanish Catholicism.

There were three main channels of reform dating from the end of the fifteenth century: the attempts of the religious orders, aided by pope and king, to change their structure in favour of the Observance; active intervention by the crown to reform both the orders and the diocesan structure; and attempts by the papacy, culminating in the Council of Trent (1545–63), to reform the whole Church. Virtually all these channels concentrated on reform of clergy rather than laity, and benefited from the spiritual movements of the fifteenth century as well as from early humanism. The changes they achieved were, unfortunately, very limited in scope.

All previous projects for reform were drawn together in the work of Philip II. His proposals to create new sees in Spain in accordance with changes in population were part of a general programme that he applied also to the Netherlands. Burgos was made into an archbishopric in 1572; Valladolid, formerly in the diocese of Palencia, was made a bishopric in 1595; and in the crown of Aragon six new sees were created. A guiding principle of the king was that Spanish clergy should not be subject to foreign jurisdiction but should have their own superiors. In 1561, accordingly, the Cistercians in Spain were removed from obedience to the (French) abbot of Cîteaux; and similar rules were applied to the Trinitarians, Carmelites and other orders. Philip was also firmly committed to uprooting Conventuals from Spain, but his proposals, set out in a memorandum of 1561 to Rome, did not coincide with Tridentine norms. In 1563, with the support of the Cortes of Monzón, he outlined to the pope the disgraceful state of some monasteries and threatened to 'depopulate them rather than let them continue living as they do'. Not until 1566, when Pius V became pope, was the Spanish programme approved. Thereafter the king proceeded with elimination of the Conventuals, reform of the orders by suppressing some and merging others and abolition of several religious houses. Force was used, and there was bitter opposition in some areas. The result, however, was a conscious nationalising of the religious impulse, and a firm emphasis on community and contemplative life. The most remarkable product of this reform period was the Observant order founded by Teresa of Ávila in the 1580s as the Discalced Carmelites.

The nationalising of Spanish Catholicism, carried out partly for political reasons and partly as a defence against heresy, was enforced by the apparatus of the Inquisition. Over the same period there was an unprecedented drive to reform the clergy and convert the people to the religion of the universal Church.

As we have seen, there was no reform of the Church in the time of the Catholic Monarchs. By 1550 the failings that the Reformation in Europe had tried to combat were also common in Spain. Clergy often held more than one post at a time, on the grounds that one benefice alone was not enough to support a priest. Absenteeism was therefore frequent (in 1549 in the diocese of Barcelona only six out of sixty-seven parish priests were resident); concubinage was widespread (in 1562, 20 per cent of the Barcelona parish clergy lived with women); clergy were notoriously ignorant and illiterate. Reforming bishops were unable to introduce reforms in so far as they themselves were non-resident: the inquisitor Fernando de Valdés visited his see of Oviedo only once between 1527 and 1539, and was almost permanently absent from his see of Seville (1546–68); cardinal Mendoza of Burgos (1550–66) did not introduce reforms until he took up residence in 1564. Where bishops wished to reform, they were often impeded by the fact that laymen were owners of the benefices: in Oviedo in mid-century the bishop reported that 'all the monasteries in this diocese are lay foundations', making interference impossible. In Mallorca in 1590 only 40 out of 500 benefices in the island, in Orense only 70 out of 700 benefices, were in the gift of the bishop or the pope: the rest were controlled by lay lords or monasteries. The ignorance of the clergy was universally recognised. In Santiago de Compostela in 1543 the diocesan visitor reported that 'parishioners suffer greatly from the ignorance of their curates and rectors', in Navarre in 1544 ignorant clergy 'cause great harm to the consciences of these poor people'. Many rural parishes lacked clergy, particularly in Catalonia and the Basque country, where ignorance of the language made it impossible for priests to communicate with their flock.

The situation of the people followed inevitably from that of their pastors. Spanish religion of the early sixteenth century was still in all essentials late mediaeval: an easy-going combination of vague theology and irregular practice, with a heavy emphasis on local rituals and folk religion. In remote districts such as Galicia, Asturias and Navarre the problem was critical. In 1510 a local writer denounced the prevalence of witchcraft in the popular religion of Navarre; Alfonso de Castro in his *Adversus haereses* (Lyon, 1546) repeated the accusation. In Oviedo the Dominicans had been at work since 1518; but a canon of the cathedral, writing in 1568 to ask Francisco Borja to send his Jesuits, could say: 'What we have here in Spain are very Indies, where great service to God our Lord may be done. . . . The clergy and curates are, in general, idiots, because the benefices are very poor. And so this land is in extreme need of the work of good labourers, such as we trust are those in the Society of Jesus'. In the same year another correspondent appealed to the Jesuits: 'There are no Indies where you will suffer greater dangers and miseries, or which could more need to hear the word of God, than these Asturias'.

The foundation of the Society of Jesus by the Basque noble Ignatius of Loyola in 1534 brought into existence the most dynamic of the new sixteenth-century orders. At first overwhelmingly Spanish in its composition and leadership (the first three generals of the society were Spaniards), the order was warmly supported by Philip II and grew rapidly in the peninsula, where it undertook important missionary work. Only after the 1580s did conflicts arise over Philip's attempts to nationalise the order, which he feared was passing into Italian control. Jesuits obtained powerful patronage in Spain, notably after their ranks were joined by Francisco Borja, duke of Gandía and viceroy of Catalonia, who rose to become third general. Outstanding for their work of conversion among the upper classes and their intellectual contribution to the Council of Trent, the Jesuits in Spain also initiated a programme of missions among the common people. The Jesuit Pedro de León, who worked all over Andalusia and Extremadura, wrote that 'since I began in the year 1582, and up to now in 1615, there has not been a single year in which I have not been on some mission, and on two or three in some years'. The need was stressed by an earlier Jesuit, reporting on the inhabitants of villages near Huelva: 'many live in caves, without priests or sacraments; so ignorant that some cannot make the sign of the cross; in their dress and way of life very like Indians'.

Reform attempts in Spain were of long standing, as the example of Cisneros shows. In 1540 the new reforming bishop of Pamplona ordered the preaching of a sermon on Sundays, reservation of the sacrament on the altar, the keeping of records, and so on. These piecemeal local efforts were reinforced by the authority of the Council of Trent, which convened in three sessions under papal direction. The last session (1561–3) benefited from the collaboration of Philip and was heavily dominated by Spaniards in both number and quality: foremost among the theologians present was Diego Laínez, second general of the Jesuits. Contrary to what is often maintained, the decrees of the council were accepted immediately in Spain: ratified by the pope in January 1564, they were issued by Philip II on 12 July as the law of the land.

By confirming previous trends, notably in the reform of religious orders, and by its own innovations, Trent revolutionised Spanish Catholicism. Of the significant material changes, the first was the abolition of variations in liturgy and the imposition of the Roman missal and breviary (decreed by Rome in 1568 and 1570). Distinctive and curious local ways of saying mass in, for example, Mallorca and Asturias, were phased out. By 1571, the nuncio reported to Rome, all the dioceses and orders (Toledo with its ancient Mozarabic rite was a permitted exception) had accepted the changes. This was certainly optimistic, for the 'nuevo rezado' (new way of praying) was not accepted without murmurs, particularly since the new missal involved the abolition of many local saints and feast-days in favour of saints recognised by the universal Church. In 1586 in the see of Mondoñedo all pre-Tridentine prayer books had to be collected and burnt. In 1588 it was reported from Mallorca that less than a third of the clergy in the diocese were using the new Roman rite, over 15 years after its introduction. Not until 1616 did the church of San Lázaro in Palencia bother to stock one of the new missals.

Secondly, the authority of bishops was strengthened. Fortified by Trent, prelates such as cardinal Quiroga in Toledo and bishop Vich in Mallorca were able to impose their wishes on parish clergy and bring about significant changes in clerical practice. Philip supported this by ordering in a decree of July 1564 that provincial synods be held regularly. In 1565 they were held in Toledo, Santiago, Tarragona, Valencia, Saragossa and Granada; but thereafter, with the outstanding exception of the Catalan province of Tarragona, the practice decayed. One reason was that bishops had to struggle to assert their powers, mainly against their cathedral chapters, which everywhere opposed their ancient rights to the new pretensions of the bishops. At a local level, episcopal authority was exercised through a strict division of the faithful into parishes, each with its own clergy and organisation.

The third material change was in education. Trent had laid particular emphasis on the need for seminaries to train an educated clergy. There was, however, considerable opposition to this programme in Spain, where many colleges for clergy were already in existence and where cathedral chapters objected to the expense of new foundations which might duplicate their work. The result was that from 1563 to the end of the century only twenty Tridentine seminaries were established, and in the whole of the seventeenth century only eight. By contrast the education of the faithful advanced significantly. In most parishes the priest was now enjoined to preach a sermon at Sunday mass, an innovation as startling for the congregation as it must have been onerous for the incumbent. At the same time religious instruction had to be given during mass, and Sunday schools for the children of the parish were made obligatory.

The achievement of Trent in Spain must not be exaggerated. Diocesan decrees were often mere wishful thinking. In the parish of San Vicente in San Sebastián, in the margin of the official record enforcing preaching on Sundays a seventeenth-century hand wrote: 'This has never been done'. Poor and ignorant clergy continued to be common, but gradually over the late sixteenth and early seventeenth centuries the combined efforts of bishops, religious orders and the Inquisition managed to coax Spaniards into the new Catholicism. A striking feature of the new parish structure was the organisation of confraternities, intended to encourage loyalty to the parish but also to heighten devotion, since confraternity rules stipulated regular confession and communion.

In appearance, nothing seemed to have changed, but there were profound differences between the new Catholicism and the old. Trent imposed on Spanish religion a revolutionary sense of the sacred that endured into the twentieth century. Where the church had been used for communal meetings and festivities, it was now totally separated from all secular use; all religious rites, and all baptisms, were to be performed in the church and in no other place; an innovation, clergy were to wear distinctive robes to separate them from laity (in Mallorca in 1578 many still refused to wear clerical dress); priests were no longer to attend wedding parties and similar celebrations; carnivals, plays and dances were banned from church; processions with any hint of non-religious ritual were abolished; certain feast days (such as Corpus Christi) which had become laicised, were reclaimed for the Church. A worshipper in post-Tridentine Spain would experience, among other innovations: whitewashed walls in church, paintings purged of sensuality, a pulpit if there had been none before, an eternal flame before the tabernacle, a sacristy to which no women were allowed access, strict separation of sexes among the worshippers, a confessional to separate priest from penitent (introduced in Barcelona, for example, from 1566), sermons and a new liturgy, including the popularisation of the rosary (1571) and the introduction of the forty-hours devotion (brought to Barcelona by the Capuchins in 1580). New rules imposed on the parish priest included having to keep a record of all baptisms, marriages and burials. Parishioners were obliged to attend mass every Sunday and take communion at Easter, all of this being recorded by the priest.

From faith and worship, the impact of these changes extended to all aspects of Christian life. The diocesan synods of Granada in 1573 and Pamplona in 1591 ordered the destruction of unseemly images. Art was encouraged to serve the faith rather than to strive for profane effect: at its best this produced the realistic sculpture of the school of Valladolid, at its worst it produced stylised religious paintings lacking in quality. The famous Seville painter Francisco Pacheco (d. 1654) reflected the new orthodoxy when he argued that 'the principal aim of painting will be to achieve a state of grace'; and he was commissioned by the Inquisition to examine the acceptability of images in public places in Seville. The reforming outlook produced a generation of composers of sacred music, culminating in the magnificent motets of Tomás Luis de Victoria (d. 1611). On literature and culture, unfortunately, the impact was equivocal. It has often – and mistakenly – been thought that the Inquisition alone was responsible for pressure on creative writers. In practice the Inquisition was more concerned with the published word, whereas the one art form

accessible to the mass of the illiterate general public – the theatre – was
more normally subject to the local civic authorities and ultimately to the
council of Castile. A clear effect of the new Catholic spirit was the evolution in the late sixteenth-century theatre of *autos sacramentales*, plays performed specially for the feast of Corpus Christi. For the dramatist and
priest Lope de Vega the auto was 'a confounding of heresy and a glory of
our faith'. On the other hand, many Counter-Reformation clergy, led by
Jesuits like Mariana and Ribadeneira, thought the stage a source of im-
morality and mounted a campaign which led to the closing of all theatres
from 1597 into the early years of the next century. The new moral spirit
extended also into family life. The rules for what constituted marriage
were clarified and enforced, and parish priests were encouraged to check
on the sex lives of parishioners.

The reform of religion was no more and no less successful than in
other parts of Europe. Thanks to the paucity of Trent-type seminaries, the
educational level of the clergy remained among the lowest in Europe. In
Pamplona in the 1650s a bishop found many of his clergy too illiterate
even to say mass; and the problem was not restricted to mountainous
areas. The right of laymen to appoint parish priests continued to be a
serious obstacle to reform. By 1700 Spain no longer had obvious areas
of unbelief, but the Catholic religion, though dominant in public life, was
not convincingly rooted among the people. Popular beliefs, customs and
sexual attitudes survived strongly enough to form the basis of the alternative culture of the nineteenth and twentieth centuries.

During its high tide, the Counter-Reformation unleashed the spiritual
creativity of Spanish society. The work of an earlier generation of theology
scholars at Alcalá and Salamanca was followed by a flowering of activity
among the religious orders, notably the Jesuits and Augustinians. The
orders likewise became the channel through which the spirituality of
the early century infused intellectual and religious thought, culminating
in various forms of mysticism and asceticism. Among the Augustinians
fray Luis de León (d. 1591), among the Carmelites St John of the Cross
(d. 1591) and St Teresa (d. 1582), among the Dominicans Luis de Granada
(d. 1588), were the outstanding exponents of a more intensely personal
Christianity. Luis de Granada was by far the most influential: his *Guide for
Sinners* (1556) was written for a broad public, and his *Book of Prayer*
(1544) went through twenty-three editions in its first five years and over
a hundred in the whole period 1554–1679, making it the most successful
religious book of the Spanish Counter-Reformation. The tradition of
spiritual writing directed to ordinary Christians was continued by the

Jesuit Juan Eusebio Nieremberg, whose works became widely appreciated in Spain and had a greater impact on everyday religion than the literary brilliance of the great mystics.

## The impact of the Inquisition

Though the sixteenth century is often considered the great era of the Inquisition, during that period its activities were not primarily directed against formal heresy. The alleged heresy of Jewish conversos had been largely dealt with by the 1530s, and 'Lutheranism' was only a momentary scare in the 1550s. Between 1540 and 1614, suspicion of Judaism arose in possibly only 5 per cent of the cases dealt with by the Inquisition, and of Protestantism in only 7 per cent. Most of the 'Protestants' prosecuted were in reality foreigners; of the few Spaniards involved, most were guilty of confused theology rather than of heresy. In the last four decades of the sixteenth century, less than a dozen people were burnt in Spain for identifiable Protestantism. In these years the only religious problem confronting the Inquisition came from the Moriscos, who produced most of the accused in the tribunals of Granada, Saragossa and Valencia, and who over Spain as a whole accounted for about one-third of the cases tried between 1540 and 1614.

Nearly two-thirds of all those arrested by the Holy Office in the period mentioned were ordinary Catholic Spaniards unconnected with heresy or with the racial minorities. This highly important conclusion confirms that at a time when in the rest of Europe Catholics and Protestants were warring against each other, in Spain the clergy and the Inquisition were devoting their energies to the re-conversion of their own people to the faith. The surprisingly mild impact of the Holy Office in this age of conflict is shown by the fact that its executions totalled no more than 1 per cent a year of those arrested, or some two to three annual executions in the whole of the Spanish monarchy including America. Without in any way relaxing its vigilance against heresy imported from abroad, the Inquisition identified itself with the religious renewal of the Counter-Reformation in two principal areas: enforcing respect for the sacred, and affirming sexual morality.

The difficulty in enforcing a sense of the sacred emerges clearly from the trial figures for the Inquisition of Toledo, where over half those arrested between 1540 and 1614 were accused of blasphemy, sacrilege, scandalous words or behaviour, and disrespect to the sacrament of marriage. These offences were by far the most important censured by the Inquisition of this area during the sixteenth century and much of the seventeenth (in other parts of Spain the inquisitors were not so worried by them). Disrespect for the Holy Office was also regularly punished. The enforcement of the new sexual morality was rendered difficult by the persistence of popular attitudes which held that sex outside marriage was permissible: as many as one-third of those who appeared before the tribunal of Toledo in 1576–90 were investigated for this offence. At the same time the Inquisition looked into cases of bigamy, which over the period 1540–1614 accounted for over 5 per cent of prosecutions in all tribunals. Of course, other Church and secular courts also had jurisdiction over matters affecting public and private conduct. The particular concern of the Holy Office was less with the crime than with the mental attitude behind the crime. Significantly, in all interrogations the Inquisition tried to correct wrong attitudes and to re-educate the accused in the basic beliefs of the faith.

The evidence found in the Inquisition papers has sometimes induced historians to suggest that success was achieved in improving the quality of religion among Spaniards. Information from the Inquisition court at Toledo seems to suggest that in the mid-sixteenth century a high proportion of people did not know the creed and other basic statements of the Church, whereas by the late seventeenth century they did so. Since the evidence comes from two wholly different groups of people, it cannot be used to make comparisons, and no conclusion can be drawn. In any case, the inquisitors of Toledo and other towns were zealous in pursuing reform only during the 1570s, when the example of Trent was there to inspire them. By the end of the century they had ceased to take much interest in the question. Fewer people were therefore prosecuted for offences, but that did not mean that Spaniards were better Catholics.

In an age when divergent beliefs were sought out and punished, the Inquisition strangely enough did not take a harsh line against witchcraft. Counter-Reformation theologians throughout Europe tended to identify 'witchcraft' with devil worship and active heresy. In Spain, where the superstition could be found mainly in the mountainous areas of the north, the inquisitors were more sceptical, and a special meeting they held at Granada in 1526 concluded that witchcraft was little more than a delusion. This attitude was in general maintained throughout the sixteenth century, with the consequence that there was little prosecution of the phenomenon. After an exceptional case in Navarre in 1610, the Inquisition further reaffirmed its refusal to treat witchcraft as heresy. The cases that it prosecuted thereafter concerned minor superstitions such as folk magic and the use of love potions and spells.

After the initial period of terror against Jewish conversos, when it enjoyed the vigorous support of the state and of Old Christians, the Inquisition evolved from an instrument of harsh repression into one of persuasion. With its limited personnel of about three inquisitors in each of the 15 tribunals in Spain, and with no secure sources of income, it did not have the capacity to develop into an oppressive institution. Nor did it ever become a secret police that spied into and controlled people's lives, since virtually all the accusations made to it were initiated not by its officials but by ordinary members of the public denouncing each other out of suspicion or malice. The punishments used by the Inquisition, moreover, were less severe than often alleged. Torture was the exception rather than the rule. The death penalty was rare, and used primarily against heretics, who were in any case numerically few after the middle of the sixteenth century. Against these considerations must be set the fact that there was always unease at the rule of secrecy in trials, at the infamy which any brush with the tribunal might bring on a man and his family, and at the continued reliance on confiscations as a source of income. Spaniards accepted the Inquisition, but it was never loved. As late as 1538 a request directed to Charles V claimed that 'if the Catholic Monarchs were still alive they would have reformed it twenty years ago'.

The Inquisition had a relevant role to play in questions of culture, through its control over censorship and the way it prosecuted select individuals. The overall impact of its activity, however, has usually been exaggerated. The censorship law of 1558 was followed in 1559 by the first Spanish-produced Index of forbidden books, drawn up by inquisitor general Valdés. This continued the suppression of Erasmus, by prohibiting 16 of his works including the *Enchiridion*. It also inevitably prohibited all heretical books and unlicensed versions of the Bible. In addition, however, the inquisitors attempted to purify Spanish literature by sweeping away inferior writings and scrutinising devotional works closely. Among the outstanding devotional works that fell prey to Valdés's Index were the *Audi filia* of St Juan de Ávila, the *Book of Prayer* and *Guide of Sinners* of Luis de Granada and the *Works of a Christian* of St Francis Borja. In addition the authors Jorge de Montemayor, Juan del Encina, Torres Naharro and Gil Vicente appeared among those with specific prohibited works; while the *Lazarillo de Tormes* was banned. Since none of these writers was suspected of heresy, and indeed all were among the foremost Hispanic authors of the period, it can be seen that the Index was intended to be not merely a defence against Protestantism but an instrument of literary control. This would explain why many prominent intellectuals, like the Jesuits

Mariana and Juan de Pineda, collaborated as censors; and Arias Montano's own contribution as a censor in the Netherlands in 1570 was precisely because he thought the task too important to be left to ignorant persons.

The somewhat limited Index of 1559 was followed in 1583 by another, issued by inquisitor general Gaspar de Quiroga. It concerned itself with books by all the famous names of the Reformation, and contained five times as many titles as the previous Index. However, most of these works had never entered Spain, and were in languages no Spaniard could read, so the real impact of prohibition was small. Only about two dozen of the hundreds of items mentioned for prohibition or expurgation were Castilian literary works. The Index by itself was not, therefore, an obstacle to culture. Nor did it interrupt the import and sale of non-controversial books. An inventory in 1591 of the stock of a bookseller of Medina del Campo, Benito Boyer, shows that two-thirds of the 26,000 books in his shop had come from France, the Netherlands and Italy. Booksellers in Barcelona also imported foreign books without any problem, and offered them for sale to the reading public.

A few intellectuals, it is true, had problems with the Inquisition. Their situation arose out of disputes with their university colleagues rather than out of conflict with the Inquisition. Where conflicts arose they were precipitated by considerations marginal to the role of the Holy Office. The reaction against Erasmus and the rising tide of anti-Semitism were the two most distinctive features of the ideological crisis faced by Spain in the early sixteenth century. The observations of Rodrigo Manrique to Luis Vives in 1533 on the subject of Vergara's imprisonment (*see* p. 122) show that humanist learning had become suspect, a development caused not by the Inquisition but by the Reformation. Cipriano de Valera, who fled from Spain and became a leading Reformer and translator of the Bible, observed that 'it has become proverbial in Spain when they hear of a learned man, to say, He is so learned that there is a danger of him becoming a Lutheran'. The Jewish connection was affirmed as follows by archbishop Siliceo of Toledo in 1547: 'It is said, and is considered true, that the principal heretics of Germany, who have destroyed all that nation and have introduced great heresies, are descendants of Jews'. Intellectuals in countries other than Spain also faced great pressures in these years. What was unique in Spain was not that the Inquisition persecuted letters – for this was not its purpose – but that it acted as a forum where protagonists of current prejudices could press their case. This created a type of indirect pressure and encouraged self-censorship, a 'law of silence' against which many individuals rebelled.

The humanist Hernán Núñez complained to Jerónimo de Zurita in 1566 that 'the worst of it is that [the inquisitors] discourage the study of letters because of the dangers said to be present in them: when a humanist corrects an error in Cicero, for example, the same error has to be corrected in Scripture. These and other similar problems drive me insane and take away from me any wish to carry on'. In practice, there seems to have been no direct clash between scholarship and the Inquisition, though individual scholars encountered problems. Fray José de Sigüenza, historian of his own Jeronimite order as well as of the Escorial, and an admirer of Arias Montano, was tried in 1592 but acquitted; and Francisco Sánchez de las Brozas, professor of grammar at Salamanca, was arrested both in 1584 and 1600. In each of these cases the conflict was provoked not by the Holy Office but by the colleagues of the accused. This was notoriously true of the prosecutions in the 1570s against noted Hebraists of the university of Salamanca. In December 1571 two professors at the university, León de Castro and Bartolomé de Medina, accused three of their colleagues to the Inquisition of Valladolid. The three were fray Luis de León, Gaspar de Grajal and Martín Martínez de Cantalapiedra. The charges against Luis de León were typical: he was accused of questioning the accuracy of the Vulgate translation of the Bible, of translating the Song of Songs as a love song instead of a divine canticle and of saying that scholastic theology harmed the study of Scripture. All were arrested in March 1572: Luis de León remained in prison for four and a half years, Cantalapiedra for five; Grajal died in the cells. 'Here envy and lies held me in prison', begins the famous poem fray Luis penned after his release. In 1572 one of their colleagues at the university of Osuna, Alonso Gudiel, was also arrested and died in prison a year later. The affair had not been precipitated by the Inquisition, but its part in the proceedings was of great significance. The arrest of Grajal, which preceded his own by five days, made fray Luis comment that 'it has given just cause for keeping silent out of fear'. After his release Cantalapiedra concluded that 'it is better to walk carefully and remain prudent'. It was a prudence that severely compromised academic life in every country where controversy might be dangerous. Moreover, fray Luis, Grajal and Gudiel were all of converso origin: there is little doubt that this prejudiced their position. The work of León de Castro was not yet done: in the same period he attacked Benito Arias Montano, who was then preparing Philip II's Polyglot Bible, eventually published by Plantin at Antwerp. Juan de Mariana's comment on the persecution of the Hebraists is well known: 'it was a sad state when virtuous men, because of their great achievements, had to undergo hostility, accusations and injuries from those who should have been their defenders. The case in question depressed many, seeing how much affliction threatened those who spoke freely what they thought. Those who agreed with current ideas did so with even greater eagerness, and entertained opinions that were approved of and were the least dangerous, without any great concern for the truth'.

Mariana, like other distinguished intellectuals, supported the Inquisition; he also worked actively as a censor for Quiroga's Index. His attitude is evidence that the role of the Inquisition in literature was not a clear-cut one. Just as St Ignatius of Loyola had once (in 1526) had a brush with the Inquisition, which suspected him in his student days of being an alumbrado; so St Teresa of Ávila, a conversa by origin, fell under suspicion and was the object of an enquiry by the Inquisition of Seville in 1575. In the same year her *Life* was seized and examined by the Inquisition of Valladolid. Both felt they had nothing to fear. The Inquisition was not consciously dedicated to the suppression of thought. Its persecutions followed current prejudices in religion as in literature, and its decisions to prosecute followed the preferences of the men who were in control at any given time.

The inevitably personal nature of many inquisitorial prosecutions is illustrated by the case of Bartolomé de Carranza, the distinguished Dominican archbishop of Toledo (1557). The year after his elevation to this see, he published at Antwerp his *Commentaries on the Christian Catechism*. His enemies, led by the theologian Melchor Cano and inquisitor general Valdés, engineered his arrest in 1559 on the grounds that the *Commentaries* were heretical, and kept him in the cells of the Holy Office for seven years, after which he was summoned to Rome and died in Italy in 1576. Leading theologians considered Carranza thoroughly orthodox: this did not prevent his work, a casualty of the doctrinal and personal rivalries at the age of the Counter-Reformation, appearing in subsequent editions of the Index of forbidden books.

## Philip II and the 'Black Legend'

If we add to the 42 years of his reign as king the 13 during which he acted as regent, Philip ruled longer than any other monarch in Spain's history. His years in power coincided with some of the most decisive events in the history of Europe, which could not fail to affect his historical reputation. During the same period of time the English were working their way up to world prominence, and consequently created in retrospect a highly favourable image of the ruler who led them there, queen Elizabeth. Spaniards felt they were already on top of the world, but their favourable image had already been created around Ferdinand and Isabella, and they failed to agree on the merits of their most famous king.

The harshest criticism came from non-Spaniards. During the reign Spain was almost continuously at war with the leading states of the west, whether Protestant, Catholic or Muslim. Not surprisingly, the hostility of other Europeans to Spain worked its way into printed propaganda (to which twentieth-century writers gave the name of the 'Black Legend', implying that the propaganda was untrue). Italians were probably the first to contribute to the unfavourable attitude, by their struggle against Spanish occupation troops from the time of Ferdinand the Catholic onwards. A further powerful impetus was given by the Dutch revolt, when protests against the 'tyranny' of the duke of Alba escalated into attacks on the king himself, notably in William of Orange's *Apologia* (1581). Subsequently, the years of the Spanish Armada encouraged the growth of government-sponsored propaganda in England against Philip II. From the 1560s Protestants also launched a particularly active pamphlet campaign against the king and the alleged misdeeds of the Spanish Inquisition. The hostile image was rounded off by insinuations directed against the private life of the king, in which Philip's former secretary Antonio Pérez, who fled from Spain in 1591, played a leading role.

The king was, quite logically, also criticised by his own subjects, notably in the last 30 years of his reign. Up to that period the country had lived in peace, and war was always far away. From the time of the intervention in the Netherlands, however, Castilians began to suffer from a number of problems, notably rises in taxation and the constant strain of military recruitment and the death of thousands of soldiers. They were negative factors that had never formed part of the experience of Spaniards, since the famous Spanish empire had come about largely through dynastic inheritance and not through blood and conquest. By the end of the reign, in consequence, disillusion was widespread. A leaflet that circulated in Madrid in the year of the king's death accused him of being 'worse than Nero'.

When some Spanish commentators looked back on those years, they claimed to see little evidence of success, and the problems and failures served only to heighten the contrast with the distant epoch, already a century away, of the Catholic Monarchs. In this way, both peninsular and foreign critics tended to agree on a negative appraisal of the reign, and Spain's best-known king was saddled with a reputation that subsequent writers continued to develop and elaborate from their respective viewpoints. The definitive unfavourable image of Philip was created in the

1820s, when Spanish, French and Belgian intellectuals who opposed the absolutist monarchies of that period united in portraying the king as a forerunner of nineteenth-century tyranny, an enemy of political and religious liberty.

# The 'Golden Age' of Spain

In 1550 Gonzalo Pérez, secretary to Philip II and translator of Homer's *Odyssey*, wrote that 'we do not have as good books as other nations . . . because of our laziness and our disregard for the public good, and because we are more inclined to war than to study'. This self-effacing comment on the limited achievement of the Renaissance in Spain must be set against the undoubted cultural successes of what later scholars were to call a 'Golden Age', roughly the early sixteenth to the mid-seventeenth century. Because many foreign influences were apparently frowned on in this period, with the exclusion of aspects of Erasmian humanism and the activity of censorship and the Inquisition, it has sometimes been argued that Spain withdrew into itself, and that its cultural achievements were produced by Spain's own genius and owed little to other nations.

The so-called 'Golden Age', however, occurred precisely during the great age of empire and owed a very great amount to that empire: there was therefore nothing mysterious about the dates when it occurred. The early years were literally an age of gold, as bullion imports stimulated monumental architecture and the decorative arts. Art was now a primary industry. Seville in particular attracted investment in building and art, in a continuous development stretching from the palace of the Medinaceli family (c.1530) to the works of Velázquez (d. 1660) and Murillo (d. 1682). It is possible that the decrees of 1558 and 1559, which imposed censorship and disapproved of education abroad, may have helped to isolate the intellectual development of Spaniards. But the isolation was certainly not significant, for in that very same decade Philip II began to upgrade the nation into an imperial power, in the Mediterranean first and then two decades later in the Atlantic. Within a generation tens of thousands of Spaniards of all ranks and conditions had travelled all over Europe, and Spanish troops were to be found in Greece, Bohemia, Flanders and Africa. The one European nation that could not be accused of insularity was Spain. Nobles serving abroad brought home with them cultural souvenirs which became the core of great collections. The duke of Alba sent back paintings from Flanders, viceroys serving in Italy brought back masterpieces in their baggage. At his death in 1655 the marquis of

Leganés had collected in this way 1,333 paintings, mostly Flemish and Italian.

In these circumstances, even while Castile and Spain continued to develop native cultural traditions, literature and art seldom lost their international dimension. The imperial experience took a generation to mature and only from the end of the reign of Philip II did it begin to bear fruit in great literary works. Italian and Flemish influences continued as they had done in the early century to infuse all aspects of creativity in Spain: Italian architects were prominent in the development of the Escorial, in Valencia the college of the patriarch included columns cut in Genoa, in Barcelona the palace of the Diputació was adapted from a design by Michelangelo. Titian influenced court portraiture; of Philip's two principal court artists one was a Fleming (Antonis Mor), the other was the sensitive and austere Alonso Sánchez Coello (d. 1588). Mannerism in Spanish painting was inevitably derived from Italian models, culminating in the magnificent achievement of El Greco (d. 1614), who came to Toledo in 1577. In the course of the sixteenth century, north European influences declined but active links with the north did not. Philip's own collection of Bosch paintings is evidence of a continuing interest, and the choice of Antwerp for the production of the Polyglot Bible edited by Arias Montano was clear recognition of Flemish superiority in printing. The triumph of Baroque at the end of the century, from Bartolome Carducho (d. 1608) onwards, reaffirmed the international sources of much Spanish creativity.

Long after the restrictive measures of 1558-9, then, Spain continued to have an active intellectual life based on a world experience vaster than that of any other European nation. Spain's elite was unusually well travelled, and nobles continued their role in the army and the diplomatic service. Garcilaso de la Vega, who died in battle in France in 1536, was of an earlier breed of soldier-poets; Hernando de Acuña (d. 1580), who fought at St Quentin and served in Germany, Italy and Tunisia, was one of the subsequent generation. Cervantes, whose *Don Quixote* (1605) was claimed by the censor to have 'met with general applause in Spain, France, Italy, Germany and Flanders', derived much of his universal vision from the very extent of the empire. He knew Old Castile and Andalusia intimately, travelled through Barcelona to Italy, worked in Rome, enlisted in Naples, fought at Lepanto, was enslaved in Algiers (for five years) and in the 1580s drifted through Orán, the Azores and Lisbon.

Contact with the wide world inevitably stimulated enquiry, including that in technical areas. Pedro Simón Abril in his *Apuntamientos* (1589) argued that mathematics directed men to 'the firm and secure truth', and

Juan Pérez de Moya publicised mathematical method (*Practical Arithmetic*, 1562). In the field of science, work produced by Spaniards was normally modelled on studies done by previous authors, usually Italians. Studies were published in mechanics, engineering (particularly the treatises on artillery by Luis Collado, 1592, and Diego Ufano, 1613), navigation (Pedro de Medina, 1545, and Martín Cortés, 1551, wrote treatises which in less than a century came out in forty-two editions in five languages), and shipbuilding (Diego García de Palacio's *Instrucción náutica*, 1587, was the world's first treatise on the subject). The expanding universe entered university teaching: in 1561 the course regulations at Salamanca specified Copernicus as a set book for second-year students of astronomy; and in 1584 the Augustinian friar Diego de Zuniga affirmed in his *Commentary on Job* that the Copernican theory 'in no way contradicts' Scripture.

America was the greatest single impetus. It stimulated geography and cartography, metallurgical method (the mercury amalgam process for extracting silver was introduced into Mexico in mid-century), and all aspects of natural science, leading in 1570 to the expedition financed by Philip II and headed by Dr Francisco Hernández, 'to study the history of living things in the Indies, sketch the plants and describe the land'. Just prior to the enormous six-year-long survey of New Spain made by Hernández, the Franciscan Bernardino de Sahagún completed in 1569 his great *History of the Things of New Spain*, a masterpiece of anthropological research, drawn up with the help of native Mexican scholars.

Between 1475 and 1600 nearly 47 per cent of new scientific studies were in medicine, making this the discipline best served with publications. The continued link of Spain with outside influences is illustrated by the career of the anatomist Vesalius (d. 1564), a Spanish subject who was born in Brussels, studied at Louvain, taught at Padua, published his work in Basel and was court physician to both Charles V and Philip II. Another itinerant was the Aragonese Miguel Servet, who first argued for the circulation of the blood and in 1553 was burnt alive by Calvin at Geneva. In practice the important centres of medical research in Spain were Valencia and Alcalá universities. At the latter the great figures were the Segovian converso (d. 1559) Andrés Laguna (who however never held an official post), physician to popes and to Charles V; and Francisco Vallés (d. 1592), whose works became authoritative in Spain, going through 17 editions there and 72 in foreign parts. The survival of practical medicine and anatomical research disproves the claim that they had totally decayed. There is, however, little doubt that medicine was practised less in Castile than in other realms, such as Valencia. We should not forget the continued role of conversos in medicine, with court physicians like Francisco López de Villalobos under the Catholic Monarchs and Juan Muñoz Peralta under Philip II.

The spread of the Castilian language was one of the foremost characteristics of the 'Golden Age'. Carried by the conquistador into central America and by the tercios into northern Europe, Castilian became par excellence the language of Spain and the medium through which Spain's personality was projected on to the world. There is no doubt over the success of Castilian in the peninsula. In 1475–1500 a third of scientific books published in Spain were in Castilian, and 16 per cent in Catalan; by 1551–1600 some 58 per cent (out of 433 works) were in Castilian, only 0.7 per cent in Catalan. In Valencia the advance of Castilian can be seen by the fact that no works published between 1474 and 1489 were in that language, but within the period 1542–64 over one-third were. This does not mean that the 'Golden Age' was exclusively a Castilian achievement. On the contrary, the development of creativity occurred only because there was a positive response to multiple internal and external influences – Arabic, Jewish, Italian, Flemish, American – that stimulated all corners of the peninsula. Cervantes apostrophised Spain as 'common mother of all nations', which was true in the sense that the many nations of Spain had through the experience of empire entered into an exchange of culture with a multitude of foreign peoples. The success of the Castilian language was more limited. Up to the nineteenth century it was used as a principal tongue by only a tiny proportion of the population of the New World, and in Europe never became an international language that could compete with Italian or French.

The achievements of Spain's imperial experience had a less positive side. Though the government depended heavily on the military and economic collaboration of the other states in the monarchy, and on technological help from foreign engineers, shipwrights and artisans, imperialistic attitudes inculcated, as in all empires, a hubris that revealed itself in contempt for other nations. The 'arrogance' that Arias Montano observed in action in Flanders was reflected in Italy by a letter to Philip II from a Spanish official in Milan in 1570: 'These Italians, although they are not Indians, have to be treated as such, so that they will understand that we are in command of them and not they are of us'. Did the official have any knowledge of how Spaniards treated Indians? The early respect for other cultures, that had been known in Spain and that even Cortés showed towards the people of Mexico, deteriorated into contempt and violence.

Spain's ambassador in Paris, Francés de Álava, commented to Philip II on
what he had seen in Granada, when 'between the consecration of the host
and the wine the priest would turn to see if the Moriscos were on their
knees and would cover them with such horrifying and arrogant abuse,
in terms showing so much disrespect for God, that my blood ran cold.
When they left mass the priests would go through the town with an air of
bullying arrogance over the Moriscos'. Spaniards often used this attitude
of superiority, to their allies in the empire and to other Catholic nations.
A leading figure such as the duke of Alba entertained a barely disguised
contempt for the French, the Italians, the English and the Germans.

The imperial experience, finally, provoked deep disagreement among
Spaniards over the direction taken by their country, whether in the
Netherlands or in America. Catalans were notoriously in disagreement
with most aspects of Philip II's policy, but even in Castile there was frequent criticism in the Cortes over rising taxes and other aspects of policy.
Philip had to permit his advisers to disagree with him on a matter as central
as religious toleration. In 1555 his chaplain, Alfonso de Castro, preached
publicly in London that the conscience of heretics could not be forced by
burning, and in 1582 another chaplain – Luis de Granada – stated in print
that force should not be used against heretics. As late as 1582, when the
matter had been virtually decided by the government, the Inquisition
of Valencia opposed the expulsion of the Moriscos on the grounds that
'they are Spaniards like ourselves'. Throughout his peninsular realms the
king was far from enjoying the favourable consensus that he would have
wished, and in 1580, at a time when it seemed that Philip was at the height
of his power, the leading Jesuit Pedro de Ribadeneira commented: 'I see
hearts very changed from their previous love and desire for the honour of
the king. The people on account of the taxes, the grandees for the apparent
neglect of their persons, the gentry, the clergy, and even the friars, all are
embittered, disillusioned and discontented with His Majesty'.

Although Spain under Philip II attained the heights of imperial authority and broadened its cultural horizons immeasurably, the 'Golden
Age' included important countervailing tendencies. The literary expansion
of Castilian took place at precisely the time that censorship came to be
accepted as a necessary restraint on cultural influences; imperial extension
over new peoples – in Portugal, in the Philippines – occurred side by side
with a refusal to understand the civilisation not only of those peoples
but of Spain's own minorities, in particular the Moriscos; championship
of the faith was taken up while the fact that Catholics in Italy, France
and the Netherlands were among the leading critics of Spanish imperial

policy was wilfully ignored. This paradoxical duality continued into the early seventeenth century, where the rich cultural influences of the previous generation produced a harvest of writers and artists, whose work however became increasingly overshadowed by the counter-productive and finally self-destructive tendencies in Spain's imperial role.

# CHAPTER 4

# The crisis of government 1598–1660

## Politics 1598–1665

Philip III (1598–1621) was aged 20 when he succeeded to the throne to which he had been heir since the death of his brother Diego in 1582. Philip II had been over-protective to the only surviving male among his children, and his son seems to have reacted by rejecting the advisers placed over him – Cristóbal de Moura had by 1599 been firmly excluded from his intimate circle – and nourishing an admiration for his grandfather Charles V. The new king was in character a contrast to his dominating father, but his several firm policy decisions suggest that he was less pliant than he has usually been painted. A pious Catholic, he was actively concerned to restore the military fortunes of the nation. Unlike his father, he was willing to give greater initiative to his ministers.

Immediately after his accession, Philip restored authority to the near-defunct system of councils, which his father had rejected in favour of a system of select committees. By 1600 a reformed council of state was in full operation: the council of war likewise was supplemented with men of known military experience. In effect the Castilian aristocracy was handed back much of the political power it had lost. One grandee remarked after Philip II's death that the world 'would see what the Spanish were worth now that they have a free hand, and are no longer subject to a single brain that thought it knew all that could be known and treated everyone else as a blockhead'. Though changes occurred there was also continuity, for Philip retained as his chief political adviser one of his father's ministers, Juan de Idiáquez, who was destined to remain the single most influential voice in the king's councils until his death in 1614. As the principal member of the council of state, Idiáquez more than any other person was responsible for the major policy decisions in both internal and foreign matters.

Unlike his father, Philip was not interested in the day-to-day business of politics and preferred to delegate responsibility to Idiáquez and the resurrected conciliar system. This withdrawal from government was foreshadowed by the king's commitment in 1599 to a long absence from Madrid (January to October), occasioned solely by the wish to meet his bride, the fourteen-year-old Margaret of Austria, already on her way from Vienna. Philip met her in Valencia; the marriage was solemnised in April. In the early summer (May–July) the court moved north to hold a session of the Cortes of Catalonia, then returned to Valencia. The high point of the whole outing (*jornada*) was the hospitality accorded to the king at Denia by the rising star of the reign, Philip's favourite, the marquis of Denia.

Francisco Gómez de Sandoval y Rojas had been a penurious noble of Valencian origin, in serious economic straits in the 1580s, when he first met the young prince and advanced in his favour. Aged 45 in 1598, he had recently been made viceroy of Valencia by Philip II, who apparently hoped in this way to remove him from his son's presence. The marquis, however, returned to court and assumed effective control of the prince's household. Thereafter his rise was sensational. When they returned from the Valencian jornada the king created him duke of Lerma. Enormous grants of money were bestowed on him. His friends and relatives were promoted, most notably his uncle Bernardo de Sandoval, who was made archbishop of Toledo and inquisitor general. Lerma accompanied the king everywhere, sold favours for profit, and dominated court patronage: he accumulated a huge fortune that by the end of the reign was probably worth three million ducats. Numerous senior posts throughout Spain were in his hands, and his children married into the wealthiest grandee families, gaining noble titles in the process (his eldest son was made duke of Uceda). 'He planted the roots of his power in the most fertile soils of Spain', commented the Venetian ambassador.

Lerma's period of influence began the seventeenth-century pattern of control through a single favoured minister, drawn from the higher aristocracy and known as a *privado* or more commonly as a *valido*. It was a significant constitutional change from the reliance by Philip II on secretaries of state, and reflected the drift of political power to the councils, which now sent their *consultas* directly to the king rather than through the mediating hands of the secretaries, who continued with only a semblance of their former influence. The king would respond to the consultas normally after consulting with the valido. Lerma held his power by virtue solely of personal friendship, but his position was later given legitimacy by Philip's decree in 1612 ordering the councils 'to comply with whatever the duke instructs or orders, and also to furnish him with any information he requires'. The decree was retrospective and confirmed that the valido had the formal powers of chief executive, albeit exercised in the king's name.

The valido was not, of course, all-powerful. In the first place, his survival depended on the support of a sufficient number of other nobles. Lerma consequently used the patronage system to build up a client group of older aristocrats as well as of newcomers. Among the latter was Pedro Franqueza, subsequently created count of Villalonga, who served as secretary to all the major councils in Madrid, made himself extremely rich and was arrested on charges of corruption in January 1607. An even greater object of popular hostility was Rodrigo Calderón, who began as a retainer in the duke's household and rose to become marquis of Sieteiglesias and Lerma's own right-hand man. Inevitably this system of clientage aroused counter-factions, and the valido had to contend with continuous political opposition. Second, though the valido might control access to the king and to major public offices, he was never in a position to control public opinion or the freely expressed views of nobles and administrators in the councils. He was therefore obliged to accept criticism (his own uncle, the cardinal of Toledo, said pointedly of his nephew's regime that 'in all that one sees, reads and hears, clear signs are in evidence which threaten the ruin of this monarchy') and sometimes to concur, as in the case of Villalonga, in the downfall of his own creatures.

Excessive attention by historians to the phenomenon of the valido, and to the activities of Lerma in particular, has diverted attention from the most striking development of the period: the fact that for 20 years Spain lived under the curious dualism of a split between court and government. Every year the king, with Lerma to escort him, spent long months away from Madrid. The country once again had a peripatetic king; but it was a king who travelled for leisure and in order to escape from the routine of administration. Lerma's role in active government was as a consequence quite small: he seems to have attended only 22 out of 739 meetings of the council of state over the period 1600–18, and no doubt preferred to exercise his influence more directly by advising the king on replies to the consultas of the councils.

As if in reaction to the removal of Philip II's personal rule, there was a remarkable reversion of power to traditional institutions: political theory was revised, the Cortes gained new initiative and authority returned to the councils.

With few exceptions, Spanish political thinkers under Philip III moved away from the concept of absolutism and stressed that political obedience was dependent upon just rule. A subject was, they argued, strictly speaking under the authority of the law, not of the king. The Jesuit Molina specified that political power derived only from the people, within the conditions and time limits set by them. 'The concept of absolute power is in fact tyranny', argued Pedro Agustín Morla in 1599, 'and was invented by the flatterers of kings'. To some degree these writers were sharing in the Counter-Reformation's defence of democratic rights against Protestant kings, a controversy to which the most famous Spanish contribution was the Jesuit Francisco Suárez's *Defensio Fidei* (1613), in which he explicitly defended tyrannicide. But there is no doubt that most were engaging in a reasoned analysis of Spain's constitution. The Catalan writer Antonio Oliván in 1600 defined Spain as a federation of sovereign states in which each had laws based on a contract between the subjects and the king. The idea of a contract, and of a right to resist, is also present in Mariana's fundamental *De rege* (1599). By the end of the reign, however, there was a return to demands for stronger royal power: the significant work in this respect was the *Royal Art of Government* (1621) of Jerónimo Zeballos.

The initiative of the Castilian Cortes arose from two considerations: by 1601 over half the crown's income came from taxes voted in Cortes; and the most controversial of these taxes were the new millones. Introduced in 1590, the millones had to be approved at regular intervals, and so made the crown dependent on the goodwill of the 18 cities represented in Cortes. Six sessions of the assembly were held under Philip III (1598–1601, 1602–4, 1607–11, 1611–12, 1615 and 1617–20). At all of them the procuradores exploited their hold over crown finance in order to voice opposition to policy. The discontent had been growing under Philip II, but reached a peak under his son. In 1599 the procurador Melchor Dávila presented a programme for tax reform and the exclusion of foreign financiers 'who are ruining and destroying the state'. In 1601 the crown actually conceded that the Cortes should determine how the money they voted should be spent. But in 1603 the procuradores complained that the agreement, which they saw as a solemn contract, had not been observed. In 1612 Pedro de Sonsoles claimed in Cortes that 'the king does not have absolute power, [but] has to submit to the wishes of the cities'. During the same session Mateo Lisón y Biedma, procurador for Granada, insisted that the people and the king had binding obligations to each other. It was the lingering voice of Castilian constitutionalism, soon to be stilled under the later Habsburgs.

What has been called a 'restoration of government' showed itself above all in the councils. Valido rule under Philip III did not mean incompetent rule. The councils, aided by select committees (juntas) for special business, functioned adequately in the hands of the men, whether aristocrats or new bureaucrats, to whom the king entrusted it. The court manoeuvres of Lerma did not seriously impede their work. Even when Lerma attended the council of state, his voice did not always carry more weight than those of the seasoned statesmen, men such as Idiáquez, the count of Chinchón, the count of Miranda and Baltasar de Zúñiga. The extra amount of business generated by the restoration of authority to the councils brought about an increase in the size of bureaucracy. Under Philip II there had inevitably been an increase in costs. Under Philip III total costs slightly more than doubled, but the really startling increase was in the number of secretaries and administrative personnel, whose wage bill nearly quintupled between 1598 and 1621. The significant increase in central government staffing rendered impossible any return to the austere personal monarchy of Philip II. For the rest of the Habsburg regime in Spain, power rested with the councils.

The king's absences, initiated in 1599, continued into 1600, when he spent eight months in the royal palaces at Valsaín, Toledo, Aranjuez and the Escorial, and the four months of summer in Old Castile and Valladolid. By the end of the year the decision was made to move the court from Madrid to Valladolid. Philip preferred the city on the Pisuerga for its climate, Lerma favoured it principally because it removed the king from the domineering and therefore rival character of his aunt the Empress Maria, who had returned to Spain in 1576 after the death of Maximilian II and lived as a nun in the convent of the Descalzas Reales. The move took place in 1601 and was intensely unpopular among the aristocracy, who spent huge sums on transferring furniture and rebuilding palaces. Eventually the court returned in 1606 (the Empress had died in 1603). From this date the town on the Manzanares blossomed into one of Europe's great cities. In 1619 the beautiful Plaza Mayor was constructed; destroyed by fire in 1631, it was soon rebuilt.

The king's travels continued even while he was in Valladolid, but the duke controlled the itinerary, which was directed towards his own interest above all. No visits were made to Portugal until 1619. Aragon, which had received a brief visit in September 1599 at the end of the Valencian jornada, was neglected and no Cortes was held there in this reign. In 1603 the king was once again persuaded to go to Valencia, where he held a Cortes in February 1604, at a time when the Morisco problem was uppermost in

many minds. The return to Madrid did not put an end to Philip's uncon-
structive absences. In 1608 and 1609 he was away for three months,
in 1610 for nearly six. Decisions were delayed while the government in
Madrid tried to keep in touch with the itinerant court.

The queen died in childbirth, at the age of 26, in October 1611. Of her
eight children, five reached maturity (Philip, the eldest boy, was born
in 1605). The king was heartbroken at her death. During this period,
he chose to direct his discontent against Lerma's unpopular protégé
Calderón, who in 1612 was sent away from court, ostensibly as an ambassador. Knowing that his position was getting vulnerable, Lerma that year
obtained from the king a royal order appointing him formally as valido.
The nobles began to form alliances around Lerma's son Cristóbal, duke
of Uceda; and in the council of state they began to defer to the views of
Baltasar de Zúñiga and others who had served abroad in the monarchy.
Having achieved the heights of worldly success, Lerma's thoughts fixed on
the bizarre wish to become a cardinal, an ambition he achieved in March
1618. On 4 October the same year he was dismissed by the king and
retired to his estates in Valencia, where he died in 1625 after being forced
to disgorge a large part of his fortune. Shortly after the valido's fall, in
February 1619, Calderón was arrested, tortured and kept in prison. Uceda
succeeded his father as valido, but this time Philip retained most of his
executive and patronage powers.

The king resolved to act as his own chief minister, so that 'papers shall
be signed by me and no other person'. The council of state in February
1619 issued a famous consulta, calling for radical reforms in the economy
and finances. The king made a belated visit to his subjects in Portugal
that year, but fell ill shortly after. He died in March 1621 aged just under
43.

His untimely death put government into the hands of his sixteen-year-
old son. Philip IV (1621–65) presided over Spain's destiny at the time of
its gravest crisis, and a recent biographer has argued that he fulfilled his
duties with 'fortitude and skill'. He grew to become a conscientious and
intelligent monarch, concerned to promote his country's interests and
to develop a cosmopolitan court; but he was also obstinate in his policy
decisions, and unduly pious. Olivares wrote of him (in 1632) that 'he has
some Latin and his knowledge of geography is outstanding. He understands
and speaks French, and understands Italian and Portuguese as well as he
understands Castilian; and though he cannot travel abroad as he would
if he were a private person, he has been all round the provinces of Spain'.
The king grew to become a good scholar (he translated Guicciardini's

*History of Italy*), and an outstanding patron of the arts: as early as 1623 Velázquez was appointed official court painter. Rubens, who was in Madrid in 1628–9, thought that Philip had 'excellent qualities', but also that 'he would be capable of governing under any conditions, were it not that he mistrusts himself and defers too much to others'. For the first 20 years of his reign the dominant influence was Gaspar de Guzmán, count of Olivares, who had joined Philip's household in 1615 and was 18 years his senior.

Olivares came from a minor branch of prominent Andalusian nobility, succeeded to the title and estates of his father in 1607, and took a leading part in overthrowing the rule of the Sandovals at the end of the previous reign. Baltasar de Zuniga, Olivares's uncle, was recalled from Vienna and resumed an active role in the council of state. As Philip III lay on his deathbed Olivares said to Uceda, 'Now everything is mine'. 'Everything?', the duke asked, 'Yes, everything, without exception', was the reply. With the accession of Philip IV the Lerma family were ousted and the interlinked families of Zúñiga, Haro and Guzmán rose to power. The death of Baltasar de Zúñiga in 1622 opened the way for Olivares's undisputed influence. In that year he entered the council of state and rapidly took control of policy. In 1625 he was created duke of San Lucar la Mayor and thereafter became known simply, by the combination of his titles, as the Count Duke.

The new regime began by setting up in 1622 a committee for reform (*Junta de Reformación*, a continuation of one that had been created under Lerma in 1618). Its aim was to 'eradicate vices, abuses and bribes'. In February the following year 23 'articles of reform' were issued: the proposals included the closing of brothels, sumptuary laws against luxury in dress and restrictions on the import of foreign manufactures. To emphasise the break with past policies, the trial of Rodrigo Calderón was resumed and in 1625 the former favourite was beheaded in the Plaza Mayor of Madrid. The urgent need for economies made the king himself set an example by cutting the costs of his court.

These austere and well-meaning policies were brusquely upset by the incognito arrival in Madrid in March 1623 of Charles, prince of Wales, seeking the hand of the infanta Maria. For the next five months Madrid was thrown into an orgy of entertainments that plunged the nobility even further into debt, blew the state budget off course and ended in mutual recrimination and an Anglo-Spanish war. Early in 1624 Olivares took the king on a state visit to his province of Andalusia, just as Lerma had taken Philip III to his native Valencia. The parallel between the two validos ends there, for Olivares was now attending closely to the urgent problems of government. At the end of the year he presented his famous secret memorandum urging Philip to become truly king of a unified Spain. In a subsequent paper he outlined a proposal for a 'Union of Arms', a force totalling 140,000 men to be raised and maintained by each component state of the monarchy in proportion to its resources: Castile and America together, for example, were to raise 44,000, Catalonia 16,000, Milan 8,000. At the end of 1625 the king and his minister began an official visit to the crown of Aragon, whose representatives were the first to be offered the proposals of the Union of Arms.

In January 1626 the Cortes of Aragon at Barbastro, and in March the Valencian Cortes at Monzón, were recalcitrant. Both eventually voted subsidies, but the sums – 72,000 ducats a year for 15 years from the Valencians, twice that figure from the Aragonese – were sufficient only for a small number of troops, who were in any case not permitted to serve outside Spain. Despite the eloquent pleas of the king, the Catalans refused to grant either men or money when the Cortes opened in Barcelona on 28 March. After several weeks of argument, the court left empty-handed on 4 May. Despite these setbacks, on 24 July Olivares decreed the implementation of the Union of Arms, which was put into effect in America, Flanders and Italy; only in Catalonia was there a total refusal to cooperate.

In May 1626 the government took the important measure of suspending all further minting of vellón coins, which had contributed greatly to inflation since they were issued under Philip III in 1599. Early the next year, in January 1627, state debts were once again repudiated, for the second time in the century. In August 1628 a sharp deflation of the vellón currency was decreed. These three measures (discussed on p. 229) helped the crown to reduce its current debts sharply, and offered it the clear option to pursue a policy of retrenchment. The years 1627–8 were the crucial turning point of Olivares's ministry: was the government going to pursue a programme of financial stability at home and low-level commitment abroad? The opportunity, however, passed. In the spring of 1628 the Count Duke committed Spain to a costly new intervention in Mantua, and in August the entire plate fleet was seized off the Cuban coast by Piet Heyn. The lack of adequate finance rapidly became a burning problem that absorbed the waking hours of the valido and precipitated all the major crises of the next decade: in Portugal, in Catalonia and in Castile itself.

The declaration of war by France in 1635 caused widespread dismay among Spaniards: few were under any illusions about the superior strength of their giant neighbour. From then on there was a rapid slide into disaster.

In 1637 tax riots broke out in Portugal in Evora and other towns, and French troops crossed into Catalonia; the year after, when the Basque fortress of Fuenterrabía was besieged by the French, Catalan troops were conspicuously absent from the force of volunteers which relieved it. The revolts of first Catalonia and then Portugal in 1640 set the seal on Spain's collapse.

The Count Duke's policy was in ruins. At court groups of nobles began plotting against him, and the grandees went on strike by refusing to attend all formal royal functions. The plot of his cousin the duke of Medina-Sidonia in Andalusia in 1641 served still further to depress the Count Duke: 'his judgment begins to break', reported the English envoy Sir Arthur Hopton. A last dramatic gesture to reverse the tide of defeat was made by Philip IV. In April 1642 he went to Aragon to direct the war effort in person; but in September Perpignan surrendered to France and in October the Castilian army under the marquis of Leganés was defeated in its attempts to retake Lérida. Back at court the count of Castrillo, of the Haro family, undermined any lingering support for Olivares. Philip IV returned to Madrid in December, and in January 1643 gave Olivares leave to retire from politics. The Count Duke retired to Toro, where he died, his mind deranged, in July 1645.

The king stated that 'such a good minister must be replaced only by me myself'. But he was reluctant to assume active control, which passed immediately to Olivares's nephew Luis de Haro. Less aggressive than Olivares, Haro exercised the full powers normally given to a valido, and was referred to by the king in the 1650s as his 'first minister' (*primer ministro*), a title used commonly thereafter for validos. Quietly, and with whatever efficiency was available to a government crippled by debt, Haro steered the monarchy on a survival course for 18 years, until his death in November 1661. The king did not entirely abdicate his responsibilities, but was adversely affected by personal problems, notably the death at the age of 17 of his only son and heir, the infante Baltasar Carlos, in 1646. Fortunately, he found spiritual consolation. In June 1643, while in Aragon, he met María de Agreda, a Franciscan nun renowned as a mystic, and for the rest of his reign engaged in a remarkable exchange of correspondence with her. Sor María advised him vigorously not only on spiritual matters but frequently also on affairs of state. Philip drew strength and comfort from her letters, but it remained a curious feature of Spanish politics that the head of the world's most powerful state should be swayed by the relatively uninformed opinions of a provincial recluse.

Philip's long and not entirely happy marriage to Elizabeth of Bourbon, daughter of Henry IV of France, ended with the queen's death in 1644. Of Philip's many mistresses the most striking was the actress María Calderón, who in 1629 bore him a son, Juan José, whom his father brought up as a royal prince. Three years after the death of Baltasar Carlos, Philip married his niece Mariana of Austria, 30 years his junior. After five pregnancies, from which only one girl survived, she gave birth in November 1661 to Carlos José, a sickly child who was expected to die at any moment. From this date, after Haro's death, government passed into the hands of Olivares's son-in-law the duke of Medina de las Torres. But already the rising star of Don Juan José, contrasting in its brilliance with the sombre last days of Philip IV and the prospect of a moribund heir to the throne of a decaying monarchy, began to raise serious doubts on the succession. When the king died, on 17 September 1665, he left Spain in grave crisis: the treasury empty, the Portuguese rebellion unsubdued and a regency under Mariana installed in Madrid.

# Foreign policy 1598–1665

Philip II by 1598 had largely pacified the Mediterranean, but in northern Europe control of events was being wrested from his grasp. The struggle against the Dutch rebels, undertaken now through the autonomous (since August 1598) government of the archduke Albert, was slowing to a halt; and the war with England seemed even less promising. The most important reversal was in France, where Henry IV was now a Catholic and supported by the papacy. The peace of Vervins (1598) released Spanish troops but identified France as a rising power towards which Spain's clients as well as enemies might gravitate. Philip III was anxious to continue the struggle against the English, and in 1601 the last of the abortive descents on Ireland (in Kinsale) was carried out. The archduke meanwhile in 1603 put out peace feelers to the new king of England, the Scot, James I. Spanish diplomacy, supported by Lerma, followed suit; and the peace treaty of London was signed in 1604.

The revolt in the Netherlands could now absorb Spain's undivided attention, but the omens were all unfavourable. From 1598 to 1601 the amount of money sent annually from Spain fell sharply, and between 1598 and 1604 every major campaign undertaken was wrecked by troop mutinies. At this juncture the Genoese general and financier Ambrogio Spinola offered to take charge. Thanks to his generalship but rather more to his loans, in 1604 Ostend was captured and further territory won. But in 1606 even his army mutinied, and the money ran out. The archduke, Spinola himself, the council of state in Madrid, all counselled peace. Spinola wrote to Philip III in 1607: 'There is only one course to take: to end this long and costly war'. In Castile war weariness had, as we have seen, led to protests in the Cortes. In 1600 an official commented that 'the provisioning of Flanders has been and is the ruin of Spain. It provokes the hostility of ministers, and the people cry that an end be put to it'. The king himself in 1604 expressed the common grief of Spaniards at 'the absence of sons, brothers, dependants and relatives, who either die or return wounded, without arms, sight or legs, totally useless'. The archduke agreed to a truce in April 1607. It was none too soon: in November that year the Spanish government again repudiated its debts. Only after long hesitation did Philip finally, in April 1609, sign the Twelve Years Truce with the United Provinces.

The truce was complemented by the decree for expelling the Moriscos, signed on the same day. Although apparently free now of enemies both without and within, and in a position to reduce costs in the Netherlands, Spain was still obliged to undertake heavy expenditure in maintaining the Spanish imperial system. In the decade that followed, Spanish diplomats achieved brilliant work in foreign capitals: Gondomar in London, Bedmar in Paris, and Zúñiga and Oñate in Vienna. Together, they created an apparently durable chain of alliances that raised Spanish influence to the highest point it ever achieved in Europe. Spanish culture became fashionable from London to Prague, and the religious progress of the Counter-Reformation seemed to be merely another dimension of the Spanish advance in Europe. In 1615, in a twin ceremony on the French frontier with Spain, the young infante Philip was wedded to Elizabeth of France and his sister Ana was married to Elizabeth's brother Louis XIII.

These triumphs, however, were not unmatched on the other side. The Dutch used the peace to build up their resources against the inevitable expiry of the truce. They consolidated their trade with Asia and began a military and commercial penetration of Brazil. At the same time they began to construct a diplomatic defence system. Their agents were in Venice in 1618 when it claimed to have uncovered a plot by Spain's viceroy in Naples, Osuna, to overthrow the republic. The year after, Holland and Venice signed a defensive alliance against Spain. More significantly, their agents were in Prague in May 1618 when two pro-Spanish ministers were thrown out of the window of the Hradčany Palace, an event that sparked off the Bohemian revolt. When the Emperor Ferdinand asked Spain for military aid against the rebels, a prime consideration in favour of granting aid was that Ferdinand had promised to cede Alsace, vital for Spanish access to the Netherlands.

The need to guarantee communications for its troops therefore pushed Spain into action in Germany. Spanish forces helped Ferdinand defeat the Bohemian rebels at the battle of the White Mountain in November 1620. Simultaneously, other contingents occupied Alsace and the strategic Alpine passes of the Valtelline; and the main body of the Flanders army under Spinola occupied the Rhine Palatinate. By the end of 1620 the Spanish army, in command of Europe's main nerve centres, was advantageously poised for a renewal of hostilities with the Dutch.

The move to war, strongly opposed by the archduke Albert, was quickened by the fall of Lerma in 1618. The duke's 'peace' policy had in reality been no more than an absence of foreign policy. Peace, his successors felt, had allowed the Dutch and English to strengthen themselves politically and economically. In Italy, America and in the Rhineland, Spanish interests were under constant threat, despite the nominal peace. The vital 'Spanish Road' between Milan and the Netherlands, on which Spain had long been dependent for movement of troops and supplies, fell under French control and could not be used after 1622. If Holland were not stopped, Zúñiga argued, 'we shall lose the Indies, then Flanders, then Italy and finally Spain itself'. His arguments were taken up by his nephew Olivares. In the United Provinces a 'war party' under Maurice of Nassau, strongly supported by Amsterdam, came to power in 1618 and made confrontation inevitable. Not that anyone wanted war. In 1619 when negotiations took place between the two sides the Spanish insisted on three conditions: a nominal recognition of Spanish sovereignty, toleration for the large Catholic minority in the United Provinces and the opening of the Scheldt so that Antwerp could trade. The government continued to make public profession of the first two claims – in 1628 Olivares reduced the essence of his demands to 'two points: religion and *reputación*' – but it was the third that most mattered; and indeed in 1621 the question of sovereignty was tacitly dropped, the matter of religion shelved and Spain's demands focused on two points: the opening of the Scheldt, and the withdrawal of the Dutch from America and the East Indies. These highly significant demands were a reflection of the worldwide successes of Dutch naval power.

Olivares consequently inherited not simply a local war in the Netherlands, but a global conflict in which the emphasis came to be more on naval warfare than on land-based strategy. For Spain the objective of the struggle was not expansion but economic survival. There was never any serious intention to recapture the rebel provinces: even Zúñiga had admitted that 'to promise ourselves that we can conquer the Dutch is to seek the impossible'. Fortunately the understanding reached with the Emperor Ferdinand brought the Spanish and German Habsburgs together for the first time in nearly a century, and helped the evolution of a continent-wide strategy. From 1625 England and France also began hostilities: the former after a strong English reaction against the abortive visit of prince Charles to Madrid, the latter after the accession of Richelieu to the king's council in 1624. The government coped remarkably, and 1625 was in effect a *Wunderjahr*: in April the port of Bahia in Brazil was recaptured from the Dutch (it was celebrated in a striking canvas by Juan Bautista Maino); in June Spinola took Breda, a feat immortalised years later in Velázquez's *Las Lanzas*; and in October the English were beaten back from Cadiz. French intervention in the Valtelline was met firmly, and by the peace of Monzón (March 1626) France agreed to withdraw. Philip IV reported with satisfaction (and some exaggeration) to the council of state: 'We have had all Europe against us, but we have not been defeated, nor have our allies lost. . . . Last year, 1625, we had nearly 300,000 infantry and cavalry in our pay, and over 500,000 militia under arms. . . . The fleet, which consisted of only seven vessels on my accession, rose at one time in 1625 to 108 ships of war'.

At the same time a concerted three-point naval campaign was launched against the Dutch. First, an attempt was made to block all Dutch trade with the peninsula, by creating in 1624 in Seville an *almirantazgo* or customs board to supervise trade with the north. Second, an armed offensive against Dutch shipping was launched from the Spanish Netherlands, using Dunkirk as the principal port for privateering operations, and leading to the capture between 1626 and 1634 of 1,835 vessels, mostly Dutch. Third, negotiations were undertaken with the emperor's general Wallenstein in the hope of launching a joint Spanish–Imperial fleet on the Baltic to cut Holland's commercial lifeline to the northern countries. These measures were only partly successful. The Dutch carrying trade to the peninsula was disrupted but soon resumed, and the scheme for a Baltic fleet never materialised, serving only to propel Sweden into the struggle against Spain. From 1628 fortunes turned against Olivares. In Italy he committed troops to secure the duchy of Mantua, leading to a disastrous war (1628–31) from which the benefits were reaped by France and its chief minister Richelieu, in full command of foreign policy after 1630. 1628 was also the year when the Dutch admiral Piet Heyn captured the entire New Spain silver fleet in the Cuban bay of Matanzas. The catastrophe earned the admiral, Juan de Benavides, trial and execution; Philip IV remarked that 'whenever I speak of the disaster the blood runs cold in my veins, not for the loss of treasure, but because we lost our *reputación* in that infamous defeat'.

At several intervals throughout the Thirty Years War discussions took place between representatives of Spain and the Dutch States General. They floundered on Spain's refusal to compromise. Failure to terminate the long struggle against Holland, which even Spinola argued could not be won, was ultimately disastrous; for as hostilities continued it became clear that an enemy far more powerful than the Dutch was looming on the horizon: Bourbon France. Philip IV's brother the cardinal infante Ferdinand led an army that joined with the troops of the emperor to inflict a crushing defeat on the Swedes at Nördlingen (1634). As a direct result France in May 1635 declared war on Spain.

Though its military resources were still relatively undeveloped, France at least entered the war fresh. Spain however had been fighting for 15 years, and the struggle was fated to endure another 25 and to encompass the peninsula itself. Already in 1626, Philip had accepted the inevitability of war: 'with as many kingdoms as have been linked to this crown, it is impossible to be without war in some area, either to defend what we have acquired or to divert my enemies'. The problem was that the tide was now turning against Spain. In 1637 the Dutch recaptured Breda, and in 1638 France's allies took the key Rhine fortress of Breisach. The reverses at sea were even more significant. In August 1638 the French wiped out a Spanish naval force in the little harbour of Guetaria (near San Sebastian); in 1639 the Dutch under Tromp defeated the Spanish fleet at the battle of the Downs (October); and in January 1640 another Dutch force defeated a much larger Hispano-Portuguese fleet off Brazil. 'God wants us to make peace,' the Count Duke wrote in a memorandum for the king in March 1640, 'for he is depriving us visibly and absolutely of all the means of war'. The revolts in Catalonia and Portugal seemed to presage the dissolution of the monarchy. Then in 1643 the governor of the Netherlands, Francisco de Melo, invaded France: his army was annihilated by a force under the young duke of Enghien (later to be famous as Condé) at Rocroi (19 May). It was 'an event', Don Luis de Haro subsequently remarked, 'which can never be recalled without great sorrow'.

Rocroi has often, and mistakenly, been regarded as the end of Spanish power. It was the first great defeat suffered by a Spanish army, but by no means the end. For nearly two decades more Spain continued to fight with varying degrees of success on a broader range of fronts than any other nation was capable of. By 1648, nevertheless, it seemed that everything had collapsed. The Portuguese and Catalan revolts were unsubdued, in Aragon there was a plot to secede, in Sicily and Naples revolution was triumphant, and epidemic and rebellion were tearing the very peninsula apart. This year of general crisis in Spain was climaxed by the long overdue triumph of the Dutch rebellion. 'Peace is necessary,' a Spanish minister had written wearily in 1645, 'whatever the cost and whatever the price'. In October 1648 by the treaty of Münster, part of the peace of Westphalia that ended the Thirty Years War, Spain recognised the United Provinces as an independent state.

Spain's weakness was all too clearly shown up by its inability to exploit the civil war – the Fronde – that preoccupied France between 1648 and 1652; requests for help from rebel Bordeaux were ignored. Where troops were already committed, however, the temporary advantage over France was pressed home, resulting in the capture during 1652, on three distinct fronts, of Barcelona, Casale and Dunkirk. These were Spain's last notable military triumphs. The unexpected outbreak in 1655 of hostilities with Cromwell's England, to whom Spain had been conspicuously friendly, helped turn the tide decisively. English naval forces seized Jamaica (it was a second best, for the real objective had been Hispaniola) and Blake's navy destroyed the Indies treasure fleets in 1656 and 1657. English troops went on to help Mazarin's army defeat the army of Flanders at the battle of the Dunes (1658) and recapture Dunkirk. Shortly after, the Portuguese defeated the Spanish army at the frontier town of Elvas (January 1659). 'I have always wanted peace', Philip IV stated in 1658, 'and desire it more sincerely every day, and will make any sacrifices on my part for it; the matter, however, depends not on my will but on that of the enemy'. Hostilities with France were suspended in May 1659, and in November the treaty of the Pyrenees ended the war.

At the peace Spain ceded to France Cerdagne and Roussillon in Catalonia, and Artois and several fortresses in the Netherlands; the infanta María Teresa was also to wed Louis XIV. Though not a humiliating treaty, it marked the end of Spanish hegemony in Europe. The war of attrition against Portugal continued, but that too was ended, after military reverses for Spain, in 1668. In rounded terms, Spain's great imperial epoch lasted just one century, from about 1560 to about 1660. The role of superpower was one for which the country had never been adequately equipped, and which many Spaniards considered to be at variance with Spain's own interests, but it was one that the nation fulfilled valiantly and sometimes gloriously: at Rocroi it was the auxiliaries who broke and ran, the Castilian tercios who stood their ground and were slaughtered.

# Olivares

The democratic and reforming trends that emerged in government during the ministry of Lerma were given their most forceful expression through the writings of the arbitristas (discussed on p. 251). The foundation of the first junta de reformación in 1618, and the famous consulta of the council of Castile in 1619, were clear indications that senior politicians felt changes to be necessary. Olivares came to power at a time when reform was in the air; not surprisingly, his own programme coincided with much that had already been proposed. In his Great Memorial of December 1624 he agreed substantially with the analyses as well as the remedies offered by arbitristas. There must, in the first place, be an end to luxury, extravagance and corruption. Second, fiscal reform was essential: the tax system needed reforming, manipulation of the coinage must end, the millones should be suppressed and substituted by a new 'single tax'. Third, an effort must be made to 'turn Spaniards into merchants', by encouraging them to invest their capital in trading companies and in savings banks; at the same time mental attitudes must change, particularly in regard to the statutes of limpieza. Finally, in order to exploit the resources of the monarchy properly, all its realms should cooperate to their mutual advantage, preferably by being united under the laws of Castile.

Apart possibly from the last one, none of these proposals was original: Olivares in 1621 had been a man with no experience of government and it was inevitable that he should derive his views from the common fund of ideas shared by reform-minded contemporaries. In the heady enthusiasm of the years 1621–5, the Count Duke and his colleagues pushed ahead with their policies. A new junta de reformación was set up in August 1622 and issued 23 articles in February 1623. Under Olivares's guidance the young king took a direct part in government: in 1625 he was estimated to be personally handling 44 out of every 50 consultas. Reform proposals were channelled for greater efficiency through small committees of the councils: a committee for trade was set up in 1622, one for population and mines in 1625. The expenses of the king's court were reduced (though they still remained close to 1.5 million ducats a year), sumptuary laws were passed and bribery restrained so that even the Count Duke's enemies admitted that his hands had been clean. The establishment of an *almirantazgo* at Seville in 1624 provided both a monopoly system for trading to northern Europe and an effective commercial weapon against the Dutch.

The achievements – Olivares himself listed them to the king in a paper of July 1625 – were those of an arbitrista who was also chief minister of the monarchy. But the Count Duke was not merely a reformer: he was also a man of vision. His hostility to the practice of limpieza, which he condemned in 1625 as 'contrary to divine law, natural law and the law of nations', arose from his conviction that all subjects of the state were entitled to equal and just treatment. He himself had converso blood (his grandmother was the daughter of the Aragonese converso Lope Conchillos, secretary to Ferdinand the Catholic), a consideration that may have helped to make him aware of the problem of discrimination. In his open favouring of Portuguese converso financiers after 1627, and in his apparently serious proposal to invite the Jews back to Spain so as to undo the bad results of their expulsion, he was stubbornly challenging contemporary opinion. This, however, was his nature, described by a diplomat in 1629 as 'very inclined to novelties, without taking account of where they may lead him'.

The most famous novelty was his proposal in the Great Memorial that Philip IV should 'become King of Spain'. 'By this I mean, Sir,' the proposal continues, 'that Your Majesty should not be content with being King of Portugal, of Aragon, of Valencia, and count of Barcelona, but should secretly plan and work to reduce these kingdoms of which Spain is composed, to the style and laws of Castile, with no difference whatsoever; and if Your Majesty achieves this, you will be the most powerful prince in the world'. Presented in this bare form, the proposal looks like an aggressive plan to do away with the fueros of the non-Castilian realms. Set in context, it was less an attempt to Castilianise the peninsula than a scheme for all Spaniards to share equally in the country's resources. The constitutional barriers between the realms were to be broken down so that non-Castilians could in future (in Olivares's words) 'equally enjoy the honours, offices and confidence given to those born in Castile'. Olivares's closest confidant, Villanueva, claimed in 1626 that royal policy was 'to familiarise the natives of the different kingdoms with each other so that they forget the isolation in which they have hitherto lived'; and in 1632 the Count Duke asserted that 'in saying Spaniards it must be understood that there is no difference between one nation and another of those included within the limits of Spain'. Behind the rhetoric lay a firm intention to harness the joint assets of the peninsula. Castilian arbitristas had long lamented the fact that Castile alone was contributing to the costs of empire. In his Art of Government (1598) Baltasar Álamos de Barrientos had complained that 'in other states all the parts contribute to the maintenance of the head; but in ours it is the head which does the work and provides the other members with their sustenance'. In 1618 in the council of finance a minister noted that 'everything is met out of the resources of Castile and out of what comes from the Indies, and literally nothing is contributed by Aragon, Valencia, Catalonia, Portugal and Navarre. As a result, Castile's revenues are pledged to the hilt'. Writing at the same time as Olivares, the arbitrista Fernández Navarrete was reflecting a common opinion when he noted that 'it is only fair that the burdens should be properly apportioned'. In practical terms, then, Olivares was calling for the non-Castilian realms to pay more taxes in return for the broader privileges he wished them to enjoy. It was a message that emerged clearly from the Union of Arms, an ambitious military scheme that gave substance to the plan for pooling resources. In the event, none of the non-Castilian realms gave unqualified support to the Union.

Within Castile, Olivares's main proposal was the establishment of a number of public banks or *erarios*, whose capital was to be drawn initially from a tax on property. The scheme, suggested to the Castilian Cortes in October 1622, was derived from plans presented to Philip II as early as 1576 by the Fleming Pieter van Oudegherste and subsequently discussed in various Cortes under Philip III. The erarios would make cash available to farmers for improvement, and at the same time offer attractive interest rates to investors. To make the scheme more attractive to the Cortes, Olivares proposed that the millones should simultaneously be abolished, and replaced by a small local tax to support a standing army of 30,000 infantry. Together, the plans for erarios and an end to the millones represented for Olivares the one way to secure 'the salvation of the monarchy'. The Cortes, despite their constant opposition to the millones, were however wary of proposals that seemed likely to offer the crown a regular income that made it independent of servicios voted by them, and rejected the proposals in 1624; so that by 1626 the government was once again collecting the millones. The latter year was also the one in which the Union of Arms failed to secure support in Aragon.

The years of success up to 1625 – the military victories of that year earned Philip IV the epithet of 'the Great' – were thus followed by long years of frustration when Olivares's reform policy ground to a halt. The failure may be in part explained by the Count Duke's thrusting and bullying nature: impatient of opposition, he raged and fumed to get his policies into operation, overworked his secretaries and drove himself relentlessly. A devoted servant of the king, he relied only on Philip for his authority, and correspondingly failed to build up a broad body of political support on the councils and in the administration. His forceful personality proved to be an inadequate guarantee of success: without a power base to support him, he quickly found that the system could and did defeat him. Within the small group of his collaborators the most prominent was Jerónimo de Villanueva, an Aragonese who rose from obscurity to become a member of the council of Aragon and the most important man in the government after Olivares. A converso by origin, Villanueva became wealthy in office, and founded in Madrid the convent of San Placido, whose nuns became the centre of a heresy scandal in the 1630s.

It is possible that the death of Olivares's only child – a daughter – in 1626 destroyed his personal hopes for the future and contributed to his austere and intense lifestyle. By the 1630s he was complaining of ill health and insomnia: 'for many days now', he admitted in 1636, 'I have been unable to sleep by night or day'. By then, too, there was widespread hatred and criticism of the valido. The public murmured, for instance, at the construction of the palace of Buen Retiro, which was begun in 1632 and cost nearly three million ducats: 'a fancy of the Conde's', was how Sir Arthur Hopton described it. The revolts in Vizcaya in 1631 and Evora in 1637 were symptoms of the general collapse of confidence in the regime, a collapse that preceded rather than followed the events of the year 1640. Lampoons against Olivares circulated throughout the country, and in 1639 the poet Francisco de Quevedo was arrested for writing a scurrilous satire that the king discovered under his table napkin. 'Everyone is complaining, both small and great,' wrote a Jesuit from Madrid in 1641, 'and nobody knows where the remedy lies'.

Universal failure in the late 1630s deprived the regime of support and caused defections among its closest sympathisers. The grandees went on strike by refusing to attend official functions and retiring in a body to their estates. A group of them led by the count of Castrillo engineered the coup that led to Philip dismissing his valido in 1643. It was apparently a move that the king had been considering for some time. Olivares had been under severe mental strain and had lost control over affairs, his own secretary Antonio Carnero admitting that 'my master is utterly worn down and broken'. The downfall of the Count Duke meant a victory for conservatism. Grandees and bureaucrats who resented his interference with their monopoly of the administration, traditionalists who objected to the appearance of conversos in public life (the Portuguese financier Manuel Cortizos de Villasante was prominent at court and contributed to the construction of the Buen Retiro), stirred opinion against him. Ironically for one whose policy has often been presented as pro-Castilian, Castilian sentiment was far from favourable to the Count Duke. In 1643, after his fall, a member of the administration, Andrés de Mena, drew up a series of charges against him, condemning his unconstitutional attacks on the laws of the Catalans no less than on the privileges of Castilians. To refute these charges Olivares issued his anonymous *Nicandro*, arguing that his policies had enjoyed the full support of the king. His critics made further moves against him (Villanueva's arrest by the Inquisition in 1644 arose officially out of the San Plácido affair) but no general purge ensued, despite changes in senior posts. Many who had been associated with Olivares, like his secretary Carnero, continued in authority, while his son-in-law Medina de las Torres made a remarkable comeback at the end of the reign.

The ministry of Olivares was (like that of Don Juan José a generation later, *see* p. 278) an unqualified failure. The collapse of his policy was not a disaster internally, for it led to a certain stability: in Castile it restored power to the local elites, in the crown of Aragon it gave initiative to autonomous interests. In foreign policy, by contrast, the decay was irreversible, and in 1660 an arbitrista was lamenting that Castile had less power by land and sea than it had enjoyed in three hundred years.

# War and finance

In every state in early modern Europe the needs of the army absorbed most public expenditure. Spain's financial situation was exceptionally bad as a result of the unprecedented effort by Philip II to make the country into a great power, and the cumulative debt he bequeathed to his successors was the principal reason forcing Lerma's government into a search for peace. But the cessation of hostilities by itself could not alleviate pressure on the treasury. To meet costs the administration resorted to a measure that Philip II had always refused to contemplate: debasing the vellón coinage by issuing coins of pure copper instead of the normal mixture of silver and copper. It was a highly unpopular move (Mariana attacked the debasements in his *De Mutatione Monetae*, 1609, was arrested by the Inquisition and his book placed on the Index), but the government found it too profitable to forgo. In 1599 copper coins worth only a fraction of their face value were minted; then in 1603 the coins were reissued at double their nominal value. The profit made on these transactions was about six million ducats; but confidence in the coinage was rapidly undermined and a new evil, that of monetary inflation, was unleashed on the public. From 1599 to 1606 about 22 million ducats of vellón were coined. The Cortes protested and minting was stopped in 1607, but ten years later they granted the king permission to coin further large sums. The issue of debased vellón now became a routine device by the government for squeezing cash out of the monetary system. The government of Philip IV between 1621 and 1626 coined the enormous sum of 19.7 million ducats, which produced a net profit of over 13 million.

By this time a rise in world copper prices – Spain imported the metal from Sweden – slowed down minting operations. But monetary disorder in Castile was so extensive that the government was forced to think again before issuing further coin. Gold and silver were driven out of circulation by the debased currency, whose premium on silver coin of the same nominal value rose to 4 per cent in 1620 and 50 per cent in 1626, thereby creating a dual currency and completely dislocating all market prices. The government itself suffered from the disparity between vellón and silver. Before the Fuggers would advance 80,000 ducats in silver in Germany, for example, they had to be promised 180,000 ducats in vellón in Spain.

Despite the good intentions of Philip IV and Olivares, the reign continued to experience uninterrupted monetary inflation and coinage manipulation. By 1641 the premium on silver had soared to nearly 200 per cent, forcing a brutal deflation in September 1642, which caused widespread losses and paralysed trade temporarily. In the last years of the reign, dominated by rampant inflation and monetary disorder, the price level attained heights equalled nowhere else in Europe. By 1650 Spain, the world's biggest importer of precious metals, had almost no gold or silver in circulation, and copper made up over 98 per cent of coinage in common use. The accepted value of the inflated currency was so low that in Seville in the 1650s a six-pound bag of vellón, irrespective of the number of coins it contained, became the normal price for ten pounds of cheese.

International payments could only be made in silver, and it was the shortage of this metal that became the biggest obstacle to Spain's imperial obligations. In the first 12 years of the reign of Philip III, from 1598 to 1609, nearly 42 million ducats in silver was spent on the war in the Low Countries alone. Unable to reimburse the financiers and also to keep up debt repayments, Philip was forced in November 1607 to declare a bankruptcy, the only one of his reign. As with the decrees of Philip II, a suspension was rapidly followed by an agreement with creditors. This resulted in the *medio general* of May 1608, which gave Genoese bankers an unshakeable hold over state finance for another 20 years.

Unfortunately, from the first decade of the century the crown began receiving less silver from America. Peak receipts of 13.17 million ducats for the crown in the five years 1596–1600 dropped to two million in 1646–50. Peace should have allowed economies to be made, but no such retrenchment occurred. In 1618, before the commitment in Germany, the head of finance reported that 'the ordinary revenues and all other resources are pledged for a greater sum than their total value'. Other advisers opposed any ambitious foreign policies. 'Everyone knows', the previous head of finance had observed, 'that Castile has been drained of men and resources; and to ruin it, and try to squeeze out of it what is simply not there, in order to make ourselves important in Germany – this is a policy which in all conscience cannot be carried out'. By 1621 the king was told that 'the money for this year's expenses has come not from present revenue but from revenue anticipated up to 1625'. The ending of the Twelve Years Truce in fact caused an immediate escalation of costs. Remittances to Flanders rose from 1.5 million to 3.5 million ducats a year, and naval expenditure doubled between 1620 and 1622 to over one million. Taking into account the reality that the government had in no way managed to cope with its outstanding juro debt, which rose from 85 million in 1598 to 112 million by 1623, its ability to cope with the renewal of war was little short of astonishing.

The first suspension of payments under Philip IV, in January 1627, was precipitated by internal monetary chaos, economic crisis and the relative failure of the Union of Arms; it formed part of the radical package of measures in 1626-8 that might have restored some stability to the Castilian fiscal system. For Olivares the suspension also had another objective: to break the hold of the Genoese, and to replace them by Portuguese bankers, some of whom had already made an asiento with the treasury the year before. From 1627 to 1647 the Portuguese, many of them conversos having invaluable links with Jewish financiers abroad, were the principal collaborators of the treasury.

After the Mantua fiasco, Olivares moved into an epoch of total war in the 1630s. By 1634, when essential budget costs were put at some 7.5 million, over 93 per cent was earmarked for the wars abroad. For 1637 essential costs were put at some four million, two-thirds for the war abroad. With inadequate tax income, and decreasing support from American bullion, the only sure source of supply was the bankers. Without their heroic efforts – in 1635 the Genoese financier Carlo Strata alone lent 2.15 million ducats – the crown would have been unable to meet its obligations. The most important financiers of the period were the Spinolas: the Genoese branch of the family produced the famous military commander, while the Spanish branch between 1615 and 1644 alone lent over 50 million ducats to the crown.

One of the more enduring consequences of the alienation of taxes in order to repay holders of juros and financiers was that the government resorted to creating new sources of income. Following the successful grant of a 'free gift' (donativo) in 1624, further such 'gifts' were levied. At the same time the sale of royal villages – the so-called 'sale of vassals' – was resumed. During his reign Philip IV was authorised by the Cortes to sell about 200,000 of his subjects out of royal jurisdiction, thus creating 169 new señoríos. Pressure was put on the grandees to contribute soldiers to the royal service: the duke of Béjar claimed that between 1625 and 1642 this had cost him about 250,000 ducats. Lesser nobles were in 1631 allowed to commute their military service obligations into cash payments: this created the *lanzas* (lances) tax. In the same year the *media anata*, or 'half-year' of income from all official posts, was introduced; and a new salt tax was created but had to be dropped after riots in Vizcaya. Then from 1636 a stamp tax on paper (the bright idea of a luckless Jesuit who was at once expelled from his order) was introduced, as well as a tax on playing-cards. Sales of offices flourished: the Cortes in 1638, for instance, gave its assent to the sale of offices and jurisdictions up to a value of two million ducats. When the matter was mentioned to the king in 1642, he replied: 'It is certainly inadvisable to sell offices, but necessity brings all these evils with it'. Most important of all, the national debt of juros was itself taxed. Where the annual sum required to pay annuities was some two million in 1574, in 1621 it was 4.6 million and by 1637 had risen to 6.4 million. In the 1620s occasional discounts had been made against these interest payments, but from 1634 the discounts became considerable and a regular source of revenue.

The new impositions were significant for two reasons. First, they effectively doubled the burden on the Castilian taxpayer between 1621 and 1642, at a time when the number of people capable of paying taxes had greatly diminished. Second, much of the new burden fell on the upper classes, partly because the taxes affected them most, partly because it was indirect rather than direct taxation that increased. The continued importance of contributions from the Spanish Church, and the role of other impositions, can be seen below in the income and expenditure table made by an official accountant.

*Hacienda income 1621–40* (in percentages)

| | |
|---|---:|
| From Cortes of Castile (servicios) | 38.0 |
| From Cortes of crown of Aragon | 1.1 |
| From Spanish Church (Three Graces) | 15.6 |
| Bullion from Indies, 1621–39 | 9.5 |
| Discounts on and sale of juros | 9.0 |
| Re-coinages | 7.5 |
| Donativos, 1624–35 | 5.5 |
| Sales of office, vassals, etc. | 3.5 |
| Salt tax | 2.9 |
| Media anata | 1.3 |
| Seizure of private bullion | 1.2 |
| Other | 4.9 |

Total 237.3 million ducats

*Hacienda expenditure 1621–40*

| | |
|---|---|
| Asientos and bankers (i.e. military and debts) | 70.4 |
| Mediterranean fleet | 5.3 |
| Atlantic fleet | 4.5 |
| Forts and frontiers | 3.7 |
| Army in Spain | 3.2 |
| Royal household | 5.0 |
| Administration | 2.5 |
| Other | 5.4 |

Total 249.8 million ducats

The extra sources of revenue failed to stem the tide of debt. In May 1646 a budget forecast showed that 12.7 million ducats were needed for the coming financial year but only 3.2 were available. In October 1647 the government, hard pressed by reverses in the north and by the revolt in Naples, declared its second bankruptcy, but exempted its principal Genoese financiers – Spinola, Centurione and Pallavicino – from the decree. The peace of Westphalia, which brought an end to 30 years of warfare in the rest of Europe, made little difference to Spain's military commitments, still at a high level as a result of the wars with France and Portugal. In his speech to the Cortes in 1655 the king himself stated that 66.8 million in silver had been spent on war abroad between 1649 and 1654. Meanwhile in July 1652 the government declared the third bankruptcy of the reign; the fourth followed in August 1662. Each suspension added to the size of the juro debt, which stood at 221.6 million ducats in 1667, the annual payments alone amounting to over nine million, or nearly three-fourths of current revenue. 'On many days', wrote the diarist Barrionuevo, 'even bread cannot be had in the royal household' of Philip IV.

The century of Spain's imperial preponderance – from 1560 to 1660 – collapsed under irretrievable debt, and the military successes of 1652 could not mask the decay within. From the mid-sixteenth century, when the imperial build-up had been undertaken in the face of overwhelming financial insufficiency, the problem never ceased to worsen. Spanish imperialism, it seemed, was doomed from the start: and perennial poverty forced peace in 1609, 1648 and 1659. In itself finance was of course not a cause but a symptom of Spain's inability to develop enough resources to support its imperial policy. The manpower problem, for example, was aggravated by the demographic crisis and by high rates of desertion on all fronts. It is possible that the burden would have been eased if a plan such as the Union of Arms had been put into effect. The income figures for 1621–40 which appear in the table (p. 230) show all too starkly the respective contributions of Castile and Aragon to the war effort. But it must be recognised that in the Spanish Netherlands, where the Union of Arms was accepted in 1627, and in the Italian dominions, Spain's allies were making a considerable contribution. A contemporary in Milan estimated that the duchy had paid some 50 million ducats to Spain over the period 1610–50. In Naples the realm in 1639 alone contributed two million ducats, and in 1640 was asked for 2.4 million more as well as 6,000 infantry. The drain on Italian men and money caused the viceroy of Naples to complain that 'Castile, Naples, and Sicily alone shoulder all the expenses . . . Your Majesty cannot carry on the war much longer in this way'. Though the crisis hit hardest at Castile, it threatened also to dismember the whole monarchy.

# The expulsion of the Moriscos

The acceptance in 1582 by Philip II's council of state of proposals that the Moriscos be expelled from Spain, would seem to have been the final signal for action. In fact a generation was to pass before anything transpired, and in that time a major debate broke out over the expulsion, which was neither inevitable nor always supported by public opinion.

The nobility in Aragon and Valencia had been tolerant of the religion of the Moriscos, whom they could exploit more readily as a depressed minority. Obstacles put by the nobles in the way of the missionaries caused a Jesuit in 1608 to complain that the tyranny of the lords was one of the main barriers to effective conversion in Valencia. Several grandees seem to have accepted that excessive religious zeal would destroy the harmony between the races. Notable among them had been Íñigo López de Mendoza, second count of Tendilla (d. 1515), grandson of the great Mendoza scholar the marquis of Santillana and himself an outstanding scholar, soldier and statesman. As captain-general of the newly conquered realm of Granada, he shared with Talavera a concern to win over the Muslims to Christianity by a policy of respect for Moorish culture. A bitter opponent of Cisneros's policy and of the harsh methods of the Inquisition, Tendilla in 1514 attacked the attempt to make Moriscos change their dress: 'What does his Highness mean by ordering the Moriscos to abandon their clothing? What clothing did we use to wear in Spain, how did we wear our hair, what sort of food did we eat, if not in the Morisco style? Did the kings cease to be Christians and saints because of this? No, sir, by God'. His son and later his grandson followed his outlook, the latter explicitly calling during the

1569 uprising for 'application rather than force, and if force then not as presently used'.

Although racial tension was high at the turn of the century, only a minority thought in terms of expulsion. Philip III was in Valencia in 1599 for his wedding and in 1604 for the Cortes: on neither occasion was an expulsion mentioned. The council of state, which had under Philip II recommended the solution, was now under Philip III divided over it. Both Lerma and the king's confessor in 1602 opposed expulsion since it 'would be terrible to drive baptised people into Barbary and thus force them to turn Muslim'. In 1606 an opinion was commissioned from the writer Pedro de Valencia: he identified all the difficulties, and proposed instead a more careful policy of assimilation. As late as 1607 two reasoned memoranda from the crown's highest ministers – Juan de Idiáquez and the count of Miranda – emphasised that the policy must be one of teaching and conversion. In all these years there was no pressure for expulsion from the Cortes either in Castile or in Valencia. All arbitristas of the period were uniformly opposed. In his *Memorial* (1600) González de Cellorigo denounced the proposal and, writing after the event, Fernández de Navarrete in 1626 regretted the expulsion and considered that 'it is a most malign policy of state for princes to withdraw their trust from their subjects'.

Nevertheless on 30 January 1608 the council of state voted unanimously to proceed to expulsion. What lay behind this astonishing volte-face? Some success must be attributed to the energetic campaign of Juan de Ribera, archbishop of Valencia, who from being a tireless supporter of conversion turned into an implacable enemy of the Moriscos and the leading partisan of expulsion. There is also no doubt that information of secret negotiations between the Moriscos and agents of Henry IV of France sent into Spain by the duke de la Force, governor of Béarn, alarmed the government. Lerma's own personal role was also important: he changed his mind, and presented to the council a proposal that the lords in Valencia – of whom he was one – should be compensated by being given the lands of the expelled Moriscos. The element of personal profit, in this as in all his policy, was crucial to the duke; but it is clear that he could not have proceeded had the lords in Valencia, who all along had bitterly opposed the move, not also changed their minds. And their position was getting desperate. Agrarian productivity rose during the good years of the sixteenth century, giving those lords and clergy who received tithes a satisfactory income from their Morisco peasantry. But where rents were fixed the nobles were barely able to cover their debts. In the area of Turís (Valencia), part of the lands of the duke of Gandía, noble rents during the sixteenth century rose four-fold, but the size of the duke's debt in censos rose thirteen-fold between 1551 and 1604. By 1600, the Valencian nobility were paying one-third of their income in censo debts, and were unable to make good their losses from the fixed tenancies of their Morisco vassals. They stood, therefore, to gain from dispossession and expulsion.

The actual decree of expulsion was passed in the council of state on 4 April 1609. The militia and navy were alerted. In September the decree was published in Valencia, giving Moriscos three days to embark. It excluded from the expulsion those certified by parish clergy as Christians, and children under the age of six whose parents consented to them remaining. Many Valencian nobles did their best to ease the travails of their former vassals; but there were thousands of tragedies, ranging from those who were robbed and maltreated to those who took up arms to resist and perished at the hands of the soldiers. Subsequent decrees extended the expulsions to the rest of Spain during 1610, despite pleas from the authorities in Aragon, Murcia and other areas. The whole operation continued in various phases up to 1614. Out of over 320,000 Moriscos resident in peninsular Spain, representing in Valencia 30 per cent of the population and in Aragon one-fifth, close to 300,000 were expelled. The great majority went to north Africa, to Moroccan and Tunisian towns where they were close to Spain; in some areas they were well received, in others they were hated as foreigners. Several thousands went to Christian lands, mainly France, but eventually moved on again to Salonika and Istanbul.

Apologists of the expulsion then and later alleged religious or security motives; but the operation was undoubtedly racial. In 1611 when it was proposed to expel the Moriscos of the valley of Ricote, a community of six towns in Murcia, a special report pointed out that the 2,500 inhabitants were truly Christian; but the expulsion went ahead regardless in 1613. It was one of the most ill-considered policy acts of the century, carried out against the views of a large body of informed opinion in Spain, denounced by foreigners – cardinal Richelieu condemned it as 'barbarous' – and very quickly regretted on all sides. Cervantes spoke for many when creating in his *Don Quixote* the sympathetic character of the Morisco Ricote, who like his people longed to return to his country: 'wherever we are we weep for Spain, because we were born there and it is our native land'. As late as 1690 a Moroccan envoy in Madrid heard court officials denouncing the expulsions and the duke of Lerma's responsibility for them.

Although the human losses of the expulsion represented little more than 4 per cent of Spain's population, the real impact in some areas was very severe. Where Moriscos had been a large minority – in Valencia (which lost nearly a third of its population), and in Aragon – there were immediate economic repercussions. But even where they were few, the fact that they had a minimal inactive population, with no gentry or clergy or soldiers, meant that their absence could lead to grave economic dislocation. In community after community tax returns fell and agricultural output decayed. Rents drawn from Morisco tenants disappeared: the income of the see of Saragossa fell by 40 per cent, that of the see of Valencia by 30 per cent. In Valencia the duke of Gandía lost 13,000 Morisco tenants, a number barely compensated by the entry of 1,300 Christian peasants in 1610. In Valencia some 14,000 new settlers entered to occupy lands left vacant by the Moriscos; 94 per cent of them were landless Christians from elsewhere in Valencia, only a fraction coming from outside the realm. Even so, some 45 per cent of Morisco villages in the province – 205 out of 453 – were still deserted in 1638, in part because they were situated in less fertile territory. Aware of the special problems in Valencia, the government intervened to help the nobles with the repopulation. They were allowed to grant resettlement charters (*cartas pueblas*), which sometimes imposed even more onerous conditions than the Moriscos had accepted. The interest rate payable on their estate debts was also reduced, though this created a crisis for the municipal bank or *Taula* of Valencia, which went bankrupt in 1613. There was considerable truth in the report made to Lerma that 'the lords have suffered greatly, but some have certainly also gained'. In Aragon, where the absence of Moriscos likewise disrupted agriculture, an official in 1635 reported that the lack of manpower 'was made up in part by French, from Béarn and Gascony'.

The expulsions were being cited a decade later by towns and arbitristas as a major cause of ruin in Spain. The truth, inevitably, was not so simple. The fecundity of the Moriscos – so often commented upon at the time – had itself been slowing down since the 1580s, in line with the falling birth rate among Old Christians, so that the expulsions worsened rather than began a depopulation that was already well under way. Moreover, in most communities agrarian production was already falling in the 1580s, and for a while the loss of the Moriscos (who did not eat much wheat and drank no wine) had a muted impact: 'the tithes', commented the Valencian Jaime Bleda in 1618, 'are not yielding a great deal less than before the expulsion'. Only with the growing crisis of production in the early seventeenth century did writers begin to point to the absence of Moriscos as a root cause of all ills. The disasters unleashed by the expulsion were serious, but in the long term merely intensified problems that were already developing in Spain's economy.

# The loss of Catalonia and Portugal

Divided by laws, customs barriers and languages, the realms of the peninsula had never been a political unity. If a Spaniard were asked what country (*país*) he came from, he would refer to the region where he was born, not to the abstract entity called 'Spain'. It would be wrong to deduce from this that Spaniards felt their primary loyalties to belong to their local provinces. Called 'realms' at that time, the provinces were in reality artificial constructs within which the people shared no moral unity, and if there was a sense of 'belonging' or a feeling for 'home', that 'home' was usually a small locality or village within the province. Within Asturias, within Andalusia, within Catalonia, different languages were spoken, different customs coexisted, loyalties were directed to the local township or seigneur rather than to the realm as a whole. Regions existed, therefore, but no effective regionalism.

Ironically, the seventeenth-century crisis aggravated the problems of the localities and helped powerfully to bring regionalism to birth. The central issue was fiscal. Olivares, like ministers before him, was aware of the unfair burden of taxation on Spain's subjects. A 1616 breakdown of revenue showed that Castile was contributing 73 per cent of imperial costs, Portugal 10 per cent, the Netherlands 9 per cent, Naples 5 per cent and Aragon only 1 per cent. The year after Philip IV's accession the Cortes were informed of a proposal to make the fuero provinces pay fairly for war expenses. 'Natural justice insists', the decree said, 'that all those who enjoy common benefits should make appropriate contributions'. Growing fiscal pressure by the central government was exemplified in the scheme for a Union of Arms, partially put into effect throughout the whole monarchy with the notable exception of Catalonia.

Since state finance had been parlous under Philip II and Philip III as well, it is not surprising to find that pressure on the regions antedated Olivares. In Castile the crown had always been concerned to raise local revenue efficiently. An important step in this direction was taken in 1608 when a royal decree reaffirmed the authority of the main cities over raising taxes in each region; the measure in effect created provincial capitals. In the northern provinces, control over taxes was put into the hands of the local oligarchies, who were formed into an assembly (or junta) for Galicia in 1599 and for Asturias a decade later. Control over raising revenue, it was felt, could be assured by collaboration with regional elites. The same reasoning probably lay behind the collective votes in Cortes granted to the cities of Galicia and of Extremadura. By granting initiative in finance to the elites, however, the government was encouraging the growth of common cause among urban oligarchies, which cultivated regionalism as a basis for their power pretensions. This precipitated conflicts all over Spain, and inevitably in Catalonia.

After Olivares's failure in the principality in 1626, a second effort was made in 1632. It was not a propitious moment. The general crisis centring around 1630 had brought plague to Catalonia and famine to all Spain; an attempt to extend the salt tax to Vizcaya brought about the first major regional revolt of Olivares's ministry (see p. 256). A Cortes was summoned to convene in May 1632 under the presidency of the cardinal infante Ferdinand, who was also appointed viceroy. Villanueva's instructions for the cardinal laboured under the same misapprehension that ministers had always had, namely that Catalonia was 'extensive, abundant and populous'. It was felt that Catalonia had about a million people – the true figure was half that – adequate to operate the Union of Arms and to contribute more to royal taxes. A dispute over Barcelona's claim to the privileges of 'grandee' status – of which the outward sign was that councillors could wear their hats in the king's presence – wrecked the Cortes, which refused to grant any money.

The outbreak of war with France in 1635 encouraged Olivares to believe that Catalonia's elite would face realities. When the French invaded Guipuzcoa in 1638 and laid siege to Fuenterrabía, however, no Catalans came to help, even though volunteers arrived from as far away as Valencia and Granada. In 1639, therefore, Olivares deliberately chose Catalonia as the principal war front and focused attention on the French siege of the border fortress of Salces. Even at this late stage the Diputación in Barcelona refused to vote more men or money, as being against the 'constitutions'. 'I am nearly at my wits' end', raged Olivares, 'but I say and shall still be saying on my deathbed, that if the constitutions do not allow this, then the devil take the constitutions!' The count of Santa Coloma, viceroy since 1638, was unable to control the situation. In January 1640 Salces was finally recaptured after a tardy effort by the Catalans, but it cost them dear: the death toll was over 4,000, including possibly one-quarter of the entire Catalan aristocracy.

Olivares felt that the initiative should not be lost; an army of 9,000 men should be billeted in Catalonia in preparation for a new campaign. The audiencia in Barcelona ruled that the billeting was illegal, but Santa Coloma went ahead despite his own reservations. Clashes between peasants and soldiers broke out all over the province, and the viceroy in February 1640 accused the Diputació of 'deliberately stirring up the people and trying to destroy the army'. Olivares was furious: 'no king in the world has a province like Catalonia', he fumed, 'it has a king and lord, but it renders him no services. This king and lord can do nothing that he wants in it. We always have to look and see if a constitution says this or that'. In April insurgent rebels began attacking the royal troops and in May they entered Barcelona, nominally to defend it against the troops. But by their conduct, and by opening all the prisons, they showed that they were equally hostile to those sections of the upper classes that had collaborated in the billeting. A wave of social revolution swept over the principality as Vic, Gerona and other cities were occupied by insurgents. On 7 June, the feast of Corpus Christi, a group of insurgents disguised as harvesters (*segadores*) entered Barcelona, started an extensive riot, pursued the viceroy from his palace and cut him down on the beach as he tried to make his escape in a galley.

From Madrid the events looked like rebellion. In reality it was chaos, as law and order in Catalonia collapsed while the upper classes feared to act against their own vassals. Olivares was powerless to use the army, since it was that against which the whole rising was directed. Unwilling to compromise with Madrid, a small group of the Diputació led by Pau Claris, canon of Urgell, and by Francesc de Tamarit, opened negotiations with France. They were joined by others who had cause for dissatisfaction with Castile, like Don Josep Margarit (later to become governor of Catalonia under the French). In October 1640 the Diputació made a formal defence agreement with the French. Unwilling to take a lenient attitude and in despair at the turn of events, Olivares drifted into open war with the Catalans. 'This year', he wrote in September, 'can undoubtedly be considered the most unfortunate that this monarchy has experienced'. The inability of Castile to cope with the new crisis was amply exposed by a poor response from the nobility to a mediaeval-style muster in 1640. 'Without reason or occasion', Olivares lamented, 'the Catalans have thrown themselves into as complete a rebellion as Holland'. In January 1641 the rebels transferred the title of count of Barcelona from Philip IV to Louis XIII, so putting themselves under the French crown.

The next ten years were traumatic ones for Catalonia. In 1642 Roussillon was occupied by the French – permanently – and the war frontier between Castile and France shifted to the Aragonese border with Catalonia. It is unlikely that the French wished to advance any further. In the principality they had a useful military and commercial colony, and French goods soon flooded the Catalan market. Coming on top of all the agonies and expense of war, this quickly disillusioned the Catalans. A murderous plague in

1650, which annihilated one-fifth of the population of Barcelona, was the final blow. When Don Juan José of Austria recovered the city in October 1652 after a lengthy siege, Catalans were ready to accept terms. Claris (who died in 1641), Tamarit, Margarit and a few others were excluded from the general amnesty, and the king swore to observe the constitutions.

The revolt precipitated the fall of Olivares and contributed to the collapse of Spain's military hegemony. In 1648–50, crisis years for France because of the Fronde, it was conceivable that Spain, now free of war in the north, might have been able to invade its neighbour; instead the army was bogged down subduing the rebellion in Catalonia. The opportunity did not recur. Catalonia north of the Pyrenees was lost forever after the treaty of 1659, and within Spain unity was permanently broken with the successful revolt of Portugal. For Catalonia the revolt was in no sense a national uprising. Rebellion was real enough, but few saw it as part of a serious aspiration to independence from Spain. The provincial cities were seldom sympathetic to the policy of Barcelona, and a high proportion of all classes remained faithful to Philip IV. It cannot be doubted, on the other hand, that by creating a common cause among some Catalans, by emphasising separateness from Castile, and by encouraging the appearance of proto-nationalist writings, the rebellion gave a major impetus to that regionalism which reared its head again in 1688 and 1705.

The revolt of Portugal in 1640 was in a wholly different category from that of Catalonia. Because Castile since Philip II had always respected the autonomy of the western realm, Portugal had retained control both over its own affairs and its vast empire. The uneasy partnership was threatened under Olivares by two problems: the demands of the war against France, and the erosion of Portuguese territory in the New World. Of these the latter created the most deep-rooted grievances. By the early seventeenth century Portugal was losing its Asian spice trade to the Dutch; for this Spain bore no responsibility. On the other hand, apart from the successful relief of Bahía in 1625, Spain was unable to offer effective protection against further Dutch invasions of Brazil, and it resisted Portuguese expansion into the interior of South America. The union of the crowns seemed to have little more to offer to the Portuguese. The war against France brought tensions to a head, when Olivares attempted to raise extra taxation, leading to riots in 1637 in Evora and other towns. Then, in 1640 when the Catalan revolt broke out, Olivares arranged for Portuguese troops, originally recruited for Italy, to be sent to Catalonia. At the same time the Portuguese nobility, like their peers in Castile, were asked to report for service in Catalonia. Their response was to stage an uprising in Lisbon in December 1640, when they proclaimed the duke of Braganza as king João IV.

The success of the Portuguese rebellion must be attributed less to Spain's military commitments elsewhere than to the determination of this small nation of one million people to break free. Active French support, both naval and military, was an immense help; but national energy alone can explain subsequent victories against the Dutch in Brazil, leading to their final expulsion in 1654; and the untiring border campaign against Spain, with victories over Spanish armies at Elvas in 1659 and Villaviciosa in 1665. Finally, in 1668 Spain recognised the independence of Portugal.

The secession of Catalonia and Portugal was, as Olivares had correctly diagnosed, a consequence of the structural weakness of 'Spain'. Further evidence of the fragility of the union created by Ferdinand and Isabella came in the plot to make Andalusia secede in 1641. The duke of Medina-Sidonia, one of the richest grandees of Spain and of the same Guzmán family as Olivares, was brother to the new queen of Portugal. Inspired no doubt by her success, he conspired with his cousin the marquis of Ayamonte to set up an independent realm in the south of the peninsula. The Andalusian nobility certainly had many interests in common – they had helped to keep the region out of the Comunidades – but the territory had never had any collective political or moral identity, and the separatist plot was doomed to fail. Ayamonte was eventually beheaded, but Medina-Sidonia escaped because of his family connections. The nobility were behind another bizarre plot in 1648, this time to make Aragon independent. The duke of Híjar, the realm's leading grandee, was influenced by the army officer Carlos de Padilla (who came from the same family as the famous Comunero) to consider the possibility of making himself king of Aragon under French protection. Padilla explained that 'I see no good reason why all Spain should be one, since what we have seen of unity has not done us any good'. The plot unfortunately lacked both money and popular support, and the unhappy duke spent the rest of his life in a prison cell in León. Both incidents reveal the absence of any regionalist sentiment, and reflect rather the feudal attitudes of Spain's aristocracy. They are evidence none the less of widespread disillusion among local elites with the policy of Castile, and are paralleled by the separatist revolt of Naples in 1647–8, which threatened to fragment the Mediterranean empire irreparably.

In Catalonia, in Portugal, in Vizcaya, in Naples, perhaps in Andalusia and Aragon, crisis forced the elites to examine what benefit association with Castile had brought them, and in each case the answer seemed to be negative. Ironically, then, while Olivares was complaining that the regions had given little to Spain, the regions themselves took the view that Spain had given them nothing. As late as 1657, reports the diarist Barrionuevo, 'in Galicia lampoons have appeared in many places, with the same complaints as we have here, and saying that if there is no remedy they have Portugal as a neighbour'. The clear threat of secession reflected the growing political maturity of Spaniards. Surmounting their intense parochialism, the local communities were beginning, however confusedly, to feel their way to broader identities. But they refused to take the step that Olivares was inviting them to advance towards: closer cooperation with each other for the sake of a fully integrated Spain.

After all, that 'Spain' seemed to promise little more than the imposition of control from Castile. Around 1650 Juan de Palafox, an Aragonese who was bishop first of Puebla (Mexico) and then of Osma in Aragon, reflected that 'our monarchy lasted barely thirty years from its completion (in 1558) to its decline. Its ruin began after 1570, and after 1630 it began to decline with more force. This is the more remarkable, when we consider the long life of other empires'. Agreeing with the view that one cause had been the excessive fiscal burden on Castile, Palafox rejected the attempts of Olivares to unify the realms, and appealed instead to the fact that Ferdinand and Isabella had never stood for a united Spain: 'Queen Isabella even changed her clothes according to the nation she was in; in Castile she was a Castilian, in Aragon an Aragonese, in Catalonia a Catalan'. Spain, he felt, would succeed only through recognition of its variety: 'in all Vizcaya you will not find an orange, in all Valencia not a chestnut'. The government must tolerate language diversity, 'governing Castilians in Castilian, Catalans in Catalan'. The views of Olivares and Palafox stand at opposite poles of the big debate that began in Habsburg Spain, and that still today in the twenty-first century has not abated, over the political destiny of the various regions comprising peninsular Spain.

# CHAPTER 5

# Spain's people in an age of crisis

## The economic recession

From the late sixteenth century the interior of Spain, in common with much of western Europe, began to experience economic problems that can be identified as a 'depression', provoked in part by frequent epidemics, harvest failures and wars, with their consequent impact on population growth and the evolution of the economy.

The rise in population during the sixteenth century had been most remarkable in the interior of the peninsula, with a 78 per cent increase in New Castile between 1528 and 1591. In the south, the population of Jaén increased 75 per cent, and that of Córdoba 83 per cent. This was the boom period for Castile, but from the 1580s the birth rate began to stagnate and fall. Parish registers show that births fell in Cáceres from 1587, in Valladolid and Toledo from 1588, in Córdoba and Ciudad Real from 1589, in Murcia from 1597. The trend was thus already descending when the major epidemic of 1596–1602 hit Spain. Entering from northern Europe through Santander at the end of 1596, by early 1599 the plague had spread throughout the peninsula along communication routes: only Catalonia and Valencia were untouched. In Santander 2,500 people, five-sixths of the population, died; in Valladolid 6,500, or nearly one-sixth. The devastation was enormous: in some towns the mortality rate was ten times higher than the average. Altogether about 600,000 people perished, most of them in the heartland of Old Castile, where the principal towns lay. The tragedy was a grim opening to a century of population reverses which struck at the roots of Spanish resources and imperial power. It took another century and a half for the nation to recover the demographic levels of 1580.

Over the next 50 years the gloom deepened. There were subsistence crises in 1605–7 in central Castile and Andalusia (in Toledo a contemporary described 1606 as 'the most fatal year ever experienced in Spain'); and in 1615–16 in Castile, Andalusia and Aragon. In 1630–1 there was a general crisis throughout the country, with famine in Segovia and hunger and extensive riots in the Basque country. In the Cantabrian provinces farmers changed to maize in order to supplement their diets, and in Catalonia the people were struck low by a plague epidemic. In 1647 Andalusia, the wheat-bowl of Spain, had its worst harvest of the century. This was the year, too, of the next major epidemic, which entered the country through Valencia, extended northwards into the crown of Aragon and southwards throughout Andalusia, dying away eventually in about 1652. Its intensity was in some areas greater than that of 1596–1602: in the kingdom of Valencia and in Mallorca one-fifth of the population died, in the cities of Barcelona and Seville approximately one-half. Perhaps as many as half a million perished altogether.

The epidemics and the Morisco expulsions were the major catastrophes, responsible between them for the loss of nearly 1.5 million souls, out of a possible total Spanish population in 1590 of eight million. But there were many lesser and more constant drains on manpower, notably the slow haemorrhage of men to the empire. Emigration to America has never been adequately measured: Navarrete claimed that 'over 40,000 people leave Spain every year', but the true figure could not have been much more than 5,000 annually. The wars in Europe, on the other hand, were a constant running sore drawing away men who (in the words of Navarrete in 1626) 'would through matrimony propagate and perpetuate the race'. From Galicia, the preferred recruiting ground, some 68,000 men left to fight abroad between 1621 and 1659, and the region of Jaén alone contributed 10,000 soldiers between 1640 and 1653. It was a burden that a nation with a falling number of births (itself in part provoked by the absence of men fighting abroad) could ill afford to sustain.

The impact of demographic disaster was plain to see. Although there was considerable emigration from depressed rural areas to the big cities, decline touched both town and country alike. Among the big cities, Burgos shrank from 13,325 people in 1591 to 3,000 in 1646, Valladolid from 40,560 to 15,000, Toledo from 54,665 to 25,000. In the rural areas, data for the villages of Segovia province show a decline of one-third between the 1590s and the 1650s. In general terms, the population totals in Spain at the end of the sixteenth century – some 6.6 million for the crown of Castile and 1.5 for the rest of peninsular Spain – fell catastrophically and were not recovered till the **mid-eighteenth** century. 'Henceforward', commented González de Cellorigo in **1600**, 'we can only expect shortages of everything, because of the **lack of people to** work in the fields and in all the manufactures the kingdom needs'. Lamenting the lack of men to recruit for the army and to till the fields, the duke of Medina de las Torres claimed in 1659 that 'over half the surface of these realms is uncultivated because of the depopulation'.

This grim picture, however, was true only of Castile and the interior of Spain. In the north-west of the peninsula, mainly Galicia and Asturias, population growth in the 1500s had been slow but the seventeenth century was one of remarkable expansion. In Catalonia, population totals rose by about 75 per cent between the 1550s and the 1620s, helped in part by immigration from France. There was then a clear difference between the interior and the periphery, which makes it impossible to state that there was a depression in the whole of Spain. Many of the problems of the subsequent decades, moreover, could be seen as a tension between a Castile prostrated by reverses and a periphery still in full command of its energies. Rather than a general 'decline', it was a crisis, but one that hit most deeply at the centre of the monarchy, Castile.

In Castile, the council of finance was inundated with memorials about deserted villages and in the Cortes of 1621 a procurador stated confidently that 'it is the weight of taxation and the oppression of the tax-collectors which are the principal causes'. In some areas, particularly the heartland of Old Castile, whole regions were abandoned. In the area of Arévalo, 30 out of 83 towns became *despoblados* (depopulated) in the early seventeenth century; in the region of Medina del Campo the tax-paying population between 1591 and 1640 fell by 73 per cent, and 19 out of 39 towns became depopulated. The contraction was obviously not so severe everywhere, but it aggravated the problems of an agrarian economy whose structural defects were of long standing. For over a century Spain with its expanding population had been unable to produce enough food to feed itself. Only a small proportion of the country's land surface was cultivable: the rest was at too high an altitude (Spain is the most elevated country in Europe after Switzerland) or too arid. The climate was, and still is, one of extremes. Droughts are common (over one-third of the peninsula the rainfall is less than 20 inches a year) and the major rivers, of which the Ebro is the most important, tend to dry up precisely when most needed, in the summer. The well-watered lands of the north and the Levant coast were not extensive enough to produce the required quantities of wheat (both the Basque country and Valencia were regular importers of grain), and the rich lands of Andalusia were very vulnerable to climatic changes. Methods of cultivation everywhere were archaic, though in the mid-sixteenth century this did not prevent some fairly good yield ratios, perhaps as much as 1:8 in New Castile. Ploughing was seldom satisfactory: though many villages used cows for plough-teams, the majority used mules. Mules were cheaper, more mobile and adaptable, and a larger area could be sown more rapidly; unfortunately they ploughed at a shallower depth and exhausted the top-soil more rapidly. The agrarian problem was above all probably one of land distribution: the overwhelming mass of the peasantry in Spain were landless labourers (*jornaleros*). In the north there were more peasant proprietors (*labradores*), though in Galicia for instance their holdings were too small to sustain a family and the men emigrated in search of extra seasonal wages. In New Castile about 70 per cent of peasants were landless and in Andalusia well over three-fourths.

The depression therefore intensified an existing long-term problem rather than created a new one. There were structural weaknesses in the economy that persisted no matter what the demographic level. In the interior the lowest levels of population in Old Castile were in the 1630s, with a firm recuperation only in the early eighteenth century. By contrast, on the periphery (below, p. 283) there were clear signs of recovery from the 1660s. The years of crisis provoked two major developments in the economy: a fall in production and rent returns, and a shift to non-wheat cereals and vines.

The first of these was mentioned in the Castilian Cortes of 1598, when a speaker observed that 'the principal cause of decrease in cultivation is the great dearth of people'. The returns from 22 villages and towns which paid tithes to the diocese of Segovia show that in wheat, which made up two-thirds of all grain, output between about 1580 and 1640 fell by 30 per cent. In Valencia, where grain (mostly wheat) made up three-fourths by value of produce from the soil, there was likewise expansion to the late 1570s, followed by stagnation and fall up to the 1640s. Periodic bad weather played some part in the crisis, but the correlation between population and production is beyond doubt. Where rents were paid in kind, the lower returns naturally affected the income of landowners: there were landlords in Segovia who complained of a decline of 50 per cent or more in returns from rentals.

According to the arbitrista Caxa de Leruela, many proprietors moved over to viticulture in order to maximise profits. More generally, as in Segovia and Andalusia, the villages shifted production from wheat to inferior cereals, principally barley and rye, which had a higher yield and could be used to sustain the valuable herds. In the diocese of Segovia, the proportion of wheat in the grain harvest fell from 61.5 per cent in 1587 to 55 per cent in 1651, while that of rye rose from 15.4 to 39.8 per cent. On the Cantabrian coast a yet more fundamental shift was made: to maize, introduced into the Basque country as a basic crop from about 1630, and constituting the bulk of grain consumed in Galicia by the late century. It was maize, indeed, with its high yield, that helped to feed the north-west and enabled it to escape from the crisis of production in Castile.

The old opinion that attention to livestock and sheep farming was somehow responsible for the agrarian crisis is untenable. The Mesta, as we have seen, frequently provoked litigation over pasture rights. But the peasantry of New Castile, as reported in the census of 1575, and all the arbitristas of the period, were at one in finding no reason to complain of the Mesta. Caxa de Leruela in 1631 pointed out that the pastoral interest in Castile was in reality highly vulnerable and required state protection, a conclusion that bore fruit in Olivares's edict of March 1633, which ordered land converted from arable since 1590 to be returned to pasture. Despite this, the number of sheep in the flocks of the Mesta continued to decline, from possibly three million in the early sixteenth century to under two million in the mid-seventeenth. The value of the tithe in cattle paid to the see of Valencia approximately halved between 1580 and 1640, and continued to fall, suggesting that there was no shift to livestock rearing. In Old Castile the evidence from Valladolid – where the Mesta was strong – confirms the picture. During the sixteenth-century phase of expansion it was arable that increased, at the expense of pasture; when the recession developed, both declined together. The Mesta bears no direct responsibility for the problems of Spanish agriculture.

The shrinking villages of rural Castile increased problems for those peasants who remained to work the land or tend the diminishing herds. Rural emigration, mostly to local cities or (in the north) to the tax-free Basque lands, became a slow drain on the communities; while those who remained had to pay the tax rates formerly levied on a full village. Whether to pay tax arrears or simply to buy more grain for sowing, villagers were obliged to borrow money through censos. In more prosperous times censos were a fruitful injection of capital into the rural economy. In times of crisis they became a liability: peasants were often unable to repay debts in time, thereby forfeiting their property to urban moneylenders. Only the most vulnerable communities suffered, but in Castile there were many of these. A common solution was to extend the area of arable temporarily into common lands, so as to raise cash. The village of Puente de Duero, near Valladolid, was typical. Already in 1503 it was illegally planting vines and ploughing up commons; by 1589 it was semi-deserted; in 1688 it had 'only six poor labourers, with no trade or crop and no harvest of either grain or wine, because the land essential to most of the inhabitants has been seized by the public officials of Valladolid to pay for the many censos upon the village and its households'.

The weight of censo debt was among the heaviest burdens on the villages. In the process a major structural change occurred in the Castilian countryside. As peasants lost their independence to urban capitalists, the big towns began to take over control of the surrounding areas. By the 1650s many cities – Ciudad Real, Jaén, Valencia, Valladolid – were in firm control of their rural hinterland. Between 1638 and 1683, for example, the town of La Guardia sold off over 83 per cent of its land to citizens of the city of Jaén to meet censo debts.

In pre-industrial Spain over three-fourths of the active working population was engaged in the agrarian economy. Less than a fifth was employed in industry, mainly in textiles. The 1560s were the peak period for cloth production, with a favourable combination of rising prices, expanding population and extra demand created by war in the Mediterranean. When the recession came its most notable casualty was the textile-producing city of Segovia, where the 600 looms existing in 1580 declined to 300 by 1640. The decay hit different centres at different times: production fell in Soria from as early as 1561, but in Cuenca only from about 1587. Unable to compete with luxury imports, manufacturers concentrated on producing lower grades of cloth for the popular market. At the same time they pressed for controls on the export of raw materials, so that they would have the right – granted by law in 1625 to factories in Segovia and Palencia – to buy quality wools that the Mesta and other traders usually preferred to export.

The crisis extended also to Spain's trading position in the world. The flourishing commerce of northern Castile had centred on the activity of Medina del Campo and Burgos. Medina was the convenient exchange centre at which bullion from fleet arrivals at Seville would be injected into the wool trade of the northern towns. But by about 1570 the fairs were in difficulties: 'the trade of Burgos is almost completely exhausted', observed Simón Ruiz that year. Irregular fleet arrivals, the wars in France, the troubles in Flanders, all hastened the decay. The royal bankruptcy of 1575 and a simultaneous increase in trade taxes (the alcabala) delivered a mortal blow to Medina, which recovered briefly in the 1580s but was in full decline by the end of the reign. Burgos, meanwhile, which had exported 21,000 sacks of wool in 1548, exported half that number in 1561 and suffered a continued fall in later years. In its great days it had issued over 2,000 ships' insurances a year; between 1594 and 1619 it issued no more than 200.

The crisis in northern Castile brought about a structural change in business activity. Financiers and traders gravitated to Madrid, permanent capital from 1601; and international bankers concentrated on Seville. In Valladolid the palaces decayed as the great lords moved to Madrid; the half-finished cathedral, begun by Herrera, remains as ghostly testimony to unachieved greatness. The epidemics of 1596–1602 gave the final blow to Old Castile.

The collapse of the trade fairs, which in their heyday had offered native capitalists the opportunity to participate in the great wool markets of western Europe, was a severe reverse for nascent Spanish capitalism. But it is important to note that Spain's position was always weak. The country exported raw materials and imported manufactures, leaving a large unfavourable balance of trade (as early as 1551 the trade with France had a balance of over one million ducats against Spain). Most trade was seaborne, but foreign textile exporters to Spain took care to charter their own ships, leaving Spanish traders dependent on their services. The important trade between Nantes and Bilbao, for example, was dominated by French vessels: only 23 per cent of the ships used by Simón Ruiz on this run between 1572 and 1576 were Spanish. Spanish financiers, finally, were relative newcomers to the world of international credit, and lacked the resources of well-established Italian firms. For Castilian traders it was an uphill struggle from the very beginning: 'these foreigners do with us as they wish', complained Simón Ruiz in 1573.

When Medina and Burgos faced difficulties the small Castilian bourgeoisie did not decline but moved: to Madrid, where many of them (like Ruiz) put their money into juros rather than into trade; and to Seville. The rise to opulence of Madrid and Seville was a bizarre phenomenon that contrasted sharply with the depression elsewhere in Castile, but there was no contradiction. In Seville the bulk of the trade to and from America was in the hands of foreigners, making the port a symbol not of Castilian but of foreign wealth and of Spain's dependence on outside capital. Madrid for its part grew bigger at the expense of the producing areas and towns around it, which fed their output into the thriving capital but reaped no benefits in return, so that the court and city became parasites contributing to the ruin of Castile.

The crisis that began in the 1580s confirmed a tendency that had been apparent since the beginning of imperial power: the dominance of Spain by the trade of other west European nations. Spanish producers of wool, of wine, of raw silk, were anxious to satisfy foreign consumers; and large sections of Spanish industry bound themselves to this obvious source of profit. Manufacturers who used the wool and silk to produce indigenous textiles found themselves hampered by the price differential, where high costs created by Spain's monetary inflation had to compete with low costs in other countries. Foreign importers of wool, on the other hand, could afford to work the material, send it back finished to Spain, and still make a profit; they also built up a chain of distributors who made foreign textiles readily available to the public. In Spain therefore the crisis of the early seventeenth century subjected the economy to foreign interests.

The Spanish kingdoms bordering France were perhaps the most liable to this subjection. Navarre and Aragon were effectively economic colonies of France, dependent more on it than on Spain for trade. In 1636 the representatives of Navarre explained that 'if our wine and wool is not carried to France and if we in return do not receive what merchandise is needed, the realm will perish'. The Flemish traveller Antoine de Brunel commented in 1655 that 'Spain cannot do without the trade of France, not only in the Basque country and Aragon, but in all regions. Provence has always had commerce with the kingdom of Valencia because of the need for its products; the same is true of Brittany, Normandy and other maritime provinces which send their goods to Bilbao and Cadiz'.

Throughout the century, therefore, Spanish trade exhibited features peculiar to a dependent economy; one, that is, in which production and trade were primarily dictated by external demand, and in which foreign investment inhibited the free growth of indigenous capital. The fall in Spain's own trading capacity led to a slump in shipping. In his *Art of Shipbuilding* (1611) Thomé Cano observed that 'twenty-five years ago more than one thousand large ships were owned in Spain, and in Vizcaya alone there were more than two hundred which made the voyage to Newfoundland and to Flanders, whereas today there is not even one'. The province of Vizcaya informed Philip III in 1610 that 'since the decline of trade to Flanders, nobody wishes to build large ships'. Smaller ships, however, continued to be built, confirming the growing preference in Europe for small vessels. In ports where sea-going trade increased, whether in Seville or Barcelona, the figures were deceptive, since they pointed less to a resurgence of Spanish commerce than to an increase in the number of foreign vessels. By mid-century important ports such as Alicante relied exclusively on foreign ships to transport their merchandise. In these circumstances, nothing was more unpopular with the merchants of France, England and Holland than war with Spain. Even in Protestant countries, the trading interest always preferred peace. In its turn, the Spanish government found it difficult to prohibit trade in items on which the public had come to rely, and connived at breaking its own bans. In 1638 alone, it earned 255,460 ducats from issuing licences permitting traders to import enemy goods. In 1642, the duke of Medina-Sidonia was sold a permit to import 300,000 ducats worth of prohibited goods from northern Europe. A state of war, or official bans on trade, did little to stop the increase in foreign control over Spanish commerce.

Various peace treaties gave formal permission to other nations to bring in their goods on favourable terms: the Dutch obtained this in 1648, the French in 1659, the English in 1667. In practice, the effective agents of control over trade were the large colonies of merchants that settled in Spain's major ports. In 1566 the Cortes had petitioned against them: 'that Genoese and foreigners not be in Spain, or at least not trade therein, since it is well known that their trade destroys Spain'. A commercial crisis in the 1620s temporarily disrupted the trade of north European merchants, who tried to set off their losses by turning their attention to the Mediterranean, where they flourished. By 1630 Alicante was home to trading representatives of all the chief northern nations; and in Bilbao the English, French and Flemish merchants controlled most of the outgoing trade.

The biggest centre of foreign attention was the group of towns operating the trade monopoly to America. Here the merchants preferred to reside not in Seville, where the official machinery of control was, but in Cadiz, which from 1535 had been granted the *juzgado de Indias* or right to unload American cargoes. Despite official vigilance, fraud rapidly undermined the whole system. In 1608 the council of the Indies reported that foreign goods in the fleets sent to the Indies accounted for two-thirds of the gold and silver brought back to Spain. By law the monopoly excluded foreigners from trading to America. This did not stop 'interlopers' from shipping goods directly to the New World and thereby undermining the trade from the peninsula. Some merchants preferred to work within the rules, acquired naturalisation (about 77 did so between 1621 and 1630) and traded legitimately from Spain. The majority, however, traded through Spanish agents and carried on large-scale smuggling to and from America. Their activities were helped by the large natural harbour at Cadiz, which made detection difficult. Gradually, shipping moved away from the inland port of Seville, as access up the river Guadalquivir became difficult for larger vessels. By mid-century, particularly after the plague of 1648, Cadiz had become the focus of the monopoly, its population rising to 7,460 in 1646 and 25,950 in 1693.

## Arbitristas and the crisis of confidence

It was a measure of Spain's political maturity that by the early seventeenth century it had a recognisable public opinion and a government that was willing to tolerate diversity of opinion. Newspapers did not exist (the first such in Madrid, called the *Gazeta*, appeared as late as 1661), but the local authorities licensed tracts and flysheets on a broad range of public issues. Some of the publications were addressed to the government and offered expedients (*arbitrios*) to solve economic problems: their writers (*arbitristas*) were drawn from the clergy, state officials, the merchant body, the professions, even from the army. Arbitristas were not the only expression of public opinion. The great issues of the day, ranging from economic ills to foreign policy, attracted considerable comment, in a political atmosphere remarkable for its freedom of expression. At the top levels of administration, both in the Cortes and in the councils, state advisers offered alternative policies; in the general public, satires were circulated by means of illicit pamphlets; and, among the intellectuals, moralists and political theorists commented extensively on public affairs.

The Cortes of Castile were summoned six times under Philip III (1598–1601, 1602–4, 1607–11, 1611–12, 1615, 1617–20), eight under Philip IV (1621, 1623–9, 1632–6, 1638–43, 1646–7, 1649–51, 1655–8 and 1660–4), one of these a session lasting six years (1623–9). To the original eighteen cities represented in the assembly the crown under Philip IV added three more, in each case in return for a considerable sum of money. The Galician cities obtained a joint privilege in 1625, Palencia in 1660 and the Extremadura cities in 1653. The municipalities were controlled by noble oligarchies, and their procuradores were uniformly hostile to indirect taxes, such as the millones, from which they were not exempt. Despite this obvious vested interest, the Cortes were not wholly unrepresentative of Castile. Their constant complaints to the government, and their criticisms of certain aspects of taxation, constitute a programme of opposition unequalled anywhere else in western Europe outside England. The crown in response was forced to employ bribery and corruption under Lerma, and Olivares found it necessary to become a procurador himself in order to intervene in debates. At a higher level the programme of opposition became virtually official policy in the famous consulta issued in February 1619 by the council of Castile; and then later in the policies of the junta de reformación and of Olivares. Typical of the leading public officials who considered it the obligation of the state to remedy defects in the economy was the ambassador to England, the count of Gondomar, who in 1619 deplored 'the depopulation, poverty and deprivation in Spain today'.

Popular criticism was widespread. In June 1640 a peasant pushed himself before the king in public and shouted: 'This country is being ruined and whoever doesn't do anything about it will burn in hell!' Moralistic criticism of this type was as a rule accepted humbly by the government. By the same token, criticism from the pulpit was permitted when it was not deemed inflammatory: the diarist Barrioneuvo reports a bitter attack on the government made by a preacher before the king, in 1657. The state, however, was not so tolerant of anonymous attacks. In the mid-seventeenth century both London and Paris became centres of agitation conducted through unlicensed pamphlets. Spain likewise became subject to propaganda, some of it reported in the pages of Barrionuevo's *Avisos*. Most surviving examples took the form not of pamphlets but of lampoons and satires pinned up on walls and public squares. Many were directed against the ministry of Olivares, whose regime appears to have been the most hated in Habsburg Spain and was obliged to resort to the arrest of its critics and their expulsion from Madrid. The diplomat Saavedra Fajardo commented that 'grumbling, although bad in itself, is good for the state. Grumbling is proof that there is liberty in the state; in a tyranny it is not permitted'.

Political theory in the course of the early century responded to the economic crisis by calling for the state to play a larger part in public policy. 'The main duty of the prince is to conserve his realms', wrote Saavedra. Though thinkers started from widely differing principles – one influential school, represented by Álamos de Barrientos and, to some extent, Olivares, derived its ideas from Tacitus – they shared a belief in greater initiative for the crown. One consequence of the ideas generated by crisis, then, was ironically a return to neo-absolutist theory; but it was theory so deeply infused by the need to accept change and reform that it cannot be categorised as reactionary. Outstanding among the works of this time were Francisco de Quevedo's *Política de Dios* (Divine Politics), which came out in 1626, going through nine editions that year; and Diego de Saavedra Fajardo's *Idea of a Prince* (more commonly known as *Political Enterprises*) of 1640. Writers also approached political problems moralistically, hence the development of satire in this period, in works such as Quevedo's *Sueños* ('Dreams') of around 1607, and Baltasar Gracián's *Criticón* (1651). Some of these writers exculpated the crown from responsibility for the ruin facing Spain, by explaining that all states were subject to an immutable law of rise and decline. The dramatist Calderón asked:

*Pero que firme estado*
*al paso que otro crece, no declina?*
*(But what strong state does not decline, while another rises?)*

All states decay, explained Suárez de Figueroa: 'there is none perpetual which will not decay after many years, no matter what good order has been practised at the beginning'. In this way the thesis of a 'decline of Spain' took root, and was officially adopted by both Olivares and Philip IV as a way to explain their failure. In 1629 the Count Duke observed that the country 'still continues on its decline', and it was to the same year that the king dated the moment when 'my monarchy began, as everyone agrees, to decline'.

Although the three preceding groups account for much of the well-informed comment on Spain's crisis, it is the reaction of arbitristas that has been most studied. The better-known writers include Martín González de Cellorigo, of Valladolid, whose *Memorial* appeared in 1600; Sancho de Moncada, professor at Toledo and author of the *Political Restoration* (1619); Pedro Fernández Navarrete, whose commentary on the 1619 consulta of the council of Castile was published as the *Conservation of Monarchies* (1626); Miguel Caxa de Leruela, whose *Restoration of the former abundance of Spain* came out in Naples in 1631; and Francisco Martínez de Mata, of Seville, whose numerous memorials were printed in the 1650s. Scores of other arbitristas may be added to this list: over 165 of their works are known to have been published between 1598 and 1665 alone.

The arbitristas, however, seldom offer a reliable guide to the Spanish crisis. Nearly all were Castilians, and reflect an exclusively Castilian viewpoint; there were very few from the other regions of Spain. Some, like Caxa de Leruela, had a specific axe to grind, in his case the problems of the pastoral industry. Others made sweeping generalisations on the basis of limited local information; Sancho de Moncada's observations, for example, are valid only for the region of Toledo. Still others, fascinated by the science of political arithmetic, produced torrents of specious statistics to make their arguments more acceptable. Contemporaries criticised them for their exaggerations and their naive belief that their pet expedient would be the *único remedio* – the sole cure – for the ills of the monarchy. Despite their distinct interests, there was considerable agreement between them on the country's problems. Most agreed that Spain was suffering a decline or a change in its fortunes, which they dated from the early years of Habsburg rule, thereby preserving the image, on which they all agreed, of the reign of Ferdinand and Isabella as the apex of Spain's glory. Starting from the fact of depopulation, which they took to be the crucial symptom of crisis, each proceeded to elaborate a specific analysis and cure. For Sancho de Moncada 'the ills of Spain rise from the new trade of foreigners. The radical cure is to prohibit foreign manufactures. Spain's remedy is in producing its own goods'. This mercantilist view was also shared by Martìnez de Mata. Of the various 'sole cures' offered by arbitristas, two are of particular importance because they quickly became part of official policy. In the early century there were proposals, made repeatedly in Cortes and eventually supported by Olivares, to abolish the millones and other harmful taxes and substitute for them a 'single tax' on a basic commodity such as flour. The plan never came into effect in Castile, partly because of opposition from holders of juros whose income was derived from existing taxes, but was introduced into Aragon during the War of Succession. The other proposal was for the formation of a trading company to dislodge foreign merchants from their control of Spain's commerce. Supported by most arbitristas throughout the century, it was also strongly favoured by Olivares and subsequent administrators.

It is customary to think of arbitristas only as writers on economic affairs. The fact is that the profundity of Spain's crisis forced thinkers to question not only economic policy but also all the postulates on which official policy was based. The leading arbitristas were, for example, uncompromisingly hostile to the statutes of limpieza. They also attacked the maldistribution of wealth. Cellorigo felt that 'there is nothing more pernicious than the extreme wealth of some and the extreme poverty of others, and our nation is much disordered by it, both because of the founding of mayorazgos and the resort to censos, since one enriches and the other impoverishes. And although it is not good to argue that all should be equal, it would not be unreasonable to avoid these two extremes'. The Madrid magistrate Mateo López Bravo in his *De rege et regendi ratione* (On the king and the kingdom) (1616) observed that 'great wealth in one person plunges many into poverty, and the opulence of a few brings disaster on the many. . . . The maldistribution of wealth is very harmful: it creates power, arrogance and idleness among those who have it and misery, humiliation and despair among those who do not'.

The long years of war had bred, as we have seen, a strong reaction against the commitment to the Netherlands, and a firm conviction among broad sections of opinion that Spain should return to its proper destiny – the one created for it by Ferdinand the Catholic – in the Mediterranean. This isolationist feeling was also directed against the very existence of empire. For Lope de Deza, discussing the *Political Government of Agriculture* (1618), the first cause of agrarian crisis in Spain was 'that so many states and realms, such as the Indies, Flanders and Italy, have been incorporated into the crown'; by which he understood that the potential labour force of Spain had been dissipated by emigration. For Sancho de Moncada in 1619, 'the poverty of Spain has resulted from the discovery of the Indies', a claim which he justified by pointing to the ruin caused by foreign trading interests which sucked the peninsula dry of American bullion. Like these writers, many fiercely criticised the negative consequences of the discovery and colonisation of America, which they felt had allowed Spaniards to rely too much on easy wealth and turned Spain into a colony of Europe. The 'depopulation, poverty and sterility', argued Martínez de Mata in 1650, prevailed because Spaniards 'spent their forces more on the riches of the Indies than on the professions which could have preserved those riches', and as a result foreign traders had rapidly taken control of the economy of the country.

The rejection of empire took many forms. With Quevedo it took the form of an introspective pessimism. 'In your country', he wrote in 1604 to a correspondent in the Netherlands, 'we consume our soldiers and our gold; here we consume ourselves'. Like Quevedo, many Castilians resented the world's rejection of Spanish power, and in reaction adopted ultra-nationalist, xenophobic and ultra-conservative views. If Spain was decaying, they argued, it was because of subversion by foreigners, Jews and heretics. Saavedra Fajardo (d. 1648), on the other hand, drew on his direct experience of European affairs to question whether the imperial experience was worth the effort: 'it has cost a great deal to wage war in inhospitable and remote provinces, at the price of so much life and money, and with such great benefit to the enemy and so little to us that it may be asked whether we would not be better conquered than conquering'. Faced after 1635 with the onset of the war against France, he set down in his *Political Enterprises* the striking opinions that 'I cannot persuade myself to suspect that the whole world should be Spanish'; and that war itself was 'a violence contrary to reason, to nature and to man's end'. Spain should, he thought, remain at peace with other nations, withdraw from Flanders and America, remain as a strong Catholic state rooted in the Mediterranean

(Saavedra's model king was Ferdinand the Catholic), and devote its genius to the arts. With the gloomy prospect of war against France in mind, in that same year, 1635, the historian Matíes de Novoa wrote, 'We have ended up as we wished, an object lesson for those to come, and for this I have taken up my pen to set down the record'.

## Popular revolt and 'seigneurial reaction'

The experience of the Comunidades and the germanías showed that the Spanish people were no strangers to popular agitation. These two movements were, however, no more than a political expression of the perennial conflict within and between communities, a conflict that expressed itself not only in revolt but through several forms of violence, of which the best known is banditry.

Revolts that transcended the limits of the local community came to prominence only during the seventeenth-century crisis, and were invariably protests against taxes. The famine conditions of 1630 provided a setting for the great Vizcaya revolt of 1631-2, which was provoked initially by Olivares's salt tax but turned into a regional defence of the fueros against Castilian rule. The movement also evolved rapidly into a social protest against economic inequalities. Labourers' wives said: 'now our sons and husbands will be the masters, not the traitors who are selling the republic; and since we are all equal in Vizcaya all property should be in common, for it is not fair for them to eat chicken while we eat sardines'. The uprising was finally suppressed by the Basques themselves, without any need for Castilian intervention. The duke of Ciudad Real entered Bilbao in April 1634, and arrested and executed six rebel leaders; the fueros were reaffirmed, and the salt tax abolished.

Endemic disorder in these years remains unstudied. There were, certainly, constant reports of riot and sedition, as in Toledo in 1634, in Navarre in 1638. The most significant revolts were those that swept over a distressed Andalusia – after years of plague and dearth – between 1647 and 1652. Typical of the minor, forgotten, uprisings of the period were those in 1647 near Granada in the towns of Lucena, Alcala la Real, Alhama and Albuñuelas. The village of Teba was occupied by the corregidor of Granada after a brief resistance and eleven rebels were hanged. In Albuñuelas the customary solidarity of popular rebels was shown when, as a correspondent reported, 'the alcaldes and regidores are imprisoned for rebellion, but they call themselves Fuenteovejuna, and the judges don't know what to do about it'. It was a remarkable instance of the theme of Lope de Vega's play *Fuenteovejuna*, which was well known at the time and in which a village claimed to be collectively responsible for the murder of its lord, being translated into historic reality. The more memorable uprisings were in the great cities, in Granada in May 1648, in Córdoba and Seville in May 1652. Each was precipitated by a subsistence crisis. In Granada the streets were full of people shouting 'Long live the king and death to the bad government', and the corregidor was replaced. In Córdoba the rising began when a poor woman went weeping through the streets, holding the body of her son who had died of hunger. The rioters sacked the house of the corregidor, broke into houses suspected of hoarding grain and elected their own corregidor. Events followed a similar pattern in Seville, where the rioters opened all the prisons and burnt all the documentation of the criminal courts. Though none of these risings lasted more than two weeks, they demonstrated that it was possible for the common people – as in Barcelona in 1640 – to take over Spain's major cities almost effortlessly. There was, however, never any fear of social revolution, since rebels invariably restricted themselves to demanding food and justice, and once these were conceded in their own community, lost interest in the continuing struggle of other communities.

Both banditry and revolt were symptoms of the economic fissures opening up between privileged and unprivileged. As the crisis hit producers and landowners, they searched around for ways to stabilise their income or invest more securely. In some areas, notably in Valencia, the lords intensified their control over their tenants in an attempt to compensate for the expulsion of the Moriscos. On the estates of the monastery of Valldigna the monks managed to increase rental income by 50 per cent between 1582 and 1648 even though the population had fallen by one-half. This success, obviously achieved at the cost of the peasants, aggravated social conflict and led to one of the great peasant rebellions of the century. To take a different example: in Villacastín, the biggest industrial centre in Segovia province after Segovia city, the recession weakened the economic and political standing of the traders and artisans, and enabled the hidalgo sheep-herders to take control of a proportion of seats on the city council. Despite the protests of the town, Philip II confirmed their position in 1581. Where all citizens had previously been taxpayers, the sheep-herders now established tax exemption for themselves. Moreover, they succeeded in quashing permanently the system of democratic assemblies (*concejos abiertos*) that the town had hitherto practised. Villacastín thereafter suffered from periodic social conflict between the new privileged and the community at large; in 1647 the elections had to be supervised by a royal official for fear of disturbances.

The process has been called a 'seigneurial reaction', though the two examples above show that one did not have to be a great lord to take part in strengthening one's economic position. Moreover, nobles were also prominent victims of the recession, and revolts were not necessarily directed against them. In broad terms, the crisis of the mid-seventeenth century caused an intensification of social conflict on an unprecedented scale, by impelling the privileged to protect their profitability but failing to protect the unprivileged. The process of popular revolt, then, was not a simple consequence of poor harvests, economic distress or excessive taxation: it was a profound response to crisis, and had long-term effects, which revealed themselves in the Catalan and Valencian peasant revolts of 1688 and 1693 (*see* p. 286).

## The crisis of the aristocracy

The higher aristocracy, like other groups in society, benefited from the favourable economic circumstances of the sixteenth century and was able to establish itself firmly in positions of privilege in political life. When the court settled down in Madrid in the early 1600s, the nobles also went there, built palaces and played their part in administration. The wealth of the great lords was legendary: though based in the area from which they drew their title, most came by marriage or purchase of señoríos to secure extensive interests right across the peninsula. Around 1600, when the average annual income of a labourer was not much more than 30 ducats, the richest grandee in Spain was probably the duke of Medina-Sidonia, with an estimated annual income of 160,000 ducats, drawn from his estates in Andalusia. Already, however, even the wealthiest nobles were complaining that their fortunes were changing for the worse. What brought this about?

Their political function had certainly changed. One of the most remarkable developments of the period is the acceptance by the Spanish aristocracy of the crown as its supreme arbiter. Unlike England and France, which had aristocratic revolts well into the seventeenth century, Spain suffered none after the Comunero period, and hesitant plots like those of Medina-Sidonia and Híjar in the 1640s never translated into action. There are possibly two explanations for this. First, beginning with Ferdinand and Isabella the monarchs laid great stress on acceptance of the rule of law. All classes of people were encouraged to bring their complaints to the royal courts, and in 1532 the Cortes was complaining that 'the number of lawsuits has grown rapidly', so much so that by the end of the century the two chancillerías of Valladolid and Granada were dealing with over 10,000 new cases annually. Charles V emphasised the role of royal justice by increasing the size of the council of Castile from twelve to sixteen, adding a new chamber of four judges to each of the two chancillerías and establishing new audiencias in the Canaries and in Seville. Neither he nor Philip II ever intervened in lawsuits involving the crown. Royal impartiality and firmness were commended by the great jurist Castillo de Bobadilla (he was also president of the council of Castile), who in 1597 claimed that in dealing with the grandees Philip II 'did not pardon them with his usual clemency, nor did he respect their estates, and there is no judge now who cannot act against them'. This, however, is only part of the story. If the nobles, powerful as they were, accepted royal justice it was because they were persuaded that their mutual interests, their binding sense of honour and their obligations to the king, were all paramount considerations. Their acceptance of royal authority was absolute and voluntary, never forced. Matters could be, of course, quite different at home in their own jurisdictions, where they usually acted in an arbitrary manner. The second aspect of control was the attendance of the nobility at court. The growth of the court after 1561 was in a way a political weapon. Philip II expected to see his nobles in Madrid, even if infrequently, and kept an eye on their behaviour. In time, the grandees accepted the need to have their residences near the king, and the aristocracy of the crown of Aragon also settled there in hopes of favour and preferment. The lesser *títulos* and nobles, by contrast, had little ambition to spend their lives in Madrid. They continued to live in the provinces, where they monopolised political office, ran their estates and acted as entrepreneurs in local commerce and industry.

The astonishing fact about the taming of the Spanish aristocracy is that it took place without any diminution of noble power. Nobles remained untouched in their personal and fiscal privileges and their control of extensive jurisdictions. Indeed, their power was extended. Sales of señoríos and of vassals were continued, royal revenue was alienated (in Segovia province alone between 1634 and 1662 the revenue from 57 towns, yielding 19,000 ducats a year, was granted to nobles), lands and offices were sold. Moreover, without any adequate state bureaucracy to serve it, the government was obliged to rely more and more on noble cooperation in the provinces, where the lords were encouraged to take on a major role in defence to balance the state's own commitments overseas. Spain therefore witnessed a phenomenon unparalleled in any west European country

outside France: the recruiting and maintaining of huge noble armies, like
the 30,000 men raised by the grandees with lands near Portugal to support
the invasion of that country in 1580, or the army raised by the Castilian
nobles for the invasion of Aragon in 1591. The armies were, it is true, no
longer private but raised for service to the king. Nevertheless, they prove
vividly that the aristocracy still had undiminished power to recruit thousands of men at will. Their capacity for violence was in no way diminished,
though their habits of violence seem to have been on the wane. Noble
crime did not normally go unpunished, and many young lords seem to
have preferred education to warfare. By 1600 the council of state was
expressing concern over 'the lack of persons qualified to command armies',
and in the same body in 1602 the constable of Castile commented that
'nobles do not join the infantry as they used to'. Olivares termed the
problem a *falta de cabezas* – a lack of military leaders.

At the same time an increase in the number of titles confirmed the
greater public role of the aristocracy. In 1520 Castile had 25 grandees
and 35 títulos; by the end of the reign of Philip III the total of both was
over 140, and Philip IV created a further 92 new títulos, explaining that
'without reward and punishment no monarchy can be preserved; we have
no money, so we have thought it right to increase the number of honours'.
Certificates of nobility (hidalguía) were sold to raise money, mainly by
Philip IV who sold over 130 between 1629 and 1652. Hábitos, or knight-
hoods of the military orders which conferred the status of caballero, were
sold on a generous scale. In the order of Santiago between 1551 and 1575
a total of 354 hábitos had been granted; between 1621 and 1645 the total
shot up to 2,288. This 'inflation of honours' was arguably an unwise
policy, but for the most part it seems to have served a useful purpose in
satisfying the pressures of social mobility and in granting to the elite due
status for their role in public life.

The *political* function of the aristocracy, then, had changed but not
decreased. Letrados were prominent at all levels of government – in the
councils, as corregidors, in the municipalities – but the great nobles still
dominated the council of state in the centre and political power in the
countryside. Much of the success of Habsburg government can be attributed to the excellent working partnership between the crown and its
ruling class. The liaison was particularly important in the circumstances of
the seventeenth-century crisis, which brought about a marked deterioration in the *economic* fortunes of the nobility.

Despite their enormous assets, most great nobles succumbed to debt by
the beginning of the seventeenth century. By 1616 the duke of Alba had to

set aside 60,000 ducats a year to repay his creditors; by 1637 the total debts of the duke of Infantado, all of them contracted within the previous 50 years, amounted to 897,731 ducats, and to meet repayments he had to set aside nearly 45,000 ducats a year. The city of Seville, remonstrating in 1627 against inflation, complained that 'it is the nobility in particular that are affected, since they have to keep themselves on incomes that will not buy today what could be bought previously with one-fourth of the same'. 'The greater part of the grandees of Spain', observed a French visitor under Philip IV, 'are ruined'.

A typical noble might draw his income from three traditional sources: his estates, jurisdictional taxes and rents; in the course of the sixteenth century he might add a fourth source of revenue: investment in censos and juros. The fact that many of these were tied up in a mayorazgo gave little protection against the cold wind of recession. As depopulation and agrarian crisis worsened, great lords found their estate revenues collapsing. The duke of Béjar's accountant complained in 1643 that 'the expenditures of the household and the wages of the servants are increasing daily while the rents are declining'. By the mid-seventeenth century, for many grandees like the duke of Gandía and the duke of Osuna, estate income did little more than pay for administering the estates. More and more they were driven to rely for ready cash on borrowing or on the income from state annuities (juros).

Debt was not caused exclusively or even mainly by a fall in production and rents. The noble lifestyle was expensive, and there was usually a large household and numerous retainers to support. Life in Madrid was particularly costly. The temporary shift of capital to Valladolid and back was ruinous: it cost the duke of Infantado 110,750 ducats. Other court functions, such as the festivities arranged for the Prince of Wales in 1623 or the regular outings to the Escorial, were notoriously expensive. Dowries could be crippling: this alone cost the Infantado family, which was blessed with many daughters, over 370,000 ducats in one generation. Above all, the demands of royal service were heavy. Aristocrats were expected to give the king money when he needed it (donativos), and to fulfil their feudal obligation of supplying armed soldiers: together these cost the duke of Infantado over 88,000 ducats in 1589–91. Military aid and levies were estimated to have cost the dukes of Arcos 900,000 ducats by 1640. Other grandees found that serving the king abroad, in the army or in diplomatic posts, could bring them close to bankruptcy.

Nobles found it difficult to repay loans, since it was not easy to realise capital out of an entailed estate. By 1623 the duke of Feria was paying

59 per cent of his outgoings for loans, and the duke of Medinaceli in 1660 was paying 84 per cent. Inevitably their standard of living fell and these great lords pleaded poverty. Failing all else, nobles could apply to the crown for a licence to raise further loans on the security of the estate. This type of credit, doubly favourable since the security could never be forfeited, encouraged some families to plunge hopelessly into debt. In these extreme circumstances the crown would supervise an arrangement (*concurso*) with creditors, whereby the noble set aside a proportion of income for loan repayments. By supporting entails, by granting licences and by supervising concursos, the crown helped powerfully to guide the aristocracy through the economic crisis of the early seventeenth century, and made sure that their estates survived almost intact into modern times. Indeed, by other means already noted above – alienating jurisdictions, taxes and land – the crown helped to turn imminent disaster into undoubted success for many aristocrats. A remarkable example was that of the duchy of Infantado, whose unredeemed capital liability of 897,731 ducats in 1637 was almost wholly paid off by 1693, a date when the then duke on his deathbed proclaimed 'that he died not a penny in debt'.

In consequence, the Spanish nobility suffered no significant decline, whether political or economic. There were many serious casualties among them, but as a class they survived and were continually reinforced by the entry of new blood. From the 1660s, when rent and production levels began to rise, they were poised to resume their leading role in the state. Charles II sanctioned the process of social mobility by approximately doubling the size of Castile's aristocracy: between 1665 and 1700 he created 328 new títulos. The infusion of new blood revived old controversies about the role of the aristocracy. Noting the great power of the grandees but their ineptitude for military service and civil or commercial posts, arbitristas argued that the honours formerly accorded to them should rightly be given to the rising elite, and that mayorazgos should be dissolved in order to release wealth. 'The nobles', complained Mateo López Bravo, 'support each other in monopolising control'. Their hold on power continued until the War of Succession, which destroyed their political role and prepared a place in the sun for the newer rising elite.

## The survival of the bourgeoisie

In the 1580s Tomás de Mercado was complaining that the trade of Spain was largely in the hands of foreigners, whose activity (he claimed) hurt the interests of native merchants. Spain was, it is true, a small country with limited resources, and the discovery of America had offered enormous opportunities that seemed to have brought little benefit to Spanish enterprise. But it would be wrong to assume that this situation came about because of the weakness or ineptitude of the middle classes. The country possessed a successful bourgeoisie that continued to play a significant, though clearly secondary, role in the major ports where foreign trade concentrated, in Cadiz, Seville, Bilbao and Alicante. In the smaller ports, like Barcelona, they managed to conserve a primary role and establish a virtual monopoly. Throughout Spain the lesser bourgeoisie held on to their role of producers and suppliers, principally of textiles but also of foods and jewellery. But all ranks of the middle classes faced serious difficulties during the period of crisis.

One problem, ironically, was that of success. Fernand Braudel has argued that the successful bourgeoisie of Philip II's Spain 'betrayed' their calling by turning their backs on trade as soon as they had made their fortunes, preferring rather to invest in status and property. The successful merchant of northern Castile, Simón Ruiz, appears to be a clear example. Another example, in Seville, is the Tenerife merchant Gaspar de Arguijo (d. 1594), who became wealthy through trading to Honduras in negroes and wine, came to own several ships, bought public office, houses and land, and dedicated his fortune to making his son, the poet Juan de Arguijo, into a nobleman of the city. The habit of exchanging commercial success for noble status and cash investments (juros) was a common one, to be found throughout the Mediterranean and even in northern Europe, so that it was no peculiarity of Spain. But it is doubtful if there was any real 'betrayal'. In the Basque country and Catalonia, business activity was respected and merchants continued in commerce long after their rise to status; while in Seville ennobled merchants did not cease to trade.

The real problem, in a period of crisis, was the search for economic security. When Simón Ruiz and his colleagues found themselves hard pressed by stronger international competition, they moved their money into loans. Similarly, when small-town investors found that inflation and economic insecurity threatened their returns, they moved into juros and censos. As foreign interests (in the slave trade, the American trade and textile imports) cornered vital sectors of Spain's business life, native entrepreneurs found it hard to compete and remain profitable. Putting assets into status and security was always an attractive alternative, and now appeared even more advisable. The crisis years after 1580, rather than any 'betrayal', should be blamed for the change in investment habits.

At the end of the sixteenth century the interest rate on censos and juros was in excess of 7 per cent per annum. The person who made a loan would not only receive a good income in annuities; if borrowers did not repay he could lay a claim to their property and lands. In some areas this produced two important developments: the urbanisation of landholdings, as town-dwellers secured rural property; and the expropriation of peasants who were unable to keep up their payments. The flow of cash into censos thus became a means of transferring property. Juros (loans to the state) in the same way offered good returns at a time when other investments were becoming risky and unattractive. Cellorigo, in common with most arbitristas, condemned this drift to non-productive investments. 'Censos', he wrote in his *Memorial*, 'are the plague and ruin of Spain. For the sweetness of the sure profit from censos the merchant leaves his trading, the artisan his employment, the peasant his farming, the shepherd his flock; and the noble sells his lands so as to exchange the one hundred they bring him for the five hundred the juro brings'. The president of the council of finance in 1617 confirmed 'the great inclination to juros and censos, which are estimated to yield more profit than trade and commerce, or farming and husbandry'.

In a period of recession, middle-class investors felt their cash was safer in annuities than in trade. The diversion of money out of industry and commerce was a well-known phenomenon that caused Cellorigo to argue that 'the riches which should have brought wealth have brought poverty'. So much money was tied up in juros, however, that the government could not pay what it owed and began lowering the interest rate. In 1608 the rate was lowered to 5 per cent, by the 1680s it was below 4 per cent. The fall in interest rates led to a reluctance to put money into the loan market. The fortunes of the wealthy members of the council of Castile consequently show after 1621 a clear decline in their juro holdings and a shift to buying up land. In other words, money was taken out of the interest market and began to flow back into productive concerns.

Those with smaller incomes also sought economic security, but for them the options were limited. People living in poor, under-invested areas of Castile had few more sensible alternatives than freezing their assets in an entail, leading Fernández de Navarrete in the 1620s to comment that 'no sooner has a trader, artisan or farmer got himself five hundred ducats income in juros, than he sets up an entail with them for his eldest son, whereupon the latter and all his brothers feel too ashamed to follow the humble callings in which the money was obtained'. A time of crisis therefore dampened initiative, but did not destroy the middle classes, who continued to function modestly within their local environment. In the small Catalan port of Tarragona we can identify by 1669 a middle class forming about 11 per cent of the taxpaying population and consisting at the top of *ciutadans honrats* trained in medicine and law, in the middle of doctors, notaries, merchants and ship-owners and at the bottom of artisans and farmers. In many other towns, too, the different levels of the middle class survived, adapted to new economic conditions, accumulated property and status and prepared modest bases for the subsequent period of expansion.

## Community and people

Traditionally the study of the past has focused on national politics and the kings and ministers who directed it, but in Spain there was little consciousness of the 'nation' and daily reality was centred almost exclusively on the local community. Social ties were formed not at a national but at a regional level, and loyalties were heavily localised, fundamentally in the rural village (*pueblo*) but at a broader level in cantons (*comarcas*) and towns. Many such communities preserved not only their own culture and language, but also their own self-government and communal exploitation of the soil. The family, the key unit in the community, was inevitably affected by the social crisis.

In most of the peninsula the basic type of family was 'nuclear', that is, a mother and father with their children; though in extensive areas, for example towards the Pyrenee mountains, households might consist of more than one family. A closer look at one region, in the west of Castile around the city of Cáceres, offers a profile – not necessarily typical – of trends during the depression. In the late sixteenth century young people in the heartland of Castile tended to marry early, girls at about 20, men at about 25. The population growth of the sixteenth century ended here in about 1590: thereafter the birth rate settled to a lower level, rising again from the 1670s. During the depression the average number of births per marriage fell to about three, but by the end of the century rose to about four. High mortality was the normal expectation of those times: during the seventeenth century between a third and a half of all children here died in infancy, and in effect two live births were necessary to produce one living adult. A comparable death rate among adults made it necessary for many marriage partners to wed again: between a fifth and a third of all marriages in the Cáceres countryside were remarriages. It was a fairly stable society, where the proportion of males to females in the population was almost equal, thereby reducing the need to emigrate in search of marriage partners; and illegitimacy was almost unknown, well below 1 per cent of all births.

Small rural communities like those around Cáceres were highly vulnerable to the seventeenth-century recession. Never economically strong, they were hit by the fall in demand, by emigration, by higher taxes. 'The state of the peasant in Spain today', commented fray Benito de Peñalosa in 1629, 'is the most poor and miserable of all, and it seems that everything has conspired to destroy and ruin him'. As output fell, the decrease in income made it difficult to repay censos, and smallholders drifted into debt. Many emigrated to the city when it became impossible for them to survive, leaving behind a decreasing population to pay the tax burden. In the villages of Bureba (north of Burgos), about a fifth of the total population disappeared, largely through emigration, between 1586 and 1597: in one village there, 'of the eighteen families here in 1593, five left because they could not pay the alcabalas'. Crop production in Bureba consequently fell between 1579 and 1595, by 30 per cent in wine and 22 per cent in cereals.

The drift from the villages aggravated the social problem in the countryside, where semi-deserted towns populated with widows and landless jornaleros became a common phenomenon. Poverty at all levels, both in town and country, intensified. An extreme but by no means the worst example is Cáceres, where already in 1557 the proportion of registered poor was close to 26 per cent, while by 1597 it had reached the level of 45 per cent. Contemporaries stepped up poor relief, set up hospitals, and wrote tracts suggesting changes in the welfare system. In response to the grave problems caused by poverty and begging, Cristóbal Pérez de Herrera published in 1598 his *Relief of the Poor*, an elaborate plan to register the poor and put them to work. It was no coincidence that the author was a friend, and fellow confraternity-member in the same Madrid parish, of the author of *Guzmán de Alfarache*, published the same year.

Banditry in these years took on new life, in post-Morisco Valencia, in Catalonia and in Castile itself, feeding on local feuds and frequently encouraged by the seigneurs. In Catalonia this was the epoch of Perot Rocaguinarda, who began his career in 1602 and makes an appearance in *Don Quixote*: 'he was', a diarist wrote, 'the most courteous bandit to have been in that region for many years: never did he dishonour or touch the churches, and God aided him'. In the mountainous areas of Granada and Murcia, and even on the highways of Castile, brigandage became common. The diarist Pellicer in 1644 reported the activities of a certain Pedro Andreu, 'who roams across La Mancha and around Ocaña. Some say he has thirty horsemen, others put it at eighty. There are curious stories about him, such as that he never kills anyone but only takes part of their money, leaving them with enough to continue their journey'. The descent into violence may well have derived in part from the thousands of ex-soldiers who came back to the peninsula and, finding little hope of economic security there, took to crime or vagabondage. In the cities the problem seemed at its gravest: a report from Madrid in 1639 commented that 'not a day passes but people are found killed or wounded by brigands or soldiers, houses burgled, girls assaulted and robbed'.

Vagrancy in Spain was aggravated by the movement of foreign workers (mostly French) southwards, in search of seasonal labour. If they failed to secure employment, they strained the resources of Spanish charity. One hospital in Burgos reported that 'every year it takes in, cares for and feeds for two or three days, from eight to ten thousand people from France, Gascony and other places', a gross exaggeration that none the less reflected a real problem. Fernández de Navarrete in 1626 lamented that 'all the scum of Europe have come to Spain, so that there is hardly a deaf, dumb, lame or blind man in France, Germany, Italy or Flanders who has not been to Castile'. Some vagabonds were idealised, in a literary genre that soon became famous, as *pícaros*. Although the lifestyle had been described as early as 1554 in the anonymous *Lazarillo de Tormes*, the pícaro as a type did not surface in literature until the epoch of depression. It was then that Mateo Alemán's *Guzmán de Alfarache* (1598) and Quevedo's *Buscón* (written 1603–8, published 1626), followed by works by Cervantes and other authors, popularised and romanticised the delinquency of the urban poor. The picaresque world of thieves, vagrants, prostitutes and swindlers was no mere construct of the creative imagination but a real dimension of the social problems faced by Spain in its age of crisis.

# The role of women

Woman's role in Spanish society was recognised as fundamental by many writers at the time: Juan Luis Vives wrote a pioneering treatise on marriage (1523), and clergy in the period of the Counter-Reformation devoted treatises to the theme. For most women the norm was matrimony, though there were many exceptions, because of a lack of eligible males or the deliberate choice of a religious life. In north-west Spain, for example, in the seventeenth century at least 16 per cent of women chose not to marry. The proportion of single females in a community was usually much higher than this, because we have to add together those who chose not to marry, those who had married and were now widows and those who either went into convents or were away in domestic service. At any given moment, nearly half the women under 50 years old might not be in a state of matrimony.

Within marriage the male usually dominated, and both Church and state aimed to strengthen the patriarchal authority of the father. But from the time of the Counter-Reformation there was an attempt to control the power over life and limb that husbands had once exercised over wives and children; and so-called 'divorces' (that is, legal separations) were granted by state and Church courts when the wife could prove systematic beating. The majority of petitions for separation in Spain cited marital violence as the reason. There were two principal grounds for granting separation in a Catholic country, if we go by the practice in Catalonia. First, if either spouse threatened the life and honour of the other (a wife from Sitges stated in 1660 that 'she is mistreated by her husband who threatens to kill her and beats her with his fists and kicks her'). Second, if the spouse refused to give economic support (the same wife stated that 'her husband refuses to work and to give her the necessary maintenance'). Impotence (that is, inability to fulfil marital duties) tended to be cited not in pleas for separation but in pleas for nullity. Impotence was difficult to prove on personal evidence alone, and more weight was put on the testimony of the community. In one case in Catalonia in 1596 the parish priest testified on behalf of the wife that 'he has heard people say many times in the village that the husband didn't have much of a member'.

Marriage in traditional Spain was not a bed of roses. 'It is no surprise', a Spanish priest observed in 1588, 'that in our time there is such unhappiness in marriages'. Nor was it permanent. Like any other secular contract, marriage could be annulled if certain conditions, such as the payment of a dowry, were not complied with. Because the contract carried no commitment to permanence, many felt themselves free to break the bonds by mutually agreed separation or even by bigamy. In the sixteenth century, the offence of bigamy made up 5 per cent of all cases prosecuted in Spain by the Inquisition. In any case, in a society where life expectancy was not high the early death of one of the partners made it necessary (as we have seen above from the case of Cáceres) for the survivor to marry again if that were feasible. In effect, marriages usually lasted around 20 years, before they were interrupted by mortality.

It was normal for women to do work both in the house and in the field. The process started from the early years, when rural families sent their daughters away from home, to spend a number of years in lifecycle service in the towns. The female presence in the urban labour market was always important. Since lifecycle workers had the specific intention of serving for only a short while, until they had saved money (for their dowry) or learnt a trade, there was a rapid turnover in their numbers. In the city of Cuenca over one-third of servants left their jobs annually, and a further one-sixth changed their dwellings every year. In global terms, country girls employed in domestic service in the towns were a significant long-term feature of the labour market. Women were also an essential part of the agrarian economy, not only in the tasks of planting, weeding and harvesting, but also in transporting produce and in buying. In the Basque lands women were an important element in agriculture. In the Mediterranean area and southern Spain, on the other hand, they appear to have been discouraged from working in the fields, as this was held to endanger the man's honour. Only men, it was felt, could direct the agrarian economy.

Women made a very special contribution to Spanish society in spiritual matters. It is true that the Counter-Reformation Church emphasised the role of the priest and tried to minimise, or at least control, the part of women in religious life. But women continued to make an impact, at a local level through their function in parish activities, and at a universal level through the many new female religious orders. Individual Catholic women made their mark. The most notable example is Teresa of Ávila, outstanding as a religious reformer in sixteenth-century Spain, whose writings became best sellers throughout the country and who, shortly after her death, was proclaimed second patron saint (after St James) of Spain. At the level of popular religion, holy women (known as *beatas*) exercised a strong spiritual influence over local communities and even, in exceptional cases, became the privileged advisers of kings. María de Agreda, a nun in a little Aragonese town, was visited by Philip IV of Spain in 1643, and came to exercise a profound influence over the king, advising him on the highest concerns of state.

Upper-class women often led enclosed lives: when unmarried they were constantly chaperoned and when married their position seldom improved. They were not even allowed to go to mass if they went alone. Though the cloistering of women was most practised among the rich, women of all conditions evaded it at every turn, and the participation of girls in public festivities was one of the delights of social life in the Mediterranean. Religion offered them a route of escape, since they went to church in order to find company, both male and female. In general, women seem to have enjoyed as much freedom of movement as men, since they emigrated without restriction to other areas of the peninsula, and many also went alone to

America. Of those who registered formally as emigrants to the New World from Seville, women constituted no more than 5 per cent prior to 1519, but by the 1550s they were some 16 per cent and in the 1560s they were as many as 28 per cent. Most were single; in the new lands they carved out their own destiny, fighting where necessary alongside the men.

## A change of perspectives

By the early seventeenth century there was growing disenchantment with Spain's imperial record, and the economic crisis forced many to reconsider the values of their own society. The stimulation once provided by inter-national contact – humanism, Italian influences, the American experience – faded and altered into a more subdued, occasionally aggressive, national chauvinism. In one sense this can be viewed as a shrinking of horizons, a major cultural contraction. From another viewpoint, however, it can be seen as a growing self-awareness, an anxiety to change course and to adopt new perspectives. There can be little doubt of the shrinking of horizons. Population decline was reflected in the figures for entrants to Castilian universities, where matriculations reached their peak at around 1620 and declined continuously into the eighteenth century. No new uni-versities were founded in Castile between 1620 and the early nineteenth century. 'The rising cost of living and the probable lack of wealth among parents' were mentioned by the corregidor of Salamanca in 1638 as explana-tions for the fall in numbers. Students preferred to go to their cheaper local colleges. The change to an emphasis on career subjects became even more marked. In the university of Alcalá in 1560, grammar had accounted for 41 per cent of all matriculations, by 1640 the proportion was under 8 per cent: canon law, by contrast, rose from 10.7 to 40 per cent. At Salamanca between the same dates, students taking grammar fell by four-fifths, and the numbers studying canon law doubled. As in all periods of economic recession, preference went to 'useful' rather than speculative studies, and the *falta de premios* or lack of prospects in certain subjects effectively doomed them. Theology was a major casualty. By 1648 it was proposed at Salamanca to suppress the chairs of Greek, Hebrew, mathematics and other subjects: Greek and Hebrew had not been taught since the 1550s.

The decline in educational institutions was not absolute. Thanks to their near-monopoly of administrative posts in the government, the colegios mayores enjoyed a sharp rise in entrants after 1620. In the same period the Jesuits stepped into the gap created by the decline of Latin grammar at the big universities. By producing a broad educational syllabus that combined academic and moral training, they quickly gained the support of parents who sought an alternative to university. Olivares relied on them as instructors for the Colegio Imperial in Madrid, founded by Philip IV in 1623 to educate sons of the nobility.

Narrower horizons were perhaps most to be seen in scientific studies. Spain lagged behind the rest of Europe not because of severe religion or censorship, for other countries had those as well, but because its ruling elites were inadequately educated at home, did not (like nobles in England or Germany) seek education abroad and failed to give cultural leadership. Other Europeans felt that the Spanish elite, both nobles and clergy, had little cultural sophistication. When Spaniards spoke of certain subjects, an imperial ambassador commented in the 1570s, they did so in the way that a blind man speaks of colours. They travelled out of Spain very seldom, he said, and had no perspective with which to make judgements. A French traveller in Madrid in 1666 came to the conclusion that people's vision of the world was limited only to that part of it controlled by Spain, 'which in their view is a world apart'. Spaniards ceased to read books written by foreigners, and did not have them translated either. When officials of the Spanish Inquisition drew up their Indices of prohibited books in the seventeenth century, they tended to prohibit the works of foreign scholars even if they were Catholics. The trend became firmer with regard to scientific and philosophical works. The social climate, rather than solely the Inquisition, was responsible for these attitudes. The works of Galileo never appeared in any Spanish Index, yet his theories evoked no interest or applause in Spain. The number of books published in Madrid on scientific subjects fell sharply: between 1566 and 1600 they were over 14 per cent of publications, but between 1601 and 1625 the proportion declined to less than 6 per cent.

The reaction against research in science – Quevedo, for example, rejoiced in his *Spain Defended* (1609) that Spain had no followers of 'that infamous sorcerer and trickster Paracelsus, who challenged the medicine of Hippocrates and Galen' – was accompanied by an almost exclusive emphasis on religious and creative literature. The influence of the Counter-Reformation emerges clearly in books published in Madrid, where the number of works with religious themes increased nearly three-fold between 1566–1600 and 1601–25. Over the same period creative literature also tripled in volume. The period of economic crisis, inevitably, also hit publishing: Madrid in 1626 was printing 112 books a year, but the figure fell to 81 in 1629 and 64 in 1631.

Some modern commentators have interpreted the self-awareness of Spaniards at this time in terms of disillusion, *desengaño*. The author most cited in support of this view is Quevedo (d. 1645), who saw the world through pessimistic eyes:

*Los muros de la patria mía*
*Si un tiempo fuertes, ya desmoronados*
*(the walls of my fatherland, once strong, now crumbling)*

Though the introspective and deeply religious outlook of Quevedo can be found in other writers, notably the dramatist Calderón, it was only one dimension of developments in Spain. The Church too was beginning to play a much larger part in the culture of Baroque Spain. The Counter-Reformation and its most brilliant agents the Jesuit order were successfully transforming the religious practices of the faithful. When the cultural leadership once supplied by great nobles like the Mendozas decayed as their economic fortunes deteriorated, the Church, which controlled a good part of the wealth of Spain, emerged as the principal patron of art outside the court. It helped talent to emerge in the provinces, and dictated the preponderance of religious themes in all branches of culture. The great age of Baroque, then, may have been in Spain one of limited creativity but was not entirely one of disillusion. Many Spaniards continued their dialogue with the outside world – the visit of Rubens to Madrid in 1628–9 was a visible sign of this cultural interchange – but at the same time developed their own perspectives and examined their own priorities more closely.

The anxiety to change course emerged as a major debate in the case of the anti-Semitic statutes of limpieza, for so long a source of conflict in Castilian society. The controversy over the statutes had been sharpened in 1547, when archbishop Siliceo of Toledo managed to adopt, against the opposition of many of his canons, a statute excluding all conversos from ecclesiastical office in the cathedral. In the course of the century, leading figures in both Church and state came out openly against the practice of limpieza. For example, the Jesuits emerged as among its firmest opponents. Both Ignatius Loyola and his immediate successor as head of the order, Diego Laínez (a converso), criticised it as *el humor español*, the Spanish peculiarity. The order came under pressure from people in Spain to accept the statutes, and in 1593 excluded conversos from membership; but thanks to a campaign by Father Pedro de Ribadeneira, the vote was reversed in 1608. It was a change of attitude sanctioned by no less a person than Philip II himself, who throughout his life had been instinctively anti-Semitic but who in the 1580s revised his views and set up a committee for the reform of the limpieza statutes. The initiative was followed by the Inquisition, which for the next half-century made strenuous but unsuccessful efforts to modify and abolish the anti-Semitic laws.

At the same period other Spaniards launched a campaign against the racialism in their society. Juan de Mariana in all his writings expressed hostility to the principle of punishing children for the sins of their fathers: 'the marks of infamy', he stated, 'should not be eternal' (*De rege*, 1599). Fernández de Navarrete, referring in 1626 to both conversos and Moriscos, commented that 'if before these arrived at the extremity of despair a way could have been found to admit them to offices, and their marks of infamy had been left forgotten, it would have been possible for them to enter the Church with honour'. 'It follows', Navarrete continued, 'that all realms where many people have been excluded from honours, are in danger of destroying themselves. Doctor Mateo Lopez Bravo put it with his customary elegance: *tot hostes, quot exclusi.*' López Bravo had indeed argued in his *De rege* (1616) that for those excluded by the limpieza laws 'there remains no way of hope except the sowing of discord'. González de Cellorigo in his *Alegación en que se funda la justicia* (Argument for Justice) (1619), defended the rights of those of Jewish origin to have access to offices and honours. Perhaps the most notable attack on the statutes was the *Discurso* (1599) of a Dominican friar, Agustín Salucio, who argued that the genealogical proofs required for limpieza were a threat to all the upper classes, who alone, unlike the lower orders, kept proofs of lineage. Discrimination against race not only excluded 'eminent subjects who have the talent to become great theologians and jurists but who do not follow these professions because they know they will not be admitted to honours'; it also bred conflict, and would make all those excluded 'discontented and ripe for rebellion'. His tract was discussed in a special committee set up by the government, and under Olivares the drive against limpieza was given official support. All books purporting to list the Jewish descent of noble families – the notorious *libros verdes* (green books) – were ordered to be publicly destroyed. In the Junta de Reformación one member claimed that the statutes were 'cause and origin of a great multitude of sins, perjuries, falsehoods, disputes and lawsuits both civil and criminal'. In the same years an inquisitor, probably Juan Rico Campofrío the bishop of Zamora, argued that proofs of limpieza were a source of moral and political scandal and had made Spain into a society of constant conflict, provoking over 90 per cent of the cases coming before the courts.

In examining their position on limpieza, many Spaniards were becoming increasingly aware that old attitudes had caused them to drift away from their common links with other peoples. 'No other nation has these statutes!' protested the arbitrista Francisco Murcia de la Llana in 1624. The Spanish ambassador to Rome in 1652 observed that 'in Spain it is held in great horror to be descended from a Jew, but here they laugh at these matters, and at us because we concern ourselves with them'. The crisis years forced a reassessment, and opened the way to new perspectives.

## The end of empire: the myth of decline

Looking back from their age of crisis and apparent failure, Spanish writers directed their nostalgia to a distant period of 'success', which they curiously identified with the epoch before the coming of their most famous rulers, Charles V and Philip II, and even before the discovery of America. Without exception they located the good times of Spain's 'Golden Age' in the reign of Ferdinand and Isabella. 'These glorious monarchs', González de Cellorigo wrote in 1600, 'raised Spain to the highest state of happiness and greatness it had ever known, in which it remained until decline began'. The theme was echoed by Pedro Fernández de Navarrete, Francisco Martínez de Mata, Diego Saavedra Fajardo and very many other writers. For them America and the Habsburg inheritance had blighted Spain's destiny. Martínez de Mata contrasted 'the happy state of Spain, in both wealth and population, in the year 1518' (that is, before the reign of Charles V and before the conquest of Mexico), with its situation in 1575, when he felt the Genoese had taken over the country's industry and trade. Like Saavedra, many Castilians in the seventeenth century welcomed the end of empire, hoping that it would give Spain the opportunity to resolve its own internal problems; though Saavedra conceded that 'the wars in Flanders have made us forget our own conflicts', allowing Spaniards to fight others rather than each other.

The challenge of imperial power outside Spain and the collapse of self-confidence within it, has passed into history as a long narrative of 'decline', a concept which gave comfort to those Spaniards who saw it as part of the changing cycle of destiny but which also confirmed non-Spaniards in their frequently negative image of Spain. In terms of what really happened, all this was more myth than reality. The Spanish universal monarchy had come into existence through inheritance rather than conquest, and Spain's limited resources had never been capable of an active imperial programme, so that its growing incapacity to fulfil that programme revealed inherent weaknesses rather than provoking a 'decline' from a position of strength. Spain moreover had enjoyed the advantage of being able to exploit the resources of its partners in the monarchy – the naval expertise and military manpower of the Genoese and Neapolitans, the weaponry of the Milanese and of Liège, the finances of Antwerp and Italy – and it was the loss of these allies, starting with the Netherlands, which served to put an excessive strain on Castile and provoked an undeniable collapse of empire. At best, the concept of 'decline' was a Castilian illusion, nurtured on the belief that they had created the empire and that they were now its primary victims. The belief became the cornerstone of the decline myth elaborated in the nineteenth century by conservative Castilian historians such as Cánovas del Castillo, and expounded by subsequent scholars, both Spanish and foreign, down to the twentieth century. They were aware of an enormous gap between the poverty of the country in modern times, and the apparent wealth and glory it had shared in the distant age of empire. The obvious explanation, it seemed to them, was that Spain had suffered a 'decline'. All that remained was to clarify the reasons why it had occurred.

The self-perception of decline, however, was a clear case of self-deception. Perceiving the universe in terms of their own aspirations, Castilians beat their breasts and assumed that they were best placed to offer an explanation of what had happened. They tried to identify the roots of failure in factors – foreign traders and capitalists, bad kings, subversive Jews – over which they claimed to have little control. It was a vision that sustained them, and that comforted subsequent generations when things started to go wrong. Even at the beginning of the twentieth century the conservative writer Ortega y Gasset was explaining, shortly after his country had lost Cuba to the United States, that 'everything that has happened in Spain since 1580 is decline and disintegration'. A version of the past was created in which the blame for what had happened was placed on Philip II, the Inquisition, contamination by Europe, capitalism and every conceivable factor that had played a role in Spain's history. The central thesis, 'decline', remained unaltered and unwavering; all that changed were the ingredients that went to make up the desired explanation.

# CHAPTER 6

# The end of the old empire 1660–1714

## The last of the Habsburgs 1665–1700

The death of Philip IV in September 1665 left the monarchy in profound crisis. His son Charles II was only four years old, and the succession of a child as king (it was the first royal minority in Spain's history) inevitably created problems. Power was vested in queen Mariana as regent and in a five-member committee of government; they were to rule until the king reached his official coming of age at fourteen. Because Mariana had little experience of ruling, decisions tended to be made by pressure groups among the grandees, of whom the most powerful up to 1668 was of the count of Castrillo, who had engineered the fall of Olivares. The king, an invalid since birth, was never a significant force. He remained chronically ill throughout his life, and proved unable to father an heir. When he was 25 the papal nuncio reported that 'he is as weak in body as in mind. Now and then he gives signs of intelligence, memory and a certain liveliness; usually he shows himself slow and indifferent, torpid and indolent. One can do with him what one wishes because he lacks his own will'.

The most significant force in politics up to 1680 was a man whom Philip in his will had deliberately excluded from government. This was Don Juan José (1629–79), Philip's illegitimate son by the actress María Calderón. Don Juan enjoyed the status of a royal prince, was grand prior of the order of St John in Castile, and had served with distinction in the Netherlands, in Italy, in Catalonia and against the Portuguese rebels. A man of great personal gifts and culture, and his country's leading general, Don Juan aspired to the power which he felt was being incompetently exercised by the regent and her supporters. For the first 13 years of the reign political life centred on the power struggle between him and the queen.

Since the grandees were divided into factions, and many were strong supporters of Don Juan, Mariana relied on 'favourites' originating from outside the noble elite and therefore always opposed by them. From 1666 she put her full confidence in her confessor, Juan Nithard, an Austrian Jesuit whom she made inquisitor general and thus ex-officio member of the committee of government. The appointment of an obscure foreigner to the highest offices of state provoked a long crisis, and Don Juan headed the campaign to get rid of Nithard. Plots by the prince to seize the confessor were discovered in October 1668, causing him to retire to Aragon and then to Catalonia, where his tenure as viceroy after the surrender of Barcelona in 1652 had earned him widespread support. After an extensive propaganda campaign that seems to have earned him enormous backing throughout Spain, particularly among the common people, Don Juan in February 1669 marched through Catalonia and Aragon towards Madrid at the head of a small force of a few hundred men. The coup was a partial success, since the crown made concessions and Nithard was dismissed and made to leave the country. Don Juan, however, was asked to retire to Saragossa with the title and powers of 'vicar general of the crown of Aragon', an obvious concession to the strength of his support in the eastern provinces. The prince remained from June 1669 to November 1675 in Saragossa, where he strengthened his position and instituted plans for economic reform.

The departure of Nithard made Mariana search for support elsewhere, in the person of Fernando Valenzuela, who began his career as a page of the duke of Infantado, but in 1661 married a lady-in-waiting of the queen and by about 1670 had a secure position in the palace. From 1673 Valenzuela and his wife were regularly consulted by Mariana. The favourite, known as 'the palace ghost' (*duende de palacio*) because of the ease with which he obtained access to the queen, was made a marquis in November 1675. This was the month that the king officially came of age, automatically terminating the powers of the regent and the committee of government. Encouraged by his private tutor, Charles decided to establish his independence, and summoned Don Juan to Madrid. The prince arrived expecting to assume power, but strong pressure from Mariana on her weak-willed son forced a complete change in circumstances. The date of 6 November is remembered as a Day of Dupes: Don Juan returned disappointed to Saragossa, Valenzuela was exiled to Granada.

By April 1676 the queen felt secure enough to recall Valenzuela, who was made a grandee and then 'prime minister'. But the united resentment of the aristocracy led 24 of them in December to issue an ultimatum to the queen, and the councils of state and Castile unanimously called for the imprisonment of the favourite. Valenzuela fled to the Escorial, and on New Year's Day 1677 Don Juan set out from Saragossa for Madrid. This time he came with a huge army, numbering 15,000 by the time it approached Madrid. Valenzuela was arrested at the Escorial and deported to the Philippines (which he never reached, since he died in an accident in Mexico in 1692). On 23 January Don Juan offered his services to a grateful king: it was the first *pronunciamiento* (military coup) of modern Spanish history.

The prince's triumph has often been presented as an intrusion by the crown of Aragon into the affairs of Castile. Circumstances had certainly given Don Juan his strongest support in the eastern realms, but his popularity in Castile was no less great. Eighteen Castilian grandees were in his army, and it was with Castile in mind that the English ambassador wrote that 'he has on his side that great Monster the People'. The prince was the first truly popular leader of Habsburg Spain, and the only one to receive the full support both of Castile and of Aragon. His tenure of power, unfortunately, lasted only two and a half years (January 1677–September 1679).

In the spring of 1677 Don Juan took the king in person to open an historic session of the Cortes of the kingdom of Aragon in Saragossa (the Cortes actually sat for two sessions, in 1677–8 and 1684–7); plans to visit Catalonia and Valencia were postponed because of Charles's health. There were no meetings of the Castilian Cortes in this reign. The prince made plans to reform the administration: orders were sent out to all corregidors in January 1678 for reports on the state of the economy, and in June a survey of depopulated villages was ordered. Early in 1679 plans were made to cure the rampant inflation by a drastic reform of the coinage. The measure, approved in August 1679 but not put into effect until February 1680, caused widespread disorder but brought an end to inflation. Finally, in January 1679, Don Juan created a committee for trade, modelled on one he had set up in Saragossa; it survived for many years and helped contribute to economic renewal in Spain.

The promise of these years was tragically left unfulfilled. It was the worst possible time for anyone to come to power: inflation was rampant, in 1677 and 1678 there was severe famine throughout Spain, and epidemic was devastating Andalusia. On top of all this there was military disaster abroad, ending in the peace of Nijmegen. The council of finance reported in the summer of 1678 that 'all the revenue has been applied to juros and other payments, leaving nothing with which to meet the many urgent expenses that arise daily'. The most pressing affair of state was the king's marriage, eventually contracted early in 1679 with Marie Louise of Orleans and consummated at the end of the year. By then Don Juan was dead: the anxieties of office took a toll on his health and he died after a two-month illness, in September 1679, at the early age of 50. One of the most promising men ever to assume command of the state in Spain, he had pursued reforming policies, in both internal and foreign policy, that could have been of real and lasting benefit.

In February 1680 the duke of Medinaceli was appointed valido and carried through the legislation of Don Juan, despite his previous hostility to the prince. The two main measures involved were the monetary devaluation of 10 February, decreed eleven days before the duke took office; and the committee for trade, which Medinaceli suspended in April 1680 but reconvened in December 1682. Following through the effects of the devaluation, the duke in 1681 sent finance officials out into each province of Castile to prepare a new tax census. The enquiry, which again was a successor to the surveys ordered by Don Juan in 1678, took some three years to complete, and in the process the burden of government taxation was reduced by over 15 per cent. It was the first time that the Habsburg state in Spain had ever reduced the burden on the taxpayer, and a sign of impending economic recovery.

Medinaceli, however, was forced to resign in April 1685 as a result of palace quarrels. The validos of this period were chosen by a sort of consensus among the grandees; the one who took over was the count of Oropesa, subsequently described by the English ambassador Stanhope as 'the ablest man I have met with in Spain'. His ministry (1685–91), like his predecessor's, concentrated on the long-standing financial difficulties of the state. In October 1686 a decree completed the measures of February 1680 by further devaluing silver coin by a fifth. Then in February 1688 the debt problem was dealt with by a budget arrangement that set aside 4.7 million ducats annually for basic expenses. The arrangement remained in force for over a quarter of a century and gave the government the security of a minimum income. Meanwhile, in Catalonia, a major peasant uprising in 1688 distracted the military authorities.

Queen Marie Louise's sudden death as the result of a riding accident in February 1689 renewed anxieties about the succession to the throne, and within six months a marriage was arranged with Mariana of Neuburg, daughter of a German prince, the Elector Palatine. She forced the resignation of Oropesa in 1691 and government then passed into the hands of a

German clique, who were tolerated because of the help being rendered by the Emperor to Spain's military effort in Flanders and Catalonia. The Germans – their principal advisers were Mariana's secretary Wiser, her lady-in-waiting the countess of Berlepsch, and two Spaniards, the count of Baños and Don Juan de Ángulo – effectively dominated the court from 1691 to 1698. Executive power however remained in the hands of the grandees, most of whom were hostile to the Germans, with the consequence that politics remained in a state of confusion, with court and councils in frequent conflict over policy.

By the 1690s the major issue was the succession to the throne. Charles II was unable to produce an heir either by Marie Louise or by Mariana, and the impending end of the male line of the Habsburg dynasty in Spain made it urgent to look around for the next king. France felt that it had a strong case in favour of the rights of Philip IV's daughter Maria Teresa, who had married Louis XIV in 1660. Both that marriage treaty and Philip IV's later testament made it clear that Maria Teresa and her issue were excluded from the succession, but Louis persisted in his claims, and many in Spain supported him. The influential position of Mariana of Neuburg fed hopes of a pro-German succession, actively canvassed in Madrid by the Imperial ambassador Harrach after his arrival in 1697. A strong pro-French grouping, which saw greater advantages in having a powerful France as an ally rather than an enemy, was however forming under the leadership of the archbishop of Toledo, cardinal Portocarrero, who had always opposed the Germans at court and from 1698, when the French ambassador Harcourt arrived in Spain, committed himself firmly to the French cause.

Charles II's health was meanwhile decaying rapidly. In 1699 there was a short-lived attempt to use exorcism to cure the king's condition, in particular his alleged impotence (the reputation he earned as a 'bewitched king' derives almost entirely from this trivial incident). Spain's sole concern now was to resolve the succession, for which the partition treaties (mentioned below) had made provision. At this juncture Oropesa was recalled to power: his ministry survived no more than a year (March 1698–April 1699) and was overthrown by serious bread riots in the capital (28 April 1699). The preponderant voice now was Portocarrero's: like him, most grandees wanted a strong king, and thought that France could provide one. There was firm opposition to the proposed partitions of the monarchy, and by June 1700 both Charles II and his councillors were agreed that the entire monarchy must go undivided 'to a grandson of the king of France, on the assurance that there will be no unification of the two crowns', to cite the vote of one grandee. Charles signed a testament to this effect on 3 October, and died on 1 November 1700.

Traditionally, historians have presented the reign of the last Habsburg as the epitome of 'decline' on the basis of the confused political situation and the weakness of the government in Madrid. In reality, politics alone provide no adequate perspective of a period that also experienced both reform and renewal. On the positive side, the reign was crucial for: the first major economic reforms of the entire century (elimination of inflation, reduction of taxation); the clearest signs of demographic recovery after the decades of crisis; the highest figures for bullion shipments from America and the first attempts to restructure the trade to the New World; the first moves towards provincial autonomy (with the Cortes of Aragon in 1677); the first major attempts to reform peninsular trade; and the beginnings of a more open approach to European thought and science. All these aspects, which give the reign of Charles II an exceptional place in Spain's history, are touched on below.

# Foreign policy 1665–1700

The peace of the Pyrenees in 1659 was the fateful hinge on which Spain's foreign policy turned in the second half of the seventeenth century. It confirmed, even more surely than the peace of Westphalia, the end of Spain's hegemony in Europe and the rise of France. Through the accompanying marriage treaty (1660), Louis XIV was given the means by which he could press a claim to the Spanish throne. The peace convinced many Spanish leaders, notably Don Juan José, that Spain should disengage from its commitments in the north of Europe and restrict itself to the Mediterranean. Symptomatic of this tendency was the suggestion, first made by Mazarin and then warmly supported in Spain, for the surrender to France of the Spanish Netherlands (Flanders) in exchange for the provinces of Catalonia lost in the treaty. It was a highly significant move, for it made clear that in Flanders the French had expansionist intentions, which the Dutch logically were determined to oppose.

From 1656, when Don Juan as governor of the Netherlands began negotiations with the Hague, the two former enemies drifted into a remarkable diplomatic revolution. The Dutch were concerned to maintain Flanders as an effective barrier against Louis's aggression, and in return offered the Spanish extensive naval protection both in the Atlantic and in the Mediterranean. For a period the two nations also had a common interest in defeating Portugal, whose territory in Brazil the Dutch occupied during the middle decades of the century. For its part, the Spanish crown did not recognise Portugal's independence until 1668.

Louis XIV was meanwhile gnawing away at the Spanish monarchy through both war and diplomacy. A partition treaty, signed secretly at Vienna in January 1668 with the Emperor Leopold I, who also claimed the Spanish throne as grandson of Philip III, agreed that if Charles II had no heir the Emperor would get Spain, the Indies and the north Italian territories including Milan; while France would get the Netherlands, Franche-Comté, the Philippines, Navarre, Naples and other dependencies. The treaty followed Louis's first substantial aggression (the so-called War of Devolution) into the Netherlands in 1667 and preceded the invasion of Franche-Comté in February 1668. The peace of Aix-la-Chapelle (May 1668), which gave France the cities of Lille, Charleroi and Tournai, confirmed the decay of Spain's military power, and pushed Spain into even closer links with the United Provinces, through the good services of the Spanish ambassador at the Hague, Manuel de Lira, a strong admirer of Dutch culture.

In 1672 France invaded the United Provinces and sparked off a major conflict with disastrous consequences for Spain, which had gallantly declared war on the side of the Dutch. Two French armies under the command of Turenne and Condé occupied the major cities of Flanders and invaded Franche-Comté. In the Mediterranean the French navy under Duquesne aided the revolt of Messina against Spain in 1674. When the Dutch sent warships to help, they were defeated by Duquesne in two naval engagements in 1676, the great Protestant admiral de Ruyter losing his life in battle for the defence of Catholic Spain. When peace was eventually signed in 1678 at Nijmegen, Spain ceded to France the territory of Franche-Comté, most of Artois and major cities including Ypres and Cambrai.

The catalogue of disaster continued for the next quarter-century. After Nijmegen Louis resorted to the legalistic device of 'reunions': frontier territories that had legal or historical links with France were declared incorporated into the state, and troops sent in to enforce the judgment. Spain retaliated by declaring war in 1683, but suffered an invasion of Catalonia and lost the duchy of Luxemburg (peace of Ratisbon 1684). France retained hopes of a French succession to the Spanish throne through the possibility that Marie Louise might produce an heir, a hope that was frustrated by Charles II's impotence and by the queen's death in 1689. In the previous year, 1688, Louis had launched another war, this time directed against Germany, which lasted for nine years and submerged the entire continent in conflict. In Flanders the Spanish and Dutch troops were put under the command of a German general, the prince of Waldeck, but the joint forces were crushed by the French in July 1690 at Fleurus. In Catalonia the French attempted to exploit the popular uprisings of 1688–9, but their barbarous naval bombardment of Barcelona and Alicante in 1691 earned them the lasting hatred of the Levant peoples. Barcelona was occupied but returned, with most other conquests, at the peace of Rijswijk (1697), which formally ceded part of the Caribbean island of Hispaniola (Haiti) to France.

In 1688, when William III of Orange took over the English throne in addition to his leadership of the United Provinces, a radical change occurred in the succession problem. The two maritime powers, England and Holland, were now united in opposition to the claims of Louis XIV and gave their support to the proposals of the Emperor. From 1692 it seemed that the most acceptable candidate might be Leopold's grandson, the newborn heir to the elector of Bavaria. In October 1698 Louis and the Dutch agreed upon a partition treaty, by which the electoral prince would receive Spain and its empire outside Europe, leaving the rest of the monarchy to the dauphin and to the Emperor's son the archduke Charles of Austria. The sudden death of the infant prince in February 1699 reopened the question, and in June 1699 Louis and William III agreed on another partition, leaving the bulk of the empire to the archduke, and the balance to the dauphin. When news of the agreement reached Madrid there was an angry reaction from the government, which agreed unanimously with the king that the crown must go undivided to a French candidate, a decision expressed in Charles II's testament of 1700 and accepted at once by Louis XIV.

## Crisis and recovery

The experience of the early seventeenth century continued to cast gloom over the reign of Charles II, and most contemporary observers saw little recovery. The Portuguese wars ended in 1668, but a quarter-century of campaigns had its effect: Extremadura in the generation after 1640 lost between one-third and one-half of its people, and remained into modern times one of the most depressed provinces of the peninsula. The rest of the peninsula also had severe problems.

The last universal crisis of early modern Spain occurred between about 1676 and 1686. Successive harvest failures from 1676 to 1679 produced famine and the highest food prices of the reign; there were floods in 1680 and 1681, then drought in 1682 and 1683. In Seville a resident reported that 'in all 1683, up to the end of November, no rain fell. The earth of almost all Andalusia dried up'. Famine in 1684 brought grain prices that were not exceeded for another hundred years. In 1687 locusts swept over Catalonia – 'people were stunned', a witness reported, 'it was as though the end of the world had come' – and precipitated a disaster that led to peasant rebellion. The chief component of the crisis was epidemic. From 1676 to 1682 a major plague swept over the south: originating in Cartagena, it moved west and engulfed Andalusia. In its wake, from 1683 to 1685, an epidemic of typhus hit Andalusia and Castile: the city of Ciudad Real lost nearly half its population. It is possible that up to half a million people died in these disasters.

The grim sequence of events masks the fact that for Spain the worst was over. From the 1660s the birth rate, both in cities and in the country-side, began to rise and maintained itself even against the reverses of the 1680s (*see* Figure 4). In the interior the recovery was slower, with virtually no growth in Aragon, and most Castilian cities showing positive signs only in the 1680s; but there were exceptions, like Medina del Campo, whose population expanded by 52 per cent between 1646 and 1683. Throughout the periphery there was no doubt of the demographic increase after the 1660s: in Galicia, Murcia, Valencia and coastal Catalonia the later century experienced rising birth rates and secure growth. The expansion continued without significant interruption into the eighteenth century, and by the 1750s Spain had regained its population levels of the sixteenth century.

Monetary inflation had soared during the century: the premium of vellón on silver in New Castile rose from 50 per cent in 1652 to 150 per cent in 1664 and 275 per cent in 1680. This meant that prices rose steeply, for more coins were required to buy the same amount of goods. The government decreed a sharp devaluation of vellón by 75 per cent in 1680, following it with another similar decree in 1686. Both decrees created widespread chaos, but they succeeded in restoring some stability to the monetary system. Manufacturers were now able to make reasonable profits without having to cope with inflationary costs. The committee for trade attempted, though with only modest success, to exploit these favourable conditions. It offered privileges, such as freedom from taxes, to foreign and domestic manufacturers wishing to establish new industries. Because its authority was restricted to Castile, additional committees with a more specialist role were set up in Granada (1683), Seville (1687), Valencia (1692) and Barcelona (1692). Possibly the most active of these was the one in Barcelona, where the guiding spirit was the lawyer Narcís Feliu de la Penya, who for nearly 20 years (1680–97) promoted schemes to resurrect the textile industry. The committee for trade attempted also to get rid of the lingering prejudice that manufacturing was a barrier to noble status, and prevailed on the crown to issue in December 1682 a formal declaration to this effect.

At the same time there was a remarkable increase in the amount of American silver shipped to the peninsula. Contrary to the impression given by official figures, shipments may have exceeded the highest totals reached in the sixteenth century. Earl J. Hamilton's classic researches suggested peak imports of 35 million pesos in the five-year period 1591–5, sinking to 3 million in 1656–60. However, there is no doubt that in the reign of Charles II the five-year totals regularly exceeded 40 million (*see* Figure 3). Most of this, it is true, did not enter Spain but went to foreign traders; much more, however, probably entered the Spanish economic system than has hitherto been suspected.

Production, and with it trade, began to expand after the middle of the century. Population growth, and higher demand for animal feed, stimulated agricultural output. A study of grain output on farms in Córdoba shows an increase, between 1650 and 1710, of over 50 per cent in wheat and over 200 per cent in barley. Even in interior Spain, there were clear signs of revival: around Segovia, output between 1640 and 1710 increased by 48 per cent in wheat and 127 per cent in other grain. The resurrection of the rural economy was paralleled by a rise in production of raw wool, Spain's most valuable commodity. Around Segovia, where the finest quality originated, output of wool from the flocks almost quadrupled between 1650 and 1700, and continued to rise throughout the eighteenth century. On the Spanish periphery the recovery was dramatic: in Valencia the decades after 1660 were years of harvest plenty, and in Catalonia there was an equally impressive rise in grain production between the 1650s and the early 1700s.

Spain's economic successes in the eighteenth century were consequently the fruit of a long period of creation and renewal that began after the middle years of the seventeenth century. Much of the progress was inevitably uneven. The increase in wool, for instance, was not followed by any significant regeneration of the textile industry. Though it is certain that manufacturing improved slightly in Segovia, Palencia, Córdoba and other centres, the bulk of the wool went abroad to the United Provinces, England and France to feed their industries, which in turn exported articles to Spain to swamp the peninsular market. It was this dependence on foreigners that

Feliu de la Penya aimed to combat, 'so that the trade of Catalonia may rise again, like a phoenix from its ashes'.

In perhaps his best-known essay, the *Fénix de Cataluña* (Catalan phoenix) (1683), Feliu and his friends proposed the establishment of a trading company to restore Catalonia's commerce. The notion of a 'company', modelled on those operated by the English and Dutch, became popular among arbitristas late in the century. A basic prerequisite was that the Seville 'monopoly' to America, now recognised to be irremediably under foreign domination, be either modified or abolished. One proposal, by fray Juan de Castro in 1668–9, was actually approved by the crown. It allowed not only Castilians and Basques but also 'Valencia, Aragon and Catalonia, since they are subjects and Spaniards', to take part in trade to the Indies. The many schemes of the period culminated during the War of Succession in the establishment by the rebel Catalans of a 'New Gibraltar Company', which included Feliu and his colleagues among its backers but collapsed after Utrecht.

Though Seville and particularly Cadiz (which became the point of departure for fleets from 1680 and to which the monopoly was officially moved in 1717) continued, like most of the peninsula's trade, to be directed mainly by foreign interests, there were signs of a new independence in the smaller ports. On the Basque coast, Bilbao began to establish itself as the chief port for the wool trade, in which, according to city ordinances of 1699, only native Basques could participate. By 1718 only two of the twenty-two richest merchants of the city were of foreign origin. In Catalonia there were similar signs of resurgence. 'In this country, within the last eight or ten years', wrote the local French consul in 1686, 'industry has begun to thrive'. Particularly interesting was the success of the seaport of Mataró, which through a policy of low customs duties and keen investment in shipping managed to achieve, as the town claimed in 1702, 'a commerce which for some years now has been almost equal to that of Barcelona'. When the War of Succession broke out, it was the thrusting bourgeoisie of Mataró and Barcelona who were the leading supporters of the archduke. The early success of the Basques and Catalans against foreign competition gave the periphery an initiative it never lost.

Internal order in Catalonia, however, was gravely compromised by peasant agitation against billeting of troops. Discontent became worse after locusts destroyed the Catalan harvest in 1687. In 1688 the agitation turned into a full-scale uprising of the peasants of lower Catalonia (the rebels were called *barretines*, after their peasant caps), who in April besieged Barcelona and extracted concessions from the authorities. The French subsidised the leaders of the revolt in an effort to make Catalonia collapse from within rather than through an expensive conquest. The Catalan ruling classes, however, refused to support either the rebels or the French, and the rising collapsed by the end of 1689. A grateful Madrid in 1690 restored to Barcelona's councillors the right (refused to them in 1632) to keep their hats on in the royal presence: it was an act that confirmed the adherence of Barcelona to the Habsburg cause. A few years later, in 1693, the oppressed peasantry of Valencia also staged a rebellion: it was quickly put down, but the agitation broke out again during the War of Succession, when the rebels helped to hand Valencia to the Allies.

The war in the peninsula did not interrupt Spain's recovery. Apart from the major subsistence crisis of 1709–11, and local epidemics that occurred both before and during it, there was no extensive loss of life. The campaigns, indeed, forced Spain to fend for itself, and stimulated industrial output. Freed now of the deadweight of its European territories, the state could dedicate its resources to internal recovery.

# Towards the Enlightenment

The later seventeenth century was a period of mediocre cultural activity: economic and political crisis in the mid-century years depressed investment in art, imperial influences that had enriched the Golden Age were on the wane, and a weak court in Madrid neglected patronage. On the periphery (notably Seville and Barcelona) writers, dramatists and artists were active, but their work found little echo beyond the confines of the province. Spain seemed to be losing touch with the outside world, and its isolation from the main currents of European thought was both recognised and regretted. In 1687 the Valencian doctor Juan de Cabriada lamented that 'like savages we have to be the last to receive the innovations and knowledge that the rest of Europe already has'. However, times were changing, and there were educated people with an active interest in European ideas. The first public mention of Descartes in Spain was in a work by a Jesuit professor in Oviedo in 1655. Books entered the country without much difficulty and facilitated contact with the work of European philosophers. Ease of communication with Italy helped this penetration of ideas. A famous converso physician, Dr Diego Zapata, helped to found in 1700 in Seville the Royal Society of Medicine, whose opponents accused it of teaching 'modern Cartesian doctrines' and of aiming 'to subvert the doctrines of Aristotle, Hippocrates and Galen'. Zapata's personal library included books by Bacon, Gassendi, Bayle, Pascal and other foreign authors. Few of these writers were actually forbidden: the Inquisition produced no Index of prohibited books between 1640 and 1707, and its activities in those years was muted. In any case, without relaxing its theoretical vigilance the Inquisition gave individual scholars permission to read authors who were generally forbidden to the public.

The new scientific movement in Spain, which extended from the late seventeenth into the early eighteenth century, was initially promoted through discussion salons during the period of Don Juan José, whose private physician, the Italian Juanini, was a leading proponent of new ideas. In Valencia in the 1670s there were literary academies like the Parnassus and the Alcázar, which were later superseded by others with a more scientific interest. In Madrid, according to Zapata, 'from 1687, there were in the capital well-known and public salons on which lustre and renown were shed by men of the highest distinction'. The most significant date for the new trends was the year 1687, when the scientific 'academy' of Baltasar de Iñigo was formed in Valencia, and when Juan de Cabriada, then aged only 20, published his challenging *Philosophical Letter* in Madrid, calling for freedom and experimentation in the medical sciences.

The controversy between conservatives and innovators continued into the reign of Philip V. Though knowledge of Descartes, Gassendi and above all Maignan continued to grow, the cultural trends remained strongly Italian rather than French. The crown – after the long hiatus under Charles II – became once more a sponsor of the arts: Philip V established the Royal Library, founded the Spanish Academy (1713) and patronised Italian artists and architects. By 1726, when the Benedictine monk from Oviedo, Feijoo, began to issue his critical writings, two generations of innovation by a determined minority had prepared the way for the cultural successes of the Enlightenment.

## The Bourbons and the War of Succession 1700–1714

The accession of Philip V, duke of Anjou and grandson of Louis XIV, was greeted with relief in Madrid. In a talk he had with Anjou shortly after accepting the Spanish testament, Louis XIV proclaimed that 'there are no more Pyrenees!' There was an exact parallel between the entry of the first Bourbon into Spain in January 1701 and that of the first Habsburg in September 1517: on both occasions a seventeen-year-old boy with no knowledge of Spain or its language, and dependent on non-Spanish advisers for guidance in matters of state, instituted the rule of a foreign dynasty.

As in 1517, resentment soon arose. Louis XIV corresponded directly with his grandson and the French ambassador, and exercised direct control over all important decisions. French advisers, notably the princess of Ursins, lady-in-waiting to the young queen Marie Louise of Savoy who married Philip in 1701, controlled all court appointments. Louis would have liked to alter the complete political and financial system of the monarchy, but refrained out of a genuine wish to proceed cautiously, and because of the outbreak of war.

The direct instruments of Louis's policy in Spain were his ambassadors, who were allowed into Philip's privy council (*despacho*) and helped to form policy. The most prominent of them was Michel-Jean Amelot, marquis of Gournay, whose term of office from 1705 to 1709 marked the highest point ever reached by French influence in the peninsula. Finances were from 1702 put into the hands of a French official, Jean Orry, who attempted to reform the fiscal system. The active role of France in Spanish affairs was made necessary by the outbreak of war. When Louis decided to accept Charles II's will rather than his own commitment to the secret partitions, the maritime powers claimed that he had reneged on his obligations and headed a grand alliance, which included the Emperor, to wrest the Spanish throne from France.

The War of the Spanish Succession (1702–13), a struggle between the powers for the inert body of the Spanish monarchy, was in effect a global war with objectives ranging far beyond the peninsula. The Emperor was primarily interested in obtaining control of the Italian possessions of the monarchy. The maritime powers were concerned to extend their trade influence in the Mediterranean and secure a portion of American wealth and territory. For Louis XIV 'the main objective of the present war', he informed Amelot in 1705, 'is the Indies trade and its wealth'. In the process the French were also concerned to strengthen their already dominant commercial role in the peninsula. In February 1704 the first French troops entered Spain to assist in the war effort, and all the major commands – including the supreme command, entrusted to the Marshal duke of Berwick – were assigned to Louis's generals. The extension of French control soon aroused opposition and divided opinion, thereby precipitating conditions of virtual civil war among Spaniards, side by side with the military campaigns. It was a situation almost without precedent, and the first time since the mediaeval Muslim invasions that the nation had suffered foreign occupation.

While Philip was touring his Italian territories from April to December 1702, the anti-French alliance declared war. In September the English attacked and destroyed the Indies silver fleet sheltering in the harbour of Vigo; fortunately for Spain all the bullion had been safely removed. Hostilities on land began shortly after the archduke, the allied candidate for the throne and now known as Charles III, landed in Lisbon in the spring of 1704. Campaigns were restricted to the Portuguese border, but Anglo-Dutch naval power was used in the capture of Gibraltar and the naval battle off Málaga (both in August 1704). In the summer of 1705 the allied fleet transported the archduke and an invasion force to the Mediterranean and opened up a second front in Valencia and Barcelona, both cities having fallen into allied hands by the end of 1705. In the spring of 1706 the allies in Portugal began a successful push to the east and entered Madrid in June; almost simultaneously, from the west, the arch-duke and his troops entered Saragossa. All major cities in the peninsula were now in the hands of the Habsburg forces. In a wry irony on the events of 1580, 1591 and 1640, troops from Portugal, Aragon and Catalonia were now occupying Madrid.

It was more difficult to make the conquest permanent. In Castile the peasantry waged highly effective guerrilla warfare against the foreign troops. French reinforcements, joining the main Franco-Spanish force under Berwick, recaptured Madrid in October 1705 and pushed south to Valencia, where in April 1707 they inflicted a crushing defeat on a smaller allied force, commanded by the earl of Galway, at Almansa. It was the most decisive battle of the war: Valencia was permanently recovered, the archduke was compelled to rely only on Catalonia, and the succession of Philip V was saved. Bourbon troops, commanded now by the duke of Orleans, went on to recover Saragossa in May 1707. The only allied victory of this period was the capture of Menorca in 1708.

The tide turned in 1709, when bad weather, harvest failure and epidemic created widespread disaster. Similar conditions in France forced Louis to negotiate for peace and withdraw his troops and ambassador from Spain. When Philip was informed of the allied demand that he vacate the Spanish throne, the young king declared: 'I shall only quit Spain when I am dead; I would prefer to perish fighting for it foot by foot, at the head of my troops'. French withdrawal left the campaigns in less experienced Spanish hands, and the allies succeeded in recapturing Saragossa (August 1710) and Madrid (September 1710).

Faced by unacceptable English demands, Louis soon realised that it had been an error to desert Spain. In August 1710 forces commanded by the duke of Vendôme poured back into the country. They defeated the English under Stanhope at Brihuega on 9 December 1710 and the main allied force under Stahremberg at Villaviciosa on the following day. Villaviciosa sealed the fate of the archduke. At the end of 1711 he left Barcelona in order to assume the Imperial crown, to which he had succeeded in the spring. Peace negotiations ended in the settlement at Utrecht (April 1713). Philip was confirmed as ruler of Spain and the Indies, but the rest of the European empire disappeared: the southern Netherlands were given to the Emperor, Sicily to Savoy, Gibraltar and Menorca to England. By the further peace of Rastatt (March 1714), to which Spain was not a party, France agreed to hand over to the Empire all Spain's Italian possessions, including Naples, Sardinia and Milan. Meanwhile in the peninsula only the Catalans were unsubdued. Although they had been given guarantees by England they were now abandoned, and after a long siege the forces of Philip V entered Barcelona on 12 September 1714.

The period of French influence did not outlast the war. Marie Louise died in February 1714 and in December the same year Philip V married an Italian princess, Elizabeth Farnese. A strong-willed queen whose chief adviser was the abbé Alberoni, Farnese immediately brought about what the French envoy early in 1715 described as 'a completely new court and a completely new system'.

# Revolution in government and the unification of Spain

The War of Succession changed the political face of Spain. After the battle of Almansa, Philip V in June 1707 issued a decree abolishing the fueros of Aragon and Valencia on the grounds of the 'rebellion and complete disloyalty' of these provinces. In September 1714 it was the turn of the Catalans, whose constitutions were abolished by Berwick as soon as he entered Barcelona. Later, in January 1716, a new constitution (*nueva planta*) remodelled the public bodies of the principality of Catalonia, established the laws of Castile, made the use of Castilian obligatory in the law courts, and imposed a military occupation on Catalonia. The crown of Aragon now ceased to exist, and for the first time in its history Spain became a politically united nation. The major exception to this unity was the Basque country, which had remained loyal to the Bourbon dynasty and continued to enjoy its fueros.

The accusation of rebellion made against the crown of Aragon was always difficult to sustain. With very few exceptions, the upper classes and the major cities of Aragon and Valencia had remained solidly faithful to Philip V. In Valencia the peasants continued their struggle, but it was

directed against their lords, not against the king. In Catalonia too there
was little evidence of rebellion. The civic leaders of the two major ports,
Barcelona and Mataró, gave their allegiance to the archduke because they
expected major commercial favours, but a large part of the principality
remained faithful to Philip V. What occurred in Aragon and indeed in
Castile during the war, was in reality something far more complex than
rebellion. The invasions shattered the uneasy relationship between local
communities and opened up a broad range of domestic conflicts, exemplified in Valencia by the sharp division between *maulets* (pro-Habsburg)
and *botiflers* (pro-Bourbon).

Abolition of the fueros had been strongly advocated by many
Castilians, notably the crown's chief legal officer Melchor de Macanaz, and
also by French advisers and Louis XIV. 'Rebellion' was in these circumstances a convenient pretext for the government to implement a measure
that continued to be long resented by the eastern realms. The end of the
fueros did not have the same impact everywhere. The internal legal systems
of Aragon and Catalonia were left largely untouched, but in Valencia they
were abolished. In 1708 and again in 1714 the customs barriers between
Aragon and Castile were also abolished, thus unifying Spain commercially.
The principal impact of all the changes on the eastern realms was financial.
The government did not introduce the unwieldy Castilian tax system but
instead imposed a single comprehensive tax, known as the *equivalente*
in Valencia (1716), the *única contribución* in Aragon (1714) and the
*catastro* in Catalonia (1717). Where the three realms had contributed
almost nothing to the crown before 1707, by 1734 their taxes represented
nearly 14 per cent of state income. In return the crown promised all
Aragonese equal access to state posts, but this soon became a pretext to
allow Castilians to occupy the principal posts in the eastern realms.

Political unity created the basis for a new national administration. At
the centre, in Madrid, the old Habsburg system of government through
regional councils was done away with. The councils of Flanders, Aragon
and Italy ceased to exist as a result of the war, the council of state declined
in importance, and the council of Castile extended its authority to become
the chief organ of government. Executive power was put into the hands
of departmental 'secretaries of state'. In order to liaise more closely with
the municipalities, the system of intendants was borrowed from France.
Introduced in 1711 by the then chief minister, the Belgian count of
Bergeyck, intendants were effective only in the ex-fuero provinces, where
their number included men, like Macanaz, José Patiño and José Campillo,
who evolved into distinguished administrators.

The war also ended the political power of the old aristocratic elite. 'Preserve all the external prerogatives of their rank', Louis XIV advised Amelot in 1705, 'and exclude them from all matters which might give them a part in the government'. The crisis of loyalty was similar to that which the Habsburgs had provoked between 1517 and 1520. A large number of prominent grandees – among them the admiral of Castile, the count of Oropesa, and the duke of Uceda – defected to the archduke; some followed him into exile. A typical casualty was the duke of Medinaceli (son of Charles II's minister): the wealthiest grandee in Spain, he was arrested for treason and died in Pamplona during the war. The old aristocracy continued to dominate social and economic life, but political direction was taken over by new gentry who distinguished themselves by service to the crown, mainly in the intendancies. It would be wrong to think of these changes as being inspired solely by principles of Bourbon absolutism. It is true that French experience was copied (in the intendants, for example), and French-style uniform and equipment became standard for the Spanish army. But in policy and personnel the early Bourbon regime in Spain was also very much Spanish: its most active theorist was the jurist Melchor de Macanaz. The Cortes of the crown of Aragon had ceased to exist along with the fueros in 1707, but the eastern realms were allowed to send representatives to the Castilian or 'national' Cortes, a purely ceremonial body that met only for formal dynastic occasions.

Its authority enhanced by a unified state, its treasury richer by substantial new revenue, its armed forces expanded and invigorated by the war, the Spanish crown emerged with confidence from the War of Succession. The loss of all the territory of the empire in Europe, including the Netherlands and Italy, was by no means looked on as a disaster. On the contrary, there was now less need to find vast quantities of silver for military payments abroad, and the crown ceased having to rely heavily on foreign bankers. It followed that more American silver now stayed in Spain. State income under the new administration also increased remarkably, from an annual 12 million escudos in 1703 to 23 million in 1713; the war actually brought about a rise in revenue. Much of the increase was inevitably spent on military needs, since Spain had signed no peace treaty with the Emperor, and undertook new campaigns in Italy after 1718. As a consequence, expenditure on the navy rose dramatically from 80,000 escudos a year in 1706 to 4.1 million in 1718, and between 1703 and 1722 the size of the army roughly quadrupled. Shorn at Utrecht of the burden of the Habsburg empire, the country could devote itself to internal recuperation and external resurgence.

# Greatness and decay

The rise and decay of Spain's empire is a theme that has always pre-occupied writers. In 1898 when the last remnants of the American posses-sions, Cuba, Puerto Rico and the Philippines, were lost to the United States, a flood tide of agonised self-examination overtook thinking Spaniards, who felt that they were in some sense diminished by imperial failure. The passion was no less intense under the Habsburgs. To preserve reputación, statesmen for years refused to come to terms with the Dutch, and only the rising power of France forced them into the humiliating settlements of Westphalia and the Pyrenees. The generation of 1648 was no less conscious of failure than that of 1898.

Arguing from these reverses, writers (both in 1648 and in 1898) at-tempted to explain why Spain could not maintain its empire, or unify the peninsula or define its own destiny. Some of them suggested that the path it had taken was a result of Spain's uniqueness, its differences from the European tradition and its consequent inability to find its destiny in Europe. Because there had been a failure to cope with the burden of em-pire, it was argued that the whole experience of empire had been a mistake, and that the 'true' Spain was in fact the pre-imperial one, its golden age being the reign of the Catholic Monarchs. The Habsburgs, who had brought only disappointment and decline, had interrupted Spain's proper destiny. The consciousness of something 'unachieved' (a key word in the vocabulary of writers after 1898) explains the relief with which, in a famous incident in 1700, a Spanish grandee embraced the ambassador of Vienna in Madrid: 'maliciously prolonging his compliment, and repeating his embrace, he said, "Sir, it is with the greatest pleasure – Sir, it is with the greatest satisfaction – for my whole life – I take my leave of the most illustrious House of Austria"'. The Bourbons, it was hoped, would supply the horizons that the Habsburgs had failed to deliver.

The succession in 1700 brought about what Saavedra Fajardo and oth-ers had argued for in the 1640s, a reversion of Spain to its Mediterranean base. It failed however to resolve the basic conflicts that had developed in peninsular society since the time of the Catholic Monarchs and that neither they nor their successors had tackled. Internal tensions were if anything further aggravated through the violence of imposing a Castilian regime on the realms of the crown of Aragon, and discriminating against the pub-lic use of the Catalan language. Nor had the dream of empire faded: war continued to be waged actively in the western Mediterranean, and efforts were still being made to impose control on the American colonies. The period ended with a strong and vigorous Spain, united and also more open to Europe, but this apparent confidence cloaked grave dissensions that would in the end bring down the new dynasty. In consequence of Spain's unending doubts over its experience of the past, the debate over its future remains as unresolved today in 2005 as it was in 1714.

# Bibliography

Books available on-line are indicated by 'e-book' after the place and date of print publication. This bibliography is intended mainly for English-speaking readers; the substantial recent work in Spanish may be looked up in references given by the latest English works mentioned here.

## General

For the late medieval background the best introduction is Angus Mackay, *Spain in the Middle Ages: from frontier to empire 1000–1500*, London 1977. The early modern period was well served by American historians of the later nineteenth century, notably William H. Prescott, Henry C. Lea and Roger B. Merriman; Merriman's *The Rise of the Spanish Empire in the Old World and in the New*, 4 vols, New York 1918, repr. 1962, still remains valuable despite its age. A stimulating perspective of the same period, limited to internal political history, was subsequently offered by J. H. Elliott's *Imperial Spain 1469–1716*, London 1963; though frequently reprinted, it has not been revised since publication and is now wholly superseded. In the same decade John Lynch produced the fullest modern survey of Spain under the Habsburg dynasty; his two volumes are available as *Spain 1516–1598. From nation state to world empire*, Oxford 1991, updated from a 1964 edition; and *The Hispanic world in crisis and change 1598–1700*, Oxford 1992, updated from a 1969 edition. The first volume is weak in sections that were not revised, the second by contrast is still the best available appraisal. Both volumes have a good treatment of foreign policy and Latin America. Stanley G. Payne, *A history of Spain and Portugal*, 2 vols, Madison 1973 (e-book) is a superb and stimulating overview. A recent brief discussion essay with bibliography is Henry Kamen, *Golden Age Spain*, London 2005.

The choice of studies in Spanish is complex, because in addition to multi-volume histories dealing with the whole country there are illustrated multi-volume histories of each region. F. Soldevila, *Historia de España*, 8 vols, Barcelona 1952–9, is old but gives useful coverage of both politics and culture. The volumes published by Ediciones Rialp, *Historia General de España y América*, vols VI (Madrid 1988) and VIII (Madrid 1986) give up-to-date coverage of the sixteenth and seventeenth centuries respectively; and in the *Historia de España* edited by A. Domínguez Ortiz, vols 5 and 6 (Barcelona 1988) cover the same period. The rebirth of interest in Spain's regional history has produced a wave of monographs of unequal value, as well as some stimulating general surveys, among them the *Historia de Andalucia*, vol. IV: *La Andalucia del Renacimiento (1504–1621)*, Madrid 1980, and similar surveys of Catalonia and of Asturias. Luis de Valdeavellano, *Historia de las Instituciones españolas, de los orígenes al final de la Edad Media*, Madrid 1968, remains a useful textbook that explains the origins of early modern institutions.

One view of the mediaeval roots of Spanish culture is expounded in Américo Castro's brilliant and controversial *The Structure of Spanish History*, Princeton 1954. The literature of Castile is analysed in the extended essay by Otis H. Green, *Spain and the Western Tradition: The Castilian Mind in Literature from 'El Cid' to Calderón*, 4 vols, Madison 1963–4; and Spanish decorative arts in the fundamental work of G. Kubler and M. Soria, *Art and Architecture in Spain and Portugal and their American Dominions 1500–1800*, Harmondsworth 1959. Spanish society of pre-industrial times is best approached through several studies in social anthropology based on the twentieth century. Among them, special mention should be made of Julian Pitt-Rivers, *The People of the Sierra*, 2nd edn, Chicago 1971. Carmelo Lisón Tolosana's *Belmonte de los Caballeros: Anthropology and History in an Aragonese Community*, Princeton 1983 (first edn, Oxford 1966), includes the seventeenth century. R. Behar, *Santa María del Monte. The presence of the past in a Spanish village*, Princeton 1986, is a recent focus. In Spanish the outstanding work on the human background has been done by Julio Caro Baroja, for example in his *Razas, pueblos y linajes*, Madrid 1957. The perception that foreigners had of the peninsula during this period is surveyed in J. N. Hillgarth, *The Mirror of Spain, 1500–1700*, Ann Arbor 2000.

There is no general economic history available, since the classic *Economic History of Spain*, Princeton 1969, by Jaime Vicens Vives, is now wholly superseded. José Antonio Maravall, *Estado Moderno y Mentalidad Social, siglos XV a XVII*, 2 vols, Madrid 1972, looks in depth at administration and society. The social dimension is surveyed in the careful and very professional study by James Casey, *Early modern Spain. A social history*, London 1999. Teofilo F. Ruiz, *Spanish society 1400–1600*, Harlow 2001, has a useful bibliography but is less wide ranging than the title suggests and omits important aspects of social activity. The history of religion has so far lacked any general survey, which makes the short analysis by Helen Rawlings, *Church, religion and society in early modern Spain*, Basingstoke 2002, particularly welcome.

A reappraisal of the nature of the Spanish empire has now begun. A useful broad perspective of Atlantic expansion was J. H. Parry, *The Spanish Seaborne Empire*, London 1966, which remains stimulating but is outdated. An enormous amount of research, mainly by American scholars, has given us new perspectives on how the overseas empire functioned. On Spanish power in Europe there is now a tendency to drop the notion of 'empire' and refer more to the dynastic principle that bound the territories together. The French historian Pierre Chaunu refers to the empire in Europe as a 'dynastic Grand Alliance of the seventeen crowns', while some British scholars refer to a 'multiple monarchy' and Spanish historians opt for a 'Catholic monarchy'. Two recent studies on how Spanish rule really functioned in Europe are C. J. Hernando Sánchez, *Castilla y Nápoles en el siglo XVI. El virrey Pedro de Toledo. Linaje, estado y cultura (1532–1553)*, Salamanca 1994, and Antonio Álvarez-Ossorio, *La república de las parentelas. El Estado de Milán en la monarquía de Carlos II*, Mantua 2002. There were no adequate studies on diplomacy until the rich and suggestive work by M. A. Ochoa Brun, *Historia de la diplomacia española*, 6 vols, Madrid 1999. A perspective of the multinational processes that created the worldwide empire is given by Henry Kamen, *Spain's road to empire. The making of a world power 1492–1763*, London 2002 (in the USA, *Empire. How Spain became a world power*, New York 2003).

Among volumes of collected essays that span the period covered here, one may mention J. H. Elliott, *Spain and its world 1500–1700*, London 1989; I. A. A. Thompson, *War and Society in Habsburg Spain*, Aldershot 1992; and Henry Kamen, *Crisis and Change in early modern Spain*, Aldershot 1993.

# The Catholic Monarchs 1469–1516

In English there are now three useful approaches to this reign. The most recent is by John Edwards, *The Spain of the Catholic Monarchs 1474–1520*, Oxford 2000. There is an excellent older study by J. N. Hillgarth, *The Spanish Kingdoms*, vol. II: *1410–1516: Castilian Hegemony*, Oxford 1978 (with a good bibliography). Finally, the pioneering work by W. H.

Prescott, *History of the Reign of Ferdinand and Isabella*, Boston 1837, can still be recommended. Unfortunately there are no satisfactory biographies in English of the chief personalities of the period. The most reliable studies of the queen are in Spanish; the fullest is by Tarsicio de Azcona, *Isabel la Católica*, new edn, Madrid 2002; and there is a stimulating short life by Alfredo Alvar Ezquerra, *Isabel la Católica*, Madrid 2002. Our understanding of the reign was transformed by the researches of M. A. Ladero Quesada, whose studies include *Granada. Historia de un país islámico (1232–1571)*, Madrid 1969, and 'Les finances royales de Castille à la veille des temps modernes', *Annales ESC*, 25, iii (1970). Mark D. Meyerson, *The Muslims of Valencia in the age of Fernando and Isabel*, Berkeley 1991, considers the largest non-Christian minority of the peninsula.

Key aspects of administration are explored in two books by M. Lunenfeld, *The Council of the Santa Hermandad*, Miami 1979, and *Keepers of the City. The corregidores of Isabella of Castile (1474–1504)*, Cambridge 1988. J. A. Maravall, 'Origins of the modern state', *Journal of World History*, 6 (1961), is suggestive. Paul Stewart, 'The soldier, the bureaucrat and fiscal records in the army of Ferdinand and Isabella', *Hispanic American Historical Review*, 49 (1969); and L. P. Wright, 'The military orders in sixteenth- and seventeenth-century Spanish society', *Past and Present*, 43 (1969), look at aspects of the army. The best analysis of Spain's military forces in the period is by Jan Glete, *War and the state in early modern Europe. Spain, the Dutch Republic and Sweden as fiscal-military states, 1500–1660*, London 2002. J. Klein, *The Mesta: a Study in Spanish economic history, 1273–1836*, Cambridge, Mass. 1920, is fundamental but has been superseded in important respects by Carla R. Phillips and William D. Phillips Jr., *Spain's Golden Fleece*, Baltimore 1997.

Studies on religious matters tend to centre on the Inquisition, on which Henry Charles Lea, *A History of the Inquisition of Spain*, 4 vols, New York 1906–7 (e-book), is still the fundamental work and a mine of information. The standard modern survey is Henry Kamen, *The Spanish Inquisition: a historical revision*, New Haven and London 1997. William Monter, *Frontiers of heresy: the Spanish Inquisition from the Basque lands to Sicily*, Cambridge 1990, looks at the Holy Office outside Castile, and Stephen Haliczer, *Inquisition and society in the kingdom of Valencia, 1478–1834*, Berkeley 1990, takes a long-range look at one peninsular tribunal. All these studies give a full guide to the literature in Spanish.

The Jewish conversos are usefully portrayed in Salo Baron, *A Social and Religious History of the Jews*, 2nd edn, New York 1952–, 17 vols, vol. 13. The big controversy has been over whether they were secret Jews or real Christians. Benzion Netanyahu, *The Marranos of Spain, from the late fourteenth to the early sixteenth century*, Ithaca 1999, suggests that they were Christians. Haim Beinart, *Conversos on Trial. The Inquisition in Ciudad Real*, Jerusalem 1981, assumes they were Jews, a view he continues to maintain in his useful volume *The expulsion of the Jews from Spain*, Oxford 2002. A recent stimulating look at various aspects of the converso problem is Gretchen D. Starr-LeBeau, *In the Shadow of the Virgin: Inquisitors, Friars and Conversos in Guadalupe, Spain*, Princeton 2003. Figures for those expelled are discussed in Henry Kamen, 'The Mediterranean and the expulsion of Spanish Jews in 1492', *Past and Present*, 119 (May 1988) (reprinted in his *Crisis and Change*). The chapters in Elie Kedourie, ed., *Spain and the Jews*, London 1992; and Moshe Lazar and Stephen Haliczer, eds, *The Jews of Spain and the expulsion of 1492*, Lancaster, Cal. 1997, look expertly at different aspects of the story.

Spain's reputation abroad is the subject of Sverker Arnoldsson's *La Leyenda Negra*, Göteborg 1960. H. F. Schulte, *The Spanish Press 1470–1966*, Chicago 1968, summarises work on printing. Ferdinand's ambassadors are discussed in Garrett Mattingly, *Renaissance Diplomacy*, London 1955, but Ochoa Brun, noted above, gives more extensive and valuable information. Two contributions to the debate on the Renaissance in Spain are Ottavio di Camillo, *El Humanismo castellano del siglo XV*, Valencia 1976; and Helen Nader, *The Mendoza Family in the Spanish Renaissance*, New Brunswick 1979 (e-book).

# Charles V and empire 1516–1558

There is a good treatment of the Spanish role of Charles in M. Fernández Alvarez, *La España del Emperador Carlos V*, Madrid 1966, vol. XVIII of the *Historia de España* originally directed by R. Menéndez Pidal. Much less satisfactory is his short biography *Charles V*, London 1975. H. Soly, ed., *Charles V 1500–1558 and his time*, Antwerp 1999, contains many useful contributions written to celebrate the 500 years since his birth. Merriman's fine volume on *The Emperor* (vol. 3 of *The Rise of the Spanish Empire*) retains its value. The classic life by Karl Brandi, *The Emperor Charles V*, London 1939, repr. Atlantic Highlands, NJ, 1980, almost totally ignores the Spanish side. James D. Tracy, *Emperor Charles V, Impresario of War*, Cambridge 2002, by contrast, superbly relates the emperor's military role in Spain to what he did in the rest of his dominions. For events in the peninsula, we have to be guided in part by Hayward Keniston, *Francisco de los Cobos*, Pittsburgh 1960. John M. Headley, *The*

*Emperor and his Chancellor: a study of the Imperial chancellery under Gattinara*, Cambridge 1983, examines the administration of Charles V.

On the Comunidades there are fine surveys by Joseph Pérez, *La Révolution des 'Comunidades' de Castille (1520–1521)*, Bordeaux 1970; J. I. Gutiérrez Nieto, *Las Comunidades como movimiento antiseñorial*, Barcelona 1973; and J. A. Maravall, *Las Comunidades de Castilla*, Madrid 1979. There is also a recent analysis in English by Stephen Haliczer, *The Comuneros of Castile. The forging of a revolution, 1475–1521*, Madison 1981. Regional conflicts are covered by R. García-Cárcel, *Las Germanías de Valencia*, Barcelona 1975; John B. Owens, *Rebelión, Monarquía y Oligarquía Murciana en la época de Carlos V*, Murcia 1980; and Eulàlia Durán, *Les Germanies als Països Catalans*, Barcelona 1982.

On finance and the economy the authoritative work is Ramón Carande, *Carlos V y sus banqueros*, 3 vols, Madrid 1949–67. The price revolution is explained by Earl J. Hamilton, *American Treasure and the Price Revolution in Spain, 1501–1650*, Cambridge, Mass. 1934, and Pierre Vilar, *A history of gold and money 1450–1920*, London 1976. Industry is examined by Felipe Ruiz Martín, 'Rasgos estructurales de Castilla en tiempos de Carlos V', *Moneda y Crédito*, 96 (1966).

On America the classic accounts of the conquest are by W. H. Prescott: *The Conquest of Mexico*, Boston 1843 (e-book), and *The Conquest of Peru*, Boston 1847. There are extended and very readable modern accounts by Hugh Thomas, *The conquest of Mexico*, London 1993, and by John Hemming, *The conquest of the Incas*, London 1970. The first steps of Spanish imperialism are considered in Felipe Fernández-Armesto, *The Canary Islands after the conquest*, Oxford 1982. The new horizons posed by America are the subject of J. A. Maravall, *Antiguos y modernos. La idea de progreso en el desarrollo inicial de una sociedad*, Madrid 1966. On emigration, *see* Magnus Mörner, 'Spanish migration to the New World prior to 1810', in F. Chiapelli, ed., *First Images of America. The Impact of the New World on the Old*, 2 vols, Berkeley 1976, and Peter Boyd-Bowman, 'Patterns of Spanish emigration to the Indies until 1600', *Hispanic American Historical Review*, 56, iv (1976). The missionary effort is detailed in Robert Ricard, *The spiritual conquest of Mexico, 1523–1572*, Berkeley 1966, and the debate over the encomienda is summarised in Lewis Hanke, *The Spanish struggle for justice in the conquest of America*, Philadelphia 1949. The mutual impact of two continents is the subject of A. W. Crosby's fascinating *The Columbian Exchange: biological and cultural consequences of 1492*, Westport, Conn. 1972. The reactions of early settlers are given in J. Lockhart and E. Otte, eds, *Letters and*

*People of the Spanish Indies*, Cambridge 1976. Aspects of ideology are looked at in the first half of Anthony Pagden, *Lords of all the world*, New Haven and London 1995.

The literary horizons of the early century are defined in Marcel Bataillon's classic *Erasme et l'Espagne*, Paris 1937. The García-Villoslada *Historia de la Iglesia* covers several themes fully. Antonio Márquez, *Los alumbrados*, Madrid 1972, is a good analysis, and Augustin Redondo, 'Luther et l'Espagne de 1520 à 1536', *Mélanges de la Casa de Velázquez (1965)*, deals with the Protestant scare. J. I. Tellechea, *Tiempos recios. Inquisición y Heterodoxias*, Salamanca 1977, contains perceptive essays. John E. Longhurst has several studies on the period, including *Luther and the Spanish Inquisition: the case of Diego de Uceda 1528–1529*, Albuquerque 1953. The books Spaniards read are assessed by Maxime Chevalier, *Lectura y Lectores en la España del siglo XVI y XVII*, Madrid 1976; and literacy is examined by Sara T. Nalle, 'Literacy and culture in early modern Castile', *Past and Present*, 125 (1989). Political theory is brought up to date by J. A. Fernández Santamaría, *The State, war and peace: Spanish political thought in the Renaissance, 1516–1559*, Cambridge 1977.

# Philip II and the power of Spain 1556–1598

Peter Pierson, *Philip II of Spain*, London 1975, gives a very useful summary of the main features of the reign, on which a more recent treatment is Patrick Williams, *Philip II*, London 2001. Gregorio Marañón in his *Antonio Pérez*, London 1954, a one-volume condensed version, analyses a murder mystery involving Philip II. I. A. A. Thompson makes an important contribution to our knowledge of government under Philip and his son in *War and Government in Habsburg Spain 1560–1620*, London 1976. He has also published two valuable collections of articles, noted elsewhere in this bibliography. Informal aspects of political life are revealed by Richard L. Kagan, *Lucrecia's Dreams: politics and prophecy in sixteenth-century Spain*, Berkeley 1990. A broad perspective of the socio-economic and military events of the reign is given in Fernand Braudel's inspiring masterpiece, *The Mediterranean and the Mediterranean world in the age of Philip II*, 2 vols, London 1972.

The fourth centenary of Philip's death inspired a large number of publications. Special mention should be made of the four massive volumes issued for the four state-sponsored exhibitions in 1998 on *Felipe II: un monarca y su época*, each full of rich illustrations and with a good bibliography. The key volume, on *La monarquía hispánica*, concentrates on the major themes. The transfer of power from Charles V to Philip II is considered in M. J. Rodríguez-Salgado, *The changing face of empire*, Cambridge 1989. Spain's difficulties in the Netherlands are excellently set in focus by Geoffrey Parker, *The Army of Flanders and the Spanish Road (1567–1659)*, Cambridge 1972, and in other studies collected in *Spain and the Netherlands*, London 1979. W. S. Maltby has examined the career of the duke of Alba in *Alba. A biography of Fernando Alvarez de Toledo, Third Duke of Alba 1507–1582*, Berkeley 1983, on whom there is also a short life by Henry Kamen, *The Duke of Alba*, New Haven and London 2004. Only one of the king's ambassadors has been studied: De Lamar Jensen, *Diplomacy and Dogmatism. Bernardino de Mendoza and the French Catholic League*, Cambridge, Mass. 1964; but important aspects of Philip's diplomatic system are examined by Friedrich Edelmayer, *Söldner und Pensionäre. Das Netzwerk Philipps II im Heiligen Römischen Reich*, Vienna 2002. The diplomatic situation at the turn of the sixteenth century is studied by Paul C. Allen, *Philip III and the Pax Hispanica, 1598–1621*, New Haven and London 2000. Only one of Philip's ministers of state has received adequate attention, by M. van Durme, *El cardenal Granvela (1517–1586). Imperio y revolución bajo Carlos V y Felipe II*, Barcelona, 1957.

J. A. Maravall, *La oposición política bajo los Austrias*, Madrid 1972, looks at (among other matters) the debate over Flanders. Montano's role is presented in Luis Morales Oliver, *Arias Montano y la política de Felipe II en Flandes*, Madrid 1927. Problems in Valencia are the theme of S. García Martínez, *Bandolerismo, piratería y control de moriscos en Valencia durante el reinado de Felipe II*, Valencia 1977; and Catalan bandits have been carefully studied by Xavier Torres, *Nyerros i cadells: bàndols i bandolerisme a la Catalunya moderna (1590–1640)*, Barcelona 1993.

There is no detailed study of 'absolutism' in Spain, but the article on Castile by I. A. A. Thompson, 'Absolutism in Castile', reprinted in his essential volume *Crown and Cortes. Government, Institutions and Representation in early modern Castile*, Aldershot 1993, sorts out confusions. There is much material in Maravall's *Estado moderno*, and in his older *La philosophie politique espagnole au XVIIe siècle*, Paris 1955, as well as in Bernice Hamilton, *Political thought in sixteenth-century Spain*, Oxford 1963, and in Gunter Lewy, *Constitutionalism and statecraft during the Golden Age of Spain*, Geneva 1960. The role of the Castilian Cortes has been revised by C. Jago, 'Habsburg absolutism and the Cortes of Castile', *American Historical Review*, 86, 2 (1981), and notably by

I. A. A. Thompson, in the articles collected in *Crown and Cortes*, noted above. J. L. Fortea Pérez, 'The Cortes of Castile and Philip II's fiscal policy', *Parliaments, Estates and Representation*, 11 (1991), resumes his own important work and supplies a guide to recent views. A good guide to the situation in Aragon is given by Xavier Gil, 'Crown and Cortes in Early Modern Aragon', *Parliaments, Estates and Representation*, 13, 2 (1993). On clientage in local government there is a pioneering study by M. T. Pérez Picazo and Guy Lemeunier, 'Formes du pouvoir local dans l'Espagne moderne et contemporaine: des bandos au caciquisme au royaume de Murcie (XVe–XIXe siècles)', in A. Mączak, ed., *Klientelsysteme im Europa der Frühen Neuzeit*, Munich 1988.

The debate over the character of Philip II originated in the 1820s among conservative scholars, the 'absolutists' (who supported traditional monarchy, which they identified ideally with Ferdinand and Isabella rather than with the Habsburgs) and the 'liberals' (who supported constitutional monarchy – which they also identified with Ferdinand and Isabella – and opposed absolute power, which they identified with Philip II). Since then, it has been politically correct to blacklist the king. The balanced, short biography by Geoffrey Parker, *Philip II*, Boston 1978, repr. Chicago 2002, was followed by his *The grand strategy of Philip II*, New Haven and London 1998, in which he argued that the king was an imperial expansionist, inspired by a 'messianic' vision. An assessment of the king's career through his own words and ideas is offered in the extended biography by Henry Kamen, *Philip of Spain*, New Haven and London 1997, who maintains that the king was neither messianic nor imperialist.

Administrative officials and their university background are discussed in Richard L. Kagan, *Students and Society in Early Modern Spain*, Baltimore 1974 (e-book); he also looks at lawyers in *Lawsuits and Litigants in Castile, 1500–1700*, Chapel Hill 1981 (e-book). The bureaucracies of the later period are analysed in detail by J. M. Pelorson, *Les letrados: juristes castillans sous Philippe III*, Poitiers 1980, and by Janine Fayard, *Les membres du Conseil de Castille à l'époque moderne (1621–1746)*, Paris–Geneva 1979. The subject is also covered in the excellent review article by I. A. A. Thompson, 'The rule of the Law in early modern Castile', *European History Quarterly*, 14 (1984) (reprinted in his *Crown and Cortes*). M. Cuartas Rivero, 'La venta de oficios públicos en Castilla-León en el siglo XVI', *Hispania*, xliv, 158 (1984), discusses and gives bibliography on the sale of office.

Thompson's *War and Government* examines the Spanish war machine from within. There are no broad surveys either of the army or of the navy, though key aspects of the navy are discussed in J. F. Guilmartin, *Gunpowder and Galleys. Changing technology and Mediterranean warfare at sea in the sixteenth century*, Cambridge 1974. A good perspective of Spanish resources is given in chapter 3 of Jan Glete, *War and the state in early modern Europe*, London 2002 (e-book). René Quatrefages, *Los tercios españoles 1567–1577*, Madrid 1976, supplemented by his 'Etat et armée en Espagne au début des temps modernes', *Mélanges de la Casa de Velázquez*, xvii (1981) 85–103, sheds light on Castilian troops in Spain's armies. The events of 1588 have launched many useful books, including C. Martin and G. Parker, *The Spanish Armada*, London 1988, and F. Fernández-Armesto, *The Spanish Armada: the experience of war in 1588*, Oxford 1988. Finance has been exhaustively covered by Modesto Ulloa, *La Hacienda Real de Castilla en el reinado de Felipe II*, 2nd edn, Madrid 1977; and there is an essential article by Felipe Ruiz Martín, 'Las finanzas españolas durante el reinado de Felipe II', *Cuadernos de Historia*, 2 (Anexos de *Hispania*), Madrid 1968. The state debt is analysed in two useful articles by Alvaro Castillo: 'Los Juros de Castilla. Apogeo y fin de un instrumento de crédito', *Hispania*, 23 (1963), and 'Dette flottante et dette consolidée en Espagne de 1557 à 1600', *Annales ESC*, 11 (1963).

The rural economy is now well studied in David Vassberg, *Land and Society in Golden Age Castile*, Cambridge 1984. Noël Salomon, *La campagne de Nouvelle Castille à la fin du XVIe siècle*, Paris 1964, examines his theme through a contemporary census. Aspects of Seville are explored in several useful studies by Ruth Pike, such as *Aristocrats and Traders. Sevillan society in the sixteenth century*, Ithaca 1972 (e-book). Two imposing studies of urban development are Bartolomé Bennassar, *Valladolid au siècle d'or*, Paris 1967, and Francisco Chacón, *Murcia en la centuria del quinientos*, Murcia 1979. On trade with America, Pierre Chaunu, *Amérique et l'Atlantique (1504–1640)*, Paris 1969, is a condensation of his major work on the trade of Seville. Eufemio Lorenzo Sanz, *Comercio de España con América en la época de Felipe II*, 2 vols, Valladolid 1979, is valuable.

On the Moriscos the most interesting survey in English continues to be the old study by H. C. Lea, *The Moriscos of Spain*, London 1901. Later research is summarised usefully by A. Domínguez Ortiz and B. Vincent, *Historia de los Moriscos*, Madrid 1978, which has a full bibliography; and cultural conflict is examined by Louis Cardaillac, *Morisques et chrétiens. Un affrontement polémique (1492–1640)*, Paris 1977, and by Anwar Chejne, *Islam and the West: the Moriscos*, Albany 1983. David Coleman,

*Creating Christian Granada. Society and religious culture in an old world frontier city, 1492–1600*, Ithaca 2003, is excellent.

The state of religion in the peninsula is at last receiving attention. The best survey of spiritual currents is by Alastair Hamilton, *Heresy and Mysticism in Sixteenth-Century Spain: the Alumbrados*, Cambridge 1992. A very useful introduction to the Church is that by Helen Rawlings, noted above. In a stimulating short study, William Christian Jr. looks at *Local religion in sixteenth-century Spain*, Princeton 1981. For the Protestants a good bibliography is supplied by Gordon Kinder, *Spanish Protestants and Reformers in the Sixteenth Century*, London 1983; and the failure of Protestantism is considered by Henry Kamen in R. Scribner *et al.*, eds, *The Reformation in national context*, Cambridge 1991. The Counter-Reformation in the peninsula is explored by Jodi Bilinkoff, *The Avila of Saint Teresa: Religious Reform in a Sixteenth-Century City*, Ithaca 1989; Sara T. Nalle, *God in La Mancha. Religion, Reform and the People of Cuenca 1500–1650*, Baltimore 1992 (e-book); Henry Kamen, *The Phoenix and the Flame. Catalonia and the Counter Reformation*, New Haven and London 1993; and Allyson M. Poska, *Regulating the People. The Catholic Reformation in Seventeenth-Century Spain*, Boston 1998. On the Inquisition, in addition to the works mentioned above there are monographs by Jaime Contreras, *El Santo Oficio de la Inquisición de Galicia*, Madrid 1982 and J. P. Dedieu, *L'Administration de la Foi. L'Inquisition de Tolède (XVIe–XVIIIe siècle)*, Madrid 1989. Censorship is the central theme of Antonio Márquez, *Literatura e Inquisición en España 1478–1834*, Madrid 1980. On witchcraft there is now a large literature in Spanish. The basic work in English is still the treatment in Henry C. Lea, *History of the Inquisition of Spain*, 4 vols, New York and London 1906–7 (e-book) supplemented by Julio Caro Baroja's old but still perceptive *The World of the Witches*, London 1964. An absorbing contribution is made by G. Henningsen, *The Witches' Advocate. Basque Witchcraft and the Spanish Inquisition*, Nevada 1981. On aspects of science, *see* J. M. López Piñero, *Ciencia y Técnica en la Sociedad española de los siglos XVI y XVII*, Barcelona 1979, and David C. Goodman, *Power and Penury. Government, technology and science in Philip II's Spain*, Cambridge 1988.

# The crisis of government 1598–1660

The best short accounts of the reigns of Philip III and Philip IV are the chapters by Patrick Williams and I. A. A. Thompson in Ediciones Rialp, *Historia General de España y América*, vol. VIII, Madrid 1986 (noted above). Thompson's chapter is reprinted in his *Crown and Cortes*. In the *Historia de España* of Menéndez Pidal the volume on Philip III is unsatisfactory, but volume XXV (1982) on Philip IV is a useful joint effort by several scholars. Francisco Tomás y Valiente, *Los validos en la monarquía española del siglo XVII*, Madrid 1963, is a good guide to the political role of ministers. Patrick Williams, 'Philip III and the restoration of Spanish government, 1598–1603', *English Historical Review*, 88 (1973), gives a new perspective. Antonio Feros, *Kingship and favoritism in the reign of Philip III*, Cambridge 2000, offers a reassessment of Lerma. Changes in political thought under Philip III are revealingly discussed by Luciano Pereña in his edition of *Francisco Suárez. De iuramento Fidelitatis*, Madrid 1979.

For Philip IV we now have the revisionist biography by R. A. Stradling, *Philip IV and the government of Spain, 1621–1665*, Cambridge 1988. Jonathan Brown and J. H. Elliott, *A Palace for a King. The Buen Retiro and the Court of Philip IV*, Yale 1980, is both illuminating and finely illustrated. Anything written by Jonathan Brown, a noted expert on Velázquez, is excellent because of the way he relates artists to their social and political context. Elliott has produced the definitive studies on Olivares: *The Revolt of the Catalans*, Cambridge 1963, and *The Count-Duke of Olivares*, New Haven and London 1988, the latter giving a comprehensive survey of foreign policy. For aspects of secret diplomacy in this period, *see* M. A. Echevarria Bacigalupe, *La diplomacia secreta en Flandes, 1598–1643*, Leioa, Vizcaya 1984. On the Catalan revolt the classic and unduly neglected study is José Sanabre, *La acción de Francia en Cataluña, 1640–1659*, Barcelona 1956. Other studies on foreign policy include J. Alcalá Zamora, *España, Flandes y el Mar del Norte (1618–1639)*, Barcelona 1975; and J. Israel, *Conflicts of Empires. Spain, the Low Countries and the struggle for world supremacy 1585–1713*, London 1997. A suggestive general discussion of foreign affairs is R. Stradling, *Europe and the Decline of Spain. A study of the Spanish system 1580–1720*, London 1981. The naval war machine in Europe is the subject of learned studies by David C. Goodman, *Spanish naval power, 1589–1665*, Cambridge 1997; C. R. Phillips, *Six galleons for the king of Spain: imperial defense in the early seventeenth century*, Baltimore 1986; and R. A. Stradling, *The Armada of Flanders. Spanish Maritime Policy and European War, 1568–1668*, Cambridge 1992. Resistance to military service is the fascinating theme of Ruth Mackay, *The limits of royal authority. Resistance and obedience in seventeenth-century Castile*, Cambridge 1999. Spain's reliance on the Dutch is analysed by Manuel

Herrero Sánchez, *El acercamiento hispano-neerlandés (1648–1678)*, Madrid 2000.

The debate over crisis and decline has been well aired. A good starting point is James Casey, 'Spain: a failed transition', in Peter Clark, ed., *The European Crisis of the 1590s*, London 1985. His study of *The kingdom of Valencia in the Seventeenth Century*, Cambridge 1979, deals with one case history. Population is surveyed by J. Nadal, *Historia de la población española (siglos XVI a XX)*, 4th edn, Barcelona 1991. The traditional thesis of decline was sustained by the conservative school of Castilian historians in the nineteenth century, then further supported by Earl J. Hamilton in an article of 1937, and later by J. H. Elliott, 'The Decline of Spain', *Past and Present*, 20 (Nov. 1961). It was criticised by Henry Kamen, 'The decline of Spain: a historical myth?', *Past and Present*, 81 (1978) (reprinted in *Crisis and Change*). A balanced examination of what Spanish decline may have been is given in chapter 6 of J. K. J. Thomson, *Decline in history. The European experience*, Oxford 1998. Perspectives of the economic problem are offered in the articles, by Spanish historians, collected by I. A. A. Thompson and Bartolomé Yun, *The Castilian crisis of the seventeenth century*, Cambridge 1994. The role of American trade is outlined in the first section of Stanley J. Stein and Barbara H. Stein, *Silver, trade and war. Spain and America in the making of early modern Europe*, Baltimore 2000. The earlier part of David Ringrose, *Madrid and the Spanish Economy 1560–1850*, Berkeley 1983 (e-book), examines the role of the capital city; and D. Reher, *Town and country in pre-industrial Spain: Cuenca 1540–1870*, Cambridge 1990, studies one case of urban development.

## Spain's people in an age of crisis

Substantial research has now been done on economy and demography, and the results have served to reveal the widely different types of regional development in the peninsula. The best overview of early modern Spanish society is James Casey's *Early modern Spain*, noted above. David Vassberg, *The village and the outside world in Golden Age Castile*, Cambridge 1996, is a pioneering book that opens up many fascinating perspectives.

A short list of scholarly studies in Spanish might include the following: E. Fernández de Pinedo, *Crecimiento y transformaciones sociales del País Vasco (1100–1850)*, Madrid 1974; Angel García Sanz, *Desarrollo y crisis del Antiguo Régimen en Castilla la Vieja: economía y sociedad en tierras de Segovia 1500–1814*, Madrid 1977; J. I. Fortea Pérez, *Córdoba en el siglo XVI*, Salamanca 1979; V. Pérez Moreda, *Las crisis de mortalidad en la España interior. Siglos XVI–XIX*, Madrid 1980; Pegerto Saavedra, *Economía, Política y Sociedad en Galicia: la provincia de Mondoñedo, 1480–1830*, Madrid 1985; Bartolomé Yun Casalilla, *Sobre la transición al capitalismo en Castilla. Economía y sociedad en Tierra de Campos (1500–1830)*, Salamanca 1987; among very many others.

On the arbitristas, Jean Vilar, *Literatura y economía: la figura satírica del arbitrista en el siglo de oro*, Madrid 1973, is essential. *See also* J. H. Elliott, 'Self-perception and decline in early seventeenth-century Spain', *Past and Present*, 74 (1977). A. Domínguez Ortiz, *Alteraciones andaluzas*, Madrid 1973, looked at riots in mid-seventeenth-century Andalucia. Some urban disturbances are well analysed by P. L. Lorenzo Cadarso, *Los conflictos populares en Castilla (siglos XVI–XVII)*, Madrid 1996. Aspects of political thought are approached in J. A. Fernández Santamaría, *Reason of State and Statecraft in Spanish political thought, 1595–1640*, New York 1983.

On population, A. Domínguez Ortiz, *La Sociedad española en el siglo XVII*, 2 vols, Madrid 1964, 1970, summarises useful material. James Casey and others contribute useful essays to *La Familia en la España Mediterránea (siglos XV–XIX)*, Barcelona 1987; and a broad perspective is offered by Robert Rowland, 'Sistemas matrimoniales en la península ibérica (siglos XVI–XIX): una perspectiva regional', in V. Pérez Moreda and D. S. Reher (eds), *La Demografía Histórica de la Península Ibérica*, Madrid 1986. Studies on demography include A. Molinié-Bertrand, *Au Siècle d'or. L'Espagne et ses hommes. La population du royaume de Castille au XVIe siècle*, Paris 1985; and M. Carbajo Isla, *La población de la villa de Madrid*, Madrid 1987.

Urban elites are considered in various suggestive chapters in *Les Elites locales et l'Etat dans l'Espagne moderne du XVIe au XIXe siècle*, ed. M. Lambert-Gorges, Paris 1993. Problems of the nobility are looked at in C. Jago, 'The "Crisis of the Aristocracy" in seventeenth-century Castile', *Past and Present*, 84 (1979), and in Ignacio Atienza Hernández, *Aristocracia, poder y riqueza en la España moderna: la Casa de Osuna siglos XV–XIX*, Madrid 1987. The excellent study on the Mendozas by Helen Nader, noted above, unfortunately has no equivalents for the seventeenth century. Marie-Claude Gerbert, *La noblesse de Castille. Etude sur ses structures sociales en Estrémadure de 1454 à 1516*, Paris 1979, studies an inland society; and Jacqueline Guiral-Hadziiossif, *Valence, port méditer- ranéen au XVe siècle (1410–1525)*, Paris 1986, examines commerce and traders. P. Molas Ribalta, *La burguesía mercantil en la España del Antiguo Régimen*, Madrid 1985, is the best survey on the middle classes. Noël Salomon, *Recherches sur le thème paysan dans la 'Comedia' au temps de Lope de Vega*, Bordeaux 1965, is an excellent literary approach to the peasantry, on whom one local study is Michael Weisser, *The peasants of the Montes*, Chicago 1976. Poor relief in Castile has been studied by Linda Martz, *Poverty and welfare in Habsburg Spain*, Cambridge 1983, and by Maureen Flynn, *Sacred Charity. Confraternities and social welfare in Spain 1400–1700*, London 1989. Literature and society are combined as themes in J. M. Díez Borque, *Sociología de la comedia española del siglo XVII*, Madrid 1976, and in J. A. Maravall, *La cultura del barroco*, Madrid 1975.

The important theme of regionalism and provincialism is now receiving the attention it deserves. For consciousness of regional identity, there are revealing essays by I. A. A. Thompson, Xavier Gil and James Casey, in R. L. Kagan and G. Parker, eds, *Spain, Europe and the Atlantic world*, Cambridge 1995. J. M. Bernardo Aries and E. Martínez Ruiz, eds, *El municipio en la España Moderna*, Cordoba 1996, and José I. Fortea Pérez, ed., *Imágenes de la diversidad: el mundo urbano en la Corona de Castilla (siglos XVI–XVIII)*, Santander 1997, are among the many studies on townships. Provincial elites are the theme of James Amelang, *Honored citizens of Barcelona: patrician culture and class relations, 1490–1714*, Princeton 1986 (e-book). Helen Nader, *Liberty in absolutist Spain. The Habsburg sale of towns 1516–1700*, Baltimore 1991, is an important study on the place of small towns in the political structure of Castile.

Little research has been done on the social and family role of women in pre-industrial Spain. Most recent work has been devoted to their part in religious life (with a heavy concentration on Teresa of Avila, and on women brought to trial by the Inquisition), or to their appearance in creative literature. Among many recent studies one may mention Magdalena S. Sánchez and Alain Saint-Saens, eds, *Spanish Women in the Golden Age: Images and Realities*, Westport CT 1996; Augustin Redondo, ed., *Images de la femme en Espagne aux XVIe et XVIIe siècle*, Paris 1994; and Beth Miller, ed., *Women in Hispanic literature*, Berkeley 1983.

# The end of the old empire 1660–1714

The most useful summary of politics in the reign of Charles II is in Lynch, *The Hispanic world in crisis and change 1598–1700*, noted at the beginning of this bibliography. The wide-ranging study by Henry Kamen, *Spain in the later seventeenth century*, London 1980, says little about politics or foreign policy; the same author has also studied 'A forgotten insurrection of the seventeenth century: the Catalan peasant rising of 1688', *Journal of Modern History*, 49 (1977). Valencian history of the same period is revised by S. García Martínez, *Els fonaments del pais valencià modern*, Valencia 1968. J. M. López Piñero, *La Introducción de la Ciencia Moderna en España*, Barcelona 1969, is a brilliant essay on the early scientific revolution. Michel Morineau, *Incroyables gazettes et fabuleux métaux, Les retours des trésors américains d'après les gazettes hollandaises (XVIe–XVIIIe siècles)*, Cambridge 1985, used Dutch consular reports to reach conclusions similar to those which the present author reached through French consular reports (*see* Figure 3).

Pere Molas, *Comerç i Estructura Social a Catalunya i València als segles XVII i XVIII*, Barcelona 1977, discusses the economic renewal on the Levant coast. On the reign of Philip V, *see* Henry Kamen, *Philip V of Spain. The king who ruled twice*, New Haven and London 2001. The best detailed introduction to the reign is given in the earlier chapters of John Lynch, *Bourbon Spain 1700–1808*, Oxford 1989. The standard study in Spanish is by A. Dominguez Ortiz, *Sociedad y Estado en et siglo XVIII español*, Barcelona 1976. The war period is covered by Henry Kamen, *The War of Succession in Spain*, London 1969, which however omits any treatment of Catalonia, an omission remedied in part by Juan Mercader, *Felip V i Catalunya*, Barcelona 1968. The standard nationalist view that Catalans revolted solidly against the Bourbons is questioned by J. M. Torras i Ribé, 'Reflexions sobre l'actitud dels pobles i estaments catalans durant la guerra de Successió', *Pedralbes*, 1 (1981) 187–209. A fundamental administrative reform is explained by Henry Kamen, 'The establishment of intendants in early Bourbon Spain', in Kamen, *Crisis and Change*. A perspective of the empire under the first Bourbon is given in chapter 10 of Kamen, *Empire. How Spain became a world power*, noted above.

# Index

The terms Spain, Aragon, Castile, France and Italy are not indexed because they occur frequently